# Reframing Organizations

# Lee G. Bolman
# Terrence E. Deal

# REFRAMING ORGANIZATIONS

## Artistry, Choice, and Leadership

 Jossey-Bass Publishers

San Francisco • Oxford • 1991

REFRAMING ORGANIZATIONS
*Artistry, Choice, and Leadership*
  by Lee G. Bolman and Terrence E. Deal

Copyright © 1991 by:  Jossey-Bass Inc., Publishers
                      350 Sansome Street
                      San Francisco, California 94104
                              &
                      Jossey-Bass Limited
                      Headington Hill Hall
                      Oxford OX3 0BW

**Library of Congress Cataloging-in-Publication Data**

Bolman, Lee G.
    Reframing organizations : artistry, choice, and leadership /
Lee G. Bolman, Terrence E. Deal. — 1st ed.
        p.  cm.—(The Jossey-Bass management series)
(The Jossey-Bass social and behavioral science series)
(The Jossey-Bass higher and adult education series)
    Includes bibliographical references and index.
    ISBN 1-55542-299-3. — ISBN 1-55542-323-X (pbk.)
    1. Management.   2. Organizational behavior.   3. Leadership.
I. Deal, Terrence.  II. Title.  III. Series.
IV. Series: The Jossey-Bass social and behavioral science series.
V. Series: The Jossey-Bass higher and adult education series.
HD31.B6135     1991
658.4'063—dc20                                    90-46853
                                                      CIP

Manufactured in the United States of America

The paper in this book meets the guidelines for
permanence and durability of the Committee on
Production Guidelines for Book Longevity of the
Council on Library Resources.

JACKET/COVER DESIGN BY CHARLOTTE KAY GRAPHIC DESIGN

FIRST EDITION

*Code 9101*
*Code 9124* (paperback)

*A joint publication in*

**The Jossey-Bass
Management Series**

**The Jossey-Bass
Social and Behavioral
Science Series**

*and*

**The Jossey-Bass
Higher and Adult
Education Series**

# Contents

# Contents

# Preface

In 1984, we wrote *Modern Approaches to Understanding and Managing Organizations.* We have been heartened by the many readers who told us that they found it helpful and even enjoyable to read. They gave us the courage to try again, and *Reframing Organizations* is the result.

The preface to our previous book outlined an ambitious objective: "Our primary audience is managers and future managers. We have tried to write in response to the question: What does organization theory and research have to say that is genuinely important and useful to practitioners? . . . We have tried to present a large, complex body of theory and research as clearly and simply as we could, without watering it down or presenting simplistic views of how to solve every managerial problem. We try to offer not solutions but more powerful ways of thinking about organizations and understanding the managerial problems that they present" (Bolman and Deal, 1984, pp. xiii-xiv).

These are still our goals. In the present volume, however, we focus more directly on both management *and* leadership. Leading and managing are distinct, but both are important. Organizations that are overmanaged but underled eventually lose any sense of spirit or purpose. Poorly managed organizations with strong charismatic leaders may soar temporarily only to crash shortly thereafter. The challenges of modern organizations require the objective perspective of the manager as well as the brilliant flashes of vision and commitment that wise leadership provides. We need more people in managerial roles who can find simplicity and order amidst organizational confusion and chaos. We need versatile and flexible leaders who are artists as well as analysts and who can reframe experience in ways that allow them to discover and express new issues and possibilities. We need managers who love their work and their organizations and care deeply about the people whose lives they affect. We need leaders and managers who appreciate that management is a deeply moral and ethical undertaking. We need leaders who combine hardheaded realism with a deep commitment to values and purposes larger than themselves. We hope to encourage and nurture such qualities and possibilities.

Even more than before, we have tried to provide a clear and readable synthesis and integration of the major theoretical traditions in the field of organizations. We concentrated on those elements of organization theory that are important and useful for managerial practice. We have also expanded the scope of the book and have drawn upon examples from almost every conceivable kind of human organization—business, military, educational, and health care organizations, as well as public agencies, religious orders, and families.

We have made other important changes. We have expanded our discussion of organizational change and leadership. Given the reality of the global economy, we thought it important to include cases and examples from different nations and cultures. In addition, we consider in more detail the role of ethics and values in management, particularly in our discussion of organizational politics. This new volume also takes advantage of important recent work in social science (and humanities) theory and research.

We also give more prominence to the idea of artistry in both management and leadership. An overemphasis on the rational and technical side of organizations has often contributed to their decline or demise. Artistry is neither exact nor precise. The artist interprets experience and expresses it in imaginative and esthetically satisfying forms. Art allows for emotion, subtlety, and ambiguity. An artist reframes the world to give us a deeper understanding of what is and what might be (Martinez, 1989). In modern organizations, quality, commitment, and creativity are highly valued but often hard to find. They can be developed and encouraged by leaders or managers who embrace the expressive side of their work. We believe that artful leaders and managers will be able to discover new organizational forms that will release the untapped potential in individuals and improve collective performance. Images rather than memos, poetry rather than policy, and reflection rather than command will help move us in that direction.

Perhaps the most significant difference between the present volume and the earlier *Modern Approaches* is the emphasis that we now place on *reframing,* as reflected in the title of this new book. Throughout this volume, we try to show how the same situation in an organization can be viewed in four different ways—from structural, human resource, political, and symbolic perspectives.

### Overview of the Contents

Part One, "Making Sense of Organizations," includes the first two chapters. Chapter One shows why reframing—the use of multiple lenses—is vital to effective leadership and management. It introduces the four basic lenses for organizational analysis and shows how artistry and reframing can lead to both managerial freedom and leadership effectiveness. Chapter Two uses a famous case, the destruction of a Korean Airlines jet plane by the Soviet Air Force, to show how managers' everyday theories for action can lead to catastrophe in the complicated world of modern organizations. It explains the basic factors that make organizational life complicated, ambiguous, and unpredictable; discusses common fallacies in managerial thinking; and spells out the criteria for effective approaches to diagnosis and action in organizations.

In Part Two, we explore the structural frame. Chapter Three describes the basic issues that managers need to consider in designing structural forms that fit an organization's goals, tasks, and context. It shows why different organizations—such as Harvard University and McDonald's—need very different structures in order to be effective in their respective environments. Chapter Four explains the major structural pathologies and pitfalls often encountered in organizations. It provides guidelines for diagnosing the structural configuration that is needed for a given situation and uses a case study to illustrate the processes that lead to successful structural change. Chapter Five applies structural concepts to the workings of groups and teams. It discusses how different tasks and circumstances require different structural forms, using cases and examples from schools, sports, and the military.

In Part Three, we examine the human resource frame. Chapter Six focuses on the relationship between organizations and human nature. It shows how managers' practices and assumptions about people can lead either to alienation and hostility or to commitment and high motivation in an organization's work force. Chapter Seven uses a case example of interpersonal conflict at work to illustrate how managers create either effective or ineffective relationships. It also discusses how groups can increase their effectiveness by attending to basic issues of group process—informal norms and roles, interpersonal conflict, leadership, and decision making. Chapter Eight provides an overview of practices that organizations can use to make work more meaningful and to build a more motivated and committed work force—including participative management, job enrichment, self-managing work groups, organizational democracy, organization development, and Theory Z.

The political frame is discussed in Part Four. Chapter Nine uses the tragic loss of the space shuttle *Challenger* to illustrate the power of political dynamics in organizational decision making. It shows how scarcity and diversity in organizations lead to conflict, bargaining, and games of power, and distinguishes constructive and destructive political dynamics. Chapter Ten explains why politics is unavoidable in organizations but need not be sordid and destructive. This chapter presents and illustrates the basic skills of the constructive politician: diagnosing political realities, setting agendas, building networks of support, negotiating, and making choices that are both effective and ethical. Chapter Eleven shows how organizations are both arenas that house political contests and political actors in their own right. It reveals how leaders and managers can shape the playing field within the organization to influence how the game is played, who the contestants are, and what rules are influence how the game is played, who the contestants are, and what rules are followed. As tools, organizations are powerful vehicles for expressing the interests of their dominant coalition.

We explore the last of the four frames, the symbolic frame, in Part Five. Chapter Twelve demonstrates the power of symbol and culture in organizations as diverse as the U.S. Congress, Procter & Gamble, and Scandinavian Air Systems. It spells out the basic symbolic elements in organizations: myths, metaphors, stories, humor, play, rituals, and ceremonies. This chapter defines organizational culture and shows its central role in determining organizational effectiveness. Chapter Thirteen reveals how organizational structures, activities, and events serve as secular theater, expressing our fears and joys, arousing our affect, and kindling our spirit. It shows how organizational structures and processes, such as planning, evaluation, and decision making, are often more important for what they *express* than for what they *do*. Chapter Fourteen uses the case of a computer development team to show what leaders and group members can do to build a culture that brings a group together in pursuit of a shared mission. Initiation rituals, specialized language, group stories, humor and play, and ceremonies all combine to transform a diverse collection of individuals into a team with purpose, spirit, and soul.

Part Six, "Improving Leadership Practice," encompasses Chapters Fifteen through Twenty-Three. Chapter Fifteen grounds the four-frame perspective in the existing body of research and scholarship on organizations and management. It discusses the historic dominance of single-frame thinking in organizational research and documents the increasing shift toward a multi-frame, pluralistic approach to understanding and managing organizations. Chapter Sixteen discusses why managers and leaders need multiple frames to survive and shows how they can blend the four frames to become more effective. It also looks at how to understand organizations as multiple realities and provides guidelines for aligning the frames with different situations that managers and leaders confront. Chapter Seventeen presents four different scenarios, or scripts, for effective leadership. It applies the scenarios to a challenging organizational case, which shows how leaders can expand their options and enhance their effectiveness by considering alternative approaches to the same situation. Chapter Eighteen describes four fundamental issues that arise in any organizational change effort: individual needs, structural alignment, conflict, and loss. It uses cases of successful and unsuccessful organizational change to develop strategies for managing human resource and structural issues in changing organizations. Chapter Nineteen provides strategies for responding to the political and symbolic dimensions of organizational change. It describes how to create arenas that encourage constructive resolution of the conflicts that accompany any significant change in an organization. It draws lessons from the failure of "new Coke" to show how change agents can use symbols, ritual, and ceremony to help people cope with loss, let go of the past, and move forward. Chapter Twenty discusses the limitations in traditional views of leadership and provides a new and more comprehensive view of what leadership is and how it works in organizations. It explains how leadership differs from authority, power, and position, and summarizes the state of current knowledge on the characteristics of outstanding leaders. Chapter Twenty-One discusses the strategies of great structural and human resource leaders. It shows how Alfred P. Sloan built General Motors into the world's largest corporation by developing a new model for the company's structure and strategy. It also describes the techniques of outstanding human resource leaders—commitment to people, visibility, and empowerment. Chapter Twenty-Two probes the artistry of great political and symbolic leaders. It explains how Lee Iacocca's understanding of political leadership enabled him to save Chrysler Corporation. It deciphers the enormous power of symbolic leadership and describes strategies that can be used for great good or enormous evil, depending on the values and vision of the leader who employs them. The epilogue, Chapter Twenty-Three, describes the strategies and characteristics needed in the leaders of the future. It explains why they will need an artistic combination of conceptual flexibility and commitment to core values. It argues that efforts to prepare future leaders will need to focus as much on spiritual as on intellectual development and demonstrates that the ability to reframe is essential for both personal freedom and organizational prosperity.

## Purpose of the Book

We hope that our approach in this work will help alleviate some of the problems that continue to plague the field of organization studies. For example, the field has long been too divided and fragmented. There are several distinct traditions, each of which remains isolated from the others. Much existing literature focuses on only one or two traditions and gives the reader a biased and incomplete sense of the state of the field as a whole. Even more important, most writing on the subject omits crucial aspects of organizations that every manager and student of organizations needs to understand. The few works that seek to provide a comprehensive overview of organization theory and research usually speak only to scholars. They often make excessive use of social science jargon and abstractions and have little to say that is of direct relevance to practitioners. We have tried to find a balance between oversimplification and complexity.

Organization theorists have also tended to focus almost exclusively on either the private *or* the public sector, but not on both. Managers need to understand the similarities and differences among organizations in both sectors. This is all the more necessary because the two sectors increasingly interact with each other. For example, public administrators who regulate airlines, nuclear power plants, or pharmaceutical companies face on a daily basis the problem of how to influence the behavior of organizations over which they have very limited authority. Public schools and private corporations need to understand and help each other if they are to solve their shared problem of ensuring that the members of each new generation acquire the skills, knowledge, and understanding that will enable them to lead productive and rewarding lives.

At the same time, corporate managers face a diverse and often bewildering array of government actions, interventions, and regulations. Private firms need to understand and find ways to manage their relationships with multiple levels of government. The situation is even more complex for managers in multinational companies, who must understand and cope with the subtleties of governments with very different systems and traditions. Across sectors and cultures, managers often cling to narrow, stereotypical conceptions of one another that impede effectiveness on both sides. We need common ground and a shared understanding if we are to strengthen public and private organizations in the United States and throughout the world. The dialogue between public and private domestic and multinational organizations has become increasingly important. Because of their generic application, the four frames provide a shared language for this exchange.

*November 1990*                                    Lee G. Bolman
                                                   *Cambridge, Massachusetts*
                                                   Terrence E. Deal
                                                   *Nashville, Tennessee*

Many of the stories and other material about organizations included in this book relate to company lore and were obtained during our consulting, training, and personal experiences as customers, consumers, and informal observers of organizations and public events. The research is based on a combination of published accounts, our own data, personal accounts, and commonly accepted knowledge and beliefs.

# Acknowledgments

In *Modern Approaches,* we noted, "Book writing often feels like a lonely process, even when an odd couple is doing the writing." This time around, the odd couple is older and, possibly, odder. Yet, for several reasons, the process seemed less lonely. Students in our introductory courses in organizations at both Harvard and Vanderbilt have continued to provide criticism, challenge, and support. A diverse set of graduate students from various schools of education, business, government, medicine, nursing, law, divinity, and public health have rarely been bashful about letting us know what parts of the book they found helpful or otherwise. A large group of undergraduates in Vanderbilt's Peabody College showed themselves delightfully unwilling to suffer turgid prose and provided many helpful suggestions. We also wish to thank each of the leaders and managers from whom we have learned in seminars, workshops, and consultations. The list of such people in business, health care, military, education, and other organizations is long in length and impressive in depth. Their wisdom is the foundation on which our work is based.

We also owe a large debt to our colleagues. The influence of all who helped us in *Modern Approaches* can still be seen in this work. But we particularly want to mention those who have made more recent contributions to *Reframing Organizations*—those with whom we have co-taught have enriched and broadened our thinking in significant ways. At Harvard, Susan Moore Johnson contributed a deep understanding of public schools, a commitment to student learning, and a critical eye. Co-teachers at Vanderbilt included Willis Hawley, whose structural and conceptual emphasis reinforced our commitment to social science traditions; John Glidewell, whose wisdom and understanding of social psychology have deepened our work in several places; Patricia Arnold, who has added important insights on families and human resource management; and Garth Andrus, whose interest in teams helped shape a chapter on the structural approach.

We have also co-taught with a number of teaching fellows and graduate assistants. At Harvard, we learned much from the contributions of Philip Cousins, Victor Friedman, Jeremiah Gule, James Honan, Cynthia Ingols, Barbara Karanian, Keith Merron, Hugh O'Doherty, Fernando Reimers, David Ross, Clarissa Sawyer, Betsy Schoenherr, Diana Smith, Lee Teitel, Margot Welch, and Dean Williams. At Peabody, we have benefited at the graduate level from the counsel and assistance of Casey Baluss, Patricia Bower, Mack McCrary, Connie Smith, Judy Waldo, Donna Wamsley, and Joan Vydra. Those who have shared the challenge of teaching organizational theory and behavior to undergraduates include Casey Baluss, Chris Briddick, Reva Chatman, Elaine Kresavage, Cheryl Lison, Janice Livengood, Mary Jane Murphy, Nicola Ritchie, Revaldo Rivera, Mark Smiley, Renee Wall, and Donna Wamsley. Our graduate students were also helpful in other ways; in particular, Casey Baluss was extremely helpful with last-minute editorial details. Mike Davis helped us locate some hard-to-find references.

Our colleagues at the National Center for Educational Leadership have provided stimulating insights to broaden and deepen our thinking, particularly around issues of leadership and schools as organizations. They include Susan Moore Johnson, Jerome Murphy, and Carol H. Weiss at Harvard; Leonard Bickman, Carolyn Evertson, Willis Furtwengler, Philip Hallinger, Willis Hawley, Catherine Marshall, and Joseph Murphy at Peabody, and Daniel Lortie at the University of Chicago.

We wish that we could thank all the colleagues and readers in this country and around the world who have provided valuable comments and suggestions, but the list is long and our memories keep getting shorter. Robert Marx, of the University of Massachusetts, deserves special mention as a charter member of the frames family. His interest in the frames, his creativity in developing teaching designs, and his eye for video material have aided our teaching immensely. Both he and Craig Lundberg of Cornell provided very thoughtful and detailed comments on an earlier draft of the book. Robert Wimpelberg, of the University of New Orleans, and his graduate student, Diane Rousell, contributed directly to the emphasis on reframing in this book. Others to whom our debt is particularly clear include Chris Argyris, Sam Bacharach, Warren Bennis, Patricia Bower, John Bransford, Barbara Bunker, Ellen Castro, Sharon Conley, Joseph Cox, Linton Deck, Brooke Derr, Peter Frost, Patricia A. Graham, Esther Hamilton, Erwin Hargrove, Ralph Kilmann, Linda Martinez, John Meyer, Harrison Owen, Kent Peterson, Robert Quinn, Phillip Runkel, Michael Sales, Marshall Sashkin, Mary Jane Saxton, Oron South, Kit Taylor, Karl Weick, and Raymond Zammuto. The Brookline Group, now in its tenth year of exploring how to find joy and meaning in a life, is devoted to the study of organizations and continues to provide support and inspiration. Thanks to L. David Brown, Philip Mirvis, Barry Oshry, Douglas T. Hall, William Kahn, and Todd Jick.

Outside the United States, we are grateful to Max Elden in Norway, Cuno Pümpin and Peter Weisman in Switzerland, Ilpo Linko in Finland, Thomas Case in Brazil, Graham Pratt in the United Kingdom, Peter Normark and Dag Bjorkegren in Sweden, and Alexei Medvedev in the USSR.

Closer to home, we owe more than we can say to Linda Corey and Homa Aminmadani Shahsavari, without whom our sanity and health would be significantly diminished. Corey, in her steady, efficient way, has endured hand-written manuscripts from Deal, abuse from Bolman, and countless meals at Japanese restaurants— where she still staunchly spurns the sushi. Shahsavari, in her Persian elegance and extraordinary determination, has single-handedly wrested as much efficiency from Deal as is possible, given the material with which she now works. She is becoming a legend in her own time, despite working for someone who is, she is sure, a "legend in his own mind."

The next generation of Bolmans in themselves represent a fascinating complex organization. Edward's commitment to his own path, Shelly's resilient good cheer and wisdom, Lori's affection and thoughtfulness, Scott's persistence and rigor, and Chris's exuberance have enriched their father's life and contributed enormously to his growth. He wishes that he could give them as much as they have given him. They probably share his wish and hope that old age will bring even more intimacy and warmth.

Janie Deal has delighted her father in becoming a fascinating and independent young woman. Her hope that advancing years will temper her father's outrageousness has not yet been fully realized; she is still waiting for maturity and wisdom to come to full flower—particularly now that her father is a card-carrying member of AARP. He is longing to see what she eventually will become.

We dedicate the book to our wives, who have more than earned all the credit and appreciation we can give them. Joan Gallos, Bolman's spouse and closest colleague, combines intellectual challenge and critique with support and love. She has been an active collaborator in the development of our ideas, and her contributions have become so integrated into our own thinking that we are no longer able to thank her for all the ways that the book has gained from her wisdom and insights. Sandy Deal's training enables her to approach the field of organizations with a distinctive and illuminating slant. Her concentration on individual and family therapy has helped us make some even stronger connections to the field of clinical psychology. Sandy is a delightful partner whose love and support over the long term have made all the difference. She is a rare combination of courage and caring, intimacy and independence, responsibility and playfulness. To Joan and Sandy, thanks again. Six years later, we love you even more.

# The Authors

**Lee G. Bolman** is lecturer on education at the Harvard Graduate School of Education and an independent management consultant. He received his B.A. degree (1962) in history and his Ph.D. degree (1968) in administrative sciences, both from Yale University. Bolman's primary research interests have been in leadership and organizational behavior, and he has published numerous articles and chapters on management development, professional education, organizational conflict, and organizational development. He and coauthor Terrence E. Deal collaborated on an earlier book, *Modern Approaches to Understanding and Managing Organizations* (1984). Bolman and Deal also codirect the National Center for Educational Leadership, a consortium of Harvard, Vanderbilt, and the University of Chicago. Bolman has been a consultant to corporations, public agencies, universities, and public schools in the United States, Asia, Europe, and Latin America. At Harvard, he has served as educational chairperson of the Institute for Educational Management. He has been director and board chair of the Organizational Behavior Teaching Society and director of the National Training Laboratories Institute for Applied Behavioral Science.

**Terrence E. Deal** is professor of education at Peabody College of Vanderbilt University. Before joining Peabody, he served on the faculties of the Stanford University Graduate School of Education and the Harvard Graduate School of Education. He received his B.A. degree (1961) from LaVerne College in history, his M.A. degree (1966) from California State University at Los Angeles in educational administration, and his Ph.D. degree (1972) from Stanford University in education and sociology. Deal has been a policeman, public school teacher, high school principal, district officer administrator, and university professor. His primary research interests are in organizational symbolism and change. He is the author of six books, including the best-seller *Corporate Cultures* (with A. A. Kennedy, 1983). He has published numerous articles on change and leadership. He is a consultant to business, health care, military, educational, and religious organizations both inside and outside the United States. He lectures widely and teaches in a number of executive development programs. He and Lee Bolman are currently codirectors of the National Center for Educational Leadership.

# *Reframing Organizations*

# Part One

# Making Sense of Organizations

# 1

# *Introduction: The Power of Reframing*

Shortly after he became chief executive officer of General Motors in 1981, Roger Smith was hailed as a bold and visionary leader. Six years later, Smith himself ruefully said, "I'm not as smart as people said a few years ago, and not as dumb as they say now" (Smith, 1987, p. 26). *Business Week* ran a cover story under the title "General Motors: What Went Wrong? Eight Years and Billions of Dollars Haven't Made Its Strategy Succeed" (Hampton and Norman, 1987).

In 1979, General Motors had earned $3.5 billion on sales of $63 billion, and it held almost half the American car market. Earnings hit $4.5 billion in 1984 and $4.8 billion in 1988, but GM's market share and Roger Smith's reputation declined steadily during the decade. In 1987, Ford earned more than General Motors for the first time in sixty years.

Roger Smith's tenure at the helm of General Motors is one chapter in the longest automobile race in America: a competition between car makers rather than cars. The race that began in 1908 continues today. The lead has changed hands several times, and each shift has illustrated a basic challenge facing every manager: How do you match the right idea to the right problem, at the right time, and in the right way? Whether you are trying to manage a business in Stockholm or a school in Kansas City, a hospital in Singapore or an army unit in Switzerland, the question is always with you.

3

The basic aim of this book is to expand and enrich the ideas and styles that leaders and managers apply to problems and dilemmas. Too often they bring too few ideas to the challenges that they face. They live in psychic prisons because they cannot look at old problems in a new light and attack old challenges with different and more powerful tools—they cannot *reframe*. When they don't know what to do, they simply do more of what they do know. Many observers described Roger Smith as a brilliant manager with a wealth of ideas, but his way of framing the challenges at General Motors rarely changed. Smith's frame was not wrong, but incomplete. As a result, the largest corporation in the world stumbled through the 1980s with a truncated vision.

The ability to reframe experience enriches and broadens a leader's repertoire and serves as a powerful antidote to self-entrapment. Expanded choice enables managers to generate creative responses to the broad range of problems that they encounter—those that they face every day, as well as the recurring challenges that periodically come back to haunt them. We cannot count the number of times that managers have told us that they handled a particular problem the "only way" it could be done. Such statements betray a failure of both imagination and courage. It may be comforting to think that failure was unavoidable and that we did all we could. But it can be enormously liberating for managers to realize that there is *always* more than one way to respond to *any* organizational problem or dilemma. Managers are imprisoned only to the degree that their palette of ideas is impoverished.

We believe that this lack of imagination is a major cause of the shortfall between the reach and grasp of so many organizations—the gap between dreams and reality, between noble aspirations and disappointing outcomes. The wide chasm between managerial intent and organizational accomplishment is an increasingly pressing problem, and one that is made all the more acute by the growing dominance of organizations in our lives.

### Virtues and Drawbacks of Organized Activity

The first humanlike primates appeared on earth about twelve million years ago. During most of the time since then, our ancestors were hunters and gatherers. Human beings evolved in a vastly simpler social context than the one in which we now live. Only in the last ten or fifteen thousand years did human beings evolve institutions more complex than small, nomadic communities. Large organizations came to dominate the social landscape only in the last century. There was little need for professional managers when people could manage their own affairs. Now, however, we live in a vastly different world: "A century and a half of technological evolution [has] produced communication and transportation technologies that make our entire planet a global marketplace. Industrial technologies, beginning with the steam engine, have led to larger and larger factories to produce products for that marketplace. The changes mean that today's executives deal with thousands of interdependent relationships—linkages to people, groups, or organizations that have the power to affect their job performance. And the diversity of goals, opinions, and beliefs among these players is typically enormous" (Kotter, 1985, pp. 22-23).

The proliferation of complex organizations has made almost every human activity a collective one. We are born, raised, and educated in organizations. We work in them and rely on them for goods and services. Many of us will grow old and die in organizations. We have built so many organizations because of what they can do for us. They produce a wide range of consumer goods, bring entertainment into our homes, raise the standard of health care and education, and provide telephone and postal service.

But we all know the darker side to organizations. They often frustrate and sometimes exploit the people who work in them. Too often, their products do not work, their students learn very little, their patients remain ill, and their policies make things worse instead of better. Many organizations infuse work with so little meaning that jobs have no value beyond a paycheck. Almost everyone, everyday, receives services or goods from someone who obviously doesn't care. We are all familiar with the indifferent flight attendant, the surly checkout clerk, and the hostile bureaucrat.

The same organization that put a man on the moon launched the ill-fated *Challenger* space shuttle. Around the world, schools are blamed for a wide range of social ills, universities are said to close more minds than they open, and government agencies are criticized for their red tape and rigidity. In the United States, the agricultural extension service helped to foster the enormous productivity of the American farmer. Across the world, Mikhail Gorbachev restructured the Soviet agricultural ministries twice in his first four years as general secretary, but the goal of better harvests remained elusive. It is often taken for granted that government agencies are badly managed. The sarcastic phrase "good enough for government work" reflects widespread cynicism about the performance of public agencies.

The private sector has its own problems. Automobile manufacturers recall faulty cars, and baby food producers apologize for adulterated fruit juice. Industrial accidents dump chemicals, oil, toxic gas, and radioactive materials into the air and water. Corporate greed and insensitivity create havoc for individual lives and communities. The bottom line is that we are hard pressed to manage organizations in such a way that their benefits regularly exceed their costs.

### Strategies for Improving Organizations: The Track Record

It is not that we have not tried. Ambitious efforts to improve organizations are commonplace. They rely mainly on at least three major strategies: management, consultation, and government intervention.

The first, and most basic, strategy for improving organizations concentrates on improving management and leadership. Modern mythology promises that organizations will work just fine if only they are well managed. Managers are supposed to have the big picture and be responsible for their organization's overall well-being and productivity. Unfortunately, they have not always been equal to the task. Managers arm themselves with decision trees, PERT charts, management information systems, management by objectives programs, performance evaluation schemes, and a panoply of other tools and techniques. They go forth with this rational arsenal to try to tame the wild and primitive social creations mundanely called organizations. Yet in the end, irrational forces often prevail. Defeated and battle-scarred managers move on to another job or retreat to management seminars and university M.B.A. programs. There they look for more sophisticated weaponry that may give them a better chance in the next encounter. They seek some way to avoid their old mistakes or, at least, to face their problems and challenges with more confidence.

A second strategy for improving organizations is to use consultants. The sheer number of consultants available today is overwhelming. Their variety is equally striking. Most consultants have a specialty: mergers, wages and benefits, strategic planning, reorganization, conflict resolution, information technology, training, organization development, and many more. For every managerial question or problem, there is usually a consultant somewhere willing to offer assistance.

Yet for all their numbers, and their fees, consultants have yet to eliminate the human problems that plague most businesses, agencies, military services, hospitals, and schools. In fact, the consultant sometimes becomes an additional barrier to solving a problem, and there is no evidence that consultants succeed more often than they fail. There are more than a few managers who wish that the Hippocratic injunction to "Above all else, do no harm" applied as much to consultants as to physicians. For their part, consultants blame clients for failure to implement the consultants' insights. Like managers, consultants retreat to their offices or to university campuses to rejuvenate their magic—or to look for another organization that will be more receptive to their message.

A third strategy for improving organizations is through government intervention: legislation, regulation, and policy making. Elected officials often become impatient with the efforts of consultants and managers. They face heat from constituents who pester them to do something about a variety of organizational ills: schools that fail to educate, public agencies that waste resources, corporations that pollute the environment or produce defective products, to name only a few. Legislatures often respond by making "policy." Schools, for example, have been a repeated target of legislative reforms. In the United States, however, an enormous increase in the educational policy establishment and in legislation has not produced a corresponding increase in public satisfaction with the schools. Similar problems occur in other nations. Before he was forced out as leader of Moscow's Communist party, and before his subsequent election as president of the Russian republic, Boris Yeltsin gave the following speech on school reform: "R. Kh. Khabibiulin, former director of School no. 528 in the Soviet District, has been sentenced to five years' incarceration. Systematic extortion of bribes from his school staff was more than just a 'hobby' with him—it was the main content of his administrative-pedagogical activities. A total of 330 educators were punished for violations of labor discipline and drunkenness in forty-seven training schools investigated by the Public Prosecutor's Office" (Yeltsin, 1986, p. 2).

Increasingly, the activities of private firms are influenced by legislative policy. Government tries to solve some problems through regulation and others through deregulation. Government regulates safety standards for automobiles, clothing, and pharmaceuticals. It regulates occupational safety and environmental pollution. In the United States, government tried to improve both the airlines and the telephone system through deregulation, on the assumption that competition would lead to better performance. In both cases, many wonder if the costs have not exceeded benefits.

It is more the rule than the exception for policies to go awry as they make their long and meandering journeys from the legislative floor to the target organizations. A literature has developed around the problem of "implementation." Essentially, it portrays a continuing saga of the perverse ways in which policies produce something other than what policymakers had in mind. Policies often create new problems that require new policies—until the time comes to develop a policy of no policies. Then, government can deregulate, and the cycle can begin anew.

The difficulties surrounding each strategy for improving organizations are well documented. Intentions are nearly always exemplary. But the human costs usually outweigh the benefits, and the problems are often far more durable than the solutions. It is as if tens of thousands of hardworking, highly motivated pioneers kept hacking away at a jungle swamp that continued to produce new growth faster than anyone could clear the old. Some day, there may be a clearing and the swamp might be drained. The basic purpose of this book is to help the pioneers improve their odds.

## Theory Base

Behind every effort to improve organizations lies a set of assumptions, or theories, about how organizations work and what might make them work better. All managers have theories, though they may not think so (we use the term *theory* broadly to refer to any set of ideas that attempts to perform the basic functions of theory in science: explanation, prediction, and control). Consultants are often hired because of their special theories. Every policy derives from a theory that legislators champion, perhaps because they have listened to an admired manager or consultant. "Ideas in good currency" generate strategies for improving organizations. Forty or fifty years ago, for example, a number of school districts in the United States tried to improve teacher performance with incentive pay schemes; almost all those plans were quietly abandoned as unworkable (Johnson, 1984). In the late 1980s the idea became fashionable again.

Managers, consultants, and policymakers formally or informally draw upon a variety of theories in their efforts to change or improve organizations. However, the organization theory base itself is relatively new. Only in the last twenty-five years have social scientists devoted much time or attention to developing ideas about how organizations work (or why they often fail to work). The theory base is also diverse. Within the social sciences, several major schools of thought have evolved, each with its own ideas about how managers can best bring social collectives under control.

*Rational systems theorists* emphasize organizational goals, roles, and technology, and they look for ways to develop structures that best fit organizational purposes and environmental demands.

*Human resource theorists* emphasize the interdependence between people and organizations. They focus on ways to develop a better fit between people's needs, skills, and values, on the one hand, and their formal roles and relationships, on the other.

*Political theorists* see power, conflict, and the distribution of scarce resources as the central issues. They argue that organizations are like jungles in which cooperation is achieved by managers who understand the uses of power, coalitions, bargaining, and conflict.

*Symbolic theorists* focus on problems of meaning. They are more likely than other theorists to find virtue in organizational misbehavior and to emphasize the limited ability of managers to create organizational cohesion through power or rational design. In this view, managers must rely on images, drama, magic, and sometimes even luck or the supernatural to bring some semblance of order to organizations.

We summarize these schools here only to point out their differences. Each body of theory purports to rest on a scientific foundation. But theories are often theologies that preach only one version of scripture. Each theory offers its own version of what organizations are like and its own vision of what they should be like. Each also provides a range of ideas and techniques to reach the promised land of effectiveness and efficiency. A modern manager who wants to improve an organization thus encounters a cacophony of different voices and visions. As an example, an executive looking for advice about how to deal with excessive turnover among middle managers could expect to receive at least four very different suggestions:

"As your firm has grown, managers' responsibilities have probably become blurred and overlapping. When reporting relationships are confused, you get stress and conflict. You need to restructure."

"You are probably neglecting your managers' needs for autonomy and for opportunities to participate in important decisions. You need an attitude survey to pinpoint the problems."

"Your real problem is that you have been ignoring the realities of organizational politics. The union has too much power and top management has too little. No one knows how to deal with conflict. There's turf protection everywhere. You have to bring politics out of the closet and get people to negotiate."

"Your company has never developed a strong value system, and growth has made the situation worse. Your managers don't find any meaning in their work. You need to revitalize your company's culture."

As another example, consider some recent initiatives to improve America's public schools. Different observers have different views on whether the schools are failing, holding their own, or succeeding. But there is even more disagreement about how to make them better. Economists favor free-market competition, political scientists recommend empowerment of major constituencies, and human resource experts emphasize the need to train teachers and administrators. Anthropologists focus on school culture, while structuralists tell us that we need longer school days, increased accountability, and more systematic approaches to the evaluation of teachers and administrators. As managers, consultants, and policy-makers turn to the theory base for help, they will find what we call *conceptual pluralism:* a jangling discord of multiple voices.

We have consolidated the major schools of organizational thought into four perspectives. There are currently many ways to label such perspectives: schemata, maps, images, and metaphors. We have chosen the label *frames* to characterize these different vantage points. Frames are both windows on the world and lenses that bring the world into focus. Frames filter out some things while allowing others to pass through easily. Frames help us to order experience and decide what action to take. Every manager, consultant, or policymaker uses a personal frame or image of organizations to gather information, make judgments, and determine how best to get things done. The more artistic among them are able to frame and reframe experience, sorting through the tangled underbrush to find solutions to problems. A critic once commented to Cezanne, "That doesn't look anything like a sunset." Pondering his painting, Cezanne responded, "Then you don't see sunsets the way I do." (Martinez, 1989) At the same time, leaders, like artists, must also bring their audience along. They must use their artistry to articulate and communicate their vision so that others are also able to see things differently.

Frames are also tools for action, and every tool has its strengths and limitations. With the wrong tool, it may be impossible to finish a job, while the right tool can make it easy. One or two tools may suffice for very simple jobs but not for more complex ones. Managers who master the hammer and expect all problems to be nails will find organizational life confusing and frustrating. The wise manager, like the skilled carpenter or the experienced cook, will want a diverse collection of high-quality implements. The experienced manager also knows that there is a great difference between possessing a tool and knowing how to use it. Only experience and practice will bring the skill and wisdom to use tools well.

Kurosawa's film *Rashomon* recounts the same event through the eyes of several witnesses. Each tells a very different story. Organizations are filled will people who have different stories about what is happening and what should be happening. Each story contains a glimpse of the truth, but each is a product of the prejudices and blind spots of the viewer. None of these versions of the truth is comprehensive enough to make the organization truly understandable or manageable.

The truly effective manager and leader will need multiple tools, the skill to use each of them, and the wisdom to match frames to situations. Consider the set of challenges facing Mikhail Gorbachev when he became general secretary of the Soviet Communist party in 1985. The Russian economy was performing badly and, in fact, had been getting worse for years. Corruption and inefficiency were rampant. Soviet agriculture had suffered six years of poor harvests, and Gorbachev himself had been responsible for agriculture (Medvedev, 1986). A growing number of managers and professionals believed that nothing short of dramatic structural change (*perestroika*) would get the economy back on track. Gorbachev and his allies launched a series of proposals for major structural reform of both the economy and the political system.

To succeed, however, this dramatic restructuring of Soviet industry would require managers with very different attitudes and skills from those that had been fostered under decades of centralized planning. In return for greater managerial and fiscal autonomy, organizations would be asked to generate revenues from sales rather than from the state budget. By Western standards, this may seem a very tame form of state capitalism, but it was a revolution for many Russian managers. The manager of a cement factory in Kiev or Novosibirsk has always been rewarded for meeting centrally planned production targets and for maintaining good relationships with party and government officials. It was less essential that her plant was producing what customers wanted or that the cement could be sold at a profit. She could always meet her payroll because the budget depended on the size of her staff rather than the efficiency of the plant. Short of a complete relearning of her attitudes, approaches, and skills—a thorough personal overhaul—how could she and thousands of managers like her cope with the new circumstances? Countless change efforts in organizations in the West have failed to meet significantly less daunting human resource challenges.

Gorbachev faced formidable political problems as well. When he came to power, he was the youngest Soviet leader since Stalin. He held a slim majority in the Communist party's Central Committee. It is true that he had the advantage of significant personal popularity both in the Soviet Union and abroad, and that he was the first Soviet leader who projected charisma and intelligence instead of terminal dullness on television. But his survival depended on retaining the support of the Communist party leadership. Nikita Khruschev, the last Soviet leader to threaten the power of the elite, had been exiled to a small *dacha* in the country. If Gorbachev moved too fast, he could easily suffer a similar fate, yet the pressing problems of the Soviet society and economy called for something more dramatic than a slow and tranquil gradualism. He faced a dilemma familiar to all leaders: How can I survive and still do what needs to be done?

Gorbachev's program also raised serious symbolic problems. The Communist party had been Gorbachev's route to leadership and remained his primary power base, yet the legitimacy of the party and the entire Soviet system was rooted in a Leninist ideology that seemed increasingly irrelevant and counterproductive. Contrary to Soviet expectations, the centrally planned, Leninist model simply was not working as well as the supposedly evil capitalist ones. And if the invention of the mainframe computer had helped to extend the life expectancy of centrally planned economies, the dawn of the microchip was their death knell. Big, centralized information-processing systems were an ideal tool for bureaucrats trying to manage large, complex economies. But the rapid spread of the microcomputer and the increasing pace of technological change in the 1980s created enormous new problems for central planners. Introduction of the microcomputer into the Soviet Union almost made it inevitable that there would be increasing pressure for decentralization, local autonomy, and experimentation, all of which are stifled by central bureaucracy.

But even if it was not working, how could a Communist leader move away from communism? How could he borrow ideas for change and reform from Western capitalism without undermining his legitimacy and provoking violent opposition from defenders of the faith? How could he unravel the centralization of power in Russia that went back to the early Tsars?

Gorbachev and his allies could succeed only by recognizing and responding to the full range and depth of the challenges that they faced. The same can be said of managers, consultants, and policymakers at every level in every nation. Whether their organization is large or small, public or private, success or failure hinges on their willingness to use multiple lenses. To cling to a single vantage point is to imprison oneself in a frustrating, self-made, and narrow intellectual jail cell. People who understand their own frame—and who have learned to rely on more than one perspective—are better equipped to understand and manage the complex everyday world of organizations. Sometimes, indeed, they can make a significant difference in how that world responds to its challenges.

The perspectives, or frames, outlined in this book are based on four major schools of organizational theory and research, and we have outlined the central assumptions and propositions of each of them. In doing so, we know that we have made omissions. Our goal is usable knowledge. Accepting elegance and parsimony as the criteria for a good theory, we have sought ideas that are powerful enough to capture the subtlety and complexity of organizational life, yet simple enough not to overwhelm the manager or leader. Simplistic ideas mislead and ultimately disappoint. In recent years, there has been a steady barrage of thin books that purport to answer all the problems of organization with a few charming stories and maxims. On the other hand, cumbersome ideas are useless in the heat of practice. Much of the social science literature is read only when it is required reading, and even then with little joy.

Our distillation drew much from the social sciences—from sociology, psychology, political science, and anthropology. It drew even more heavily from our own experience in working with managers and organizations. Thousands of managers and scores of organizations have been our mentors. They helped us to sift through the social science research to identify the ideas that work in practice.

We have sorted the insights drawn from both research and practice into four major ways in which both academics and practitioners make sense of organizations.

The structural frame, drawing mainly on the discipline of sociology, emphasizes the importance of formal roles and relationships. Structures—commonly depicted by means of organization charts—are created to fit an organization's environment and technology. Organizations allocate responsibilities to participants ("division of labor") and create rules, policies, and management hierarchies to coordinate diverse activities. Problems arise when the structure does not fit the situation. At that point, some form of reorganization is needed to remedy the mismatch.

The human resource frame, based particularly on the ideas of organizational social psychologists, starts with the fundamental premise that organizations are inhabited by individuals who have needs, feelings, and prejudices. They have both skills and limitations. They have a great capacity to learn, as well as a sometimes greater capacity to defend old attitudes and beliefs. From a human resource perspective, the key to effectiveness is to tailor organizations to people—to find an organizational form that enables people to get the job done while feeling good about what they are doing.

The political frame, invented and developed primarily by political scientists, views organizations as arenas in which different interest groups compete for power and scarce resources. Conflict is everywhere because of the differences in needs, perspectives, and life-styles among various individuals and groups. Bargaining, negotiation, coercion, and compromise are all part of everyday organizational life. Coalitions form around specific interests and change as issues come and go. Problems arise because power is concentrated in the wrong places or because it is so broadly dispersed that nothing gets done. Solutions are developed through political skill and acumen—as Machiavelli suggested they should be centuries ago in *The Prince*.

The symbolic frame, drawing on social and cultural anthropology, abandons the assumptions of rationality that appear in the other frames. It treats organizations as tribes, theater, or carnivals. In this view, organizations are cultures that are propelled more by rituals, ceremonies, stories, heroes, and myths than by rules, policies, and managerial authority. Organization is theater: various actors play out the drama inside the organization, while outside audiences form impressions based on what they see occurring onstage. Problems arise when actors play their parts badly, when symbols lose their meaning, when ceremonies and rituals lose their potency. Improvements in rebuilding the expressive or spiritual side of organizations come through the use of symbol, myth, and magic.

Each of these frames has its own vision or image of reality. Only when managers, consultants, and policymakers can look through all four are they likely to appreciate the depth and complexity of organizational life. Galileo discovered this when he devised the first telescope. Each lens that he added contributed to a more accurate image of the heavens. Successful managers take advantage of the same truth. They frame and reframe until they understand the situation at hand.

### Our Objectives

A behavioral view of objectives holds that we should specify with as much precision as possible what managers will be able to do as a result of their learning (for example, managers will be able to describe the four basic organizational frames and specify how the frames can be applied to specific managerial cases). But different individuals have different backgrounds, face different challenges, and need to learn different things. In a rapidly changing, turbulent world, moreover, the behaviors that work today may be irrelevant tomorrow.

Our goal is different: we do not want to produce specific kinds of behavior but to cultivate habits of mind and to enrich managerial thinking. In particular, we want to reduce the gap between how managers, consultants, and policymakers typically think and how they might think. We have witnessed this gap repeatedly in the painful, poignant, and sometimes tragic experiences of the many managers who have contributed to our own learning. We continually learn from them—in universities, in executive-development programs, and in the unruly world of managerial life.

Our collaboration began with a doctoral course on organizations at the Harvard Graduate School of Education. Since then, the range of people and places that have contributed to our learning has been enormous. In the public sector we have worked with small school districts, sprawling community colleges, and enormous government agencies. In the private sector, we have worked with airlines and banks, with manufacturers in the Rust Belt, and with high-flying consumer marketers, as well as with high-tech, low-tech, and no-tech companies. Our work has taken us to Latin America, Asia, and Europe (both eastern and western). We have tested our framework against managerial cases and dilemmas from Belgium and Brazil, China and Czechoslovakia, Kenya and Korea, Singapore and Switzerland, to name a few.

All those experiences have impressed us with the richness and diversity of organizations, cultures, and managerial life. The chancellor of schools in New York City, the president of Stanford University, and the director of Vocational-Technical School no. 628 in Moscow are all expected to provide educational leadership, but their situations are vastly different. Skoda, the state automobile monopoly in Czechoslovakia, faces a set of challenges quite distinct from those of Toyota in Japan or General Motors in the United States. Management strategies that might work brilliantly in Sweden could lead to disaster in Colombia. Managers ignore the power of such differences at their peril. But we have also been struck by the commonalities. Issues of structure and people, of politics and culture are important *everywhere,* and the costs of impoverished managerial thinking can be observed in organizations throughout the world.

In every country that we have visited, we have found managers who think in ways that limit their vision and impede their ability to understand and respond to the complexities of everyday life in organizations.

The alternatives in Exhibit 1 represent two distinctive ways of approaching management and leadership. One is a rational-technical approach that emphasizes certainty and control, the other is a more expressive, artistic conception that encourages flexibility, creativity, and interpretation. The former sees managers as mechanics, the latter sees them as leaders and artists.

Managers who master the ability to reframe report a liberating sense of choice and power. They are able to develop new alter-

**Exhibit 1. Expanding Managerial Thinking.**

| *How Managers Think* | *How Managers Might Think* |
|---|---|
| 1. Managers often have limited views of organizations (for example, many attribute most organizational problems to the defects of various individuals and groups). | 1. They need a holistic framework that encourages inquiry into a range of significant issues: people, power, structure, and symbols. |
| 2. Regardless of the source of a problem, managers often choose rational and structural solutions: rational discourse, restructuring, facts, and logic. | 2. They need a palette that identifies a full array of options: bargaining as well as training, ceremony as well as reorganization. |
| 3. Managers have often been taught to value certainty, rationality, and control, and to shun ambiguity and paradox. | 3. Managers need to become more creative and more willing to take risks in response to the dilemmas and paradoxes of organizational life. They need to focus on finding the right questions as much as the right answers, on finding meaning and pattern amidst clutter and confusion. |
| 4. Leaders often try to change organizations by finding the one right answer and the one best way; they are stunned by the turmoil and resistance that they thereby generate. | 4. Leaders must be passionately committed to their principles but also flexible in understanding and responding to the events around them. |

natives and new ideas about what their organization needs. They become better attuned to and more able to learn from the people around them. They are less often startled by organizational perversity, and they learn to anticipate the turbulent twists and turns of organizational life. The result is managerial freedom—and more productive, humane organizations.

We would be foolish to expect that simply reading a book will produce dramatic outcomes for everyone. But the artful combination of the four frames with insightful instruction in classrooms, seminars, and workshops will enable people to reflect in more profound ways on their experience. With the help of case studies, videotapes, simulations, and role plays, they are able to learn a great deal about personal and organizational possibilities.

The lessons often continue long after the "students" have left the classroom because the frames provide a way for them to continue to learn from their experience.

Broudy (1981) observed that learning can be guided by several different purposes. Learning directed to recall or application is the easiest to accomplish. Learning that creates associations that come to mind in subsequent experience is more difficult to achieve, but it is also more important. The highest order of learning in Broudy's view, however, involves the development of *stencils* that frame and give meaning to experience. It is by far the most difficult kind of learning to master but it is also the most effective. The frames serve as stencils. They provide the opportunity to learn and relearn from organizational experience. With multiple stencils, managers, consultants, and policymakers can make use of different frames, blending them into a coherent, pragmatic, personal theory of organizations. We believe that an explicit introduction and grounding in all four frames can enrich native intuition and improve the chances of success even for those who were not born with all the right stuff to be brilliant managers or artistic and charismatic leaders.

Artistry is neither exact nor precise. The artist interprets experience and expresses it in a form that can be felt, understood, and appreciated by others. Art allows for emotion, subtlety, ambiguity. An artist reframes the world to help us see new possibilities. Modern organizations rely too much on engineering and too little on art in their effort to foster such attributes as quality, commitment, and creativity. Art is not a replacement for engineering, but an enhancement. Artistic leaders and managers are essential in helping us see beyond today's organizational forms to those that will release untapped individual energies and improve collective performance. The leader as artist will rely on images as well as memos, poetry as well as policy, reflection as well as command, and reframing as well as refitting.

# 2

# Simple Ideas,
# Complex Organizations

Early in the morning of August 31, 1983, Kim Eui
Donz, a Korean Airlines flight engineer, entered the
cockpit of Flight 007. His responsibility was to program
the INS (inertial navigation system) that would direct
the automatic pilot on the 4,100-mile flight from Anchorage to Seoul. Routinely, he entered the plane's run-
way ramp position into the computer. Unknowingly,
his entry was ten degrees off; he noted the plane's position as W139 instead of W149. A warning light blinked
on when he entered the incorrect position, but he assumed that the computer had malfunctioned. That ten-
degree error programmed the INS to believe that the
plane was actually starting from a position some 300
miles *east* of Anchorage. The error should have been
caught. Elaborate cross-checking is built into the work
of airline pilots, but pilots are people—and people
sometimes take shortcuts. The aircraft commander,
Captain Chun, revised his flight plan at the last minute,
and the crew had to rush through their routine flight
checks.

    The Anchorage control tower cleared Flight 007
to proceed directly to the Bethel checkpoint, and Cap-

tain Chun switched on the INS without verifying the
settings. After takeoff, air traffic control gave the flight
a more direct route to save time and fuel. But the new
route bypassed Bethel, the last checkpoint before they
flew over water on a route with no checkpoints until
they reached Asia. The crew and passengers were now
en route to an unknown destination. Even then, the error might still have been detected if Captain Chun had
stayed on the flight deck. But after the seat belt sign was
turned off, he went back to the first-class cabin to mix
with dignitaries and talk to deadheading KAL pilots.
The "finger error" of ten degrees in fact put the plane
on a course similar to that flown by American recon-
naissance flights near Soviet airspace. To Soviet radar,
KAL 007 looked like a routine and familiar blip until it
did the unexpected. Instead of turning away, Flight 007
crossed the border into Soviet territory.

Another human organization came into play—
the Soviet Air Defense Force. Because radar operators
could not identify the intruding aircraft, four intercep-
tors were sent up. Soviet commanders were thrown into
panic and confusion. An unidentified intruder was as
dangerous as it was puzzling. If this was a reconnais-
sance plane, why wasn't it turning away? When they
still could not identify Flight 007, still more fighters
were dispatched. The flight was now well inside Soviet
airspace, following a course that would take it between
two major Soviet air bases. At 3:12 A.M. a Soviet SU-15
fighter locked on to the KAL 747. The pilot was ordered
to identify the aircraft. Unable to do so, he switched on
his weapon system and carried out an order to signal
the intruder with machine gun fire. No response. At
3:26 A.M., the pilot fired two missiles. He reported to
ground control: "The target is destroyed." Two
hundred sixty-nine people fell to their deaths [based on
Hersch, 1986].

The ensuing outrage produced charges and countercharges.
Was the plane on a spy mission for the United States? Had the

Russians intentionally shot down a civilian aircraft? The KAL 007 incident is a dramatic version of an old story. At first glance, it is simply one more example of human error, but it is actually much more than that. Korean Airlines had systems to prevent such errors from occurring, and those systems failed. It had procedures that were designed to detect and correct error if it did occur, and those also failed. Similar examples can be found in other well-publicized disasters: Three Mile Island, Chernobyl, and the destruction of the space shuttle *Challenger*. Each illustrates a similar chain of error, miscommunication, and misguided actions.

The endless spate of conspiracy theories to explain John F. Kennedy's assassination suggests that we often prefer to believe that a dramatic and bizarre outcome must have been produced by extraordinary antecedents. But the tragedy of KAL 007 can be traced to ordinary processes that occur routinely in and between organizations. Error and chaos are the everyday stuff of managerial life. But many of these errors are insidious because they are subtle or even invisible. A good example is the following case, a true story that has been disguised to protect both the innocent and the guilty.

> Helen Demarco arrived in her office to find a clipping from a local newspaper. The headline read, "Osborne Announces Plan." Paul Osborne had been brought in two months earlier as chief executive of the organization with a mandate to "revitalize, cut costs, and improve efficiency." After twenty years with the organization, Helen had achieved a senior management position. She had not yet talked directly with Paul Osborne, but her boss reported directly to him. Like other long-term employees, Helen waited with curiosity and some apprehension to learn what the new chief would do. She was startled when she read the plan. Many of its most important aspects rested on technical assumptions that related directly to Helen's area of expertise. Helen knew that Osborne was a professional manager with no particular technical skills, and she immediately saw that the new plan contained fatal technical flaws. "If he tries to implement this, it will be the most expensive man-

agement mistake since the Edsel," Helen thought to herself.

Two days later, Helen was one of the several senior managers who received a memo from Paul Osborne instructing them to form a committee to begin immediate work on implementation of the Osborne revitalization plan. The group met, and everyone agreed that the plan was "crazy."

"What do we do?" they said to one another.

"Why don't we just tell him that the plan can't work?" said one manager.

Several others rejected that approach: "We can't do that! He already thinks we're too conservative and not really creative. Besides, he's on record saying that this plan will be great. If we tell him it's no good, he'll just think that we're defensive."

"Well, we can't just go ahead with it. It's bound to fail!"

"That's true," said Helen, "but we could tell him that we are making a study of how to implement the plan."

Helen's suggestion was overwhelmingly approved by the committee members. They told Paul Osborne that the study was starting, and were able to get a substantial budget to support the "research." But the real purpose of the study was more subtle (or more sinister): to discover a way to kill the plan without alienating Osborne.

Over time, the group developed a strategy. They developed a very lengthy, technical report, filled with graphs, tables, numbers, and impenetrable technical jargon. The report offered Osborne two options. Option A, his original plan, was presented as technically feasible, but the price tag was phenomenal—well beyond anything the organization could possibly afford. Option B, billed as a "modest downscaling" of the original plan, turned out to be much more affordable.

When Paul pressed the members of the group for

an explanation of the extraordinary difference in costs
between the two proposals, they responded with technical jargon and extensive quotations from the charts.
They did not mention that if he were able to wade
through all the data in the report, he might see through
the smoke screen that even Option B would provide
very few benefits at a very high cost.

Osborne thought and argued and pressed for
more information. He finally agreed to proceed with
Option B. Since the plan took more than two years to
implement, Paul Osborne had moved on to another organization before the plan was fully operational. In
fact, the "Osborne plan" was widely described as an extraordinary innovation that proved once again Paul Osborne's ability to revitalize ailing organizations.

Helen came away from this experience with deep feelings of
frustration and failure. The Osborne plan, in her view, was a wasteful mistake, and she had participated in the charade. But, she said
to herself, I really didn't have much choice. Osborne was determined to go ahead with the plan. It would have been career suicide
to try to stop it.

In fact, Helen did have other choices; there are always alternatives in any managerial quandary. Tragedies occur because managers cannot foresee the issues, are unaware of their options, or lack
the artistry and skill to chart a different course. Helen Demarco,
Paul Osborne, and the crew of KAL 007 all thought that they were
performing effectively. They were tripped up in part by human
fallibility, but they were also misled by their limited understanding
of the circumstances. The first step in managerial wisdom and artistry is to understand the nature of the beast—the situation—you are
up against.

## Properties of Organizations

Human organizations can be exciting and challenging places, and
that is how they are usually depicted in management texts and
annual reports. But organizations can be snakepits as well as rose

gardens. To assume that they are always one or the other distorts reality. Managers need to be mindful of several basic characteristics of organizations that can be opportunities for the wise or traps for the unwary.

*Organizations Are Complex.* This statement is true for a number of reasons. First, organizations are populated by people, and our ability to understand and predict human behavior is still very limited. Second, the interactions among different individuals, groups, and organizations can be extremely complicated. The transactions among the flight crew of KAL 007 show the intricacies that can arise even in a three-person cockpit. Larger organizations usually have a bewildering array of people, departments, technologies, goals, and environments. The complexity is compounded even further when a number of different organizations are involved. In the case of KAL 007, disaster resulted from a chain of events within and among several organizations. Almost anything can affect anything else in a collective activity. The permutations produce complex, causal knots that are very hard to disentangle. Osborne probably never understood the real story of what happened to the plan that bore his name. Even after exhaustive investigation, our explanation of what happened to KAL 007 is still woven from conjecture and supposition. We may never know the real story.

*Organizations Are Surprising.* It is hard to predict the outcome of decisions or initiatives in an organization. Paul Osborne believed that his plan represented a significant improvement for the organization. Helen and her group thought that it was an expensive albatross. If Helen was right, Osborne actually made matters *worse* by trying to improve them and might have produced better results by leaving things alone.

The solution to yesterday's problem often creates impediments to getting anything done in the future, and it may even create new possibilities for disaster. Think of the procedural hurdles and bureaucratic obstacles that are often put in place in an organization after a disaster such as Flight 007 or the loss of the space shuttle *Challenger*. A friend of ours is the president of a chain of retail stores. In the firm's early years, he had a problem with two sisters who worked in the same store. To prevent this kind of problem from recurring, he established a nepotism policy that prohibited two members of the same family from working for the company. Some years later, two of his employees met at work, fell in love, and began to live together. The president was stunned when they came to ask him if they could get married without being fired. Taking action in an organization is like firing a cue ball into a large and complex array of billiard balls. So many balls bounce off one another in so many directions that it is hard to know if the final outcome will bear any resemblance to what was intended.

*Organizations Are Deceptive.* Not only do organizations defy expectations, they often camouflage the surprise. The Soviet Air Defense did not want to admit how surprised and confused it was by Flight 007. To do so could reveal vital weaknesses in its defense system. Paul Osborne expected that Helen and her colleagues would work hard to implement his plan. He would have been surprised to learn that their "research" was really a holding action and that the "technical report" was actually artful camouflage.

Helen did not engage in deception because of a character flaw or a personality disorder. She knew deception was wrong and later regretted her actions. Yet she still believed that her behavior was the only moral choice under the circumstances. Sophisticated managers know that what happened to Paul Osborne happens routinely in organizations. Even though programs for improving an organization might be counterproductive, subordinates usually do not say so. Challenging the authority of a KAL captain would violate a strong core value of East Asian cultures. It is a taboo that a first officer or flight engineer will often honor even when faced with catastrophe. Such sensitivity to one's place in the formal pecking order is not confined to Asia. People in almost any culture are reluctant to offend their superiors. They often feel that the boss would not listen to them or might even punish them for being resistant or insubordinate. A friend who occupies a senior position in a large government agency puts it simply, "Communications in organizations are rarely candid, open, or timely."

*Organizations Are Ambiguous.* Because organizations are complex, surprising, and deceptive, they are often highly ambiguous. Figuring out what is really happening in businesses, hospitals, schools, or public agencies is difficult. Even if we do know what is happening, it is hard to know what it means or how we should interpret it. Helen Demarco was never sure how Paul Osborne really felt, how receptive he would be to other points of view, or what kind of compromise he would be willing to accept. She and her peers then added to the ambiguity by trying to keep their boss in the dark. When you add additional organizations—or nations—to the human equation, as was illustrated in the KAL case, the level of ambiguity increases.

Ambiguity comes from a number of sources. Sometimes, information is incomplete or vague. Sometimes the same information is interpreted in different ways by different people. At other times, ambiguity is deliberately created as a way to hide problems or avoid conflict. Much of the time, organizational events and processes are so complex, scattered, and uncoordinated that no one can fully understand—let alone control—what is happening. McCaskey (1982) lists the following sources of ambiguity in organizations:

1. *We are not sure what the problem is.* Definitions of the problem are vague or competing, and any given problem is intertwined with other messy problems.
2. *We are not sure what is really happening.* Information is incomplete, ambiguous, and unreliable, and people disagree on how to interpret the information that is available.
3. *We are not sure what we want.* We have multiple goals that are either unclear or conflicting or both. Different people want different things, leading to political and emotional conflict.
4. *We do not have the resources that we need.* Shortages of time, attention, or money make a difficult situation even more chaotic.
5. *We are not sure who is supposed to do what.* Roles are unclear, there is disagreement about who is responsible for what, and things keep shifting as players come and go.
6. *We are not sure how to get what we want.* Even if we agree on what we want, we are not sure (or we disagree) about what causes what.
7. *We are not sure how to determine if we have succeeded.* We are

not sure what criteria to use to evaluate success. If we do know the criteria, we are not sure how to measure them.

## Coping with Ambiguity and Complexity

When an event is clear and unambiguous, it is relatively easy for different people to agree on what is happening. A fact is a fact. It is fairly easy to determine if a train is on schedule, if a plane landed safely, or if a clock is keeping accurate time. But many of the most important issues confronting managers are not so clear-cut. Harold Geneen, the chief executive of the American conglomerate ITT, used to hound his subordinates for the "unshakable facts" (Deal and Kennedy, 1982). But in any organization, solid facts are often hard to find. Will a reorganization work? Was a meeting successful? Why did a decision made by consensus turn out not to work? When the issues are complex and the evidence incomplete, individuals must make judgments or interpretations. The judgments they make depend on their perceptions—their beliefs, expectations, and assumptions—of the issues at hand. Most often, a fact is a social interpretation, largely based on what people expect and want their world to be like.

We can see the influence of social interpretation by considering a relatively straightforward task: asking people to determine the suit and number of a playing card. In a classic experiment, different playing cards were projected on a screen and people were asked to identify each card. The color of the cards was reversed in some instances, so that people were seeing a red nine of clubs or a black jack of hearts. People usually reinterpreted the reversed cards to make them "right"—the red club became either a black club or a red heart.

When people were given more time to view the anomalous cards, many became uncomfortable. They knew that something was wrong, but they had trouble saying what it was. Some could not determine why the cards were incorrect, no matter how much time they had to study them. People's perspectives influence what they see. What is internal to them is as important as what is outside—sometimes more so. Given the fuzzy realities of everyday life in organizations, it is hardly surprising that people try to make that world conform to their internal maps.

The world of most managers is an unending series of puzzles or "messes." In order to act decisively—without creating more problems—managers need first to determine what is happening. They then need to proceed to a deeper level: "What is *really* going on here?" (Goffman, 1974) This important diagnostic distinction is often overlooked in the rush to make decisions. Managers tend to make superficial analyses of "what is happening" and then immediately look for a solution to the putative problem. More often than not, the solution is selected from those in vogue at the time. Market share declining? Try strategic planning. Quality a problem? Experiment with quality circles.

A better alternative is to probe more deeply into the situation. "What is *really* going on here?" These more careful assessments sometimes show that we have a problem. In other situations, we find that we are locked between the horns of a dilemma. The first possibility stimulates the search for a satisfactory solution. The second requires a choice based on values and ethics, or enough patience to wait until circumstances change on their own.

Suppose that you consult a physician with symptoms of a fever and a runny nose. You would probably not be happy to hear the physician say, "Let me call around and see what others are doing." Physicians are prohibited from taking such a course by the aforementioned principle of the Hippocratic Oath: Above all else, do no harm. Physicians are trained to find recognizable patterns in presenting symptoms. A bacterial infection is treatable with antibiotics, but the normal prescription for a virus—which means roughly that the doctor does not know much more than you do— is "rest, drink plenty of liquids, and call me in a week if things don't clear up." It is just as crucial to make the correct diagnosis in organizations. Flight 007 is one of countless examples of the costs of acting without knowing what is really going on. According to Admiral Carlisle A. H. Trost (1989), who currently serves as chief of U.S. Naval Operations, figuring out what is going on in a complex world is the heart of leadership. Otherwise leaders are caught off guard and put off balance by events they do not really understand. In Trost's words, they "lose the bubble" (1989, p. 2).

People rarely enjoy losing the bubble or feeling out of control. They want their world to be understandable, predictable, and manageable. Even in the face of inconsistent evidence, as in the playing card experiment, people will try to make the world fit their current theories about it. They may be right, or, like Captain Chun, they may be dead wrong. What they want above all is a theory that works for them and helps them figure out what is going on in a particular situation.

The theories that we learn and carry with us determine whether a given situation is confusing or clear, meaningful or cryptic, a disaster or a learning experience. Theories are essential because of a simple—but very basic—fact about human perception in organizations: There is simply too much happening in any given situation for an individual to attend to everything. To understand what is going on and to take action, the individual needs theories that will do two things:

1. Tell the individual both what is important and what can be safely ignored.
2. Group a great deal of different pieces of information into patterns or concepts.

To someone who is not a pilot, the cockpit of a 747 jetliner is a very complex and confusing array of controls, switches, and gauges. But an experienced pilot can glance at the instruments briefly and know a great deal about the status of the aircraft. A nonpilot could stare at the same instruments indefinitely and learn almost nothing. It is not that the pilot is necessarily more intelligent or has a better memory than the nonpilot. But the pilot has learned a set of patterns that group a lot of information into a few manageable chunks. It takes hundreds of hours to learn the concepts, but once they are learned, they can be used with enormous ease, speed, and, usually, accuracy.

While you are learning a pattern, you have to spend a great deal of time concentrating on it. Whether you are learning to program a computer, prove a theorem, play a musical instrument, or return a tennis serve, learning is a slow, frustrating, self-conscious process. But once you have learned the pattern, you can use it quickly and easily without conscious thought or effort. Experienced managers can often size up a situation very rapidly, decide exactly what needs to be done, and either do it or artfully persuade others to take the correct action. Their intuition and skill are based on prior learning of effective patterns of thought and action.

What this all means is that we have to develop patterns in order to make sense of the complexities of everyday life. It takes time and effort to learn how to frame patterns, so we invest heavily in them once they are developed. Helen Demarco's experience provided her with a set of theories for interpreting the meaning of Paul Osborne's behavior and for what she should do about it. She may have misinterpreted the situation, and chosen a poor course of action, but because she had no alternative frame, she could see no other option. To give up a theory is to sacrifice one's investment in learning it. Theories shield us from confusion, uncertainty, and anxiety. People get completely stuck when they have tried every lens that they know, and none of them works. They "lose the bubble," and are caught off balance, no longer in control of themselves or their circumstances.

We experience a dilemma whenever our current theories do not work. Revising old patterns is costly in terms of time and effort and may even lead to a temporary loss of confidence and effectiveness. The dilemma exists even if we are not aware of the flaws in our current theory. The card experiment shows that a theory often blocks recognition of its own errors. We see the world through the filters and perspectives that we already have. Those theories lead us to attend to certain kinds of information, while ignoring other important details, and to interpret everything in the light of what we already believe. Consider the following example in the light of the KAL 007 tragedy:

> A DC-8 jet airplane was approaching the airport in Cold Bay, Alaska, under poor weather conditions. Results from the navigation equipment were erratic because of the mountainous terrain. At 5:36 A.M., the captain asked the first officer, "Where's your DME?" (pilot jargon for, "How far are we from the airport on the distance-measuring equipment?"). The first officer

indicated that he did not have a reading, but his previous reading was forty miles. The captain, an experienced pilot, was off course for the approved approach into the Cold Bay airport but said nothing to the first officer about what he intended. The following conversation occurred:

*First officer:*   Are you going to make a procedure turn?

*Captain:*   No, I . . . I wasn't going to.

(Pause)

*First officer:*   What kind of terrain are we flying over?

*Captain:*   Mountains everywhere.

(Pause)

(At 5:39 A.M.)

*First officer:*   We should be a little higher, shouldn't we?

*Captain:*   No, forty DME [forty miles from the airport], you're all right.

(At 5:40 A.M.)

*Captain:*   I'll go up a little bit higher here. No reason to stay down that low so long.

(The captain climbed briefly to 4,000 feet, then began to descend again.)

(At 5:41 A.M.)

*First officer:*   The altimeter is alive. [The radio altimeter, which measures the airplane's distance from the ground, shows that we are not very far above very mountainous local terrain.]

(At 5:42 A.M.)

*First officer:*   Radio altimeters. Hey, John, we're off course! Four hundred feet from something!

(Six seconds later the airplane was destroyed when it crashed into a mountain.) [Based on "World Airways, Inc.," n.d.]

The captain—like Captain Chun of Korean Airlines—was a senior pilot who had flown into this airport a number of times. He assumed that his knowledge of the terrain and approach procedures was accurate. He had a "theory" of how to land the plane safely, one that he never communicated to his copilot.

The first officer, in the dark about the captain's intentions, gently suggested that they might not be making a safe approach. Apparently, the probes were too gentle—the captain never responded to the message. The captain did not *expect* difficulty, because he had flown into this airport before. The conversation suggests that he did not *want* to examine the possibility of a mistake. When the first officer questioned the captain's actions, the captain said, in effect, I'm in charge here, and I know what I'm doing.

The Cold Bay incident, like Flight 007, is a chilling demonstration that experienced and competent people can use incorrect theories without realizing their error (at least until it is too late). Such errors are most likely to occur in situations that are complex, ambiguous, or stressful, and these are exactly the conditions that organizations create all the time.

Most of us recognize that our mental maps influence heavily what we see and how we interpret the world around us. What is less widely understood is the Pygmalion effect—that differences in theory can actually create differences in reality. Rosenthal and Jacobson (1968) studied schoolteachers who were led to expect—and subsequently perceived—dramatic growth on the part of "spurters," that is, students who were labeled as "about to bloom." Even though the so-called spurters had been chosen at random, they still made above-average gains on achievement tests. They really *did* spurt. Somehow, the teacher's expectations were communicated to and felt by the students. What you believe can determine what you see and what you get. The same Pygmalion effect has been replicated in countless reorganizations, new-product launchings, or new-and-improved approaches to performance appraisal.

## Commonsense Organizational Diagnosis

We have asked a number of students and managers to develop diagnoses of cases such as those involving KAL 007 or Helen Demarco and Paul Osborne. We find that most of them use one of three limited perspectives to develop their diagnoses.

Most common is the *people-blaming approach*. In this view, most of what happens in organizations can be explained by the characteristics of individuals. Problems are caused by individuals' bad attitudes, abrasive personalities, neurotic tendencies, or incompetence. People with this view may label Paul Osborne authoritarian and Helen Demarco "gutless" for not standing up to her boss. They blame the Flight 007 disaster on the flight engineer's incompetence or the callousness of the Russian military. As children, we all learned that it was important to assign blame for every broken toy, stained carpet, or wounded sibling. To know who is at fault is comforting. In one stroke it resolves ambiguity, explains mystery, and makes clear what must be done next: punish the guilty.

When it is hard to single out a guilty person, a popular alternative is to *blame the bureaucracy*. Whatever went wrong is seen as the result of either red tape and rigidity or insufficient policies and procedures. Or, if an organization is not too bureaucratic, then it must be too disorganized. The solution for disorganization is simple enough: develop a rational, clear-cut set of procedures and role expectations. The problem between Helen Demarco and Paul Osborne would not have developed if roles had been clear and everyone had behaved rationally. Tragedies such as KAL 007 can be prevented if we verify cockpit procedures and make sure that pilots fly "by the book." The problem is that all those rules and regulations are what we dislike about bureaucracy. They inhibit freedom and flexibility. They stifle initiative and generate reams of red tape. The solution then is to "free up" the system so that red tape and rigid rules do not limit creativity and the ability to respond quickly. But many organizations find themselves on an endless round-trip between structures that are too loose and too tight.

Still a third fallacy attributes all organizational problems to a *thirst for power*. This view emphasizes that it is a dog-eat-dog world, the fix is always in, and everyone has an axe to grind. Power becomes a central preoccupation: who has it, and how to get more. From this viewpoint, Paul Osborne and Helen Demarco are both playing power games, and the winner will be the one who is the most adroit—or the most treacherous. In its extreme form, the political approach assumes that organizations are nothing more than jungles full of predators and their prey. Problems are constantly attributed to political game playing and petty bickering. The solution is to join the game before you fall victim to it.

Each of these three everyday approaches is based on a partial truth. Blaming people does point to the perennial importance of individual differences. Some organizational problems *are* caused by personal characteristics: rigid bosses, slothful subordinates, bumbling bureaucrats, greedy union members, or insensitive elites. A personalistic perspective may make sense whenever we are trying to understand why two people do the same thing differently. But in organizations we often find that different people behave the same when placed in the same situation. People blaming has no explanation for that. Moreover, blaming individuals often provides a diagnosis that is not very helpful, even if it is correct. If, for example, the cause of a problem is someone's personality, what do we do? Even psychiatrists find it a difficult, long-term task to alter someone's personality, and firing everyone whose personality is less than ideal would rarely be a viable solution.

The overly rational, blame-the-bureaucracy perspective starts from a reasonable assumption: Organizations are created to achieve certain goals. They will be most effective when the goals and policies are clear (but not excessive), jobs are well defined (but not *too* well defined), control systems are in place (but not oppressive), and employees behave like reasonable and prudent people. Any disagreement between Helen Demarco and Paul Osborne should be resolved through reasonable discussion and careful consideration of the facts. If people always behaved that way, human organizations would presumably work a lot better than most of them do. Standard operating procedures in commercial aircraft are designed for virtually every foreseeable contingency. If they were always followed, a safe flight would be almost a sure thing.

The problem with the rational perspective is that it is very good at explaining how organizations should work but very poor at explaining why they often do not. Managers who employ the rational perspective often become discouraged and frustrated when confronted by intractable and irrational forces. Year after year, we witness the introduction of new control systems, we hear of new studies and new ways to reorganize, we are dazzled by new management consultants and new management methods. Yet the same old problems persist, seemingly immune to every rational cure that management can devise.

The thirst-for-power approach also points to some enduring features of organizations. Helen Demarco and Paul Osborne actually do have different self-interests and sources of power. Helen is a career employee with a stake in protecting her status in the organization. She can afford to take a long-term view of organizational improvement. An unrealistic crash program that fails in the long run could hurt her career. Paul is in a different situation. He has been brought in with a mandate for change and will probably not stay very long. Five- or ten-year programs will not bolster Paul's reputation as a leader who gets results. He needs a dramatic and visible initiative that promises big improvements quickly.

The power perspective provides a plausible analysis of why the situation turned out the way it did. Helen and her colleagues played their political cards adeptly and, apparently, achieved a significant victory. But Helen and Paul would, no doubt, prefer that political games did not dominate decision making. In that sense, both lost. The naive political approach does not provide much help in knowing how to prevent such tragedies. Nor would it provide much help to KAL executives who were trying to figure out how to change communication patterns on the flight deck.

Each of these commonsense views points to important phenomena in organizations, but each is also incomplete and oversimplified. Each leads to a false sense of both clarity and optimism. The surprises, complexities, and ambiguities of organizational life require more powerful and comprehensive approaches. Determining what is really going on in an organization requires more sophisticated lenses than many managers currently possess. It also requires the flexibility to look at organizations from more than one vantage point.

In Western cultures, particularly, there is a tendency to em-

brace one theory or ideology and to try to make the world conform
to it. If it works, we continue in our view. If discrepancies arise, we
try to rationalize them away. If people challenge our view, we ignore them or put them in their place. Only if events go against us
dramatically and over a long period of time are we likely to question
our theories. Even then we may quickly convert to a new worldview,
triggering the cycle again.

In Japan there are four major religions, each with its own
beliefs and assumptions: Buddhism, Confucianism, Shintoism, and
Taoism. While the religions conflict dramatically in their basic
tenets, many Japanese feel no need to choose only one. They use
them all—taking advantage of the strengths of each for suitable
purposes or occasions. The four organizational frames can play a
similar role for managers in modern organizations. Rather than
portraying the field of organizational theory as fragmented, we present it as pluralistic. Seen this way, the field provides a rich palette
of lenses for viewing organizations. Each theoretical tradition is
helpful. Each also has its blind spots. The ability to shift from one
conceptual lens to another provides a way to redefine situations so
that they become manageable. The ability to reframe situations is
one of the most powerful capacities of great artists. It can be equally
powerful for managers.

The management theories that you choose will influence
what you see, what you understand, what you do, and, ultimately,
how effective you are. In this book, we will not attempt to teach the
one true theory of management. Rather we will present an array of
four very important and powerful theories about how organizations
work and how they can be made to work better. Our approach to
learning is based on an idea from cognitive psychology theory—the
idea, namely, that people know more than they think they know
(Bransford, Franks, Vye, and Sherwood, 1989). Through experience,
managers learn what works and what does not. The problem is that
much of this wisdom remains inert. Partly because their theories
cancel out many of their own hard-earned insights, managers draw
upon only a fraction of what is available to them. The frames provide "contrasting sets" that help people gain access to, express, and
apply inert knowledge. In this sense, the book is not designed

simply to impart knowledge. Rather, we emphasize helping managers frame, understand, and use what they already know.

## Summary

Because organizations are complex, surprising, deceptive, and ambiguous, they are formidably difficult to understand and manage. We have to rely on the tools at hand, including whatever ideas and theories we have about what organizations are and how they work. Our theories, or frames, determine what we see and what we do and can generate self-fulfilling prophesies and Pygmalion effects.

Perspectives that are too simple or too narrow become fallacies that cloud rather than illuminate managerial action. Some managers overuse a people blaming approach that attributes everything to personalities. Others rely too much on a rationalistic view that assumes that all organizational problems can be solved through restructuring and reasonableness, or on a power perspective that sees all of organizational life as a power game in which the strongest survive.

The world of most managers and administrators is a world of complexity, ambiguity, value dilemmas, political pressures, and multiple constituencies. In such worlds it is easy to experience failure, frustration, cynicism, and powerlessness and hard to experience growth, achievement, and progress. Managers need better theories, as well as the ability to implement those theories with skill and grace.

In succeeding chapters, we will examine four perspectives, or frames, that have helped many managers and leaders find clarity and meaning amidst the confusion and equivocality of organizational life. We cannot guarantee your success as a manager or a change agent. We believe, though, that you can improve the odds in your favor if you have a clear understanding of each of the four lenses and how they can be used to determine what is really going on in your organization. As a manager, you *can* make a significant difference. You can develop a broader understanding of human organizations—how they work, their limitations, and their possibilities. There is always more than one way to think and act in any given situation. The artistry of management is to see new possibilities and to express these in a form that can be shared with others. Some situations may still turn out to be impossible dilemmas, but most of them should reveal surprising possibilities for creativity and effective action.

# Part Two

# THE
# STRUCTURAL
# FRAME

# 3

# *Getting Organized*

In the dingy gray of a Moscow winter morning, the new McDonald's restaurant is an otherworldly presence, huge and sleek and lighting up Pushkin Square with a red and yellow Technicolor glow. When this ultimate icon of Americana opens to the ruble-paying masses on Wednesday morning, it will represent not just an architectural curiosity, but a triumph of capitalist determination.

Already the missionaries of the fast-food chain have taught farmers in this potato-addicted country how to grow potatoes. They have drilled hundreds of Soviet teenagers in habits of unrelenting cheer and fanatic cleanliness that contradict every dour instinct of Soviet service personnel.

The prices will be high for customers raised on subsidized food—a "beeg mek," french fries, and cola will run about five rubles, half a day's wage for an average Soviet worker—but no one doubts the attendance will smash company records [Keller, 1990a, pp. 1, 12].

McDonald's, which made the Big Mac a household word, is an enormously successful organization that dominates the fast-food business. McDonald's has a relatively small staff at its world headquarters outside Chicago. The vast majority of its employees are spread across the world in thousands of McDonald's outlets. Despite its size, however, McDonald's is a highly centralized, tightly coupled organization, and most of its major decisions are made at the top.

The managers and employees of each McDonald's restaurant have limited discretion about how to do their jobs. Much of their work is controlled by technology—machines time french fries and even measure soft drinks. Cooks are not encouraged to develop creative new versions of the Big Mac or the Quarter-Pounder (although the Egg McMuffin and some other items were created by local franchises). The parent company makes strenuous efforts to ensure that food and service in every franchise conform to standard specifications. The customer is assured that a Big Mac will taste virtually the same whether it is purchased in New York or Los Angeles, Toronto or Mexico City, Hong Kong or Moscow. The guarantee of standard quality inevitably limits the discretion of the people who own and work in individual outlets. Creative departures from standard product lines are neither encouraged nor tolerated among McDonald's employees, except when a new item is being tested for adoption throughout the chain.

McDonald's makes little effort to offer different products in different markets. They assume that their hamburgers—or newly added salads and sandwiches—will sell in the same form almost anywhere, regardless of local traditions and culture. There are occasional concessions to local tastes—we once ordered *saimin* (a Japanese noodle soup) from a McDonald's in Hawaii. But the McDonald's on the Champs Elysées in Paris makes no attempt to conform to French culinary style.

Harvard University is also widely regarded as a highly successful organization. Like McDonald's, Harvard has a very small administrative group at the top, but in most other respects the two organizations are structured differently. Even though Harvard is much more geographically concentrated than McDonald's, its administrative structure is significantly more decentralized. Virtually all of Harvard's activities are concentrated in a few square miles of Boston and Cambridge. Most of its employees are spread across the several different schools of the university, including Harvard College (the undergraduate school), the graduate Faculty of Arts and Sciences, and the various professional schools. Each of the separate faculties has its own dean, and, in accordance with Harvard's philosophy of "every tub on its own bottom," largely controls its own destiny.

Harvard is one of the few universities in the world in which different faculties choose to operate on different academic calendars. The fall semester in the law and business schools usually begins a week or two earlier than in the schools of government or education. Each school also has a large measure of fiscal autonomy and has responsibility for its own budget. Just as the separate schools are highly independent of one another, individual faculty members have enormous autonomy and discretion. In many schools, they have almost complete control over what courses they teach, what research they do, and what, if any, university activities they pursue. Faculty meetings are often sparsely attended. When a dean or department chairperson wants a faculty member to chair a committee or offer a new course, the request is more often a humble request than an authoritative command.

The contrast between McDonald's and Harvard is particularly obvious at the level of service delivery. No one expects individual personalities to influence the quality of a McDonald's hamburger. But everyone expects each course at Harvard to be the unique creation of an individual professor. For example, two different schools might offer courses with the same title, covering entirely different content and employing widely divergent teaching styles.

Why do McDonald's and Harvard have such radically different structures? Is one more effective than the other? Or has each organization evolved a structural approach that fits its circumstances? The structural perspective focuses on such questions and seeks to understand the complex nature of formal organizational design and operation.

## Structural Forms and Functions

Different organizations may display distinct patterns of human architecture yet at the same time share a number of characteristics. All organizations have goals, boundaries, levels of authority, communication systems, coordinating mechanisms, and distinctive procedures. This is true whether the organization is a bank, a church, a family, or the U.S. Army. Structural profiles, however, vary widely across different types of organizations. Educational organizations such as Harvard typically have multiple, diffuse goals, unclear boundaries, a weak technology, and informal mechanisms for coordinating work. In contrast, many large firms such as McDonald's have clearer goals and boundaries, more unified chains of command, and more sophisticated and extensive control systems.

How to structure itself is one of the central issues facing any organization. A structure is more than boxes and lines arranged hierarchically on an official organizational chart. It is an outline of the desired pattern of activities, expectations, and exchanges among executives, managers, employees, and customers or clients. The shape of the formal structure very definitely enhances or constrains what an organization is able to accomplish. On the one hand, if the Harvard faculty produced hamburgers, each would be a novel surprise. On the other hand, students would not fight to gain entrance to a university that offered mass-produced courses, each controlled by standards set at the top.

We often assume that people prefer structures that give them more choices and more latitude to communicate with others in the organization (Leavitt, 1978). But this is not always the case. A study by Moeller (1968), for example, explored the effects of structure on morale in two very different school systems. One was structured very loosely and encouraged wide participation in decision making. The other was tightly controlled with a centralized hierarchy and clear chain of command. Moeller expected to find lower morale in the more bureaucratized district but instead found exactly the opposite. Morale in the more tightly structured organization was higher. Teachers apparently enjoyed the sense of certainty and predictability that this kind of structure gave. They liked knowing the official channels for influencing decisions or obtaining resources. Rationality and clarity, it seems, are often preferable to the ambiguity and instability of more decentralized structural forms.

Structure can also play an important role in an organization's performance. Small groups trying to accomplish a complicated, nonroutine task (such as research at the frontiers of knowledge) do better with a decentralized structure. But groups working on a simpler, more routine task (such as producing a reliable product) do better with a more centralized structure (Leavitt, 1978).

### Origins of the Structural Perspective

The structural view has two main intellectual sources. The first is found in the work of industrial psychologists who wanted to determine how organizations could be constructed for maximum efficiency. The most prominent of these researchers was Frederick W. Taylor. In his approach to scientific management, Taylor (1911) attempted to break a given task into minute parts and to retrain workers to get the largest payoff from each motion and each second spent at work. Taylor is considered the father of time-and-motion studies. Another group of theorists who contributed to the scientific management approach included Henri Fayol ([1919] 1949), Lyndall Urwick (1937), and Luther Gulick (Gulick and Urwick, 1937). Their primary focus was on developing a set of principles about specialization, span of control, authority, and delegation of responsibility.

The second branch of structural ideas is rooted in the work of the German sociologist Max Weber. Weber wrote at the turn of the century, when formal organization was a relatively new phenomenon. Patrimony, rather than rationality, was still the customary organizing principle. Patrimonial organizations usually had a father figure—a single individual with almost unlimited power over others, who could reward, punish, promote, or fire solely on the basis of personal whim. Weber (1947) saw some of the major limitations of patrimonial organizations and sought to conceptualize an ideal organizational form that maximized norms of rationality. Weber himself was anything but a narrow rationalist, and he offered bureaucracy as an image not of how organizations *should* be but of how they might be if rationalizing tendencies were carried to their logical conclusion. His model outlines six major dimensions of bureaucracy: (1) a fixed division of labor, (2) a hierarchy of offices, (3) a set of rules governing performance, (4) separation of personal from official property and rights, (5) technical qualifications for selecting personnel (not family ties or friendship), and (6) employment as a long-term career.

After the Second World War, Weber's work was rediscovered by organization theorists and has since spawned a substantial body of theory and research. Among others, Blau and Scott (1962), Perrow (1986), and Hall (1963) have contributed significantly to the extension of the bureaucratic model. Their work has examined the relationships among the elements of structure, looked closely at why organizations choose one structure rather than another, and examined the impact of structure on morale, productivity, and effectiveness.

## Assumptions of the Structural Perspective

The structural perspective is based on the following set of core assumptions:

1.  Organizations exist primarily to accomplish established goals.
2.  For any organization, a structural form can be designed and implemented to fit its particular set of circumstances (such as goals, strategies, environment, technology, and people).
3.  Organizations work most effectively when environmental turbulence and personal preferences are constrained by norms of rationality. (Structure ensures that people focus on getting the job done rather than on doing whatever they please.)
4.  Specialization permits higher levels of individual expertise and performance.
5.  Coordination and control are essential to effectiveness. (Depending on the task and environment, coordination may be achieved through authority, rules, policies, standard operating procedures, information systems, meetings, lateral relationships, or a variety of more informal techniques.)
6.  Organizational problems typically originate from inappropriate structures or inadequate systems and can be resolved through restructuring or developing new systems.

These assumptions depict organizations as relatively closed systems pursuing fairly explicit goals. Such conditions make it possible for organizations to operate rationally, with high degrees of certainty, predictability, and efficiency. Organizations highly dependent on the environment are continually vulnerable to external influence or interference. To reduce this vulnerability, a variety of structural mechanisms are created to protect central activities from fluctuation and uncertainty (Thompson, 1967). Devices that buffer the organization and reduce unpredictability include the following:

- Coding—creating schemes for classifying inputs.
- Stockpiling—storing raw materials and products so that inputs and outputs can be controlled by the organization.
- Leveling—motivating suppliers to provide inputs or creating a higher demand for outputs.
- Forecasting—anticipating changes in supply and demand.
- Growth—striving for a scale of activity that will give the organization leverage over its environment.

Business enterprises regularly employ these techniques to manage unpredictable external elements. McDonald's, for example, codes its inputs into categories such as ground beef, chicken, potatoes, and condiments. These inputs are stockpiled to ensure that customer requirements can always be met. McDonald's negotiates with suppliers to guarantee a steady flow of raw materials and uses extensive marketing and sales efforts to bring customers to its restaurants. The company monitors and anticipates fluctuations in the price or availability of raw materials and grows through establishing new outlets and adding new products. Its first outlet in the Soviet Union posed unusual problems:

> The real key to the venture is a $4 million Finnish-built processing center, situated on the northern outskirts of Moscow, which is transforming locally available ingredients into a McDonald's menu. Here, at a glistening new complex encompassing a bakery, dairy, potato-processing line, meat plant, sauce cookers, laboratories and vast storage freezers, McDonald's will turn its rubles back into fast food. Finding acceptable local raw materials has entailed a year-long hunt through the dismal and sometimes stomach-turning landscape of the Soviet

food industry. One McDonald's meat scout, no stranger to slaughterhouses, was sickened by his visit to a Soviet abattoir.

To get the large white potatoes specified for its french fries, the company imported Russell Burbank seed potatoes from the Netherlands and installed an agronomist on a local collective farm to supervise the crop from planting to harvest. Other farmers were induced to grow hothouse Iceberg lettuce, not part of the Soviet diet, and pickle cucumbers from imported seed. By luck, the company found a dairy in Volgograd that makes cheddar cheese, which is brought to Moscow and processed into bricks for cheeseburgers [Keller, 1990a, p. 12].

The same buffering strategies are also used in other types of organizations. Harvard also codes its inputs (distinguishing, for example, between undergraduates and graduate students); stockpiles important resources (Harvard's endowment is a particularly prominent example of this); tries to find markets for its outputs (for example, the university established a program several years ago to help graduating Ph.D.'s find jobs in the private sector); monitors, predicts, and attempts to influence supply and demand (both university personnel and alumni are aggressively involved in recruitment of undergraduates); and grows through the addition of new programs or schools (continuing education and professional schools have been a growth industry for Harvard in recent years).

The structural approach is often associated with red tape and routine, and the word *bureaucracy* often conjures up images of inefficiency and rigidity. But the structural perspective is not as machinelike or as inflexible as many believe. One has only to deal once with a poorly structured organization to appreciate the perspective's virtues. Its assumptions reflect a belief in rationality and a faith that the right formal arrangements can minimize problems and increase quality and performance. Where the human resource perspective emphasizes the importance of changing people (through training, rotation, promotion, or dismissal), the structural perspective focuses on how to find some arrangement—a pattern of formal roles and relationships—that will accommodate organizational needs as well as individual differences.

## Basic Design Elements

The contrasting structures of McDonald's and Harvard are a mixture of history, accident, and design. Of these, the last is the main concern of management. How to design the formal structure of roles and relationships occupies an especially prominent niche in managerial priorities. Managers spend hours and hours trying to determine the best response to the two central issues in structural design: (1) how to divide the work, and (2) how to coordinate the work of different people and units after it has been divided.

The first issue centers on dividing work or responsibilities into manageable jobs or positions. Division of labor—or differentiation—is the cornerstone of the modern organization. But every living group finds a way to create different roles. Consider an ant colony: "Small workers . . . spend most of their time in the nest feeding the larval broods; intermediate-sized workers constitute most of the population, going out on raids as well as doing other jobs. The largest workers . . . have a huge head and large powerful jaws. These individuals are what Verril called soldiers; they carry no food but constantly run along the flanks of the raiding and emigration columns" (Topoff, 1972, p. 72).

Human beings, like ants, long ago discovered the virtues of specialization and finding the right task for every individual or group. Who does what and who reports to whom are critical features of horizontal and vertical differentiation in any organization.

How to integrate the different roles within an organization is the second issue in structural design. Specialized jobs focus an individual's attention, but only on one part of the total operation. We all know the frustration of trying to get help from someone who tells us, "That's not my responsibility." In addition to finding the right division of labor, an organization must develop a reliable method of linking individual efforts into a unified whole. In part, coordination is achieved through vertical differentiation, that is, by creating administrators whose role is to supervise work rather than actually do it. But as the McDonald's and Harvard examples both illustrate, other methods of coordinating different positions and groups are also needed. McDonald's is highly differentiated geographically, yet each restaurant is much like the next and the total organization is tightly integrated. Harvard is highly differentiated by division and market (law school, education school, undergraduate college) but is very loosely integrated both vertically and horizontally. Coordination is achieved mostly by committees and the professional training of its professors.

Structurally, every manager is looking for the best combination of differentiation and coordination. As the formal structure of McDonald or Harvard evolved, a number of fundamental questions had to be answered—whether by systematic planning or by just muddling through. The following questions will guide managers in designing formal structures that will suit their organization's unique circumstances (Mintzberg, 1979):

1.  How many tasks should a given position in the organization contain and how specialized should each task be?
2.  To what extent should the work content of each position be standardized?
3.  What skills and knowledge should be required for each position?
4.  On what basis should positions be grouped into units and units into larger units?
5.  How large should each unit be, and how many individuals should report to a given manager?
6.  To what extent should the output of each position or unit be standardized?
7.  What mechanisms should be established to facilitate mutual adjustment among positions and units?
8.  How much decision-making power should be delegated to managers of line units down the chain of authority?
9.  How much decision-making authority should pass from the line managers to the staff specialists and operators?

Creating a position or role constrains individual behavior. Formal expectations outline what a person is to do—or not do—to accomplish a task. These formal expectations take the form of standardized job descriptions, procedures, or rules (Mintzberg, 1979). While such formal constraints often create human problems such as apathy, absenteeism, and resistance (Argyris, 1957, 1964), they also help ensure predictability, uniformity, and reliability. If manufacturing standards, airline maintenance, hotel housekeeping, or prison sentences were left solely to individual discretion, the problems of quality and equity would arise repeatedly. Formal expectations can also be established and communicated through training done by the organization itself or by other agencies. The consistent quality of American Airlines flight attendants is largely a function of their intensive preservice and in-service training. The behavior of pilots, surgeons, and other professionals is shaped as much or more by their training as by the organization for which they work. In hospitals, the performance of physicians and nurses is governed primarily by professional norms, while most other positions are shaped by formal job descriptions, procedures, and rules—or by training provided by the hospital itself.

Consider again McDonald's and Harvard. As a McDonald's customer, you deal directly with counter staff, whose job is to take your order, collect your money, assemble the items, and give them to you. Both McDonald's and you, the customer, have expectations about how counter help will fill their role. If they are slow, surly, or uncooperative, they violate these expectations. If they are efficient, fast, and cheerful, however, the counter help meet your expectations. If you order a Big Mac and none is available, they will communicate this to a cook, whose job is to provide a steady supply of cooked items. Each restaurant also has managers, who are responsible for hiring and supervising the help, ensuring that the restaurant adheres to standards, and ordering raw materials. The jobs of the counter help are highly structured, narrowly defined, and highly repetitive. Few skills are required, and there is limited discretion. Although the job of manager is more complex, varied, and demanding, McDonald's creates consistency among its unit managers through training at Hamburger University.

Harvard University also delineates roles but the definitions are very different. Where the counter help is the primary provider of direct service at McDonald's, the professor occupies that pivotal role at Harvard. The role of professor is complex, ambiguous, and loosely structured. Professors are expected to show up for classes, conduct research, and fulfill vaguely defined goals of "university service." Beyond that, the role is mostly what each individual chooses to make it. In fact, people *expect* professors to be unusual or idiosyncratic, as witnessed by the long life of the "absentminded professor" stereotype.

Once an organization has defined its positions or roles, the next question is how to group the positions. Organizations have several basic options (Mintzberg, 1979). They can create *functional* groups based on knowledge or skill, as in the case of Harvard's academic departments. In the classic functional structure for industrial firms, groupings include manufacturing, engineering, sales, marketing, research, and finance. Units can also be created on the basis of *time;* police departments, for example, group their officers into three main shifts: day shift, swing shift, and graveyard. Groups can also be created on the basis of the *product* they produce or the *market* in which they sell. Procter & Gamble creates units around its different brands: Colgate, Tide, Scope, and Bounce. So does General Motors with its Buick, Chevrolet, and Cadillac divisions. Many professional organizations organize around *clients.* Hospital wards are often created around a certain kind of patient—pediatrics, intensive care, or general wards. Mental health organizations often have separate units for adults, adolescents, and children. Finally, organizations often create groupings around *place* or *geography.* Hospital Corporation of America has several domestic regional divisions as well as an international division. Many hospitals group patient care around specific floors or other physical locations (Mintzberg, 1979). Government agencies typically have regional offices situated in different geographical areas.

Every arrangement has advantages and disadvantages. Grouping professors by departments, for example, creates social interaction, stimulates new research ideas, and encourages integration within disciplinary boundaries. But professors may then talk only to colleagues who think the same way they do. Research agendas may become narrowly specialized, and reduced interdisciplinary options for students often create costs that outweigh the advantages of departmental grouping. An organization that organizes primarily by function often gains substantial benefits of efficiency within each function but may also incur substantial costs of bickering and conflict between different functional groups. For example, in manufacturing firms, there is a classic tension between production and sales—production works best with predictability and long lead times while sales often needs to respond to unpredictable customer pressure for quick turnaround.

## Structural Configurations

Structure is often depicted on a one-dimensional organizational chart that reveals primarily where positions fit horizontally and vertically. Mintzberg offers a more sophisticated picture in his five-sector "logo" (Figure 1).

At the base of Mintzberg's image is the *operating core,* which performs the basic work of the organization. The operating core consists of the manufacturing, service, professional, or other workers who produce or provide what the organization offers to

**Figure 1. Mintzberg's Model.**

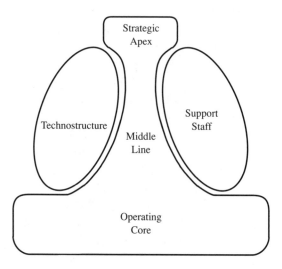

*Source:* Henry Mintzberg, THE STRUCTURE OF ORGANIZATIONS, © 1979, p. 20. Reprinted by permission of Prentice-Hall, Inc., Englewood Cliffs, N.J.

customers or clients. The operating core includes the teachers in schools, the assembly-line workers in factories. In hospitals, the operating core includes physicians and nurses; in the airline industry it is the flight crew.

Directly above the operating core is the *administrative component*. The middle line is composed of those managers who supervise, control, and provide resources for the operating core. School principals, foremen, and other first-line supervisors fulfill this role. Above the middle managers are the top-level managers at the strategic apex. Positions at this level relate primarily to the organization's external environment; they create the mission and provide strategic direction. Superintendents and school boards are the main players in the strategic apex of school systems. In private corporations the apex includes the chief executive officer, the chairman of the board, and officers of the board of trustees.

Mintzberg adds two other parts to the administrative component of organizations. The *technostructure* consists mainly of analysts whose role is to standardize the work of others by inspecting outputs and processes. Quality control departments in industry, auditing departments in government agencies, and flight standards departments in airlines all perform such functions. The final administrative component is the *support staff*, which performs tasks that indirectly facilitate the work of the operating core. In schools, for example, the support staff includes nurses, secretaries, custodians, food service workers, and bus drivers.

Successful organizations employ a variety of methods to link individual and group efforts in pursuit of desired goals. Defining appropriate positions and groupings is important, but the various parts must also work together. Otherwise, individual or unit subgoals may displace collective ends and products or services may suffer. For example, the public relations coordinator of a large hospital remarked in a recent meeting that cost reductions had forced his unit to reduce significantly the quality of paper used in the weekly newsletter. The hospital's chief executive asked, "What is the relationship between high-quality paper and high-quality patient care?" The red-faced coordinator had no response.

Organizations must create mechanisms to coordinate groups and link individual efforts to shared goals of quality service or products. The reputation of a restaurant can suffer even if the chef produces culinary masterpieces. Waiters need to get the food to the table while it is still hot and bring the check without too much delay. Busboys need to keep water glasses filled and remove empty plates to make way for the rest of the meal. The wine steward needs to serve the right vintage at an appropriate temperature at the right time. The efforts of valets, hostesses, maitre d's, and busboys need to mesh. An enjoyable meal depends as much on how well a restaurant coordinates multiple activities as on the quality of food it serves. Food quality also requires tight coordination among the various actors in the kitchen. The more highly the actions of one group or individual depend on those of others, the more important coordination becomes in a successful enterprise.

Organizations attempt to achieve formal coordination and control in two primary ways: (1) vertically, through commands, supervision, policies, rules, planning, or control systems and (2) laterally, through meetings, task forces, standing committees, special coordinating roles, or matrix structures. Basically, vertical coordination occurs when people at higher levels coordinate and control the work of subordinates. Lateral coordination is more informal. It occurs when those at similar levels respond to one another face-to-face. A restaurant manager who develops policies about how cooks and waiters should work together is using vertical coordination. When the waiter and the cook talk directly to one another, they are coordinating laterally.

The relative importance of vertical and lateral coordination depends mainly on the organization's task and environment. Vertical coordination is more likely to be significant when the environment is relatively stable, the task is predictable and well understood, and uniformity is a critical need. McDonald's ensures that its restaurants meet standards largely through such vertical coordination mechanisms as commands, written procedures and quality standards, control systems, and regular inspections of every restaurant. Inspectors are provided with detailed checklists that they use to rate every aspect of a restaurant's functioning: Do employees, for example, greet customers with a smile? Even in individual restaurants, activities are prescribed and proscribed by procedures, systems, and the authority of the local manager. Very little lateral coordination occurs between different outlets.

Lateral communications are likely to dominate in organizations that perform complex tasks in environments of high uncertainty and rapid change. In a university such as Harvard, the loose structure and the high levels of faculty autonomy make it very difficult for the president or the deans to coordinate activities through the chain of command. No dean would dare to send inspectors armed with checklists into a professor's classroom. Instead, Harvard relies extensively on faculty committees for almost every academic decision that requires coordinated efforts among various faculties or departments. Faculty often lament the loose and inefficient work habits of the proliferating committees, but few would greet commands, rules, or standardized procedures from the administration as an improvement. Even formal evaluations of teaching can be ignored or embraced depending on the personal disposition of an individual faculty member. Common lore has it that even though such evaluations are often made public, they have little to do with salary or other personnel decisions.

## Vertical Coordination

This kind of coordination can be implemented by creating a chain of command; establishing rules, policies, and standard operating procedures; or implementing planning and control systems.

*Authority.* The most common method of linking the efforts of individuals, units, or divisions is to create a position with authority over other positions. Establishing a chain of command yields a hierarchy of managers and supervisors with legitimate power to shape the behavior of others, especially when the authority is endorsed by subordinates as well as authorized from above (Dornbusch and Scott, 1975). Those in positions of authority are formally charged with integrating the activities of an organization and keeping them in tune with its goals. Executives, managers, and supervisors control activity by making decisions, resolving conflicts, solving problems, evaluating performances and output, and distributing rewards and penalties.

Not all organizations have the same number of links in their chains of command and not all centralize authority to the same degree. In some, such as Harvard, the chain of command is short, and workers or professionals have considerable discretion in dealing with day-to-day operations. Teachers and professors, like policemen and social workers, are "street-level bureaucrats" with almost unlimited authority and discretion in the classroom, unless they egregiously violate accepted norms of practice (Lipsky, 1980). In other organizations, such as McDonald's or the U.S. Army (which has seven levels between a four-star general and a squad sergeant), the chain of command is lengthy; many operational, as well as strategic, decisions are made at the top. In McDonald's, that makes it possible for the customer to purchase a hamburger that will meet the same standards and taste basically the same, whether it is bought in Kansas City or Kuala Lumpur.

The same degree of centralization can be much less effective in one context than in another, and too many levels of command can displace as well as reinforce an organization's goals. In one mental health organization, for example, decisions to administer drugs had to be made at the top of the hierarchy. One night, a patient became violent, and the staff requested permission to administer a tranquilizer. The person at the apex of the chain of command could not be reached for several hours. By the time permission was granted, the patient had been subdued and was asleep. Since the staff had no discretion about such decisions, it was necessary to awaken the patient and administer the tranquilizer.

***Rules and Policies.*** Another way to limit discretion and ensure predictability and uniformity is through rules, policies, or standard operating procedures. Rules govern the conditions of work and outline standard procedures for carrying out tasks, handling personnel issues, and adjusting relationships with the external environment. Policies are intended to minimize the differences that result from personalities or irrational forces and to ensure that similar situations will be handled the same way, regardless of the people, place, or time of year involved. A complaint from a citizen about a tax bill is supposed to be handled according to the same procedure, whether the citizen is a prominent politician or a shoe clerk. Once a situation is defined as one in which a rule applies, the steps become clear, straightforward, and almost automatic. If the rule does not apply, one simply finds someone in the chain of command who can interpret the policy or who has the discretion to make a decision. An example from the British income tax office provides an illustration:

> Faced by an income tax problem because I have an income from writing and broadcasting and the like, in addition to a salary, I decided to take my problem to the local income tax office. A young clerk sees me come in and . . . comes toward the desk to receive me. I tell her I have problems, and I bring out my income tax form. She immediately answers by saying, "Well, you fill this one in here, and fill that one in there." This cannot solve my problem, and she does not know how to solve it either, whereupon she lifts up the flap in the counter and takes me through the office into a room in which sits somebody I take to be the chief clerk, by reason of his oak desk and ten square feet of carpet. He examines my problem and takes out a large book of rules governing income tax. I should give an answer on my return according to section 23, paragraph A, but unfortunately, this does not quite suit my particular case.
>
> I am then taken into a room which belongs to someone I assume to be a chief inspector because he has a mahogany desk and the carpet is filled to the walls. He sees that my case is unique and the answers lie between paragraphs A and B; therefore he decides (because he has the right to) that I should answer somewhere in between . . . he makes a decision lying between the limits set by the rules. Such rules have been laid out, in the first instance, by people in the Inland Revenue of London, so as to give limits within which chief inspectors may make such new, unique decisions, or regulations which the chief clerk can obey precisely [Paterson, 1969, pp. 28–29].

The scope and application of rules or standard operating procedures vary widely across different organizations. Commercial airlines typically fly with a different set of pilots at the beginning of every month. Since interdependence is high, and mistakes are critical, standard operating procedures govern every significant aspect of pilots' work. Each pilot has been extensively trained in the same procedures. So long as each follows the rules that they all know, they will not surprise each other or fail to coordinate their activities. A significant percentage of aviation accidents occur because someone violated standard operating procedures. More than one airplane has crashed on takeoff simply because the crew neglected to cover all the items on their required checklists.

The areas regulated by rules differ across organizations. Since rules are a key strategy for coordinating activities, one could expect rules to be established around areas of importance, uncertainty, or conflict—the areas central to an organization's mission or survival. Rules are often explicit about questions of hiring and firing, relationships with the environment, and key aspects of the flow of work. But rules are sometimes established in areas that seem less important. In schools, for example, policies and rules are extensive and explicit around student discipline, but vague or nonexistent around curriculum and instruction. (We discuss reasons for apparent perversity in later chapters.)

*Planning and Control Systems.* The third vertical strategy seeks coordination through planning and control systems. Ever since sophisticated computer technology made its appearance, PERT, management by objectives, and other management information systems have permitted a flow of information up and down the formal hierarchy that standardizes outcomes, actions, or behavior.

Mintzberg distinguishes between two different systems of control or planning. *Performance control* imposes outcome standards, without regard for how the outcomes are achieved. A goal to "increase sales by 10 percent this year" would be an example. Performance controls both motivate and measure. They can be very effective when the goals and objectives are reasonably clear and measurable, but they can be more hindrance than help if the goals are ambiguous, hard to measure, or of dubious relevance. A controversial example was the use of "body counts" by the U.S. Army as a measure of combat effectiveness in Vietnam. Field commanders often became obsessed with "getting the numbers up," regardless of whether the numbers reflected any real military progress.

*Action planning* specifies the decisions and actions to be carried out in a particular way or at specific times; for example, "increase sales by conforming to a uniform sales approach" (Mintzberg, 1979, pp. 153–154). Action planning is very useful when it is difficult to measure outcomes and easier to assess *how* a job is done than whether the objectives were achieved. This is often true of service jobs. McDonald's has very clear specifications for how a counter employee is to greet customers (for example, with a smile and a cheerful welcome). The intended outcome is customer satisfaction, but it is easier to monitor the employee's behavior than the customer's frame of mind.

### Lateral Coordination

As almost anyone who has worked in an organization knows, vertical strategies by themselves are not enough. Vertical coordination tends to be less costly than lateral approaches, but it is not always effective. In many complex organizations the behavior of people seems virtually untouched by commands, rules, or systems. Lateral techniques are developed to fill the coordination void. They include (1) formal and informal meetings for developing plans, solving problems, and making decisions; (2) task forces that bring together representatives from different areas and specialties to work together on a specific problem or project; (3) coordinating roles that work through persuasion and information negotiation rather than through authority or rules; and (4) matrix structures in which people have more than one boss.

Lateral forms of coordination are typically less formalized and more flexible than authority systems and rules. They are also often simpler and easier to employ. If the guards on a basketball team decided that they would pass the ball to the forwards only on direct orders from the coach, the team would vividly illustrate the limits of vertical coordination. If the guards are not working well with the forwards, the coach may need to intervene, but a successful intervention would be one that established effective lateral communications among the players.

Informal communications are the most basic form of lateral coordination, and they are vital in every organization. Equally necessary are formal meetings. All organizations have formal groups that meet regularly to make decisions. Boards meet to make policy. Executive committees meet to make academic decisions. In some government agencies, review committees referred to as "murder boards" meet to examine proposals from lower-level officials. Formal and informal meetings can provide most of the lateral coordination in relatively simple, stable organizations—for example, in a railroad with a stable market, a company manufacturing a product that changes very little (such as paper clips or cardboard boxes), or a school system in a town with a fixed population.

As organizations become more differentiated, their technologies become more sophisticated, and their environments become more turbulent; however, the need for horizontal communication increases and is likely to be met by additional devices. Task forces are used when organizations face new problems or opportunities that require the resources of individuals from a number of different organizational specialties or functions. High-technology organizations make frequent use of project teams to coordinate the development of new products or services. Those same organizations also make extensive use of coordinating roles and units, that is, individuals and groups whose sole purpose is to help other people work effectively and integrate their efforts.

> Ellen Fisher is a product manager responsible for the introduction of new soap products. She works through several functional departments, including market research, the development laboratory, production, and sales. In designing the new product, market research usually conducts a test of consumer reactions. In this case, the market research head, Hank Feller, wants to run the standard field test on the new brand in two preselected cities. Ellen is opposed to this because it would delay the product introduction date of September 1; if that date can be met, sales has promised to obtain a major chain-store customer (using a house-brand label) whose existing contract for this type of soap is about to expire.
>
> At the same time, manufacturing is resisting a commitment to fill this large order by the date sales established because "new-product introductions have to be carefully meshed in our schedule with other products our facilities are producing. . . ."
>
> Ellen's job is to negotiate with market research and manufacturing. This means assessing how important their technical criteria are, which ones are modifiable, and, overall, what is best for the new product's introduction. . . . Her goal is to

balance the legitimate objections of manufacturing and sales as
she perceives them against her need to get the new product off
to a flying start [Sayles, 1976, pp. 11–12].

Many organizations move to matrix structures that formally
spell out both vertical and lateral coordinating responsibilities. J.C.
Penney, for example, has a permanent matrix structure "contain-
[ing] two sets of managers, with relatively equal power and somewhat opposed interests, who are supposed to negotiate their
differences. The systems managers are the store- or regional-level
executives, responsible for operating a diversified department store
that is responsive to the consumer tastes of particular communities
and areas. They are dependent for their merchandise on equivalent
functional managers—divisional merchandise managers. The latter
identify, specify, and purchase the major categories of merchandise
the stores will carry—furniture, for example, or tires or women's
fashion apparel. These two sets of managers have separate performance responsibilities, report up separate lines of authority, and see
the world from separate perspectives—the former from a store in a
particular place or geographical area, the latter from the perspective
of the overall market" (Sayles, 1976, p. 13).

Other organizations, such as NASA, have shifting matrix
structures that draw members from functional departments (Mintzberg, 1979, p. 172). Each of these lateral coordination strategies has
its own strengths and weaknesses. Formal and informal meetings
provide structural opportunities for dialogue and decisions but can
absorb an excessive amount of a manager's or employee's time. Task
forces provide a source of integration around a specific problem but
can detract attention from ongoing operating issues. Liaison roles
or groups can effectively span different positions or divisions but
are heavily dependent on the skills and credibility of those who
carry out the boundary-spanning activities. Matrix structures can
provide a continuing source of lateral linkage and integration but
are notorious for creating undue costs and confusion. The right
blend of these strategies for an organization depends on its unique
coordination problems. Coupled with the vertical options outlined
earlier, every organization either finds a design that works, or reor-
ganizes, or fails.

### Structural Imperatives

What determines the shape of an organization's structure? Why are Harvard University and McDonald's structured so differently, even though each is viewed as an effective organization? What structural arrangements work best under which kinds of conditions? There are several forces that affect the design of an organization: its size, core technology, environment, goals or strategy, information technology, and the characteristics of its people. Each of these are issues, or contingencies, that must be taken into account in designing a formal structure that will allow individuals to work well as a group.

*Size of the Organization.* Mintzberg (1979) illustrates the importance of this characteristic:

> Ms. Raku made pottery in her basement. That involved a number of distinct tasks—wedging clay, forming pots, tooling them when semidry, preparing and then applying the glazes, and firing the pots in the kiln. But the coordination of all these tasks presented no problem: she did them all herself.
>
> The problem was her ambition and the attractiveness of her pots: the orders exceeded her production capacity. So she hired Miss Bisque, who was eager to learn pottery. But this meant that Ms. Raku had to divide up the work. Since the craft shops wanted pottery made by Ms. Raku, it was decided that Miss Bisque would wedge the clay and prepare the glazes, and Ms. Raku would do the rest. And this required coordination of the work, a small problem, in fact, with two people in a pottery studio: they simply communicated informally [p. 1].

Ms. Raku's pottery studio was just beginning to feel the effect of size on structure. As the studio continued to flourish, more assistants were added. This time they were selected from the local pottery school. Their training made coordination easier—even with five people working together. But two more assistants were needed to deal with the backlog of orders. Increasing the size to seven began to tax the limits of the existing structural configuration:

> One day, Miss Bisque tripped over a pail of glaze and broke five pots; another day, Ms. Raku opened the kiln to find that the

hanging planters had all been glazed fuchsia by mistake. At this point, she realized seven people in a small pottery shop could not coordinate all of their work through the simple mechanism of informal coordination [Mintzberg, 1979, pp. 1–2].

Because she was occupied with her formal duties as the president of what was now called Ceramics Limited, Ms. Raku appointed Miss Bisque as the studio manager, giving her the responsibility to coordinate the work of the others. As the firm continued to grow, a work study analyst was hired. His recommendation was to divide the work around each product into steps, allowing workers to specialize. Standard procedures for wedging, tooling, and glazing were developed so that a pot could move easily from one stage to another.

As pot sales continued to increase, Ms. Raku added ceramic tiles, bathroom fixtures, and clay bricks to her product line. Three divisions were created around the different products: consumer, building, and industrial. Ms. Raku no longer supervised work directly. She relied mainly on quarterly reports and discussed matters with employees only when production or costs deviated from preset outcome standards. As her pottery studio continued to prosper, eventually becoming "Ceramico," its structure became even more complex and formalized.

Ms. Raku's case illustrates an important structural principle: The size of an organization affects the shape and character of the formal structure. Unless growth (or downsizing) is matched with corresponding alterations to the formal structures, problems inevitably arise. In the beginning, McDonald's was not the complex, standardized, and tightly controlled company that it is today. It began as a single hamburger stand in San Bernardino, California, owned and managed by the McDonald brothers. It was, however, a phenomenally successful operation. The McDonalds had tried to expand their concept by selling franchise rights to others, but got almost nowhere. The brothers were making about $100,000 a year, disliked travel, and neither had a family. If they made even more money, said one brother, "We'd be leaving it to a church or something, and we didn't go to church" (Love, 1986, p. 23).

The idea only took off when Ray Kroc came into the picture.

Kroc had been in the business of selling milk shake machines to restaurants. He came out from Chicago to visit the McDonald brothers, simply because he wanted to know why they had bought more milk shake machines than any other restaurant in the country and why he was getting calls from people who wanted to buy whatever milk shake mixer the McDonalds were using. As soon as he saw the original McDonald's stand, Kroc realized the possibility of building a great business: "Unlike the homebound McDonalds, Kroc had traveled extensively, and he could envision hundreds of large and small markets where a McDonald's could be located. He understood the existing food services businesses, and understood how a McDonald's unit could be a formidable competitor" (Love, 1986, pp. 39-40).

Kroc persuaded the McDonald brothers to let him take over the franchising effort, and the rest is history.

*Core Technology.* What an organization does to transform raw materials into finished products also has an effect on its structure—independently of the size of the organization. Every organization has a central activity, which is referred to in the organization literature as its core technology. A core technology involves three parts: raw materials, technical activities that transform raw materials into desired ends, and underlying beliefs about the cause-effect relations that link materials, activity, and outcome (Dornbusch and Scott, 1975). Organizational technologies vary in clarity, predictability, and effectiveness. Assembling a Big Mac is a relatively routine and programmed activity. The task is clear, most of the potential problems are known in advance, and the probability of a successful outcome is high. McDonald's relatively simple technology allows it to function successfully with mostly vertical coordination.

In contrast, Harvard's two core technologies—research and teaching—are much less routine and predictable. The teaching objectives in a university course are usually complicated and amorphous. Unlike hamburger buns, students are active agents. Their needs and skills vary widely; their moods fluctuate in response to the weather, the time of day, and the season of the year; their preoccupation with extracurricular activities is well known to Harvard professors. Confidence about what teaching strategies will yield desired outcomes is more a matter of faith than of fact. Even if students could be molded in predictable ways, it would be hard to know which ways were the correct ones. Where will the students go, and what will their jobs or graduate programs demand of them? Harvard's complex technology is one factor behind its highly decentralized, loosely coordinated structural arrangements.

Differences in technologies are particularly striking in the field of medicine. In surgery the clarity of the technology varies with the difficulty of the procedure. Appendectomies are fairly straightforward, heart surgery is much less routine. But something can go wrong with even the simplest surgeries, because the human body is so complex and its reactions are so difficult to predict. In addition, the success or failure of an operation can depend on a host of postoperative conditions, including the attitudes of the patient's family, the kind of nursing care that the patient receives, and so forth.

As a rule, more complex technologies require more elaborate structures. In a hospital that performs only routine procedures, the levels of specialization and coordination are much less complex than in a hospital where lung and heart surgery is done on a regular basis. A cardiovascular surgical team typically consists of several specialties, and the diverse efforts of the team must be tightly coordinated. After the surgery, heart patients require more highly specialized and coordinated care than do patients who have had simpler surgery.

As the pace of technological change has accelerated in recent decades, organizations' differential ability to integrate new technologies has become fateful for their effectiveness and sometimes their survival (Henderson and Clark, 1990). The introduction of new technology affects what people do at work, which in turn alters the relationships between individuals and groups. Technical change implies structural change (Barley, 1990), but existing structures often impair an organization's ability to adapt. When high-strength-low-alloy steel was introduced into the manufacture of automobiles in the 1970s, one firm's engineers continued to use traditional methods to design engine hoods out of the new steel. Eventually it became clear that traditional methods would not work with the new materials (Henderson and Clark, 1990). Henderson and Clark note that this is one reason that new entrants often have an advantage over established firms in exploiting new technologies. Established firms are tempted to treat the new technology as an incremental change that requires no fundamental change in structure.

*Environment.* A third influence on structure is the environment in which the organization operates. Although organizations employ a host of strategies to buffer internal activities from external fluctuations and interference, the environment is still a force to be reckoned with. The environment provides raw materials to an organization and receives its outputs. Schools receive students from the local community and later return skilled graduates to the local labor pool or send them on for advanced training. But the relationship between educational organizations and their environment does not end with a simple economic transaction. The boundaries between schools and their external constituencies, for example, are especially nebulous and permeable. Local as well as state and national governments and interest groups attempt to influence the educational process. As a result, the external world often directly shapes the structure of local districts and schools, as the following example from a school with which we worked illustrates.

> In a suburban school district, the environment of a middle school changed significantly over a five-year period. Once a school that served a fairly homogeneous population of blue-collar workers, it now found itself confronted by children from professional families as well as those of a very conservative faction of religious zealots. The school was originally constructed as three instructional pods, each with four classrooms. As the environment changed, what once was a quiet, smoothly functioning school quickly became one in which internal conflicts were only superseded by waves of angry parents—of all types—descending on an increasingly embattled principal. The principal had tried human relations and political strategies—all to no avail. During the summer, he decided to reorganize. Instead of randomly assigning teachers to pods and students to

teachers, he created three different classroom groupings—each with its own philosophy. One pod consisted
of regular teachers, conventionally organized, employing fairly traditional instructional strategies. To the second pod, he assigned his strictest disciplinarians and
encouraged them to adopt a reading, 'riting, and 'rith-
metic approach, using McGuffey readers and other instructional materials. The third pod was a totally
unstructured instructional environment with unconventional teachers and a roomful of play equipment, comic
books, and animals. The curriculum was designed
around the learning-by-doing philosophy of John Dew-
ey. Students were assigned to pods on the basis of parental preference and learning style. Most conflict subsided.
The next structural task was to create different evaluation and supervisory approaches and to develop schoolwide rules for the cafeteria, playground, and other
common areas. Most faculty meetings are held in individual pods. The entire faculty assembles only when
schoolwide decisions need to be made. Tailoring the
school's structure to the environment permitted the
school to perform at high levels with a highly diverse
population.

Not only do organizations vary in the extent to which the
environment penetrates into their internal workings, but environments themselves can be very different. Some are highly diverse,
unstable, and unpredictable. Organizations with rapidly changing
technologies or markets—such as high-technology electronics corporations—must cope with high degrees of uncertainty. A new
state-of-the-art product may be obsolete in six months. Any organization that finds itself in rapidly changing economic or political
conditions must also deal with high levels of uncertainty. In contrast, a stable, mature business such as a railroad or postal department deals with a much more homogeneous, stable, and predictable
set of environmental circumstances.

Organizations that face highly uncertain environments need
high levels of flexibility and adaptability to cope. They are likely

to be less bureaucratic and more decentralized. A well-known example is Digital Equipment Corporation, for many years a fast-growing manufacturer of minicomputers. Historically, Digital had no organization charts, paid little attention to job titles, and encouraged creative entrepreneurship in its employees. (One of the major industry magazines called Digital to check on the title of one of its executives and was surprised to learn that the company was not sure what his title was and did not care because it would probably change soon, anyway.) As the company matured and growth began to slow, however, Digital went through a period of reappraisal, and pressures to tighten up began to appear.

All organizations are dependent on their environment, but the degree of dependence varies. Some organizations, such as public schools, have very low power with respect to their environment, and it is difficult for them to get the resources that they need. Organizations are likely to be dependent if they are relatively small, if they are surrounded by more powerful competitors or well-organized constituencies, or if they have little flexibility and few slack resources in responding to environmental fluctuations. An organization such as Harvard University is insulated from its environment by its size, elite status, and large endowment. A small private college with no endowment is much more dependent on external fluctuations and outside expectations. Harvard can afford to give low teaching loads and a high degree of freedom to its faculty. A small college with serious financial pressures is likely to have tighter controls, higher work loads, and limited discretion in using its funds. Harvard can afford to maintain well-financed academic programs in classical Greek and Latin, even if most of the courses are under-enrolled. The poorer college will be forced to eliminate courses that do not attract students and pay their own way.

Generally speaking, organizations in more uncertain, turbulent, and rapidly changing environments will develop more sophisticated architectural forms. New specialties and roles are required to deal with emerging problems. A more specialized and diversified role structure requires more elaborate, flexible approaches to vertical and lateral coordination. The effectiveness of an organization is therefore contingent on how well its structure matches or can deal with the demands of the environment.

Compare the structural arrangements developed by three multispecialist medical clinics, each operating in different environments. For the most part, the core task of each is the same. Five or six specialists operate in each of ten to twelve departments, supported by four laboratories and x-ray facilities. Full utilization of these specialized services is important, but scheduling patients with the right specialist in the right sequence of the right amount of time creates a real structural dilemma: How do you achieve the best possible balance between full utilization of physicians' time and quality patient care? The first clinic deals with the problem by creating slack time: "Patients flow through medical departments. The waiting lines guarantee full utilization of doctors and equipment. The cost is that the patient spends a good deal of his time waiting. The cost is minimized in a way because patients travel to this clinic, which is located in a rural setting. Patients arrange their affairs so as to have time available. While they are at the clinic, there are few competing uses of their time and they have the expectation of a relaxing wait" (Galbraith, 1977, p. 43).

The other two clinics are located in large metropolitan areas where people are usually in a hurry and not interested in visiting with others. Each clinic adopted a different structural design. One clinic used an elaborate questionnaire to code incoming patients into different diagnostic categories. In this environment, patients were willing to complete the questionnaire, which permitted the clinic to do scheduling in advance. The other clinic created a twenty-person scheduling unit that used computer-generated estimates to assign patients to the appropriate specialists.

Different environments thus create different structural issues. The most efficient levels of differentiation, as well as the appropriate mix of vertical coordination strategies, are highly contingent on the organization's external terrain.

**Strategy and Goals.** An organization's decisions may be divided into two broad categories. Tactical decisions must be made about day-to-day problems that might threaten the smooth functioning of the organization and its ongoing viability. Strategic decisions are oriented to the future and are concerned with the long-term health of the organization (Chandler, 1962). Most organizations, particularly in the business world, devote at least some effort to developing strategies. Chandler defines strategy as "the determination of long-range goals and objectives of an enterprise, and the adoption of courses of action and allocation of resources necessary for carrying out these goals" (p. 13).

Organizations vary considerably in the strategies they develop and pursue. This is especially obvious in the different strategies that businesses employ. Alcan Aluminum, for example, has based its strategic position on producing suitable quality aluminum at a very low cost. Rolls Royce and Rolex produce very expensive products aimed at consumers who are willing to pay for products of high quality and strong image. Kodak's strategy is to produce low-cost goods that nevertheless carry an assurance of high quality because of the company's strong image (Pümpin, 1987). Each of these strategies has structural implications. For example, consider Zellweger AG, a Swiss manufacturer of specialty electronics products. Its strategy is based on producing top-quality high-technology equipment. In order to ensure high quality, the company has created so-called quality work groups that are composed of development engineers, designers, foremen, and others who meet regularly to coordinate their efforts and focus on quality. The managing director holds his management staff directly accountable for ensuring high quality and presides over "product conferences" in which all levels of management deal with any threats to the high-quality products and image that are part of the company's strategic plan (Pümpin, 1987).

Embedded in an organization's strategy are its goals. From a structural perspective, organizations are created almost exclusively to accomplish goals. Goals are conceptions of desired end states. They are projections of what the organization wants to produce or reach. Goals vary in how specific they are. In business organizations, goals such as profitability, growth, and market share are relatively specific and easy to measure. That is why McDonald's is able to structure its resources so tightly. However, the goals in educational and human services organizations—goals such as producing well-rounded individuals or improving individual well-being—are much more diffuse. That is another reason Harvard adopts a more decentralized, loosely integrated system of roles and relationships.

Organizations vary in the number and complexity of their goals. The goals of McDonald's are fewer, less complex, and less controversial than those of Harvard. That is part of the reason it is so much harder to get agreement on goals among members of an educational or human services organization. To complicate matters further, the stated goals of the organization are not the only, or the most important, goals it pursues. Westerlund and Sjostrand (1979) suggest a variety of other possibilities:

- Honorific goals—fictitious goals that credit the organization with desirable qualities
- Taboo goals—goals that are real but not talked about
- Stereotypic goals—goals that any reputable organization should have
- Existing goals—goals that are quietly pursued even though they are inconsistent with the organization's stated values and its self-image

To understand the appropriateness of an organization's structure for its strategy or goals, one has to look beyond its formal statement. Schools, for example, are often criticized because their structure does not focus enough on the goal of scholastic achievement. But schools have other goals, even though they may not always be a visible part of day-to-day activities. One of these is character development. Another is the "taboo" goal of certification and selection. While this goal is usually veiled, it is well known that schools channel students into different tracks and sort them into different careers. Still a third goal is custody and control—keeping kids off the streets and out from underfoot. Finally, schools often herald the stereotypical goal of achieving excellence, like almost every organization in the wake of Peters and Waterman's influential work (1982). Strategy and goals do shape structure, but the process is more complex and subtle than many managers realize.

*Information Technology.* During the past decade, modern computers revolutionized the amount of information available to an organization as well as the time it takes to move information from place to place. Information once available only to top-level or middle managers is now easily accessible and widely shared across all levels.

Many decisions that were once made at upper levels can be made closer to the immediate situation.

The implications of improved technology for the design of organizations are far reaching. Galbraith (1977), for example, argues that uncertainty is central in determining the structure of an organization. He defines uncertainty as the difference between the information that an organization already has and the information that it needs. As uncertainty increases, more information is needed to make decisions—information that may be hard to get. An organization can plan in advance how to handle simple, predictable tasks because the information needs can be anticipated. But preplanning is harder when uncertainty is high and decisions have to be made as the task is unfolding.

As uncertainty increases, Galbraith argues, organizations are confronted with two choices: (1) reduce the need for information processing or (2) increase the capacity to process information. Organizations can reduce information processing by creating slack resources or by establishing self-contained units that can work independently. If every project in a research firm is given its own editor—and the various units no longer have to rely on a centralized editorial department—the organization has created a slack resource (more editors than it needs) and at the same time has made each department more self-contained. Although the organization must now spend more money on editors, researchers will waste less time coordinating their efforts with those of the editorial department.

An organization can increase its capacity to process information by investing in vertical information systems (computers and staff personnel to collect information and direct it to decision makers) or by developing lateral relations (direct contacts, liaison roles, project teams, and matrix structures).

As organizations face more complicated situations, they must choose one or a combination of those strategies. Advances in computers and information systems are making investments in vertical information systems more attractive. Direct contact and lateral relations, because of their expense, may become far less prominent. In fact, computers and information technology often significantly reduce the need for middle managers and make it possible to create much flatter structures: "Only five years ago it was treated as sensational news when I pointed out that the information-based organization needs far fewer levels of management than the traditional command-and-control model. By now a great many—maybe most—American companies have cut management levels by one-third or more. But the restructuring of corporations—middle-sized ones as well as large ones, and, eventually, even smaller ones—has barely begun" (Drucker, 1989, p. 20).

*People: Nature of the Work Force.* Many of our prevailing ideas about designing formal structures are based on outmoded assumptions about the nature of the work force. There was a time when the typical worker was unskilled or semiskilled and had minimal education. Decisions were made at the top. Work was divided into fairly routine chunks and then allocated to employees. The main job of managers was to supervise the work closely and ensure that standards of quality were maintained.

But human resource requirements have changed. Even the lowest jobs in many organizations require high levels of skill. People are now better educated than they were in the past and they expect, and sometimes demand, more discretion in their daily work routines. Even more significant is the increasing specialization of knowledge that has created an ever growing number of professionals, who, as is well known, are different from other workers. They often know more about the technical aspects of their jobs than do managers. They are socialized to expect autonomy in their work. If they have to be supervised, they prefer reporting to professional colleagues. Lawyers who report to engineers, or engineers who report to lawyers, are likely to doubt their boss's competence to judge their work.

Hospitals, for example, have two official structures, each with a different design. One is a more traditional hierarchy of authority that controls and coordinates the work of relatively unskilled people such as receptionists, custodians, food service workers, record clerks, and secretaries. At the apex of this hierarchy is the hospital administrator, who is responsible for nonmedical operations. The other is the collegial structure, governed primarily by professionals. A medical director (an M.D.), along with various committees of physicians, oversees and coordinates medical care. A director of nursing (a professionally trained nurse) supervises and makes decisions about how nurses provide care. Tension between these administrative and collegial structures is a regular part of day-to-day relationships in hospitals.

The changing nature of the work force will increasingly put pressures on traditional hierarchical forms of organizations. Add to that changes in technology and the increasing emphasis on symbolic approaches to control in organizations, and we can anticipate dramatically different structural forms in the near future. Deal and Kennedy (1982) predict the emergence of the atomized organization—small, autonomous (often geographically dispersed) work groups tied together by information systems and organizational symbols. Drucker makes a similar observation in noting that businesses will increasingly "move work to where the people are, rather than people to where the work is" (Drucker, 1989, p. 20).

### Summary

The structural frame looks beyond individuals to examine the context in which they work together. The perspective is sometimes misunderstood or undervalued because it is equated with red tape, mindless memos, and rigid bureaucrats. In reality, the structural approach is a complex and subtle one that encompasses the free-wheeling, loosely structured entrepreneurial task force as well as the railway company and the postal department. Unfortunately, it is also a perspective that is often overlooked, with one result being that organizations engage in massive training programs to solve problems that have more to do with structure than with people.

The structural frame focuses on the two central dimensions of organizational design. Organizations divide work by creating a variety of specialized roles, functions, and units. They must then tie all those elements back together by means of both vertical and horizontal methods of integration. There is no one best way to organize, and the right structure depends very much on an organization's goals, strategies, technology, and environment.

In general, organizations operating in simpler and more stable environments are likely to employ less complex and more centralized structures, with authority, rules, and policies as the primary vehicles for coordinating the work. Organizations that operate in rapidly changing, turbulent, and uncertain environments are likely to need much more complex and flexible structures. Understanding the complexity of organizational contexts and the variety of structural possibilities can help to create structures that work for, rather than against, both people and the purposes of organizations.

# 4

# *Structuring and Restructuring*

For every combination of goals, technology, people, and circumstances, there is a formal structure that will work, but there are many others that will not. How, then, does a manager decide what structure is needed? One approach is to bring in consultants.

> Tomorrow in Manhattan, Harvard Business School professor Michael Porter and McGraw-Hill president Joseph Dionne will share the dais at a World Management Council forum on "Managing Innovation." The setting—and the pairing—is ironical, as Michael Porter is the architect of a costly and ruinous restructuring of McGraw-Hill. After reading Porter's best-selling management manual, *Competitive Strategy,* Dionne invited the wispy-haired HBS *wunderkind* to devise a strategy for pumping new life into the moribund, billion-dollar publishing giant. In 1984, Porter suggested a sweeping reorganization of the company, which had been divided up into book, magazine, and financial services divisions, into twenty-one "market focus" segments. But Porter's scheme backfired. The elaborate mixmastering of McGraw-Hill assets cost hundreds of staffers their jobs, but has fallen far short of management's expectations. Revenues in 1988 grew only 3.8 percent to $1.8 billion, trailing the rate of inflation. McGraw-Hill is no longer a leader in trade magazine publishing, an industry it once dominated [Beam, 1989, p. 40].

The divisions that performed best were those that were reorganized least. A McGraw-Hill executive commented ruefully, "Market focus was the atom that blew the company apart. It was like our first whiff of coke, this seductive idea that the solution to our problems could be found inside the company, by reorganizing the pieces. Now, when things are going badly, we reorganize" (Beam, 1989, p. 40).

## Structural Issues and Dilemmas

Finding a workable arrangement of roles and relationships is an ongoing struggle in all organizations. Miller and Friesen (1984), for example, identified a number of structural patterns, some of which worked, while others did not. Firms that were in trouble typically fell into one of three major structural patterns:

1. Impulsive firms. Typically these are fast-growing organizations, controlled by one individual or a few top people, in which the structures and controls have become too simple and primitive for the size and complexity of the firm. In such cases, the firm often grows to the point that it gets out of control. Profits may then fall precipitously, and the firm's survival may even be at stake.

2. Stagnant bureaucracies. These are usually older organizations controlled by past traditions and turning out obsolete product lines. A predictable and placid environment has lulled the organization to sleep, and top management is heavily committed to the old ways. Information systems are not sophisticated enough to detect the need for change. Lower-level managers feel ignored and alienated. Many old-line corporations and public bureaucracies have these characteristics.

3. Headless giants. These are made up of loosely coupled, independent departments or divisions. Most of the management and leadership is in the departments, and the organization, with no real strategy or leadership at the top, simply drifts. There is little collaboration because the departments compete for resources, and most of the problems are handled by crisis management.

Each of these dysfunctional patterns exhibits inadequate resolution of the major structural dilemmas that every organization confronts. We will discuss nine of these dilemmas below.

*Differentiation vs. Integration.* This is the classic structural tension between the need to divide the work and the difficulty of coordinating work after it has been divided. Lawrence and Lorsch (1967) studied three different types of organizations, each facing a different set of environmental challenges. They found that effective organizations developed structures that mirrored their environments. In the container industry, which is relatively stable, effective organizations had simple structures. In the more unstable food industry, however, successful organizations were more differentiated and had developed more elaborate mechanisms for coordination and control. In the highly volatile plastics industry, the effectiveness of an organization seemed contingent on an ability to develop highly complex systems of roles with correspondingly sophisticated strategies for coordinating diverse efforts.

In addition, Lawrence and Lorsch found that even within the same industry different divisions developed different structures. The structure of manufacturing in many industries was decidedly more bureaucratic, for example, than that of research and development units. When different parts of an organization faced different environments, they needed different structures. If the same structure is used for both the research and manufacturing departments in a plastics manufacturer, at least one of the departments will be organized incorrectly: research will have a structure that is too tight and bureaucratic, or manufacturing will have one that is too loose and freewheeling. The more the two departments differ, however, the more difficult it will be to coordinate their efforts. In such situations, the more effective firms found ways to attain higher levels of both differentiation and integration, despite the inherent tension between them.

*Gaps vs. Overlaps.* In designing an effective structure, an organization must assign key responsibilities to individuals or groups. Otherwise, important tasks are not carried out and performance suffers. In many public schools, for example, pressing issues such as discipline or transportation divert attention from instruction. Students learn less than they might if instruction had a higher priority. By the same token, roles and activities can overlap, creating unwanted redundancies, wasted effort, and conflict. In one experimental high school, all staff members took it upon themselves to call the district office when problems arose in the school. This created considerable confusion for district office personnel, and the teachers and principal were constantly stepping on one another's toes. The overlap was eliminated when staff members agreed to communicate through the formal channel.

*Underuse vs. Overload.* In many organizations, some individuals have too little work. They often become bored and get in other people's way. In one physician's office, for example, the clerical staff members were able to complete most of their tasks during the morning. After lunch, they had very little to do. They filled their time by talking to family and friends. As a result, the office's telephone lines were constantly busy, making it very difficult for patients to schedule appointments. At the other extreme, it is possible to overload positions or units and thus make it impossible to get everything done or done well. In the same physician's office, the nurses were swamped with patients and paperwork. They were so busy that they rarely had time to talk informally with patients. They were often brusque and curt when asked to go beyond routine, clinical conversations. A better structural balance was accomplished by reassigning many of the nurses' clerical duties to the office staff.

*Lack of Clarity vs. Lack of Creativity.* A common problem in organizations is that people do not fully understand what they are supposed to do. As a consequence, they shape their roles to fit their personal needs rather than to further organizational goals. At the same time, however, too much clarity can undermine creativity. It is equally common for people in organizations to conform in a "bureaupathic" way to their official roles. They rigidly do what they are supposed to do even though the service or product thereby suffers. In contrast, an American Airlines flight attendant once delighted first-class passengers by asking them how they wanted their filets cooked. She had observed that cooking them for the formally prescribed twenty-five minutes resulted in dry, overcooked meat. By reducing the cooking time, she could custom tailor each filet to a passenger's taste.

*Excessive Autonomy vs. Excessive Interdependence.* In some organizations, the efforts of individuals or groups are so loosely coupled that they come to feel isolated and unsupported. In schools teachers often work in isolation and rarely see other adults during the school day. But it also happens that some units or roles are more tightly connected than they need to be, so that each group (or individual) has difficulty concentrating on its own work and wastes time on unnecessary efforts to coordinate activities. One mental health clinic had designed a sophisticated system of interdependencies among its professional staff. But the nature of the patient population made such tightly coordinated care unnecessary. In fact, the staff spent so much time in underproductive meetings that the quality of individual patient care began to deteriorate.

*Too Loose vs. Too Tight.* One of the most critical tasks in structuring human resources is finding a balance between vertical and horizontal looseness or tightness. Typically, this means creating a system of rules and other coordinating strategies that hold an organization together without holding it back. In some organizations the structure is so loose that no one knows what it is, and people go their own way with little sense of what others are doing. Schools, for example, have long been criticized for structural looseness. But in other organizations the structure is too tight, stifling flexibility and ensuring that people spend much of their time trying to escape from control. When Rene McPherson became the CEO of Dana Corporation, he allegedly took all the policy manuals and dumped them into a wastebasket (Peters and Austin, 1985). He then set out to loosen those controls that had prevented the company from achieving high levels of productivity.

*Diffuse Authority vs. Overcentralization.* In some organizations, no one really knows who has authority over what. The resulting confusion limits individual initiative and creates conflict. At the other extreme, layers and layers of formal authority remove decisions so far from their source that decision making is both excessively slow and inaccurate. Digital Equipment Company's authority patterns are very diffuse, yet the company has found a balance that promotes tolerance of reasonable levels of confusion. Northwest Orient was able to reduce its passenger complaints significantly by giving personnel with direct passenger contact discretion in making payments for lost luggage or meals when flights are delayed. The awards can be made on the spot rather than requiring approval by higher-ups.

*Goal-Less vs. Goal-Bound.* In some organizations, few people know what the goals are; in others, people cling to goals long after they have become irrelevant or outmoded. The film *Bridge Over the River Kwai* initially depicts the delaying tactics of American and British prisoners of war who are working under Japanese supervision to construct a strategic bridge. In a sense the group was goalless—or at least did not accept the goals of their captors. When Alec Guinness took over command, he announced to his men that the bridge would be built, and he held to this goal even though it went against the Allied war effort. In *The Bridge,* a corps of young German adolescents, recruited late in World War II to fill gaping vacancies in Hitler's army, were assigned to defend a bridge. Someone, however, forgot to tell them when the command was given to withdraw. They defended that bridge to their deaths.

*Irresponsible vs. Unresponsive.* When people are unclear about their responsibilities, or uncommitted to them, their performance suffers. However, adhering too rigidly to one's job description can also reduce performance. In public agencies, the "street-level bureaucrats" (Lipsky, 1980) who meet the public are often asked questions such as, "Could you do me this favor?" or "Couldn't you bend the rules a little bit in this case?" If they turn down every such request, no matter how reasonable, they will alienate the public and perpetuate images of bureaucratic rigidity and red tape. But if they are too accommodating, they will create other problems. Airline flight attendants, for example, continually get various special requests from passengers. If they respond to all such requests with, "That's not my job," a lot of passengers will look for another airline. But if they accommodate an unruly passenger who insists on another shot of Jack Daniels or a passenger who refuses to follow safety regulations, they are not doing their job.

Attempting to resolve these structural dilemmas is an ongoing task of management. Which dilemmas are most pressing depends on an organization's situation: its history, its current environment, and the structural configuration that it has developed.

## Structural Configurations

Because they encounter different circumstances, organizations evolve different structural forms. Mintzberg (1979) has developed five possible configurations: simple structure, machine bureaucracy, professional bureaucracy, divisionalized form, and adhocracy. Each form creates a unique set of management challenges.

*Simple Structure.* The simple structure is just that—simple. It has only two levels: the strategic apex and an operating level.

### Figure 2. Simple Structure.

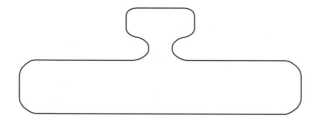

Source: Henry Mintzberg, THE STRUCTURE OF ORGANIZATIONS, © 1979, p. 307. Reprinted by permission of Prentice-Hall, Inc., Englewood Cliffs, N.J.

Coordination between levels and among employees is accomplished primarily through direct supervision. The simple structure is found in mom-and-pop operations. Either mom or pop is constantly aware of what is going on in the store and has almost total authority over what happens on a day-to-day basis. Mintzberg (1979, pp. 310–311) describes a typical business with a simple structure:

> Chez LeThin, located in the North of France . . . sells notions and novelties in five stores, four of which were opened in a five-year period. . . . Both product lines are simple, but the market for novelties is extremely dynamic. Novelties include fashion

clothing—turtlenecks, scarves, belts, and the like—that require frequent and rapid response, in high season almost weekly, because of the uncertainty of supply and demand. The technical system—retail selling—is, of course, extremely simple and nonregulating; the only equipment required are cash registers, an automobile that doubles as a truck, and a telephone. Chez LeThin is owned and managed by a husband-and-wife team—a dual chief executive—the husband looking after control and administration, the wife, purchasing and inventory. Fifty salespeople report directly to the owners, despite the fact that these people are dispersed in the five different stores across a thirty-mile radius. There are no store managers. Instead, the owners visit each store every day. The only other employees—support staff, so to speak—are one secretary and one woman who works part time to balance the inventory among the stores. There is hardly any information system—problems are communicated verbally to the owners during their visits. Sales for each store are, however, reported daily, although overall sales and cost figures are generally run about twelve months late. There is no training of salespeople, no differentiation among them (except for the cashiers), no planning, and hardly any rules.

The simple structure is prominent in nearly all start-up companies. William Hewlett and David Packard began their business in a garage; General Electric had its humble beginnings in Edison's laboratory. The virtues of simple structure are its flexibility and adaptability—one person can change the entire operation. But the virtues can also become structural vices. The operation is highly dependent on one individual who can block change as well as initiate it, or punish capriciously as well as reward handsomely. Because the boss is so close to day-to-day operations, he or she can easily become preoccupied with immediate problems and neglect long-range strategic decisions.

*Machine Bureaucracy.* We have already described a classic machine bureaucracy—McDonald's. Here, most important decisions are made at the strategic apex of the organization; the day-to-day operations of the local restaurants are controlled by managers and by standardized procedures developed by analysts housed at the corpo-

**Figure 3. Machine Bureaucracy.**

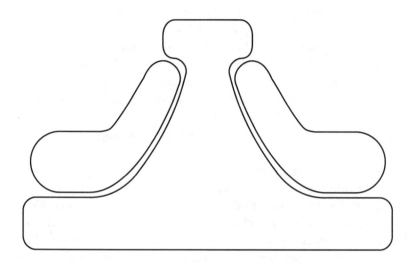

*Source:* Henry Mintzberg, THE STRUCTURING OF ORGANIZATIONS, © 1979, p. 325. Reprinted by permission of Prentice-Hall, Inc., Englewood Cliffs, N.J.

rate headquarters. Unlike simple hierarchies, machine bureaucracies have a large support staff and technostructure; there are many layers between the apex and the operating levels.

For routine tasks such as making hamburgers or manufacturing automotive parts, the structure of a machine bureaucracy is enormously efficient and effective. The primary structural issue develops around motivating and satisfying workers in the operating core. Most people tire quickly of repetitive work and standardized procedures. But to introduce more creativity and challenge in a McDonald's outlet could easily undermine the consistency and uniformity that have made the company so successful.

Like every machine bureaucracy, McDonald's must also deal with tensions between middle managers in the individual outlets and the executives at the headquarters. The tendency is for middle managers to adapt their unit to local circumstances. But as problems flow up the chain of command for resolution, and top executives rely more and more on abstract information produced by analysts in the technostructure, their solutions may not always match the needs of individual units. McDonald's handles this tension by allowing individual restaurants to experiment with new ideas. The McDonald's Egg McMuffin was originally developed by a local franchisee who believed he could enlarge his market by serving breakfast. The McDonald's breakfast is now standard across its restaurants. By permitting such experimentation, McDonald's has solved one of the most difficult problems for this structural form—innovation. This machine bureaucracy is created for efficiency, not flexible adaptation to a changing environment.

*Professional Bureaucracy.* Earlier, Harvard University provided a glimpse into the inner workings of a typical professional bureaucracy. Its operating core is very large relative to its other structural parts—particularly the technostructure. There are few levels between the strategic apex and professors. Professional bureaucracies are flat, decentralized structures; control is provided mainly by the professional indoctrination of their members. The support staff exists to serve the professionals, who carry out the primary responsibilities.

The professional bureaucracy insulates its key players from formal interference, allowing them to concentrate on using their expertise. That produces many benefits, but it also leads to problems of coordination and quality control. Because a tenured professor at Harvard is largely immune to formal sanctions, Harvard, like many universities, has to find other ways to deal with incompetence and irresponsibility.

Professional bureaucracies often respond slowly to changes in the environment. Multiple waves of reforms and reformers have tried with little success over several decades to reform and restructure public schools. Although individual teachers may adapt rapidly to new developments in their fields, their schools change at a glacial pace. These are two sides of the same coin: the autonomy and adaptability of the professional make it very hard for the organization to make systematic changes. Professional bureaucracies rarely succeed when they try to standardize the performance of those in the operating core, by means of policies, supervision, or output controls, and instead often upset the delicate relationship between

**Figure 4. Professional Bureaucracy.**

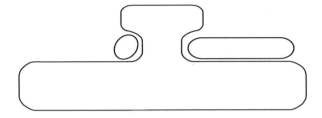

*Source:* Henry Mintzberg, THE STRUCTURING OF ORGANIZATIONS, © 1979, p. 355. Reprinted by permission of Prentice-Hall, Inc., Englewood Cliffs, N.J.

professionals and their clients (Mintzberg, 1979). It would be futile to require Harvard professors to follow standard teaching methods; such an approach would be more likely to harm performance than to improve it.

***Divisionalized Form.*** In this organizational form, the bulk of work is done in quasi-autonomous units—the campuses in a multicampus university, the different specialties in a large multispecialty hospital, or the divisions in *Fortune* 500 companies (Mintzberg, 1979). The structures of the divisions themselves may represent any of the other possible configurations, although the machine bureaucracy is most commonly found. The divisions serve specific market areas and house their own functional units. The strategic apex strikes a deal with each division. The divisions get considerable autonomy, but they are responsible for achieving certain measurable results: profits, sales growth, and return on investment (Mintzberg, 1979). Divisional general managers, although they serve at the pleasure of the chief executive, are given wide latitude as long as they deliver results. Headquarters usually gives divisions relatively free rein as long as they perform at preset levels. Headquarters manages the strategic portfolio and allocates resources based on its assessment of the appropriate mix of market opportunities.

The headquarters of General Motors, departing from Alfred Sloan's original model, governs its divisions more tightly than many divisionalized companies. L. Wrigley (1970, p. V-33) describes

**Figure 5. Divisionalized Form.**

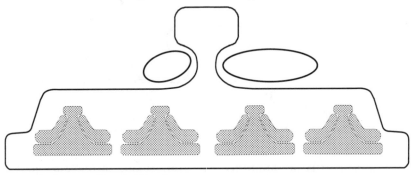

*Source:* Henry Mintzberg, THE STRUCTURING OF ORGANIZATIONS, © 1979, p. 393. Reprinted by permission of Prentice-Hall, Inc., Englewood Cliffs, N.J.

this integrated closed system: "Neither GM nor Fisher Body can be permitted to sell their facilities to the market, nor the car divisions (Chevrolet, Pontiac, Buick, Oldsmobile, Cadillac) to buy the kind of facilities they need from the open market. No break is allowed in the chain. The central office controls labor relations, market forecasting, research engineering, quality control, styling, pricing, production scheduling, inventory levels, product range, and dealer relations. It decides what plants are to be built, and what cars; it styles them (all must have a 'General Motors' look), and tests them at the corporate proving grounds. It is of note that the Engineering Policy Group of General Motors does not include division managers." General managers make decisions about marketing and distribution, but even those are tightly controlled by the central office.

In theory, the divisional structure offers economies of scale, ample resources, and responsiveness without undue economic risks. But it creates its own structural tensions. One is an ongoing cat-and-mouse game between headquarters executives and division managers. Headquarters tends to favor tighter control over the divisions, while divisional general managers continually try to find ways to evade those controls: "Our top management likes to make all the major decisions. They think they do, but I've seen one case where a division beat them. I received for editing a request from the division for a chimney. I couldn't see what anyone would do with a chimney, so I flew out for a visit. They've built and equipped a whole plant on plant expense orders. The chimney is the only in-divisible item that exceeded the $50,000 limit we put on plant expense orders. Apparently they learned that a new plant wouldn't be formally received, so they built the damn thing. I don't know exactly what I'm going to say" (Bower, 1970, p. 189).

Divisionalization also leads to concentrated efforts in other organizations such as unions or regulating agencies. Because of its sheer mass, the corporate headquarters of a huge divisionalized company or conglomerate can lose touch with its operations and its social responsibility. As one GM manager put it, "headquarters is where the rubber meets the air." While the divisional form is often used in the not-for-profit sector, it is unwieldy unless goals are measurable and a reliable vertical information system can be de-signed (Mintzberg, 1979).

*Adhocracy.* The final structural configuration developed by Mintz-berg is the adhocracy. This is a loose, flexible, self-renewing organic form tied together mostly by lateral coordination. An adhocracy can exist at either the operating or the administrative level. Usually found in diverse, freewheeling environments, the adhocracy func-tions as an "organizational tent" that "exploits benefits hidden within properties that designers have generally regarded as liabil-ities. Ambiguous authority structures, unclear objectives, and con-tradictory assignments of responsibility can legitimize controversies and challenge traditions. . . . Incoherence and indecision can foster exploration, self-evaluation, and learning" (Hedberg, Nystrom, and Starbuck, 1976, p. 45).

Ad hoc structures are most often found in conditions of tur-bulence and rapid change. Examples include advertising agencies, think-tank consulting firms, and the recording industry. Perhaps one of the best-known corporate examples of an adhocracy struc-tural form is found in Digital Equipment Corporation (DEC): "In many ways [DEC] is a big company in small-company clothes. It doesn't believe much in hierarchy, rule books, dress codes, company cars, executive dining rooms, lofty titles, country club member-ships, or most trappings of corpocracy. It doesn't even have assigned parking spots. Only the top half-dozen executives have sizable of-fices. Everyone else at the company headquarters in Maynard,

**Figure 6. Adhocracy.**

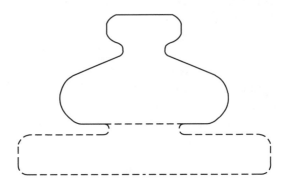

Source: Henry Mintzberg, THE STRUCTURING OF ORGANIZATIONS, © 1979, p. 443. Reprinted by permission of Prentice-Hall, Inc., Englewood Cliffs, N.J.

Mass., makes do with dinky doorless cubicles" (Machan, 1987, p. 154).

These unusual trappings reflect the company's diffuse structure authority: "It's hard to know who's in the pecking order. When Personnel Director John Sims joined the company thirteen years ago, he sat in on a meeting and could not determine who was the boss" (Machan, 1987, p. 154). Instead of being determined by the strategic apex, organizational strategy emerges from decisions made by a variety of units in different parts and at different levels of the organization. Ideas and decisions from the lowest levels in the organization "bubble up" to the top: "Employees think nothing about jumping several levels of authority to get support for an idea. Some newcomers have written lengthy memos to Olsen [Kenneth Olsen, CEO] himself, to which he has responded" (p. 154).

Digital is a highly successful company largely because of its unusual structural arrangements. But like every structural form, adhocracy creates its own set of managerial issues:

1. An adhocracy's ambiguity can tax even the most flexible individuals and units: "Digital's structureless, informal environment could drive outsiders nuts" (Machan, 1987, p. 156).

2. An adhocracy can create conflict and chaos. At DEC, "projects started at first-rung levels can overlap and bump into each

other. And at some jobs, employees may have dotted-line relationships to several bosses. That's great for creative exchange, but it's trying when an employee can't be in two places at once" (p. 156).

3. An adhocracy relies on extensive training of its employees and promotes from within: "Lots of training goes on in-house, too [in addition to DEC's strong encouragement of advanced education externally]. Engineers are expected to spend at least five days a year attending training sessions, and salespeople must spend at least twice that amount boning up on company products and services. DEC has an educational services department that provides instructions for employees and customers alike. DEC prefers to develop its managers in-house, rather than go outside" (p. 156).

Adhocracies are not good at the routine and the repetitive. They often produce duplication and inefficiency and make it difficult to coordinate activities. Adhocracy works best when individuals in an organization must perform creative tasks in a rapidly changing environment. DEC continues to operate in a highly turbulent environment, but that environment became increasingly competitive in the late 1980s. A marked slowdown in DEC's growth put new pressures on its adhocracy.

### Generic Issues in Restructuring

Restructuring efforts need to take account of the differences inherent in different configurations. Consultants and managers sometimes apply general principles without recognizing key structural differences. Restructuring an adhocracy is radically different from restructuring a machine bureaucracy. Subjecting radically different organizations to the same organizing principles is a sure-fire recipe for the kind of difficulty that Michael Porter experienced in his work with McGraw-Hill.

Mintzberg's imagery suggests the kind of general principles needed to guide restructuring across a range of circumstances. He notes that the various components of an organization exert structural pressures. In any restructuring effort a multidirectional tug-of-war will eventually determine the shape of the structure. Unless the various "pulls" are acknowledged and managed effectively, the resulting structural form may turn out to be wrong for the organization's task and environment. Some observers, for example, argued that the marketing failure of Lockheed's L-1011 jet airplane was a function of too little tension between its engineering and marketing units. The plane was (and still is) one of the most sophisticated in the air, and analysts generally agreed that it was a better airplane than its chief competitor, the Douglas DC-10. But Douglas got its plane to market first, and a number of airlines immediately ordered it. Because of this, many observers argue that Lockheed was never able to sell enough airplanes to justify its enormous investment.

Mintzberg discusses a generic set of "pulls" that exist across different structural forms. The strategic apex tends to exert centralizing pressures on the organization. Either through commands, rules, or less obtrusive means, those at the top continually try to develop a more unified mission or strategy. Deep down, they prefer a simple structure.

By contrast, those in middle management tend to "pull" the organization toward Balkanization. School principals, general managers, department heads, or bureau chiefs become committed to their own domain. It is their job to protect and enhance their unit's interests. The tensions between centripetal forces from the top and centrifugal forces from middle management are especially prominent in divisionalized structures but are critical issues in any restructuring effort.

The technostructure of an organization typically exerts pressures to standardize, because analysts want to be able to measure and monitor the organization's activities. Depending on the circumstances, they can counterbalance (or complement) the forces of the top administrators, who want to centralize activities, or those of the middle managers, who seek greater autonomy. Technocrats feel at home in the machine bureaucracy.

The support staff component pulls the organization in the direction of greater collaboration. Its members usually feel happiest when decision-making authority is given to small work constellations. There they can influence, directly and personally, the shape and flow of everyday decisions. They prefer adhocracy.

Across the various structural forms, those in the operating core seek to minimize pressures from the other components. Their preference is for professional autonomy so that they can control the conditions of work. They often look outside—to unions or to their professional colleagues—for support.

Anyone who attempts to restructure an organization needs to understand these natural tensions among the various structural parts or territories. Depending on the structural configurations— simple structure, machine bureaucracy, professional bureaucracy, divisionalized form, or adhocracy—different organizational territories will have more or less influence on the final outcome. In a simple structure, the boss undoubtedly has the edge in determining the shape of the structure. In machine bureaucracies, the technostructure and those at the strategic apex possess the most clout in shaping structural arrangements. In professional bureaucracies, the chronic tension between administrators and professionals is the dominant organizational tension, while those in the technostructure play an important role in the wings. In the adhocracy, a number of different actors can play pivotal roles in shaping the emerging structural patterns.

Beyond internal negotiations lurks a more central issue. A workable structure is ultimately a function of how well it fits an organization's environment and technology. Natural selection weeds out survivors from victims. It is always a poker game among the major players to negotiate a structure that will meet the needs of each component and still work in the organization's environment.

### Pressures for Restructuring

Why then do organizations restructure? In fact, Miller and Friesen (1984) argue that organizations typically go for fairly long periods of time with relatively little structural change but then experience intervals of major restructuring. Organizations try to retain their existing form as long as possible in order to maintain internal consistency and to avoid upsetting the existing equilibrium. But, if the environment changes while the organization remains static, the structure gets more and more out of touch with the environment. Eventually, the gap becomes so wide that the organization is forced to do a major overhaul. Restructuring, in this view, is like spring cleaning: We accumulate debris over months or years, and finally we have to face up to the mess. The changes that lead to restructuring include the following factors:

- The environment changes. In the case of AT&T, a shift in the environment from regulation to competition has required a major reorganization of the Bell System.
- The technology changes. The replacement of piston engines by jet engines in the aircraft industry profoundly affected the relationship between engine and airframe. Some established firms faltered because they underestimated the complexities; Boeing rose to lead the industry because it understood them (Henderson and Clark, 1990).
- Organizations grow. DEC thrived with a very informal and flexible structure during the company's early years, but the same structure produced major problems when DEC grew into a multibillion-dollar corporation. Reluctantly at first, it was forced to develop more formal procedures and relationships.
- The political climate changes. Public agencies often reorganize to attune their structure to the priorities and expectations of the legislature. In recent years, for example, the National Institute of Education was reorganized to tailor its research units to the areas that Congress was most interested in trying to improve.
- Leadership changes. Reorganization is often one of the first initiatives of new leaders. At times, there are clear task-related reasons for a new structure.

Sometimes, several of these factors converge at the same time. A reorganization of the operations at Citibank, currently the largest bank in the United States, illustrates many of the issues in structural change.

The back room at Citibank was in trouble when John Reed took charge of it in 1970 (Seeger, Lorsch, and Gibson, 1975). Productivity was disappointing, errors were frequent, and expenses were rising at a rate of almost 20 percent every year. Reed soon determined that the back room needed dramatic structural change. Traditionally, the back room (which processes checks and other financial instruments) was viewed as a support service for the customer-contact offices of the bank. But even though it was part of the support component of the bank, it was internally structured as a machine bureaucracy. Reed decided to think of it not as a support function but as a factory: an independent, high-volume production process. To implement the new plan, he imported high-level executives from the automobile industry. One of them was Robert White, who came over from Ford Motor Company and became the primary architect of a new structure and systems for the back room. White arrived with a strong faith in top-down management: "We use a pass/fail system as a management incentive. A manager passes or fails in terms of the objectives he himself has set within the top-down framework. He is rewarded, or not rewarded, accordingly. No excuses or rationalization of events 'beyond one's control' are accepted" (Seeger, Lorsch, and Gibson, 1975, p. 3).

White began by developing a Phase I Action Plan that called for cutting costs, putting in new computer systems, and developing a financial control system that could both forecast and measure performance. In effect, the strategy was to retain the machine bureaucracy, but to tighten it up. After the Phase I program was implemented, White concluded "We hadn't gone back to the basics enough. We found that we did not really understand the present processes completely" (Seeger, Lorsch, and Gibson, 1975, p. 8). What followed was an intensive, detailed study of how the back room's processes worked. White and his associates developed a detailed flowchart that covered the walls of a room. They realized that the current structure was, in effect, one very large, functional pipeline. Everything flowed into "preprocessing" at the front end of the pipe, then to "encoding" and on through a series of functional areas until it eventually came out at the other end. Reed and White decided to break up the pipe into several smaller lines, each carrying a different "product" and each supervised by a single manager with responsibility for the entire process. The key insight was to change the structure from machine bureaucracy to divisionalized form.

White also instituted extensive performance measures and tight accountability procedures: "We currently measure 69 different quality indicators, and we are meeting the standards 87 percent of the time. When a given indicator is met or beaten consistently, we tighten the standard; we expect to continue this process indefinitely. We have defined 129 different standards for timelines, and we expect

that number to continue to grow. Today, we are meeting 85 percent
of those standards. Moreover, we also continually tighten these
standards as soon as they can be consistently met. I think it is fair
to say that our service performance has improved greatly since we
began to hold costs flat—if for no other reason than that we really
know what we are doing" (Seeger, Lorsch, and Gibson, 1975, p. 8).

Not surprisingly, this demanding, top-down approach produced fear and loathing among many old-timers in the back room
and nearly led to rebellion. As Mintzberg's model predicts, the technical core strongly resisted this major intrusion into its autonomy.
Reed and White decided to implement the new structure virtually
overnight, and the short-term result was chaos and a major break-
down in the system. It took two weeks to get the system functioning
normally, and five months to fully recover from the problems generated by the transition. But, once past that crisis, the new system led
to a dramatic improvement in operating results: production was up,
costs and errors were down. The back room was unexpectedly making a major contribution to corporate profitability.

The basic concepts behind the restructuring in the back room
were not new. The change from a large, functional bureaucracy to
a divisionalized form had first occurred in the 1920s at General
Motors and Du Pont. By the 1970s, it had become the dominant
form for large organizations. What was unusual was to take the
basic concept of a divisionalized organization and apply it to the
back room of a bank.

No one knows whether more reorganization efforts succeed
than fail, but even casual observation makes it clear that the percentage of failures is high. Reed and White were successful where
others failed because they followed several basic principles of successful structural change. First, they developed a new conception of
the organization's goals and strategies. Instead of being a service
function, the back room was to be a "factory," a highly efficient
production operation. Second, they carefully studied the existing
structure so that they understood how it worked. Many efforts at
structural change fail because they are premised on an incomplete
picture of how the current patterns operate. Third, they designed
the new structure in light of changes in goals, technology, and
environment. Finally, they experimented. When their initial, Phase

I redesign failed to achieve what they hoped, they went back to the drawing boards, did a more thorough study, and implemented a more thorough reorganization.

In both the Citibank and McGraw-Hill cases, restructuring led initially to confusion, resistance, and an initial decrease in effectiveness. In the short term, these are the expected by-products of rearranging the parts of an organization or developing new schemes for coordinating across different positions or groups. Success or failure depends, to a large extent, on developing a microscopic view of the typical structural problems as well as a topographical sense of the structural options.

## Summary

Restructuring is one of the most common approaches to organizational change, despite the fact that all reorganizations produce disruptions and many never produce long-run benefits that justify the short-term costs. The impulse to restructure arises in response to a variety of structural tensions: differentiation/integration, gaps/overlaps, underuse/overload, clarity/creativity, autonomy/independence, loose/tight, diffuse/overcentralized, goal-less/goalbound, and irresponsible/unresponsive.

The possibilities and dynamics of restructuring depend on an organization's configuration. Mintzberg identifies several major forms of organizational configuration: simple structure, machine bureaucracy, professional bureaucracy, divisionalized form, and adhocracy. Each fits particular circumstances and creates a different set of internal dynamics. An understanding of those dynamics is essential to successful restructuring.

# 5

# *Organizing Groups and Teams*

Much of the work of large organizations is done in small units, teams, or groups. The scale is smaller and structural elements are often more subtle, but such units must respond to the same basic structural questions that face larger organizations: (1) how should their members divide responsibilities across different roles and (2) how can they integrate diverse activities into a unified effort?

Small groups are microcosms of large organizations. Smoldering interpersonal friction, emotional outbursts, confusion, competing agendas, power struggles, conflict, and disputes over values and symbols frequently prevent small groups from performing optimally or from providing needed psychological support. This chapter examines the structural features of small groups and shows how redesigning structure can often improve a group's performance, as well as its ability to respond to the needs of its members.

### A High-Performing Commando Unit

During the Second World War a U.S. Army commando team compiled a distinctive record. It successfully accomplished every mission it was assigned, including some extremely high-risk behind-the-lines operations. It had one of the lowest rates of battle-related deaths or injuries of any unit in the U.S. military services. A research team was asked to find out what made the unit so successful. Were the enlisted men and officers especially talented? Had their training been longer or more intensive than normal? Or was the group just lucky?

The researchers found that the group's success resulted from its ability to change its structure to fit the situation. In planning for missions, the group functioned democratically. Anyone—irrespective of specialty or rank—could volunteer ideas and make suggestions. Decisions were arrived at by consensus, and the features of an engagement were approved by the group as a whole. As far as planning went, the structure of the unit resembled a research and development team or a creative design group. Amorphous roles and a flat hierarchy encouraged participation, creativity, and productive conflict. Battle plans thus reflected the best ideas that the group could produce.

Executing the plan was another story. When the group carried out its mission, the structure changed from a loose creative confederation to a well-defined and tightly controlled bureaucracy. Each individual had a specific task to do. Every task had to be done with split-second precision. Operational decisions and changes in the plan were solely the responsibility of the commanding officer. Everyone else obeyed orders without question, although if time permitted, they might offer suggestions. In battle, therefore, the group relied heavily on the traditional military structure: responsibilities were clear-cut, and decisions were made at the top and executed by those at the bottom.

The group's ability to redesign its structure to fit the circumstances provided the best of both worlds. Participation encouraged creativity and ownership of the battle plan. Authority and clarity of roles enabled the group to operate with speed and efficiency when executing the plan. Like all organizations, small groups must arrange people vertically and laterally to deal with the immediate task and environment. In the case of the commando unit, changing the structure to fit the strategy won battles and saved lives.

## Tasks and Linkages in Small Groups

The commando team's experience is consistent with what we have learned from several decades of research on small work groups. In dealing with their tasks, groups have a number of structural options. The one they choose—or the one that evolves—must allow individual members to pool their efforts so that the task can be completed successfully and without creating the pathologies that often accompany work in small groups. Tasks vary in their clarity, predictability, and stability. Complex tasks, such as planning a commando mission or doing open heart surgery, present different challenges from simpler tasks—for example, building a house or performing an appendectomy.

Simple tasks are usually best performed with simple structures—clearly defined roles, simple forms of interdependence, and coordination by plan or command. More complicated tasks generally require more complicated structures—flexible roles, reciprocal interdependence, and coordination by means of lateral relationships and mutual feedback. When tasks become exceptionally complex, particularly in cases where time is a major factor, more centralized authority is often needed. Otherwise the group will be unable to decide quickly enough how to deal with rapidly changing circumstances. Unless a group is able to work out a structure that fits its task, performance and morale will suffer, and the pathologies so familiar to anyone who has worked in small groups will multiply.

Finding the right structure for the circumstances is always challenging. It requires careful consideration of a number of situational variables, some of which are apt to be ambiguous or hard to assess. We will illustrate some of the issues by following a school superintendent through the process of designing an organizational structure for her school board.

> Dr. Roberta Summers stared pensively at the circles and lines on the legal pad in front of her. To her, each circle had a unique personality, and each line represented a potential relationship. Her job was to arrange the lines and circles into an effective system of communication between five elected officials. This was her first formal task as superintendent of schools. Roscoe Larson, president of the five-member school board, had asked her to recommend how the district's formal decision-making body should organize itself. Dr. Madeline Creecy and

Leonard Williams had just been elected to three-year terms. They joined Melissa Roden and Virginia Corey, two long-term board members. Larson was anxious to formalize a set of working relationships at their first official meeting together. Larson wanted to hear Summers's ideas about how to structure communications among members, particularly in the intervals between formal meetings. Board membership was a part-time responsibility for everyone; and, in the past, Larson had often found that getting information out to everyone resulted in frustrating rounds of telephone tag. Larson and Summers both knew that the quality of communication would have a major effect on how the board and superintendent worked together.

Drawing upon her knowledge of small groups, Summers pondered the options. Three main considerations were uppermost in her mind:

1. What are we trying to accomplish?
2. What do the board members care about most? (time? quality? participation?)
3. What are the special skills and talents of each board member?

She believed that those questions were central to working out an effective organizational plan for the board. She had five different options in mind.

In the first of these, the board chairman would be the official "boss" of the other members—the hub of the communications flow. In this structure, information and decisions would flow through the chairman (Figure 7). Group members would provide information to him, and he would be responsible for communicating information from the superintendent to them. Members would communicate primarily with the chairman rather than with one another. Summers knew this arrangement would be efficient and would facilitate com-

**Figure 7.
One-Boss
Arrangement.**

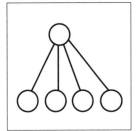

**Figure 8.
Middle Managers.**

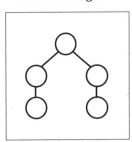

munication among board members. She
also knew that the one-boss structure
works best on tasks that are relatively simple and unambiguous. But this structure
often foundered on more complex and ambiguous tasks unless the leader had unusual levels of skill, expertise, and energy
(Bavelas and Barrett, 1951; Leavitt, 1951,
1978; Collins and Guetzkow, 1964).
Summers was not fully confident about
Larson's abilities and was aware that he
could give only a limited amount of time
to the job. If the work became too demanding, he might find himself over-
whelmed by it. She also questioned
whether the other board members would
feel comfortable about going through him
to talk with her. Each board member was
elected to represent a constituency, and it
was important that each member have
equal opportunity to influence her.

Summers then considered another
option: to create a second managerial level
(Figure 8). In this arrangement, two board
members would be responsible for specific
areas of the board's work, and information
would flow back and forth through them.
This pattern seemed sensible, since Creecy
was particularly interested in issues of instruction, while Williams was an accoun-
tant with considerable experience in
business and finance. Each of them could
take one of the new members under his or
her wing and serve as a communications
link between them and Summers. The addition of the new layers might reduce the
load on the board chairman (though that
was not a sure thing), possibly freeing him

to put more energy into issues of mission and community relations. But the new board members would have less direct access to the chairman, and he to them. This could be very troublesome, since Summers was not sure how much the new members trusted their more senior colleagues. She knew that in such an arrangement, the morale of "middle managers" is often higher than that of lower-level participants. The addition of the new levels might make communication more difficult and increase the time it takes to get things done. The board's performance would become more dependent on the skills and abilities of Creecy and Williams. Summers did not want to alienate the new members and worried about overburdening already busy board members.

Still another possibility was to put Williams between Larson and the other members—creating, in effect, a simple hierarchy (Figure 9). This relationship would let Larson focus on managing relations with the community, which he did well, while Williams could focus on managing the board's internal dynamics. Since Williams was a manager in a respected accounting firm, he had ample experience in managing groups. This design tended to be more efficient than the previous one, but it also created its own problems. Fewer people would have direct access to the chairman, and it would also give Williams considerable power, possibly even tempting him to try to usurp Larson's position. Williams had expressed interest in chairing the board, so Summers recognized po-

**Figure 9.
Simple
Hierarchy.**

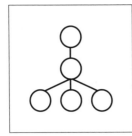

Figure 10.
Circle.

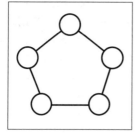

tential political pitfalls in this arrangement.

Summers turned to a fourth possibility—a circle network in which information would flow sequentially from one member to another (Figure 10). Information would pass around the circle from one person to another. Each person would add to or modify whatever passed through the channels. This design had some attractive features—it was egalitarian, and it simplified communications so that each member only had to worry about communicating with two others. Summers could get information to Larson, and he could get it to the rest of the board with one phone call; the message would then be passed around the circle. But there were risks. One weak link could ruin the whole process. Summers doubted that this option was feasible given the time constraints and differing skills and personalities of the board members.

A final possibility was to create a highly interactive all-channel or "star" network that would allow each member to talk to everyone else (Figure 11). Information would flow freely, and decisions would require touching base with everyone. Summers knew that an all-channel network tended to produce high morale. But it can also be a slow and inefficient method of communication. If everyone could talk to everyone else, the members might spend inordinate amounts of time in meetings and on the phone, and yet there would still be times when someone got left out of the loop. Even so, this

Figure 11.
All Channel.

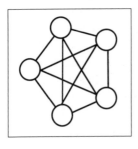

might be an effective structure for the board, since it
works best for tasks that are ambiguous and complicated or are heavily dependent on everyone's full understanding. That seemed to fit a lot of the work of the
board. At the same time, the all-channel arrangement
works best when the group members have well-honed
communications skills, enjoy participation, can tolerate
considerable ambiguity, and are not plagued by too
many conflicts. On those criteria, the all-channel arrangement seemed like a dubious fit.

As Summers considered all the possibilities, she
realized that none was especially well suited to the
board's specific set of circumstances. She finally decided
to recommend a modified version of the last model: The
board would use an all-channel network, but she herself
would be in the middle of the network as a sixth player.
She recognized the risks in this arrangement but felt
that it would best fit the complex and turbulent times
that the district was entering.

### Teamwork and Interdependence

The importance of teamwork is an article of faith across organizations, and "team building" has become a major activity in organizations around the world. But just what is a team? Do all successful
team structures look alike? What criteria are important in deciding
how to structure a team?

The fact is that all team structures are not alike (Keidel,
1984). Teams, like organizations, need to be structured to accomplish the task at hand. The structures of a baseball team, football
team, and basketball team are remarkably different. Unique patterns of differentiation, interdependence, and coordination are required for each of them.

*Baseball.* As Pete Rose once noted, "Baseball is a team game, but
nine men who meet their individual goals make a nice team" (Keidel, 1984, p. 8). Baseball teams are loosely coupled systems. Individual efforts are mostly independent, seldom involving more than two

or three players. Particularly on defense, players are separated from one another by significant distances. Individual efforts are pooled, with little reciprocal interdependence, and the success of the team depends heavily on the skills of individual players.

Because of the differentiated, loosely linked nature of a base-ball team, very little coordination is required among the various positions. Of course, the pitcher and catcher must each know what the other is going to do. And, at times, infielders must have an idea of how others will act, particularly in the case of a double play or "squeeze" situation. But most managerial decisions are tactical and normally involve individual substitutions or actions. Managers themselves can come and go without seriously disrupting the team's playing ability. Players can be transferred from one team to another with relative ease, and newcomers can carry out their responsibil-ities without making significant adjustments.

John Updike summed it up very well: "Of all the team sports, baseball, with its graceful intermittence of action, its im-mense and tranquil field sparsely salted with poised men in white, its dispassionate mathematics, seemed to be best suited to accommo-date, and be ornamented by a loner. It is an essentially lonely game" (Keidel, 1984, pp. 14-15).

*Football.* Football (that is, American football) is a different story. Compared to a baseball team, players perform in close proximity to one another. Lineman and offensive backs can hear, and often touch, one another. Each play involves every player on the field. Their efforts are sequentially linked in the sense that the actions of the linemen pave the way for the movements of the backs, the out-come of the defensive team becomes the starting point for the of-fense, and so forth. In between these transitions, specialty platoons play a pivotal role (Keidel, 1984). Unlike baseball, the efforts of individual players are tightly coupled. George Allen, coach of the Washington Redskins, put it this way: "A football game is a lot like a machine. It's made up of parts. If one part doesn't work, one player pulling against you and not doing his job, the whole ma-chine fails" (Keidel, 1984, p. 9).

Because of the tight linkages among individual efforts, a football team must be well coordinated. Coordination is achieved mainly through planning and hierarchical control. The primary unit of coordination is the individual group. Offensive, defensive, and specialty platoons often have their own coordinator within the coaching staff. Under the direction of the head coach, the team uses scouting reports and other surveillance to develop a strategy or game plan in advance. During the game, strategic decisions are typically made by the head coach. Tactical decisions are made by assistants or by the designated player on either offense or defense (Keidel, 1984).

Because of a football team's systemic characteristics, players are not easily swapped from one team to another. Irv Cross of the Philadelphia Eagles once remarked, "An Eagles player could never make an easy transition to the Dallas Cowboys; the system and philosophies are just too different" (Keidel, 1984, p. 15). Coaches also are not easily replaced. Tom Landry, Vince Lombardi, and Don Shula led the Cowboys, Packers, and Dolphins for many years. Their success came, in part, from their ability to create a well-coordinated team from the available talent. Unlike baseball, sound strategy and collective execution are necessary ingredients in winning at football (Keidel, 1984).

*Basketball.* Basketball players perform in even closer proximity than do football players. With only a quick, rapidly moving transition (if any at all) offense becomes defense—with the same players. The efforts of basketball players are highly reciprocal; each player depends on the efforts of all the others. Each player may be involved with any of the other four. Anyone can handle the ball or attempt to score.

Basketball teams require a high level of mutual adjustment on the part of every player. Everyone is on the move, often in a direction that is spontaneous rather than predetermined. The key to a successful basketball season is a flowing relationship among team members who can "read" and anticipate one another's moves. Players who play together for a long time develop a better sense of what each will do in given circumstances. A team of newcomers experiences difficulty in trying to adjust to individual predispositions or quirks. Keidel (1984) notes that coaches are integrators whose periodic interventions reinforce team cohesion. They help the players coordinate themselves. Unlike a baseball team, a basketball team cannot function with individual stars. Unlike football, there are no platoons. Basketball is wholly a team effort. After a talented group of Philadelphia 76ers lost to a more cohesive Portland Trail Blazers team, Bill Bradley commented, "Maybe someday a team will have so much individual fire power that on that alone it can win a championship. It hasn't happened yet" (Keidel, 1984, p. 12).

Teamwork is not a universal concept that provides a unified set of principles applicable to all situations. The right team structure depends on what the team is trying to do. All games are not the same, nor are the tasks and environments of teams in different settings the same. Keidel (1984) suggests several questions that are important in determining an appropriate structural design: (1) What are the nature and degree of task-related interaction among unit members? (2) What is the geographical distribution of unit members? (3) Given a group's objectives and constraints, where does autonomy reside? (4) How is coordination achieved? (5) What words best describe the required structure—conglomerate, mechanistic, or organic? (6) What sports expression metaphorically captures the task of management—filling out the lineup card, preparing the game plan, or influencing the game's flow?

Even within the same organization, team structure may shift according to changes in the task. A senior research manager in a pharmaceutical firm, for example, noted this progression in the discovery and development of a new drug: "The process moves through three distinct stages. It's like going from baseball to football to basketball" (Keidel, 1984, p. 11). In the basic research stages, individual scientists work independently to develop a pool of knowledge. As in baseball, individual efforts are the norm. Once a promising drug has been identified, however, the process moves from developmental chemists, to pharmacy researchers to toxicologists. If the drug receives preliminary approval from the federal government, it moves to the clinical researcher for experimental tests. The sequential relationships here are reminiscent of play sequences in football. In the final stage of "new drug application," physicians, statisticians, pharmacists, pharmacologists, toxicologists, and chemists work closely and reciprocally to win approval for the drug from the federal Food and Drug Administration. Their efforts resemble the closely linked and flowing patterns of a basketball team (Keidel, 1984).

## Choosing a Structure

In any work group or team, a structure of roles and relationships will evolve over time. Often, the patterns that emerge informally make it possible for a group to accomplish a task efficiently and effectively. Just as often, however, the structure that evolves makes it difficult for individuals to do their best or for the group to perform at a high level. Many communication, morale, or political problems can be traced to poorly designed roles, relationships, or coordination strategies. It usually makes sense for a group to discuss and select a structure that will work best for a given set of circumstances. In making such decisions, the group needs to consider several issues:

*What Is the Nature of the Task?* Tasks vary in complexity. Designing a cost-accounting procedure is more straightforward than developing an overall corporate mission. Deciding how to distribute supplies to an operating room is easier than doing sophisticated surgery. Some tasks are fairly routine; others are complicated, unpredictable, and highly ambiguous.

One of a group's first jobs is to figure out what it is going to do. Getting agreement on the nature of the task is an important step that groups often ignore. As a consequence, everyone has his or her own opinion about the means required to achieve a given end. Agreeing on the task is different from simply setting goals for the group. Goals are an important component of tasks. But the nature of the linkage between the desired ends and the means to achieve them is equally critical.

A group needs to ask itself a number of questions: What are we being asked to do? What are the desired goals? How clear are the goals and how easy will it be to determine when we have accomplished them? Can the task be broken down into subtasks? Do some steps have to be completed before others? How predictable are the issues that we will consider? Are some of the subtasks more routine than others? How do we allocate specific subtasks? How dependent are specific subtasks on other subtasks? What criteria or standards will govern a subtask? What are the minimal levels of work that will be acceptable? What is the optimum level of accomplishment? If a group takes the time to construct a flowchart outlining the various steps that need to be taken to get the job done, the critical structural issues will then become fairly obvious.

*What Is the Nature of Our Environment?* Groups or teams never operate in isolation. For some groups, the relevant environment is the rest of the organization. Other groups have a more direct relationship with constituencies outside the organization. Developing a map of the environment and understanding the key external relationships are as important as determining the task at hand. Who are the key players or what are the key events outside the group? Who or what in the external environment is critical to getting the task accomplished? What resources will we need? How certain can we be that the resources will be there when we need them? What do external players or groups expect from us? How stable are external circumstances? Are there some foreseeable changes in the near future? in the distant future?

Mapping the environment also carries structural implications. Relationships between a group and its environment are as important as the relationships inside the group.

*How Can We Clarify Roles and Relationships and Coordinate Our Efforts?* Once the task and environment have been defined, the formal structure can be shaped and molded. An organization chart can identify roles and authority relationships. But in most groups or teams a more detailed understanding of who is going to do what and their relationships with others is needed. Before beginning work, a group can negotiate a set of responsibilities and working relationships. Task, environment, time, skills, and individual needs are all important factors in designing a structure that will work.

In negotiating roles and relationships, a group needs a framework and a language to pinpoint the key issues. One possibility is to use responsibility charting (Galbraith, 1977). Responsibility charting assigns responsibility (an R) to a given individual or group and then outlines how that role or unit will relate to other roles or units. Does some person or group need to approve their actions (an A)? Are there individuals or groups that the person needs to consult (a C)? Are there people that the responsible person needs to keep informed (an I)?

RACI becomes a language for designing the formal structure of roles and relationships. Consider a family we will call the Smith family. For years, family members had engaged in acrimonious battles on a daily basis. Very little ever got done, and when it did, one person (the mother) usually did it. Husband and wife were about to file for divorce. Before taking this final step, however, they sought the assistance of a marriage counselor. She recommended family therapy. After several sessions, it became clear that, individually, each member of the Smith family was in good psychological health. But it was also obvious that the structure of the family had collapsed. Everyone had a different understanding of what was to be done and who was supposed to do it. When the individuals first charted family roles, it was as if each of them came from a different family. Everyone had a different perception of who needed to approve an action, be informed of it, or be consulted about it. Under the family therapist's supervision, the family negotiated a structure for itself, as shown in Table 1.

Responsibility was now clearly assigned. Everyone knew who needed to approve specific actions, to be informed of them, or to be consulted about them. Outsiders might question some of their

**Table 1. The Structure of the Smith Family.**

| | Roles | | | | |
|---|---|---|---|---|---|
| *Tasks* | *Father* | *Mother* | *Brother* | *Sister* | *Family* |
| Making money | R | C | I | I | |
| Spending money | A | R | I | I | C |
| Cooking food | A | R | A | A | |
| Cleaning house | I | R | I | R | |
| Family vacations | A | A | A | A | R |
| Caring for pets | | C | R | | |
| Relations with relatives | C | R | C | C | I |
| Mowing the lawn | C | A | R | | |

decisions. Mother appears to carry a very large share of the load, and the family's structure seems influenced by gender stereotypes. But, from the family's point of view, the more significant question is whether the process will work for it.

The following guidelines are important in developing a group structure:

- Determining responsibility is critical. The R specifies who is responsible for making a particular decision or conducting a particular activity. Shared responsibility is sometimes necessary but it also carries the risk of ambiguity and diffusion of responsibility. (The family chose to make only one item—family vacations—a shared responsibility. Vacation planning will be time consuming, but the time may be well spent, given the importance of having everyone support the decision.)
- Approval (A) gives someone authority over someone else's action. The more people whose approval is needed, the more time is required to make decisions. (The arrangement whereby mother is responsible for cooking, but everyone else needs to approve what she does, may turn out to be a cumbersome decision-making process.)
- Assigning a C is important when responsibilities are pooled or sequentially interdependent, or when one party has information that another party needs. But consultation also takes time and requires reasonable interpersonal skills.
- Assigning an I is important when responsibilities are reciprocally interdependent. The family decided, for example, that father and brother needed to be kept informed about housecleaning. Otherwise, they might get in the way of the cleaning process, or it might get in their way.

***What Are Acceptable Standards for Completing the Task and How Will Group and Individual Rewards Be Allocated?*** Before a group begins its work it should settle on some quality standards and determine in advance how rewards will be distributed. Quality standards are an important determinant of organizational slack, that is, the amount of "extra" resources that an organization has at its disposal. High standards may be motivating, but very high standards mean that organizational slack may be zero or even negative. Organizations with little slack have little tolerance for error or surprise, and they also have little or no latitude in structural design: the structure has to be right or the standards will never get met. For example, a group of students working on a class project might say to themselves, We want to produce a product of such unquestioned excellence that it is certain to get an *A* grade. We also want our group process to be completely responsive to the needs of every member. And, of course, we want to make all decisions by consensus. But, we don't want to spend a lot of time in meetings. Such a set of aspirations almost guarantees negative slack: all the aspirations cannot be met, and something will have to give.

### Summary

Every group will evolve some structural form as its members work to accomplish a task, but the design that emerges may or may not be effective. Many of the typical problems of small work groups arise from inappropriate structures. Consciously choosing a structure or revising emerging roles and patterns can make an enormous difference in a group's performance. Many groups fail to learn the lesson of the commando team: vary the structure in response to changes in task and circumstance. A group that meets to study a problem and develop a report for higher management will need to go through several phases, each of which suggests a different structural form. The structure of roles, linkages, and interdependence that will work best is likely to change significantly over the course of the group's life. Nonhierarchical forms may work extremely well in the early phases of goal setting and brainstorming, particularly if the group has enough time to work through the inevitable challenges of any task, while the later phases of report writing and editing may require a more centralized and differentiated structure.

When a group encounters the inevitable vicissitudes of group life—such things as overload, conflict, confusion, communication gaps, or bungled handoffs—the members often try to pin the blame on each other. Few groups are blessed with flawless members, but many groups will find that it is much easier and more profitable to restructure the group than to reconstruct each other's personalities.

# Part Three

# THE HUMAN RESOURCE FRAME

# 6

# *People and Organizations*

*Vancouver Sun*                                    January 29, 1981

### Whistle Stops Anger Office Staff

BOISE, Idaho (AP)—Seven times a day, someone blows a whistle at the Idaho health and welfare office. The secretaries have to stop and fill out a form saying what they're doing at the moment.

Administrators in the state department of health and welfare say it's a good way to check office efficiency, part of a drive to eliminate three secretarial positions in an economy move.

Secretaries call it insulting, degrading, and disruptive.

The procedure began on Monday. That was when Theo Murdock, chief of the state's welfare division, instructed aides to blow the whistle—literally—on the secretarial staff. He said the "random moment time study" would enable him to judge how the secretaries spend time on the job.

Complained Angie Stelling: "Yesterday morning, there wasn't a single whistle. They all blew in the afternoon, and everybody was afraid to take a break or go to the bathroom" [Cited in Frost, Mitchell, and Nord, 1986, p. 279].

The structural perspective focuses on the way that structure develops in response to an organization's tasks and environment.

**119**

The human resource frame adds an additional dimension—the interplay between organizations and people. It starts from the premise that people's skills, insights, ideas, energy, and commitment are an organization's most critical resource. Organizations, however, can be so alienating, dehumanizing, and frustrating that human talents are wasted and human lives are distorted. Employees may respond by devoting much of their time and effort to beating the system. When a manager starts blowing whistles to find out what the employees are doing, the employees start looking for ways to defend themselves and even to get revenge. But it does not *have* to be that way. At their best, organizations can be energizing, exciting, productive, and rewarding for the individual, as well as for the system.

Literature and film often focus on the alienating and brutalizing aspects of systems. In Franz Kafka's *The Trial*, the protagonist faces a mysterious, impersonal, unpredictable, and hostile organization that destroys individuals at its own time and for its own mysterious reasons. Frederick Wiseman's documentary film *High School* shows a world in which insensitive adults tyrannize students. In such Hollywood films as *Norma Rae, Nine to Five, Silkwood,* and *Wall Street*, organizations are presented, at best, as ineffectual, and, at worst, as oppressive and inhuman, places dominated by insensitive and selfish bosses who care only about accumulating money and power. A similar view is succinctly summarized in the popular song, "Take This Job and Shove It!" How accurate are these popular views of organizations? Is the reality of organizations as bleak as it is often depicted to be? Are human beings inevitably the pawns of organizations, sacrificed to the organization's purposes and thrown out when they are no longer needed? Can individuals only hope to protect themselves or to exploit the system before it exploits them?

These questions are particularly important in light of the enormous size and power of modern institutions. Government spending represents an increasing percentage of the total wealth of virtually every developed nation, and much of that spending goes to support large public bureaucracies. The twentieth century has witnessed an extraordinary growth of large private corporations, including giant multinational companies. General Motors, the world's largest corporation, generates revenues each year that exceed the gross national product of most of the world's nations. In a world whose political and economic decisions are increasingly dominated by such gigantic institutions, how can individuals find freedom and dignity? How can they avoid the fate of Kafka's K, of Wiseman's students?

The answers to such questions are not easy. They require an understanding of people and organizations, as well as of the complex relation between the two. The human resource frame draws on a body of research and theory built around the following assumptions:

1.  Organizations exist to serve human needs (rather than the reverse).
2.  Organizations and people need each other. (Organizations need ideas, energy, and talent; people need careers, salaries, and work opportunities.)
3.  When the fit between the individual and the organization is poor, one or both will suffer: individuals will be exploited, or will seek to exploit the organizations, or both.
4.  A good fit between individual and organization benefits both: human beings find meaningful and satisfying work, and organizations get the human talent and energy that they need.

Exploring the fit between people and organizations must, however, begin with a discussion of the concept of *need*—what, in fact, do people need from their experiences with organizations?

### Human Needs

The concept of need is controversial. Some scholars reject the whole idea. They argue that the concept of need is too vague, that it refers to something that is difficult to observe, and that human behavior is so heavily influenced by environmental factors that the need concept is really of no help in explaining how people behave (Salancik and Pfeffer, 1977).

From a human resource perspective, the concept of need is important, even though needs are hard to define and difficult to measure. Moreover, the idea that people have needs is a central element in commonsense psychology. Parents talk about the needs of their children, politicians try to respond to the needs of their constituents, and managers try to meet the needs of their workers.

Common sense makes sense in this case, but in everyday language the term *need* is used in a variety of different ways, many of them imprecise and ambiguous. An analogy may help. Gardeners know that every plant has "needs." Certain combinations of temperature, moisture, soil conditions, and sunlight will allow a plant to grow and flourish. Within the limits of its biological capabilities, a plant will do its best to satisfy its basic needs. It will orient its leaves to the sun to get more light. It will sink deeper roots to get more water. A plant's capabilities generally increase as it matures. Highly vulnerable seedlings become more self-sufficient as they reach maturity (for example, they become better able to fend off insect damage and crowding from other plants). Those capabilities decline as the plant nears the end of its life cycle.

Human needs can also be defined as conditions or elements in the environment that allow people to survive and develop. Without oxygen, water, and food, human beings cannot survive. A more complicated question is whether there are also basic psychic needs. There are two sides to this issue. One position is that certain psychological needs are in fact basic to being human. Such needs are presumably present in everyone. The opposing viewpoint is that humans are so molded by environment, socialization, and culture that it is fruitless to talk about generic human needs.

This is one form of the nature-nurture controversy, which has long been a hotly debated issue in the social sciences. The "nature" team argues that human behavior is mostly determined by biological and genetic factors, while the "nurture" team takes the opposite view: human behavior is largely determined by learning and experience.

The debate is often heated because the stakes are high. Is mental illness caused by one's genetic inheritance or by growing up in a disturbed environment? The answer is critical to deciding whether drugs or psychotherapy is a more appropriate form of treatment. Are behavioral differences between men and women determined by biology or culture? (Do women have greater maternal "needs"? Do men have greater needs to engage in combat and competition?) The answers are important in understanding the possibilities for redefining male and female roles.

In their extreme forms, the nature and nurture arguments both mislead. A degree in psychology is not required to know that people are capable of enormous amounts of learning and adaptation or that what people learn is influenced by the situations in which they find themselves. Nor is advanced training in biology needed to recognize that many of the differences among people are present at birth. Since genes determine so many physical characteristics, it is surprising that so many environmentalists are wedded to the argument that differences in behavior are *always* caused by environmental factors.

At present, a consensus is emerging in the social sciences that human behavior results from the interaction between heredity and environment. Genes may determine the initial trajectory, but subsequent learning has a profound effect in modifying or even reversing the original instructions. Nature-nurture interaction suggests another way of thinking about human needs. A need can be defined as a genetic predisposition to prefer some experiences over others. Needs energize and guide behavior, and they vary in strength at different times. We usually prefer temperatures that are neither too hot nor too cold. We do not like being alone all the time, but we are also not happy if we are constantly surrounded by people. Since the genetic instructions cannot anticipate all the specific situations that an individual will encounter, the form and expression of each person's needs will be significantly modified by what happens after birth.

Needs perform other central functions—they influence how we feel and they guide learning. We are likely to have positive emotions—happiness, contentment, joy, and love—in situations that are need fulfilling (Tomkins, 1962). We experience negative emotions—anger, fear, depression, and boredom—in situations where important needs are frustrated. We are also more likely to learn about things that are relevant to our needs. If you are motivated to become a successful manager and believe that organization theory can help you achieve that goal, then you are likely to learn a lot about it. If you have little desire to be a manager, or believe that social science is mostly common sense disguised in polysyllabic words, you are not likely to learn very much.

In sum, people try to satisfy their needs, become unhappy when their needs are frustrated, and are more likely to learn things that are relevant to their needs than things that are irrelevant. Individuals flourish and develop in environments where they can satisfy important needs but become psychologically undernourished in situations where major needs are consistently thwarted.

### What Needs Do People Have?

If all human beings have needs, what needs do they have in common? One of the most influential theories about human needs was developed by Abraham Maslow (1954). Maslow started from the notion that human beings have a variety of needs, some more fundamental than others. He noted, for example, that the desire for food dominates the lives of the chronically hungry but that other forms of satisfaction are more significant for those who have enough to eat.

Maslow grouped human needs into five basic categories, arranged in a hierarchy from "lower" to "higher." Lower needs dominate behavior when they are not satisfied. Higher needs become salient only *after* the lower needs have been satisfied. Maslow's categories were:

1.  Physiological needs (such as needs for oxygen, water, food, physical health, and comfort)
2.  Safety needs (to be safe from danger, attack, threat)
3.  Belongingness and love needs (needs for positive and loving relationships with other people)
4.  Needs for esteem (needs to feel valued and to value oneself)
5.  Needs for self-actualization (needs to develop to one's fullest, to actualize one's potential)

In Maslow's view, lower needs are "prepotent" and have to be satisfied first, although they do not have to be completely satisfied. Once lower needs are satisfied, an individual begins to focus more on higher needs. Maslow acknowledged exceptions. Parents who sacrifice themselves for their children and martyrs who give their lives for a cause are emphasizing higher needs over lower ones. Maslow believed that such exceptions occurred only when lower needs were very well satisfied early in life, so that they fell into the background. Needs for belongingness, esteem, and self-actualization then became dominant.

Maslow's ideas have had an enormous impact on the thinking of both managers and behavioral scientists. While they are intuitively plausible, that does not mean they are right. A number of researchers have tried to assess the validity of Maslow's theory without complete success. The biggest problem is that needs are hard to measure. Testing Maslow's theory requires assessing both the strength and the level of satisfaction of each need. Should you ask people questions such as, "How strong is your need for self-actualization, and to what degree you are filling that need?" It is not clear how much people know about their own needs. And even if they know what their needs are, will they give truthful answers? What if people think the researcher will have a better opinion of them if they say they are concerned about self-actualization rather than such mundane matters as salary and benefits?

Several systematic attempts to assess the validity of Maslow's theory have failed to show conclusively that Maslow was right *or* wrong (Alderfer, 1972; Schneider and Alderfer, 1973). Still, his is one of the most influential views of motivation in organizations. It has become a widely accepted conception, and its validity is often assumed, despite the lack of convincing empirical evidence.

### Theory X and Theory Y

Douglas McGregor (1960) took Maslow's theory of motivation and added another central idea, namely, that the perspective from which a manager views other people determines how they respond. McGregor suggested that most managers subscribed to Theory X. The central proposition of this theory is that managers need to direct and control the work of subordinates. According to Theory X, subordinates are passive and lazy, have little ambition, prefer to be led, and resist change.

McGregor believed that virtually all conventional management practices were built on Theory X assumptions, which limited managers to possibilities ranging from "hard" Theory X to "soft" Theory X. Hard Theory X emphasizes coercion, tight controls, threats, and punishments; in McGregor's view, it results in low productivity, antagonism, militant unions, and subtle sabotage. In contrast, soft Theory X is a permissive style that tries to avoid conflict and satisfy everyone's needs. It may produce superficial harmony but leads to apathy and indifference and causes people to expect more and more while giving less and less. Either way—hard or soft—Theory X creates self-fulfilling prophesies. Both approaches generate signs that the theory is correct and that even more Theory X management is needed to cope with workers who "just don't seem to give a damn any more" and "are never satisfied."

McGregor argued that new knowledge from the behavioral sciences challenged these conventional views. The evidence was inconclusive, he acknowledged, but it suggested a different view, which he called Theory Y. Maslow's need hierarchy was the foundation: "We recognize readily enough that a man suffering from a severe dietary deficiency is sick. The deprivation of physiological needs has behavioral consequences. The same is true—although less well recognized—of deprivation of higher-level needs. The man whose needs for safety, association, independence, or status are thwarted is sick just as surely as the man who has rickets. And his sickness will have behavioral consequences. We will be mistaken if we attribute his resultant passivity, his hostility, his refusal to accept responsibility to his inherent 'human nature.' These forms of behavior are symptoms of illness—of deprivation of his social and egoistic needs" (McGregor, 1960, pp. 35-36).

McGregor argued that managers needed a new theory about people. Theory Y, like Theory X, accepted the proposition that "management is responsible for organizing the elements of enterprise . . . in the interest of economic ends" (p. 38). McGregor did not challenge capitalism or the role of private industry; he challenged managers to behave differently. Theory Y argues that people are not passive or indifferent by nature, but that they sometimes become so as a result of their experience in organizations.

The key proposition of Theory Y is that "the essential task of management is to arrange organizational conditions so that people can achieve their own goals best by directing their efforts toward organizational rewards" (p. 61). In other words, the job of management is to arrange things so that the organization's interests and the employee's self-interest coincide as closely as possible. Theory X relies too much on external control of people, while Theory Y relies on self-control and self-direction. Theory X treats people like children, whereas Theory Y treats them like adults.

### Personality and Organization

Chris Argyris (1957, 1964) provided another classic statement of the human resource frame. Argyris saw a basic conflict between the human personality and the ways that organizations were structured and managed. Though Argyris did not base his view directly on Maslow, his ideas were similar. He argued that individuals have basic "self-actualization trends" and that they develop in specific directions as they mature from infancy into adulthood. They move from high levels of dependence on others to high levels of independence. They move from a narrow to a much broader range of skills and interests. They move from a short time perspective (in which interests are quickly developed and quickly forgotten, and there is little ability to anticipate the future) to a much longer time perspective. People develop from low levels of self-awareness and self-control to higher levels of both. Argyris proposed that all individuals are predisposed to move from the infant toward the adult ends of all these criteria, "barring unhealthy personality development" (1957, p. 51). That is very much like Maslow's idea that people move up the needs hierarchy unless their lower-level needs are frustrated.

Like McGregor, Argyris saw a conflict between individuals and organizations because organizations often treat people like children. This view was anticipated in Charlie Chaplin's film *Modern Times*. Early in the film, Chaplin's character works furiously in an assembly-line job trying to tighten each bolt on each piece that goes past him. The time perspective of the job can be measured in a few seconds. The range of skills is minimal, and the worker has virtually no control over the pace of his work. A researcher uses Chaplin as the guinea pig for a new machine to increase efficiency. The machine is designed to feed Chaplin his lunch while he continues to tighten bolts, but it goes haywire and begins to assault Chaplin with the food. The message is clear—the logic of industrial organization is to treat adults as much like infants as is technologically possible.

Argyris argued that such problems were built into the traditional principles of organizational design and management. The principle of task specialization carried to its logical extreme leads to defining jobs as narrowly as possible. "You put the right-front tire on the car, Joe will tighten the bolts, and Bill will check to see if it was done right." Task specialization requires a chain of command to coordinate the work of all the people who are doing narrowly specialized jobs. The chain of command requires that people at higher levels be able to direct and control people at lower levels, creating a situation of passivity and dependence. Argyris believed that under such conditions, people experience "psychological failure." They are unable to define their own goals or the way in which they might achieve their goals. Organizations create a situation that is fundamentally in conflict with the needs of healthy human beings. The conflict gets worse as one moves down the hierarchy, as jobs become more mechanized, as leadership becomes more directive, as formal structure becomes tighter, and as people attain increasing maturity.

Argyris added that employees can be expected to find ways to resist or to adapt to the frustration that organizations create. He suggested several options:

1.  They might withdraw from the organization—through chronic absenteeism or simply by quitting.
2.  They might stay on the job but withdraw psychologically, becoming indifferent, passive, and apathetic.
3.  They might resist the organization by restricting output, deception, featherbedding, or sabotage.
4.  They might try to climb the hierarchy to better jobs. (But the pyramidal structure of most organizations means that there are far more jobs at the bottom than at the top.)
5.  They might create groups and organizations (such as labor unions) that try to redress the power imbalance between person and system. (Argyris cautions, however, that the new organiza-

tions are likely to be designed and managed like the old ones. In the long run, the employees may feel equally powerless with company and union.)

6.   They may socialize their children to believe that work is unrewarding and that hopes for advancement are slim. (Researchers in the 1960s began to find that the children of farmers were more likely to believe in the merits of hard work than the children of urban, blue-collar workers. One reason that many U.S. companies moved manufacturing facilities south in the 1960s, and off shore in the 1970s, was to find still-uncontaminated rural workers. Argyris's theory predicted, however, that industry would eventually demotivate whatever work force it found unless management practice changed.)

Argyris and McGregor both argued that management practices were inconsistent with employee needs and that this conflict produced resistance and withdrawal. Both believed that managers misinterpreted employee behavior to mean that something was wrong with the employees rather than with the organization. Withdrawal and resistance confirmed Theory X assumptions that employees are lazy, uninterested, incompetent, or greedy. If managers assumed that the problem was "in" the employees, then the solution was to change them.

Argyris described three strategies that managers typically used, all of which made the problem worse instead of better. One approach was "strong, dynamic leadership," an approach based on the assumption that employees are a relatively passive flock of sheep. Argyris saw the strategy as self-defeating—it put more and more responsibility on managers, and less and less on workers. A second solution was to install tighter controls—quality control inspectors, time-and-motion studies, and so forth. But tighter controls deepen and reinforce the conflict between individual and organization and lead to escalating competitive games between managers and employees.

The first two solutions correspond to the tough version of Theory X. The third was softer: human relations programs. These programs often took the form of selling management's philosophy (through company newspapers and films, for example), pseudo-participation ("make the employees *feel* that their ideas are valued"), and communications programs that rarely communicated what employees really wanted to know. Trying to make employees feel better without solving the underlying problems just made matters worse.

What could be done? Argyris found potential in job enlargement (making jobs more varied and challenging) and participative management, but also saw limits to both. Many employees were already socialized to be passive and dependent at work. They might resent and resist efforts to make their work more challenging and responsible. Ultimately, Argyris said, "reality-centered leadership" was needed—leadership that took account of the actual needs of the employees, as well as the needs of the organization. In addition, Argyris and McGregor both believed that much more needed to be learned about the design and management of organizations in order to reduce the conflict between the system and the individual.

In the three decades since Argyris and McGregor developed their classic statements of the human resource frame, legions of writers, consultants, and managers have pursued the questions that they raised. Their efforts have led in two primary directions, one focuses on individuals and the other on organizations. We discuss those directions in the next two chapters.

## Summary

Organizations and people depend on one another. People look to organizations to satisfy a variety of economic, personal, and social needs, and organizations in turn cannot function effectively without the energy and talent of their employees. Human resource theorists argue that the central task of managers is to build organizations and management systems that produce harmony between the needs of the individual and the needs of the organization. When they succeed, both the organization and its employees will benefit. When they fail, one or both sides will suffer. The individuals will feel alienated, apathetic, or exploited. The organization may find that its employees arrive late and leave early, on the days when they even get to work, and put in little effort while they are there.

Human resource theorists argue that managers need to understand and respond to the needs that human beings bring with them to work. Maslow's influential hierarchy of motivation suggests that, as people satisfy lower-level needs for food and physical safety, they move to higher-level needs for self-esteem and self-actualization. Human resource theorists such as Argyris and McGregor note that traditional managers often treat employees like children, satisfying only their lower-level needs. Such techniques as participative management can satisfy higher-level needs and tap higher levels of employee motivation and capacity.

# 7

# *Interpersonal and Group Dynamics*

Anne Barreta was both excited and apprehensive when she became the first woman and the first Hispanic-American ever promoted to district marketing manager at the Hillcrest Corporation. She felt confident that she had the experience and skills to be successful in the job, but she knew that she would be watched carefully. Her boss, the regional marketing manager, was very supportive, but not everyone at Hillcrest was as enthusiastic. She remembered one male colleague who smiled as he patted her on the shoulder and said, "Congratulations! I just wish I was an affirmative action candidate."

Anne was responsible for one of two districts in the same eastern city. Her counterpart in the other district, Harry, was twenty-five years older and had been with Hillcrest twenty years longer than Anne. Some people said that the term "good old boy" was probably invented to describe Harry. Genial much of the time, Harry had a temper that flared quickly when others got in his way. Anne made repeated efforts to maintain a positive and professional relationship with Harry, but she felt his response was at best cool, at worst condescending and arrogant.

Things came to a head at a meeting of Anne, Harry, and their immediate subordinates. As they discussed marketing plans for the next quarter, Anne and Harry were disagreeing politely. Then Mark, one of Anne's subordinates, directly criticized Harry's ideas. Harry was particularly incensed by Mark's closing line: "If you'd think things through a little before you open your mouth, we'd make a lot more progress." With barely controlled fury, Harry declared that "this meeting is adjourned" and stormed out.

A day later, Harry phoned to demand that Anne fire Mark. Anne tried to reason with him, but Harry was adamant. Worried about the fallout, Anne talked to Steve, their joint boss, about the incident. Steve agreed with Anne that firing was too drastic a step, though he suggested that she reprimand Mark for his lack of tact. Anne agreed and let Harry know of her decision. He again became angry and practically shouted at her, "If you want to get along in this company, you'd better fire that guy!" Anne calmly replied that Mark reported to her and that she would not fire him. Harry's final words were, "You'll regret this!"

Three months later, Steve called Anne to a private meeting away from the office. He told her he had just learned that the company had hired a private detective to investigate a rumor that the two of them were involved in a sexual relationship. The detective had, of course, found no evidence to support the rumor, and senior managers planned to drop the matter. But, said Steve, "Some of the damage is done, and you should realize that Harry must be behind this."

Although the human resource frame focuses on the relationship between the individual and the organization, people relate more to each other than to the organization. Managers spend most of their time with other people: in conversations and meetings, in groups and committees, over coffee or over lunch, in person or on the telephone (Kotter, 1982; Mintzberg, 1973).

Psychological theory and folk wisdom agree that social needs and interpersonal styles are substantially influenced by experiences in infancy and childhood. Those patterns do not change quickly or easily in response to organizational requirements. Thompson (1967) and others have argued that the socializing institutions of a bureaucratic society shape individuals to make them better suited to organizational life. Schools, for example, attempt to train students in bureaucratic skills such as being punctual, completing assignments, and following rules. But schools are not always successful, and the human inputs of organizations are shaped initially by a decentralized cottage industry known as the family. Families seldom produce raw materials exactly to organizational specifications.

To be human is to be an imperfect cog in the bureaucratic machinery. People conduct their interpersonal relationships in ways that fit their own styles and preferences, sometimes disregarding what the organization or anyone around them wants. They may work on organizational tasks, but they never work *only* on organizational tasks. They also work on whatever personal and social needs are important to them. Those needs often conflict with organizational rules and requirements. As Anne Barreta's case illustrates, gender and sexual dynamics are among the many human characteristics that managers and organization theorists often try to ignore but that will not go away (Burrell and Hearn, 1989).

Individual differences and interpersonal dynamics continually spawn organizational muddles. Critical projects falter because no one on the team likes the manager's style. Departments engage in protracted warfare because of friction between their respective heads. Committees get little done because of tensions that everyone is aware of but no one mentions. School principals spend an inordinate amount of time trying to deal with a handful of abrasive or ineffectual teachers who are responsible for most of the discipline problems and almost all the parental complaints.

### Interpersonal Dynamics

In organizations, as in the rest of life, many of the greatest joys and most intense sorrows, the highest peaks and deepest valleys, occur in relationships with others. The complexities of interpersonal behavior go well beyond the confines of a book about organizations, but there are at least three recurrent questions that haunt managers in their relationships at work:

- What is really happening in this relationship?
- Why do other people behave as they do?
- What can I do about it?

All were questions for Anne Barreta. What was happening between her and Harry? Did Harry really start such a vicious rumor? If so, why? How should she deal with someone as difficult and devious as Harry? Could she talk to him? What options did she have?

Some observers might assume the obvious: Harry resented a young, minority woman who had become his organizational peer. He became even more bitter when she rejected his demand that she fire Mark. Harry sought revenge by means of a sneak attack. The case resembles several provided by Collinson and Collinson (1989) to demonstrate their assertion that male sexuality dominates and victimizes women in organizations. The point is valid, but it is less clear what Anne Barreta, or women in similar circumstances, can do about it. Should she try to confront the larger organizational issues? Such confrontation might help to change organizational norms in the long run, but Collinson and Collinson (1989) show that women who initiate such confrontations are likely to pay significant personal costs and be branded as "troublemakers." Or should Anne start to assemble her own political weapons and try to get Harry before he gets her? If she follows that course, Anne might win or lose. Either way, she will escalate the interpersonal struggle. Revenge is tempting, but it often leads to wars that no one wins.

Human resource theorists offer a more hopeful view. They acknowledge the political dynamics in organizations but suggest that constructive responses are possible. Argyris (1962), for example, emphasizes the importance of "interpersonal competence" as a basic managerial skill. His research showed that managers' effectiveness was often impaired because they were overcontrolling, excessively competitive, uncomfortable with feelings, and closed to ideas other than their own.

Argyris and Schön (1974) carried the issue of interpersonal effectiveness a step further. They argued that individuals' behavior is controlled by personal "theories for action," that is, assumptions and ideas about the nature of effective action. A theory for action is a program, or cognitive map, that informs behavior and tells a person what to do. Argyris and Schön distinguished two versions of the theories that inform action. *Espoused theory* is what individuals use whenever they try to describe, explain, or predict their behavior. *Theories-in-use* predict what individuals will in fact do. A theory-in-use is an implicit program or set of rules that specify how we should behave in different situations.

Argyris and Schön found significant discrepancies between the theories that most managers espoused and the theories that they actually used. What managers say they do is often unconnected to their actions. They typically see themselves as rational, open, concerned for others, and democratic. Yet their behavior is often governed by such values as competition, control, and self-protection. Managers are often blind to these gaps between what they say and what they do.

How does such self-deception occur? The case of Anne and Harry offers some clues. From the moment of her promotion, Anne felt that she had entered a dangerous and competitive world where she was surrounded by enemies. The rumored affair with her subordinate simply proved that her fears were justified. Managers often feel as Anne did, and events regularly confirm their suspicions.

Argyris and Schön contend that most managers have a self-protective model of interpersonal behavior. Implicitly, managers adopt a political view: resources are scarce, and competition and conflict are the dominant features of organizational life. They employ a "mystery-mastery" model of effective interpersonal behavior. Mystery-mastery is a theory-in-use intended to let managers get what they want while protecting themselves from the hazards of organizational life (we are indebted to our colleague William R. Torbert, of Boston College, for the mystery-mastery label). The model includes a simple series of steps that can be applied to almost any interpersonal problem:

1. *Assume that the problem is caused by the other person(s).* Harry, for example, apparently believed that all his problems were caused by Mark and Anne: Mark was insulting and Anne protected him. For her part, Anne blamed Harry for being sexist, demanding, and devious.

2. *Develop a private, unilateral diagnosis and solution.* Harry developed his own diagnosis and solution—Anne should fire Mark. When she declined, he apparently developed another, more private strategy: undermine Anne without her knowledge.

3. *Since the other person is the cause of the problem, get him or her to change, using one or more of three basic strategies: facts, logic, and rational persuasion (argue the merits of your point of view or your solution); indirect influence (ease in, ask leading questions, manipulate the other person); direct critique (tell the other person directly what he or she is doing wrong and how he or she should change).* Harry started with logic, moved quickly to direct critique, and finally employed covert strategies.

4. *If the other person resists or becomes defensive, that confirms the original diagnosis (that the other person caused the problem).* When Anne refused to fire Mark, this apparently proved to Harry that she was both ineffective and a troublemaker.

5. *Respond to resistance through some combination of intensifying pressure, protecting the other person, and rejecting the other person.* When Anne resisted, Harry intensified the pressure. Anne tried to back off and reassure him but did not agree to fire Mark. Harry apparently concluded that she was impossible to deal with and that the best solution was to get rid of her.

6. *If your efforts are unsuccessful, or less successful than hoped, it is the other's fault. You need feel no personal responsibility.* Harry did not succeed in getting rid of Mark or Anne. He stained Anne's reputation but damaged his own as well. The outcome hurt everyone, but Harry probably never realized that he hurt himself as well as Anne. The incident probably confirmed to Harry's colleagues that he was too temperamental and defensive, that he let personal needs intrude on his work, and that he could not be fully trusted. Such perceptions would block Harry's promotion to a more senior position. But who would want to say all that to someone as defensive and cranky as Harry?

What else can be done about situations like Anne's? Argyris and Schön propose Model II as an alternative way of achieving interpersonal effectiveness. The model offers these guidelines:

*Emphasize common goals and mutual influence in relationships.* Even in a situation as difficult as the relationship between Anne and Harry, there are likely to be shared goals. Both want to be effective managers. Neither is likely to benefit from a fight to the finish. At times, each needs the help or collaboration of the other and might well learn and profit from the other. To emphasize common goals, Anne might ask Harry, What kind of relationship do we want to have? Do we want an ongoing battle? Wouldn't we both be better off if we worked together instead of undermining each other?

*Communicate openly and publicly test assumptions and beliefs.* Harry apparently decided to go behind Anne's back. She could be equally devious, but would more of the same help anyone? Model II suggests that she talk directly to Harry and test her assumptions. She *thought* that Harry deliberately started the rumor, but she was not *certain* that he had. She suspected that Harry would lie if she confronted him, but that was another untested assumption. Model II insists on being honest and testing assumptions, even in situations like this one. Anne might say, for example, "Harry, someone started a rumor about me and Steve. What do you know about that story and how it got started?"

Though such directness seems startling and dangerous to many managers, Model II says that Anne has little to lose and much to gain. Even if she does not get the truth from Harry, she lets him know that she is aware of his game and that she is not afraid to confront him.

*Combine advocacy with inquiry.* Advocacy includes statements that communicate what an individual thinks, knows, wants, or feels. Inquiry includes behavior whose purpose is to learn what others think, know, want, or feel. Figure 12 provides a simple model of the relationship between advocacy and inquiry.

Model II emphasizes actions that communicate a high degree of both advocacy and inquiry. It asks managers to express openly what they think and feel and to seek actively to understand the thoughts and feelings of others. Harry's demand that Anne fire Mark combined high advocacy with low inquiry. He told her what

Figure 12. Advocacy and Inquiry.

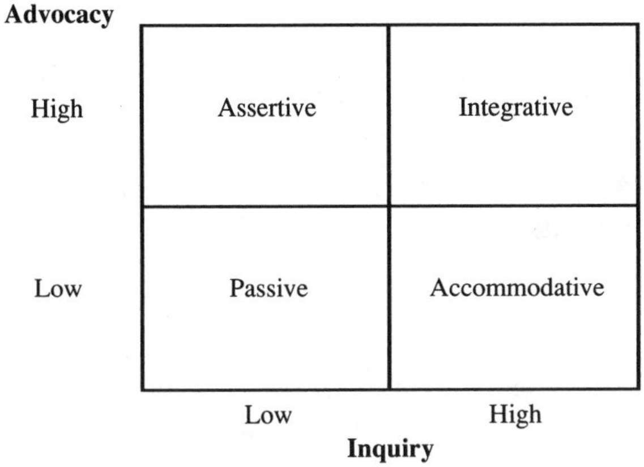

**Advocacy**

| | Low | High |
|---|---|---|
| **High** | Assertive | Integrative |
| **Low** | Passive | Accommodative |

Low                    High

**Inquiry**

he wanted while showing no interest in her point of view. Such behavior tends to be perceived as assertive at best, dominating or arrogant at worst. Anne's response was low in both advocacy and inquiry. In her discomfort, she mostly tried to get out of the meeting without making any concessions. Harry might have seen her as apathetic, unresponsive, or weak.

A Model II Anne would initiate a meeting with Harry to discuss the situation. She would combine advocacy and inquiry. She would tell Harry what she thinks and feels, while testing her assumptions and trying to learn from Harry. This is not an easy prescription. Model II is difficult to learn and practice. Such openness carries risks, and it is hard to be effective when you are ambivalent, uncomfortable, or frightened. It is much easier if you are reasonably confident that you can cope with others' responses. But Anne is likely to be comfortable confronting Harry only if she thinks her skills permit her to cope with interpersonal challenge. Such beliefs can be self-fulfilling prophesies. If you tell yourself that you do not deal well with people who are demanding, critical, angry, or manipulative, you will probably end up being right.

Because such situations are demanding and challenging, and because they doubt their interpersonal skills, managers often revert to self-protection or mystery-mastery. They avoid dealing with the issue, deal with it indirectly, or attack the other person. The result, according to Argyris and Schön (1978), is escalating games of camouflage and deception. Faced with conditions of ambiguity, uncertainty, and conflict, managers often feel inadequate and develop tactics to camouflage their inadequacy. To avoid detection, they pile camouflage on top of the camouflage. This, in turn, creates even more uncertainty and ambiguity and makes it difficult or impossible to detect errors. As a result, organizations can persist in a course of action for months or years, even though many managers know they are on a path to disaster. No one knows what to say or how to say it; no one wants to be the messenger who is slain for bringing bad news.

Even in the short term, such behavior can be catastrophic. Think back to the Cold Bay accident in Alaska (Chapter Two). The copilot, who was worried about the captain's approach to a mountainous airport, used gentle questions such as, "What kind of terrain are we flying over?" The copilot combined low advocacy and high inquiry, and his message never got through. He could have combined advocacy and inquiry in a statement such as "What approach are you following? I think we're off course and need to get higher immediately." We do not know why he was not more direct. Perhaps he feared upsetting the captain. Perhaps he was not sure whether he or the captain was mistaken. But a different response might have saved the airplane and its crew.

Many change efforts fail not because managers' intentions are incorrect or insincere but because they lack interpersonal skills and understandings. A good example is management by objectives (MBO). The MBO philosophy of performance improvement calls for a focus not on *how* a manager performs but on *what* the manager accomplishes. Typically, managers and subordinates meet to discuss the subordinate's major objectives. They reach an agreement that is acceptable to both. Later, they meet to evaluate their success in fulfilling the objectives. MBO theory calls for subordinates to develop realistic goals and to participate in their own performance assessment. Evaluation is supposed to be fairer because it is based on objective, observable results instead of on subjective assessments of personality traits.

At least, that is the theory. In a company with an extensive MBO program, we asked a group of middle managers how well it worked. The reply was immediate: "We don't have MBO. We have MBT."

"What is MBT?" we asked.

"Management by terror" was the reply. The managers said that, in practice, they were manipulated into agreeing to unrealistic goals and then punished for not achieving the goals that they had "set for themselves." Even though the intentions of the program were honorable, managers lacked the skills to realize the noble aspirations.

### Management Styles

Differences in individual character and style present another important managerial challenge. A long line of research has tried to determine what kinds of individual behaviors and styles will be most effective in task settings. In a classic experiment, Lewin, Lippitt, and White (1939) compared autocratic, democratic, and laissez-faire leadership in boys' clubs. They found that autocratic leadership produced dependence or frustration. Laissez-faire leadership led to aimlessness and confusion. Not only was democratic leadership strongly preferred by the boys, but it also produced a more positive group climate.

A number of subsequent researchers have examined leadership in work settings (much of that work is reviewed in Stogdill, 1974, and Bass, 1981). Fleishman and Harris (1962) conducted a series of studies focusing on two dimensions of leadership: consideration (how well a leader showed concern for and sensitivity to people) and initiating structure (to what degree a leader actively structured subordinates' activities). Their research, and many subsequent studies using their leadership variables, produced a complex pattern of findings. High consideration for employees is generally associated with lower turnover, fewer grievances, and less absenteeism. Overall, the most effective supervisors tended to be high on both consideration and structure. Similar results were produced by Likert (1961), who presented evidence that "employee-centered" managers were more effective in the long run than "task-centered" managers.

Countless theories, books, workshops, and tests have been

devoted to helping managers identify their own and others' personal or interpersonal styles. Are leaders introverts or extroverts? Are they friendly helpers, tough battlers, or objective thinkers? Do managers care more about control, inclusion, or affection? Do they behave more like parents or children? Are they superstars who are concerned for both people and production, "country club" managers concerned only about people, or hard-driving taskmasters who are insensitive to human needs and feelings (Blake and Mouton, 1969). In the 1980s, the forty-year-old Myers-Briggs Type Inventory (Myers, 1980) took thousands of Americans by storm. Built on principles from Jungian psychology, the inventory categorizes individuals into one of sixteen "types." Are you, for example, an ISTJ (serious, quiet, thorough, practical, and dependable), or an ENFP (warmly enthusiastic, high-spirited, ingenious, and imaginative), or perhaps an ENTJ (hearty, frank, decisive, and inclined to take leadership)?

Despite the risk of turning managers into undertrained amateur psychologists, it often helps to have concepts that make sense of the elusive, complex, and sensitive phenomena of individual behavior and style. Research has shown that managers are often blind to their own management style (Argyris, 1962; Argyris and Schön, 1974) and unable to learn about it without some help from their friends. Their friends may be more helpful if they have some way to talk about the issues.

### Groups in Organizations

Anne Barreta's case shows how demanding even a two-person relationship can be. But managers face a more complex challenge in that they spend much of their time in groups. Groups take many forms: standing committees, task forces, project teams, boards of trustees, faculty committees, advisory groups, and cliques, to name only a few. Whatever their labels, groups constantly challenge and frustrate their members. The oldest management joke defines a camel as a horse designed by a committee. We know a marketing professor who gleefully tells students that the only group that ever gets anything done is a "committee of one." Organizations are full of people who believe that nothing is worse than working in groups, because groups are invariably inefficient, confused, and frustrating.

But there is another side to the story. Even people who hate groups can often recall at least one group experience that was a high point in their lives. Research on task groups (Collins and Guetzkow, 1964) has shown that blanket condemnation of groups is unduly harsh. Groups have both assets and liabilities. Compared to individuals, groups have greater knowledge and diversity of perspective, as well as more time and energy. Groups are often a good way to improve communication and increase acceptance of decisions. Nevertheless, groups sometimes overrespond to social pressure or individual domination, and personal goals can smother collective purposes (Maier, 1967).

Depending on whether their assets or liabilities dominate, groups can be wonderful or terrible, productive or stagnant, imprisoning or freeing, conformist or creative. At best, they are places of loyalty, mutual commitment, excitement, and motivation. Many problems with groups result from interpersonal dynamics, but those problems can be minimized if they are identified and effectively managed. For better or worse, organizations cannot function without groups.

Groups always operate at two different levels: a more overt, conscious level where they focus on the *task,* and a more subtle, implicit level of *process,* where the focus is on group maintenance and interpersonal dynamics (Bion, 1961; Leavitt, 1978; Maier, 1967; Schein, 1969; Bales, 1970).

Many people see only confusion in group processes. The informed eye sees much more. Groups, like modern art, are complex and subtle. Every group is unique, yet each reveals the kinds of order, meaning, and beauty that reflect fundamental elements of the human experience. It is a matter of knowing what to look for. A few basic dimensions of group processes can provide a map for bringing clarity and order out of apparent chaos and confusion. Our own map emphasizes four central issues in group processes: (1) informal roles, (2) informal norms, (3) interpersonal conflict, and (4) leadership and decision making.

*Informal Roles.* A role is a position in a group or organization that is defined by expectations: the person who occupies a particular role is *expected* to behave in ways that fit the role. *Leaders* are expected to be confident and to take initiatives; *followers* are expected to be loyal and supportive. For example, *professors* are expected to show up for class and to give lectures; *students* are expected to take notes. *Politicians* are expected to promise that things will get better if they are elected; *voters* are expected to respond skeptically but vote anyway.

In the structural frame, he learned that formal roles are often defined by means of a title and a job description. In small groups, roles are often much more informal and implicit. In fact, every small group that meets for any length of time develops an informal role system. Undefined by title or written job description, such roles can have a strong, if subtle, influence on the group.

Roles in small groups have both task and personal dimensions. Every work group needs a structure of *task* roles to enable it to do its job. Take a typical group of four or five people who come together to do some research and to prepare a report on their results. They will need to decide who is going to do what. Everyone could do exactly the same thing, but because people are not alike, that seldom happens. They have different interests (some love research but hate writing), different skills (some may communicate better in writing than face-to-face), and different degrees of enthusiasm (some may be highly committed to the project, while others may be dragging their feet). Structurally, groups do better when they recognize and respond to those differences. It is normally a mistake, for example, to assign the task of writing the final report to someone who dislikes writing and writes poorly.

Beyond task roles, every group also evolves *personal roles.* When we enter a group, we face the problem of finding a comfortable and satisfying role. Imagine a three-person task force. One member, Karen, is only happy when she feels influential and visible. Another member, Bob, feels comfortable when he has permission to be quiet and inconspicuous. Teresa finds it hard to participate until she feels liked and valued. As the group begins to meet, members send signals to each other about the roles that they want. The signals are implicit and no one recognizes what is happening. In the first meeting, Karen jumps in, takes the initiative, and pushes hard for her point of view. Teresa smiles, compliments other people, asks questions, and says that she hopes everyone will get along. Bob watches the others and speaks only when someone asks him a direct question.

If members' preferred roles are well matched, things often go well. Karen is happy to have a Bob who will listen to her, and Bob is happy to have a Karen who will let him be inconspicuous. Teresa will be happy if she feels that Karen and Bob like her. But suppose Tony joins the group. Tony always likes to be in charge. Karen and Tony may collide. They may dislike each other without knowing why. Both want the same role, and neither wants to give it to the other. The prognosis for the group now looks bleaker. But suppose one more member signs on. Susan simply *loves* to help other people get along. If Susan can assist the group so that Karen feels visible, Teresa feels loved, Tony feels powerful, and Bob feels left alone, everyone will be happy—and the group may be very productive.

In groups, as in organizations, a central human resource issue is the fit between the individual and the larger system. A group's ability to develop an appropriate role system is critical to developing a good fit. The right set of task roles helps to get the work done and make optimal use of each member's resources. But without the right set of informal roles, individuals will feel frustrated and dissatisfied. They may then become unproductive or disruptive.

Some groups are blessed with a rich set of resources and highly compatible individuals, but most groups are not that lucky. They have limited quantities of talent, skill, and motivation. They have areas of both compatibility and potential conflict. Many groups never become aware of the role issues that need attention. Others see them but never talk about them.

People avoid discussing informal roles for fear of offending someone or of descending into an abyss of unmanageable conflict. But this kind of avoidance often backfires. The issues come back to haunt the group, particularly when task pressures increase. It often works better to deal with those issues early in the group's life. All members can be asked what roles they want, how they would like to see the group operate, and what resources they think they bring.

If Karen and Tony learn right away that both of them like to be in charge, they can see the potential for difficulty and discuss how to deal with it. If everyone knows that the group could become a battleground in a power struggle between Karen and Tony, everyone has an incentive to look for a better alternative. The relationship between Karen and Tony becomes a group responsibility, not a subterranean struggle that everyone notices but no one mentions.

*Informal Group Norms.* Every group develops a set of rules to live by—norms that govern how the group will function and how the members will conduct themselves. We once observed two families who were in adjacent sites in the same campground. At first glance, both were very similar: two adults, two small children, and California license plates. Further observation, however, made it clear that they had very different norms. Family A practiced a strong form of "do your own thing." Everyone did what he or she wanted, and no one paid much attention to anyone else. Their two-year-old boy wandered around the campground until he fell down a fifteen-foot embankment. He cried for a while, while we pondered the costs and benefits of intervening in the affairs of someone else's family. Finally, we pulled him up and returned him to his parents, who seemed oblivious to what had happened to him.

Family B, in contrast, was a model of interdependence and efficiency, operating like a well-oiled machine. Everything was done collectively, and each member had a role in every activity. An army drill sergeant would have admired the speed and precision with which they packed up their camping gear when they were ready to depart. Even the youngest, a three-year-old girl, approached her tasks with purpose and enthusiasm.

Every group, including families, evolves a set of informal rules for "how we do things around here." Eventually, those rules come to be taken for granted. They are not viewed as "how we choose to do things" but as unchangeable social facts. The parents in Family A envied Family B. They were plainly puzzled as they asked, "How did they ever get those kids under control? *Our* kids would never tolerate that."

Individuals then carry those unchangeable social facts with them into new experiences. When new groups form, different members may have very different ideas about how things should work. Returning to our small task force, suppose Karen grew up in family A; she wants autonomy and spontaneity in the group. Tony grew up in family B, and pushes for efficiency and clear structure. From a structural perspective, the norms should fit the task. From a human resource perspective, it is equally important that they fit the people. While it may be difficult it is essential that the group meet *both* Karen's needs for space and Tony's needs for clarity.

With norms, as with roles, it often helps to discuss early on how to proceed. Do we want to be task oriented, no nonsense, and get on with the job? Or would we prefer to be more relaxed, playful, and responsive to individuals? Do we expect everyone to attend every meeting, or should we be more flexible? Must people be unerringly punctual, or would that cramp our style? Do we prize boisterous debate or courtesy and restraint? Every group needs to answer these and many other questions as it develops its norms.

*Interpersonal Conflict in Groups.* Many of the worst horror stories about group life center on personal conflicts. Interpersonal strife can block progress and waste time. It can make group activity unpleasant at best and painful at worst. A few exceptional groups are blessed with little conflict and never have to worry about it. In most groups, however, diversity among the members inevitably results in differences in goals, perceptions, preferences, and beliefs. The larger and more diverse the group, the greater the potential for conflict.

The question is what to do about differences when they arise. The mystery-mastery model discussed earlier in the chapter suggests two basic strategies: "pour oil in troubled waters" and "might makes right." Each can make things worse instead of better. The oil-on-troubled-waters strategy views conflict as something to avoid at all costs: minimize it, pretend that it does not exist, smooth it over, bury it, circumvent it. Suppose, for example, that Tony says that the group needs a leader, and Karen replies that a leader would selfishly dominate the group. Teresa, dreading conflict, might rush in to say, "I think we're all basically saying the same thing," or, "We can talk about leadership later, but right now why don't we find out a little more about each other's backgrounds."

Smoothing tactics may work if the issue is temporary or pe-

ripheral. In such cases, conflict may disappear of its own accord—
much to everyone's relief. But conflicts that arise in the first hour
or so of a group's life have a remarkable tendency to come back
again and again if they are not dealt with.

If smoothing tactics fail and conflict continues, another option is "might makes right." If Tony senses conflict between him
and Karen, he might think:

1. Since we disagree, and my view is right, she is the problem.
2. Since she is the problem, the only way to get anything done is
   for her to change.

Tony may try any of several strategies to change Karen. He
may try to persuade her of the validity of his position. He may try
to get others in the group to side with him and put pressure on
Karen. He may subtly, or not so subtly, criticize or attack her. If
Karen thinks that she is right and that Tony is the problem, the two
of them are headed for collision. The result may be very painful for
both the two individuals and the group.

If mystery-mastery is a costly way to deal with conflict, what
else might a group do? The following guidelines may prove
helpful:

1. *Agree on the basics.* A group needs to take time to work
out agreement on its goals and how to achieve them; this means
agreeing on basic issues of both task and process. The human resource frame suggests that groups need to make sure that every
member is comfortable with his or her role and with the norms that
govern the group's activities. Shared commitment provides very
powerful glue to hold a group together in the face of the inevitable
stresses and strains of group life.

2. *Search for interests in common.* How does a group reach
agreement if it begins with differences? It often helps to keep asking,
What do we have in common? If we disagree on this issue, where
can we agree? If Tony and Karen disagree on the need for a leader,
can they find other areas where they do agree? Perhaps both agree
on the task to be done, and both believe that it is important to do
it well and to work well together. Recognizing what they have in
common may make it easier to discuss where they differ.

It is important to remember that some interests in common are rooted in differences (Lax and Sebenius, 1986). Karen's desire to be visible and Bob's desire to be invisible made them different from each other, but those differences actually made them compatible. Conversely, it was the very similarity between Karen and Tony (both wanted to lead) that produced conflict.

3. *Experiment.* If Tony is sure that they need a leader and Karen is sure that they do not, the group could bog down in endless debate. Susan, the group's social specialist, might therefore propose an experiment: Since Karen sees it one way, and Tony sees it the other, how could we get more information to help us decide? Could we *experiment*, maybe try one meeting with a leader and one without, to see what happens?

Experimentation can be a very powerful tool for dealing with conflict. It is a way to move beyond a stalemate without forcing either party to lose face or admit defeat; the parties may agree on a test of their differences when they cannot agree on anything else. Equally important, Karen, Tony, and the other group members may all learn something from the experiment that moves the conversation forward to a new, perhaps more productive, point.

4. *Doubt your own infallibility.* This was the advice that Benjamin Franklin offered his fellow delegates to the United States constitutional convention in 1787: "Having lived long, I have experienced many instances of being obliged by better information, or fuller consideration, to change opinions even on important subjects, which I once thought right, but found to be otherwise. It is therefore that the older I grow, the more apt I am to doubt my own judgment, and to pay more respect to the judgment of others" (Rossiter, 1966).

Groups have the advantage of diverse resources, ideas, and perspectives. A group that sees differences as an asset and a source of learning has a better chance for productive discussion of those differences.

In the heat of the moment, though, a five-person group can turn into five teachers in search of a learner. At such times, it can help if at least one person in the group asks, Are we all sure that we're infallible? Are we really hearing one another?

5. *Treat differences as a group responsibility.* If Tony and

Karen are on a collision course, it would be tempting for others in the group to stand out of the way: It's their problem. Let them solve it. But since everyone is riding the same vehicle, all will suffer if it careens off the road. The debate between Karen and Tony does reflect their personal feelings and preferences. But they are also conducting a conversation on behalf of the group: leadership is an issue that the *group* needs to resolve, not just Karen and Tony. Even if the issue were entirely personal, it still has the potential to spill over into the group's ability to get on with its work. If Karen and Tony need help in working through their differences, it is in everyone's interest to make sure that the help is provided.

*Leadership and Decision Making.* A final problem that every group has to resolve is the question of navigation: How will we steer the ship, particularly when the weather is stormy? Groups often get lost. Groups often expend large amounts of time and energy in directionless activities. Such group meetings may be punctuated with statements such as, I'm not sure where we're going, or, We've been talking for an hour without getting anywhere, or, Does anyone know what we're talking about?

The task of leadership in small groups is to help the group develop a sense of direction and a commitment to that direction. If that task is not performed, the group will be rudderless, or it may move in directions that have little support and commitment from the members. Leadership is essential, but it does not always have to be provided by a single person. In small groups, there are advantages and disadvantages to having a single, designated leader. The model of a single leader is relatively simple and well understood. It focuses responsibility for leadership in a single person so that everyone knows who is accountable. But there are costs as well. A single individual is often unable to provide leadership in all the situations that the group may encounter. Sometimes, groups do better with a shared and fluid approach to leadership, always asking, Who can best lead in *this* situation?

Sharing leadership is also a way to respond to different individual needs. When we last saw Karen and Tony, they were feuding about the need for a group leader. Both assumed that the term *leader* referred to a single individual who would become the "boss" of the group. But Karen and Tony, as well as others in the group, may *both* be able to provide leadership, perhaps in different ways, for different tasks, or at different times.

Whether leadership is shared or individual, research on task groups has shown that it plays a critical role in group effectiveness and member satisfaction. Maier (1967) found that leaders who either overcontrol or understructure tend to produce frustration and ineffectiveness. Effective leaders are sensitive to both the task and the process dynamics, and they enlist the group in actively managing both. Maier found that effective leaders focused on helping group members communicate and work together, while less effective leaders tried to dominate and get their own ideas accepted.

### Summary

Employees are hired to do a job, but they always bring other social and personal needs with them to the workplace. Moreover, they spend much of their time in organizations interacting with other people—one-on-one and in groups. Both individual satisfaction and organizational effectiveness depend heavily on the quality of those interactions.

Argyris and Schön argue that interpersonal dynamics in organizations are often counterproductive because people employ theories-in-use (behavioral programs) that emphasize self-protection and the control of others. They therefore developed an alternative model of effectiveness—a model built on the values of mutuality and learning.

Small groups are often condemned for their tendency to waste time while producing little output, but groups *can* be both satisfying and efficient. In any event, organizations cannot function without them. Managers need to understand that groups always operate at two levels: task and process. Both levels need to be managed if groups are to be effective. Among the significant process issues that groups need to manage are informal roles, group norms, interpersonal conflict, and leadership.

# 8

# *Improving Human Resource Management*

High-involvement management is the competitive advantage
available to countries with educated, achievement-oriented
work forces who want to perform effectively, whose core values
support participative decision making, and who can engage in
substantial amounts of self-regulation. At this point, it is more
of a concept than a reality, but many of the practices have been
proven in the sense that they have worked in new plants and
in plants with gain sharing. The key question at this point is
not whether high-involvement organizations will work. It is
how to create such organizations [Lawler, 1986, p. 215].

For more than a quarter century, human resource theorists
and practicing managers have confronted such questions as, How
can we make this a better place for people to work? How can we
improve morale, reduce turnover, or improve absenteeism? How
can we improve employees' confidence in management and the organization? What could we do to make better use of the human
resources in our organization? This chapter discusses some of the
approaches to organizational improvement that have been developed in response to such questions, including job enrichment, participative management, and organizational democracy.

The theories of Maslow, McGregor, and Argyris suggested
that conflict between individual and organization would get worse

as organizations became larger (with greater impersonality, longer chains of command, and more complex rules and control systems) and as society became better educated and more affluent (producing more people whose higher-level needs are salient). As they anticipated, more and more organizations, including many of the largest, are making major efforts to address human resource issues. An example is General Motors, which had little investment in human resource applications until the late 1960s and early 1970s. The company then entered a period in which profits began to decline even though sales were increasing. Just as Argyris and McGregor had predicted, the internal system was becoming increasingly expensive and difficult to manage. In 1972, GM's new plant at Lordstown, Ohio, gained notoriety as an example of conflict between individual and system.

Lordstown was GM's newest and most heavily automated plant when it opened in 1970. A year later, the plant had failed to achieve its production targets. New managers were brought in to solve the problem. They reduced the number of workers and increased the work load for those who remained. Although wages and benefits were excellent, the grievance rate soared (from 500 grievances a year to more than 500 a month). Employee sabotage slowed or stopped the assembly line several times, and the local union finally voted to strike over working conditions. One of the major issues was an employee practice known as "doubling-up." One employee covered two jobs on the line for a period of time, so that another could take a break. Then the second person returned the favor. Since cars moved down the line at a rate of 100 per hour, each worker normally had about thirty-six seconds to perform one job. Doubling-up reduced that to eighteen seconds. That was a fast pace, but many employees preferred working faster with an occasional break to facing another car every half-minute all day long. Management, fearing that doubling-up would produce inferior work, wanted to eliminate the practice. When employees were interviewed about the strike vote, they said that wages were not the issue: "The job pays good, but it's driving me crazy." "It's just like the army. No, it's worse than the army, 'cause you're welded to the line. You just about need a pass to piss."

After a costly wildcat strike at Lordstown, GM began to get

the message. In 1973, three years after the strike, GM and the United Automobile Workers (UAW) signed a contract that established a union-management National Committee to Improve the Quality of Working Life. Since then, GM has invested substantially in such programs (Maccoby, 1981; Kanter, 1983; Lawler, 1986). In the wake of both failures and successes, GM continued to believe that the program was essential to corporate well-being, despite lukewarm enthusiasm from Roger Smith, GM's chief executive. The extent of the change in philosophy is symbolized by the appointment of Patricia Carrigan as a plant manager in 1982. Carrigan is a woman (in itself a remarkable break from GM tradition) trained in clinical psychology and human resource management. She turned out to be a remarkably successful plant manager—at least until her sudden, mysterious retirement in May 1990. We tell more of her story in Chapter Twenty-One.

General Motors is only one example of the trend toward human resource management. Major organizations around the world— both public and private—have experimented with a variety of new approaches to this kind of management. The most prominent forms have included participative management, job enrichment, self-managing work teams, organizational democracy, training and organizational development, and Theory Z. Each is discussed below.

### Participative Management

McGregor and Argyris both believed that organizations created systems that forced employees to be highly dependent on superiors and gave them little control over their work. Adults were treated like children. One solution to that problem is *participation*—giving workers more opportunity to influence decisions.

The basic idea behind participation is illustrated in the classic case of a group of manual workers—all women—who were responsible for painting dolls in a toy factory (Whyte, 1955). The job had just been redesigned. In the new system, each woman took a toy from a tray, painted it, and put it on a hook passing by on a belt. The women received an hourly rate, a group bonus, and a learning bonus. Although management had expected no difficulty with the new system, production was less than anticipated and many hooks went by empty. Morale among the women was very low. They especially complained about the heat in the room and the speed of the belt.

Reluctantly, the foreman followed a consultant's advice to meet with the employees. After several meetings, the foreman agreed to bring in fans, though he and the industrial engineer both doubted that fans would help. In fact, the fans led to a significant improvement in morale. Discussion continued, and the employees eventually came up with a radical suggestion—they asked that they be allowed to control the speed of the belt. The engineer resisted this proposal, since he had carefully calculated the optimal speed for the belt. The foreman was skeptical but agreed to give it a try. The employees met and developed a complicated schedule—the belt ran fast at some times of the day and slow at other times.

Morale shot up. Production increased so much that it exceeded the engineer's calculations and began to overload the rest of the plant. The same was true of the workers' bonuses: they went up so much that the women now earned more than many workers with higher levels of skill and experience. Their high production and high pay upset the rest of the plant, and the experiment had an unhappy ending. To solve the overpay-overproduction problems, management reverted to a fixed speed for the belt. Production dropped again, morale plummeted, and most of the employees quit within a few months.

Many other studies of participation at work have found that it leads to significant improvements in both morale and productivity. Participation is one of the very few ways to increase both morale and productivity at the same time (for a review of this literature, see Blumberg, 1968, and Katzell and Yankelovich, 1975). Even when it works, however, participation can have unfortunate side effects because it may create the need for changes that are resisted by other parts of the organization.

Participative management became a fad in the 1970s. Managers throughout the world went off to seminars to learn how to become more participative. An example was the sudden "discovery" in the United States of Japanese quality circles. The Japanese had actually taken the idea of quality circles from two influential American consultants, Joseph Juran and W. Edwards Deming, who worked in Japan in the 1950s and 1960s. Japan had quickly moved away from its status as a low-cost, low-quality producer (in the late 1940s and early 1950s, the words "Made in Japan" meant "cheap and probably defective" to American consumers). The Japanese had used quality circles extensively in their remarkably successful drive to improve quality.

Hundreds of U.S. companies seized on this latest example of Japanese management success, often with little attention to the possible cultural differences between Japan and the United States. For example, loyalty to the group is revered with the same fervor in Japan as rugged individualism is in the United States. Nevertheless, a study in 1982 found that about two-thirds of large American corporations were using quality circle programs (Lawler, 1986).

Typically, a quality circle consists of employees from a particular work area. Management solicits volunteers and, in most cases, finds there are too many rather than too few volunteers. Programs usually begin with training in group processes and problem solving. The agenda of the meetings focuses primarily on issues of product quality. Sometimes the groups are also asked to explore ways to reduce costs or improve productivity, but they are rarely asked to look at broader ways to make the organization more effective (Lawler, 1986). Members usually receive no direct financial rewards for the success of their team's effort, though they often receive various kinds of recognition (award ceremonies, T-shirts, publicity, and so on).

As with most fads, quality circles have met with variable success. When implemented thoughtfully and with due regard to the needs of both employees and organization, they have often achieved significant results. When employed simply because everyone else was doing it, they achieved very little. Lawler (1986) argues that quality circle efforts usually have a much shorter life cycle in the United States than in Japan, partly because of problems of implementation, partly because of cultural differences. Employees generally enter quality circles with enthusiasm, but their feelings change to disappointment and disillusionment if their suggestions for change are rejected or poorly implemented. Quality circles may be useful as one step in a long-term move toward participative management, but they should not be seen as ends in themselves.

American managers are often attracted to quality circles for the wrong reasons: because they are structured, bounded programs and because they do *not* change the organization (Lawler, 1986).

Although the participation fad has reduced the number of autocratic managers, participative management often exists more at the level of myth than reality (Argyris and Schön, 1974; Bolman, 1975), and managers often believe in participation more for themselves than for their subordinates. Many efforts at fostering participation have failed not because participation did not work, but because it was not really implemented. This failure of implementation often reflects the difficulties of designing workable participative systems, managers' ambivalence about power, and the gap between espoused theory and theory-in-use discussed in the previous chapter. Managers may believe in sharing power but may also fear that subordinates will misuse it. As a result, their attempts to implement participation are often inconsistent and contradictory: quality circles and many other forms of "participation" are often implemented in a controlling, top-down fashion that almost guarantees failure.

## Job Enrichment

If jobs are too narrow, fragmented, and restrictive, another approach to reducing conflict between the individual and the system is to redesign work. *Job enlargement* and *job enrichment* are two labels often used to describe efforts in this direction. Herzberg (1966), for example, asked employees to talk about the times when they felt best and worst about their jobs. The dominant themes in "good feelings" stories were achievement, recognition for performance, responsibility, advancement, and learning. The "bad feelings" stories featured such themes as company policy and administration, supervision, and working conditions.

Herzberg called those aspects of work that produced job satisfaction *motivators* and those aspects that produced job dissatisfaction *hygiene factors*. In effect, Herzberg proposed a two-level need hierarchy. The hygiene level included the physiological, safety, and belongingness needs in Maslow's hierarchy. The motivators included needs for self-esteem and self-actualization.

Herzberg's hygiene factors all have to do with the work environment, while the motivators mostly deal with the work itself. Herzberg argued that attempts to motivate workers with better pay and fringe benefits, with improved working conditions, with communications programs, or with human relations training were all based on what he called the KITA approach to motivation—the belief that the quickest and surest way to get someone to do something is to kick the person in the tail. In Herzberg's view, KITA approaches do not motivate—they may get the person to move, but it takes another kick to get the individual to move again.

Herzberg saw job enrichment as central to motivation. But this kind of enrichment is not the same as "horizontal job enlargement." Adding more dull tasks to an already-dull job does not enrich it. Herzberg argued for "vertical job loading," that is, giving the individual more freedom and authority, more feedback, and more challenges, while also making him more accountable and allowing him to use more skills.

Herzberg's theory has been heavily criticized, particularly because his research was based entirely on what people said about good and bad work experiences. People often attribute unpleasant events to forces outside themselves, while taking personal credit for successes. Psychologists call this an *attributional bias*. But even if Herzberg's approach oversimplifies the question of human motivation, it is broadly consistent with the work of Maslow, McGregor, Argyris, and other human resource theorists. All point to job enrichment as a way to produce a better fit between individual and organization.

Hackman and his colleagues extended Herzberg's theory and argued that three variables were critical to the success of job redesign experiments: individuals needed to see their work as meaningful and worthwhile, they needed to feel personally accountable for the consequences of their efforts, and they needed feedback that would give them knowledge of results (Hackman, Oldham, Janson, and Purdy, 1987). Whether a job meets those requirements depends on several core dimensions. One dimension is skill variety, that is, the degree to which a job challenges an individual's abilities. A second core dimension, task identity, has to do with whether the job produces a "whole." It is more meaningful, for example, to produce a complete toaster than to attach an electrical cord to every toaster that passes on the line. Next, task significance has to do with how much impact the work has on others' lives, so that "the worker who tightens nuts on aircraft brake assemblies is more likely to perceive his work as significant than the worker who fills small boxes with paper clips" (Hackman, Oldham, Janson, and Purdy, 1987, p. 320).

Two other dimensions that affect the quality of a job are autonomy and feedback. A job possesses autonomy if it gives the worker discretion in scheduling work and determining how to carry it out. "People in highly autonomous jobs know that they are personally responsible for successes and failures" (Hackman, Oldham, Janson, and Purdy, 1987, p. 320). Feedback is knowledge of results, or the degree to which the workers get information about how well they are doing.

Does job redesign work? A number of experiments have been tried (some going back to the mid 1940s), and the answer has mostly been yes. In most of these experiments, the majority of workers preferred the redesigned jobs, though some workers liked the old jobs better. Argyris, McGregor, and Hackman all predict that some workers will resist job enrichment. Argyris and McGregor both noted that many workers have been trained to accept Theory X assumptions, and will resist a change toward more responsibility. Hackman emphasized the importance of distinguishing between employees with "high growth needs," who would welcome job enrichment, and employees with "low growth needs," who would not.

Kopelman (1985) and Lawler (1986) provide reviews of the research on job enrichment experiments. Job enrichment usually has more impact on the quality than on the quantity of production. Kopelman (1985) reported an average quality improvement of 28 percent across twenty-one job enrichment experiments. Gains are stronger for quality than productivity probably because workers get more satisfaction from doing a job well than from doing more work (Lawler, 1986). Job enrichment often produces other benefits. It increases staffing flexibility (making it easier to move tasks between workers as the need arises) and makes it easier to attract and retain workers.

It is likely that the coming years will see a gradual reduction in the percentage of jobs that are overwhelmingly dull, routine, and unchallenging. Increasingly, such jobs will either be redesigned or turned over to machines and computers. But, there are significant barriers to the progress of job enlargement, and dull jobs will not entirely disappear. One source of resistance is the philosophy of *technological determinism*—the belief that jobs should be organized on the basis of technical imperatives and people then trained to perform the jobs correctly. Another barrier is the durability of Theory X. Right or wrong, many managers continue to believe that their workers will be most productive in a Theory X environment. A third barrier is economic. Many jobs cannot be significantly altered without major investments in the redesign of physical plant and machinery.

A fourth barrier is that job enrichment experiments, when they work, often lead to pressures for broader and more basic changes in the organizations, as the doll case vividly illustrates. Workers on enriched jobs often come to see themselves differently and to demand more from the organization—sometimes increased pay and benefits, sometimes new career opportunities and training for new tasks (Lawler, 1986).

## Self-Managing Work Teams

One limit to the enlargement of individual jobs is that in many organizations, no single person can produce more than a small part of the product or service. No one is likely to propose, for example, that an automobile plant be broken into a series of self-contained garages, each with a single worker responsible for the production of an entire automobile. In many cases, meaningful job enlargement may be possible only if responsibility can be given to autonomous or self-managing work groups. Much of the early research on autonomous teams occurred in Scandinavia under the guidance of Einar Thorsrud (Thorsrud, 1977, 1984; Lawler, 1986), but in recent years a number of major firms in the United States (including Cummins Engine, Digital Equipment Corporation, General Foods, General Motors, and Shell Oil) have experimented with autonomous teams. Some of these experiments have been conducted in existing facilities, others in new facilities that were designed from the outset to accommodate the work team concept.

The idea is to give a team responsibility for a whole product or a complete service, and its members are provided with enough autonomy and resources so that they can be held accountable for their output. Teams meet regularly (at least weekly) to discuss work assignments, scheduling, current production problems, and so forth. Supervision is provided by a team leader who may be appointed or who may emerge from the group. The amount of discretion given to a team varies. At one end of the spectrum, a team may be given the authority to hire, fire, determine pay rates, specify work methods, and manage inventory, all with the assistance of a computerized system that provides information on the team's results. In other cases, decisions about the pay and selection of workers remain with management, but the workers still make decisions about production, quality, and work methods. Installation of the team concept is always accompanied by considerable training. The training focuses in part on group process to help make the team meetings effective, and in part on increasing workers' abilities to perform multiple jobs. In many cases, incentive systems are changed to base workers' pay on the range of different tasks they can perform (Lawler, 1986).

### Organizational Democracy

Especially in the United States, participative management has been viewed as a matter of organizational style and climate rather than as a way to share authority. A manager may choose to be participative, or choose not to, with no change in managerial prerogatives. In both public and private organizations in the United States, managerial thinking has resisted the idea of organizational democracy, namely, that the rights of workers to participate should be built into the formal decision-making process and protected from managerial discretion. Doing so is often viewed as structurally unwise.

Organizational democracy has been carried further in a number of European nations. In Norway and Sweden, for example, industrial democracy is increasingly accepted as a fact of life by both managers and workers, and efforts to introduce organizational democracy have moved ahead rapidly (Elden, 1983, 1986; Thorsrud, 1984). Ironically, the two Scandinavian nations have taken the lead because they were able to borrow the expertise of British social scientists who had considerable understanding of participative systems but whose ideas were not particularly welcome in Britain. For example, they brought to Norway the idea that legal participation in the management of the enterprise was not enough. Changes were also needed in what they called the sociotechnical system—the interplay between the social and the technical aspects of how work is performed.

In both Sweden and Norway, worker participation in decision making is now legally mandated, and there is extensive experimentation with new forms of work and employee participation. In 1977, Norway passed a law with the ambitious purpose of outlawing alienating and dehumanizing jobs, while requiring quality-of-work-life (QWL) councils in Norwegian firms. In the 1980s, a special commission appointed by the Norwegian government recommended further democratization as a national industrial strategy (Elden, 1986).

Major Scandinavian corporations have been at the forefront of experimentation with QWL and democratization. Both of the major Swedish automakers—Saab and Volvo—have experimented with radical changes in the traditional assembly-line approach to producing automobiles. Volvo built an entire plant at Kalmar, Sweden, around the concept of self-managing work groups.

In describing the evolution of sociotechnical thinking in Norway, Elden (1983) suggests that there has been a gradual shift from a focus on "empowerment as structure" to "empowerment as process." In earlier experiments, participative structures were put in place through a process that was often managed primarily by expert consultants: "The manifest goal of the change efforts based on first-generation ideas was to change organizational structure from a hierarchical, centralized form to a more self-managed, autonomy-based form. The change process itself, however, was based on a model of hierarchical organization and expert authority. The first-generation change agents provided the model of a nondemocratic organization even as they attempted to install democratic organizations. Democratizing the change process itself was thus considered one means of improving diffusion and learning" (p. 243).

More recently, Norwegian efforts have emphasized concepts

such as participatory research, in which the employees take primary responsibility for the change process. Expert consultants, if they are used at all, provide counsel rather than managing the process. In Elden's view, "the process of inquiry, learning, and self-study can empower participants because it creates new definitions of what is possible, new explanations of why things are as they are, and, therefore, new possibilities for action" (p. 243).

Industrial democracy has been viewed both as an enormously powerful idea whose time has finally come and as an overrated fad. In truth, the debate has been clouded by too much rhetoric, ideology, and emotion, and too little evidence for either view has been brought forward. But several points seem reasonably clear:

1.  There has been an enormous increase in experiments in industrial democracy. (Prior to the late 1950s, there were many experiments in benevolent paternalism, as well as state ownership of work organizations, but neither did much to increase employees' control over decisions.)
2.  Most of the empirical investigations of industrial democracy show more positive than negative consequences. Workers almost always prefer more power to less power.
3.  Experiments with industrial democracy sometimes show an initial decline in productivity, but in the long run most experiments either result in a gain in productivity or maintain a level of productivity roughly comparable to that under the previous system.
4.  The process is usually irreversible. When workers gain more power, they are rarely willing to give it up and often press for its expansion.
5.  Despite the mostly favorable evidence, many managers, scholars, and trade union leaders continue to oppose the idea.

Managers resist democracy for fear of losing the powers and prerogatives that they currently enjoy (and believe to be essential to organizational success). Traditional union leaders sometimes see organizational democracy as a management trick: a way of getting workers to accept gimmicks instead of real gains in wages and benefits. Union resistance also stems from fear that organizational democracy might produce closer collaboration between workers and management, thus undermining the role of the union. Moreover, some unions, while formally democratic, are internally as authoritarian as their corporate counterparts. Democracy in the corporation leads to questions about democracy in the union as well. Lawler (1986) cites a union leader who began a QWL experiment at his local because the national union was encouraging such initiatives. But he tried to pull out when his members argued that the local union should also be run on the basis of QWL principles. At the same time, a number of pioneering union leaders, such as Irving Bluestone of the UAW, have taken prominent leadership roles in pushing for union-management collaboration. Many unions in the United States and elsewhere have supported QWL efforts.

### Training and Organization Development

As a result of the early research on human relations in industry, it came to be generally accepted that managers needed more skills in human relations. Training programs and departments began to proliferate rapidly in the 1950s and 1960s. Many of the early programs focused on training managers how to be more sensitive, how to be better listeners, and how to communicate more effectively, and they usually consisted mostly of lectures about the importance of good human relations. However, while the programs produced a great deal of enthusiasm, they seemed to be short on substance. After enough failures, the question was asked, Is there a problem with our methods of teaching human relations? If people cannot learn to play tennis or a violin by listening to a lecture, why should they be able to develop human relations skills that way?

This line of questioning led to the idea of experiential learning and learning by doing. One of the most provocative examples of experiential learning was laboratory human relations training, often known as "sensitivity training" or "T-groups." The T-group was a serendipitous discovery made by a group of social psychologists at a conference on race relations in Connecticut in the late 1940s. During the conference, participants met in groups, and researchers were stationed in each group to take notes. In the evening, the researchers reported their observations to the program staff.

When the participants heard about the evening sessions, they asked to be invited. When they came, they were fascinated to hear reports about themselves and their behavior in groups that they had never heard before.

The researchers recognized that they had discovered something important and began a program of so-called human relations laboratories. These laboratories attempted to provide training for participants and research opportunities for social scientists. The first such laboratory, held in 1946, had six trainers and thirty researchers on the staff. The participants were assigned to basic skills training groups that met for several hours a day. Each group had a trainer and a training observer. During the last half hour of each meeting, the observer discussed his observations of the group. One year later, when another laboratory was held, the observer had become a trainer, and his or her observations were reported as events occurred. Trainers and participants joined in the common task of working in a group and learning from the work at the same time. That became the basic model for the T-group. It was a powerful, even startling, educational model.

In the early years, most of those who came to T-groups had very little idea of what to expect. They found themselves in a group with some twelve other participants and one or two trainers. The opening minutes often went like this:

*Trainer:*   We'll be together for many hours during the laboratory. This gives each of us a chance to learn more about ourselves, and how we can participate effectively in groups. I think the best way for us to do that is to focus on the here and now: on what we do and how we do it. I'm here to help as much as I can, but I don't plan to serve as the group leader.
[Silence ensues, becomes increasingly uncomfortable, and lasts for anything from a few seconds to a few minutes.]

*Member A:*   I don't think I understood everything that you said, Trainer. Could you repeat it?

*Trainer:*   [Repeats, in essentially the same words.]

*Member B:*    What are we supposed to do?

*Trainer:*    I see that as something for the group to
decide.
[Another silence.]

*Member C:*    Well, I think this whole thing is a waste
of time! If we're going to get anything done, we have to
get organized. We need a leader. Every group has to
have a leader to get anything done. Why don't we
choose someone to chair the meeting?
[More silence.]

*Member D:*    [Carefully.] Maybe it would be a good
idea if we all introduced ourselves.

*Member A:*    Yeah, I don't know anyone's name.

*Member D:*    [More confidently.] Good, A. Why don't
you start? Then we'll go around the table.
[A introduces himself, and others follow around the
circle.]

Later, the trainer would ask the members of the group to
examine how they felt when C suggested a leader. C would be surprised to learn that there were many who agreed with him but that
others had mistrusted his motives. The group might examine how
D, with a little help from A, had made a decision that everyone then
followed. They might discover that some members disagreed with
D's procedure but that no one felt willing to question it.

The T-group had several features that made it a powerful
experience for participants. The trainer's refusal to fill the customary role for group leaders created a vacuum, and the group began
with little in the way of rules, organization, leadership, or content.
The only definition of the task was to learn from examining events
in the group, and this definition had little meaning for most participants. In order to function, the group had to create its own
agenda, goals, and procedures. This was enormously frustrating
and unsettling at first but led to a great sense of achievement and
satisfaction when groups began to create for themselves a structure

that worked. It also came as a surprise to many that a group with so little structure and such unorthodox leadership could actually work.

A second source of the power of the T-groups was interpersonal feedback. In a culture where it is rare for people to communicate direct reactions to one another's behavior, the high levels of feedback in a T-group constituted a powerful intervention. Countless members of T-groups found themselves saying, I never knew that's how people see me.

As word spread, T-groups began to replace lectures as an approach to improving human relations skills in organizations. T-groups also attracted a large body of research on their impact (mostly because so many T-group leaders were trained as social scientists). Through a haze of controversy, charges, and counter-charges (T-groups had more than their share of zealous proponents and equally zealous critics), the evidence began to suggest two basic conclusions: T-groups could and did have an effect on people's feelings about themselves, on their self-perceptions, and even on their behavior. But those effects rarely led to very much in the way of organizational change (Gibb, 1975; Campbell and Dunnette, 1968).

Because research and experience showed that the training effect of T-groups often did not persist, many laboratory trainers began to experiment with new approaches. If participants were not applying what they learned in their organizations, perhaps it was because the individual needed support from others in the workplace. If so, might the effects be better if an entire work team were included in the same T-group? A number of such experiments were tried, and they represented a very important early experiment in what has come to be called organization development (OD).

Many of these "family" T-groups worked very well in promoting communication and trust within the group, although sometimes at the cost of an in-group climate that alienated others in the organization. The research evidence was never very clear (and still is not) whether the use of T-groups in work organizations produced positive results, but many practitioners increasingly came to believe that the T-group was too specialized and atypical to be a vehicle for organizational change. Though some writers (such as Heffron,

1989) still see OD and sensitivity training as synonymous, the two have in fact become quite distinct. OD practitioners have taken some of the basic elements of laboratory training (for example, the use of face-to-face groups, the emphasis on open communication, and the use of interpersonal feedback) and adapted them to a variety of organizational contexts. Thus, so-called conflict laboratories are designed for situations involving conflict between departments, and team-building programs are used for groups that wish to increase their ability to work as teams. A host of other OD intervention techniques have gradually been created.

### Survey Feedback

At about the same time that laboratory training was getting its start (the late 1940s), a group of researchers at the University of Michigan began the first of a long series of efforts to develop surveys to measure human elements in organizations—elements such as motivation, communications, leadership styles, and organizational climate. Rensis Likert was a founding member of the Survey Research Center at Michigan, and his 1961 book, *New Patterns of Management,* became a classic work in the human resource tradition.

Likert argued that many commonsense beliefs about effective management were simply wrong because they neglected the human element in organizations. He distinguished between *job-centered* and *employee-centered* management styles. The job-centered manager decides how the job should be done, instructs the employee, and monitors the employee to make sure that he or she does the job right. In contrast, the employee-centered manager focuses on the human aspects of employee performance and on building effective work groups with high performance goals. Likert pointed to a large body of evidence—most of it derived from survey research—that showed employee-centered supervisors usually managed higher-producing units than did job-centered supervisors. The issue, according to Likert, was *not* satisfaction. In some studies of routine jobs that required a low skill level, job satisfaction was a little higher in those units that were low in production.

Likert's distinction between job-centered and production-centered supervision bears a strong resemblance to McGregor's Theory X and Theory Y. Likert developed a prescription for organizational effectiveness that included employee-centered supervision and an "overlapping group" organizational structure. The overlapping group structure viewed every manager as a member of two work groups and as a "linking-pin" between those groups. One group consisted of the manager's boss and peers; the other group included the manager's subordinates. Each was to be a high-performing group that emphasized openness, cohesiveness, democratic supervision, and high production goals (Likert was involved early on in the T-group movement, and his views of effective groups were presumably influenced by those experiences). Likert's new management system retained the basic hierarchical structure of organizations but put great emphasis on groups and on the quality of interpersonal relationships. If every supervisor was an effective, employee-centered leader, he argued, the quality of life in organizations would be dramatically improved.

Likert's theory rested heavily on survey data and was instrumental in the evolution of survey feedback as an approach to organizational improvement. The survey feedback process begins with the administration of questionnaires concerning human and organizational issues. The questionnaires are tabulated, and the results are then computed for each work unit and subunit. A consultant meets with each work unit to report the results for that unit and for similar groups in the company. In a given unit, the results might show that information flows well and that members of the group are highly motivated, but that decisions are often made in the wrong place and on the basis of the wrong information. The consultant would ask the group members to discuss the results, test the data against their own experiences, and look for solutions to any problems that might arise.

## Evolution of OD

Likert's emphasis on openness, interpersonal relations, and effective groups was consistent with the basic assumptions of laboratory training. T-groups and survey research became the parents of organization development (OD), and understanding the parentage helps to explain why OD has developed into its current form. Both parents were very much in the human resource tradition. The only other major perspective in organization theory at the time was the structural approach, and most structural theorists were more interested in studying organizations than in trying to improve them. Human resource theorists had the field of organization development almost to themselves, and that fact is still reflected in current OD practice.

Since the 1960s, OD has continued to evolve. Mirvis (1988) describes OD of the 1960s as essentially a process-oriented philosophy built around the values of human expression. In the 1970s, OD shifted to an emphasis on technique and attempted to develop different interventions for different organizational problems. In the 1980s, Mirvis believes, OD shifted from a facilitative, person-centered approach to a more directive, organization-centered one, and it came to be viewed as a strategy for helping organizations achieve and maintain stability in the face of changing and turbulent environments. "In OD of the 1960s, it was assumed that by developing people we could create healthier and more effective organizations. Today, many advocate that we must develop organizations to create healthier and more effective people" (Mirvis, 1988, pp. 17–18).

In the meantime, OD consultation has grown enormously. In 1965 few managers or organizations had heard of OD. By 1975, there were few managers who had not, and few major organizations (particularly in the United States) that had not tried it in some form or other. General Motors and the U.S. Post Office, IBM and the Internal Revenue Service, Texas Instruments and the U.S. Navy had all made significant investments in one or another form of OD.

OD's popularity does not entirely result from its enormous success. Both the research evidence and the feelings of clients point to a mixed record—there have been notable successes, as well as dramatic failures. There is still scant evidence to provide firm conclusions about what form of OD works best under what conditions. Yet OD continues to grow in significance and for a fairly simple reason. It may not be the best solution, but for many human resource problems, it is just about the only solution. A professor of medicine once offered the opinion that doctors probably killed more patients than they cured until about 1940. For centuries, physicians employed cures that did not work to treat illnesses that they did not understand, because no one else could do better. People recognized many of the limitations of the medical profession, which was held in much lower repute in the past than it is now, but they still turned to doctors when ill.

Something similar is happening to OD. Systematic research on organizations is a few decades old, and most OD practice has evolved in the past twenty-five years. OD, like air, is all around us, but it is hard to define or pin down. The research base is growing, but it is still primitive and controversial. OD is also a highly personalized activity—the style of the consultant is a significant determinant of the nature of the consultation.

Fullan, Miles, and Taylor (1981) provided an excellent review of OD practice, although they focused primarily on OD in public schools. They concluded that OD is so ill defined and amorphous that it is important to distinguish it from organizational training and other organizational improvement approaches. They argue that the label OD should only be applied to a program that has all the following characteristics: It is *"simultaneously . . .* planned, long-range, involves a change agent or agents, focuses on organizational processes, tasks, and structures; addresses the development of individuals as well as the organization; and uses behavioral science techniques to generate valid data for both individual and organizational decisions" (p. 6). On the basis of their review of the literature, Fullan, Miles, and Taylor concluded that the probability that any given OD project will be successful is about 50 percent. But many of the failed projects appear to have been "ineptly conducted," while the success rate was high for those programs that adequately met their definition of a systematic approach to OD.

It is fairly easy to predict the general future of OD. It will continue to grow, and it will evolve as its knowledge base improves. It will become more precise and differentiated and develop more specific cures for specific organizational illnesses. It is also likely to become more professionalized.

Currently, OD is a two-tier profession. One tier consists of a relatively small number of researchers and theorists, usually based in universities, who write most of the books on OD and garner most of the prestige. The second tier consists of a much larger number of OD consultants who work full time as practitioners. Some are internal consultants who work for one organization only. Others are external consultants who work with a number of different organizations. Members of the university tier usually have doctoral degrees and extensive training in the social sciences. Members of the consultant tier have learned much of their craft from hands-on experience and from attendance at workshops. OD training programs are becoming more common in universities, and several organizations have attempted to certify the competence of OD practitioners. Even though there are counterpressures from within the field, the future is likely to bring more formalization of training and credentials and a greater emphasis on professionalism.

## Theory Z

William Ouchi's *Theory Z*, published in 1981, was the first book by an organizational behavior researcher to attain a long stay on the best-seller lists in the United States. The book was published at a time when the American economy was sagging and many were comparing American organizations and American management unfavorably to their Japanese counterparts. As a student of both Japanese and American approaches to management, Ouchi was able to isolate several major differences between American and Japanese organizations:

1.  While American organizations have relatively high mobility and turnover, Japanese organizations provide lifetime employment for their basic work force.
2.  In American organizations, evaluation is relatively explicit, and promotion is often rapid. In Japanese organizations, performance evaluation is relatively subtle and implicit, and promotion is infrequent.
3.  American organizations are much more likely to provide highly specialized career paths for different managers—a financial manager always works in finance, while a manufacturing manager never leaves manufacturing. In Japanese organizations, specialized career paths are unusual, and most employees move through a variety of different functions in the course of their careers.

4. Where decision making in American organizations is frequently seen as an individual responsibility, decision making in Japanese organizations is a collective process that involves everyone who will be affected by the decision. This leads to an important contrast: American organizations make decisions more quickly but encounter problems of implementation. Japanese organizations take longer to make decisions but implement smoothly and rapidly.

5. Whereas American culture highly prizes individuality, Japanese culture prizes collective effort.

Ouchi believes that differences between American and Japanese culture make it impossible to import the Japanese approach to American organizations in its entirety. But his research also revealed that (1) a number of Japanese organizations had successfully adapted their system to American conditions when they established subsidiaries in the United States and (2) a number of successful American organizations employed techniques that were very similar to those used in Japanese organizations.

Ouchi, mindful of McGregor's Theory Y, coined the term *Theory Z* to describe a management philosophy that successfully blended Japanese and American approaches to management. His Theory Z incorporates many of the central assumptions of the human resource frame: "Of all its values, commitment of a Z culture to its people—its workers—is the most important. . . . Theory Z assumes that any worker's life is a whole, not a Jekyll-Hyde personality, half machine from nine to five and half human in the hours preceding and following. Theory Z suggests that humanized working conditions not only increase productivity and profits to the company but also the self-esteem for employees. . . . Up to now American managers have assumed that technology makes for increased productivity. What Theory Z calls for instead is a redirection of attention to *human* relations in the corporate world" (Ouchi, 1981, p. 165).

Ouchi acknowledges that Theory Z organizations have potential weaknesses. Because they put heavy emphasis on close, harmonious working relations, they often tend to exclude people who are different, and this can lead to distrust of ideas that originate outside the organization. Paradoxically, it can also lead to racism and sexism. Even though Z organizations put a strong emphasis on egalitarian relations within the organization, a predominately white male management might exclude women and nonwhites to avoid disturbing existing interpersonal relationships.

The process of implementing Theory Z is time consuming and not yet well understood: "Going from A to Z reaches down to touch every worker in every plant within perhaps ten to fifteen years. The large-scale successful developments are to date so small in number that it is not possible to gauge these estimates reliably. The process of participative management, once begun, is largely self-sustaining because it appeals to the basic values of all employees. And in fact the process promotes greater productivity and efficiency through better coordination and will flourish unless intentionally stopped by a disenchanted or threatened union or by top management" (Ouchi, 1981, p. 110).

Ouchi's theory incorporates and restates many classical elements of the human resource frame, but it also makes important additions, particularly in its emphasis on the importance of organizational philosophy and culture and in its questioning of many values long held by American management theorists. As we will explore later in this chapter, American organizations will never become mirror images of their Japanese counterparts because of the significant differences between the cultures, but in the same way that the Japanese have shown an ability to learn from other cultures, Americans may learn a great deal in return from the Japanese that can help in enhancing the effectiveness of American management and organizations. For most of the century, American models have dominated management theory, but a global economy requires theories of management that transcend the American experience. Increasingly, creative managers and sensitive researchers around the globe will contribute to a shared pool of ideas about management and leadership.

### A New Twist in the Longest Auto Race: NUMMI

In 1985, New United Motor Manufacturing, Inc., more commonly known as NUMMI, reopened an old General Motors plant in Fremont, California, and began to produce automobiles. It hired its work force from 5,000 workers who had been laid off the previous year by General Motors. These workers had a reputation at GM for militance, poor attendance, alcohol and drug abuse, and even fist-fights on the assembly line (Holusha, 1989; Lawrence and Weckler, 1990; Lee, 1988). Two years later, however, the plant was producing cars of higher quality but lower labor content than any other GM plant, and absenteeism had declined from 20 percent under GM to 2 percent under NUMMI. Moreover, the car produced at NUMMI ranked second among all cars sold in the United States in initial owner satisfaction; no other GM car was even in the top fifteen.

What accounted for this manufacturing miracle? The answer, in a word, was Toyota. NUMMI was a joint venture of General Motors and Toyota. General Motors provided the plant, the workers, and an American nameplate, but the car and the production processes were designed in Japan. Toyota managed the plant, and production was split fifty-fifty between Chevrolets and Toyotas.

NUMMI implemented many human resource management innovations. Workers and executives wear the same uniforms, park in the same lots, and eat in the same cafeteria. Workers are grouped in small, self-managing teams. They participate in designing their own jobs and rotate through different jobs. NUMMI's motto is, "There are no managers, no supervisors, only team members."

Lee (1988) used images of dance and poetry to capture NUMMI's approach to designing the production process: "Every motion should be flowing and natural, like a ballet. If a worker has to bend awkwardly to do his job, then the symmetry of his motion is disturbed, and he will tire. 'One should never have to fight the car to build it,' the NUMMI trainer explains. 'If you must hold nine bolts in one hand and fumble with an air wrench in the other, that is clumsy and wasteful.' One understands that the sin of awkwardness, of assembly in fits of effort, is as much an esthetic fault as it is a flaw in the quest for efficiency. The entire system is pure oriental poetry that emphasizes the beauty of the process of life, the grace of 10,000 stalks of rice bending in unison in the winds" (pp. 234–235).

Both union and management stress collaboration. If a worker takes a complaint to the union, the union representative is likely to be accompanied by a member of the company's human relations staff, and the three try to work out the problem on the spot (Holusha, 1989, p. 1). If workers fall behind, they can pull a cord to stop the line; help will arrive quickly. NUMMI's president, Kan Higashi, sees the cord as a sign of trust between management and labor: "We had heavy arguments about installing the cord here. We wondered if workers would pull it just to get a rest. That has not happened" (Holusha, 1989, p. 1).

When car sales slumped for a while in 1988, NUMMI laid no one off. Workers were sent off at full pay to attend training sessions on problem solving and interpersonal relations. One worker commented, "With GM, if the line slowed down, some of us would have been on the street" (Holusha, 1989, p. 1).

Even union leaders like NUMMI. Bruce Lee, a UAW official, said that the team system liberated workers by giving them more control over their jobs and that it is "increasing the plant's productivity and competitiveness while making jobs easier" (Holusha, 1989, p. 1). UAW president Owen Bieber said when he toured the plant, "I was most struck that there is hardly any management here at all" (Lee, 1988, pp. 232–233).

But NUMMI is not paradise. A dissident group within the union says that the brisk work pace at NUMMI amounts to "management by stress" and that the plant's policy on absenteeism is inhumane. A worker absent on more than three different occasions within a three-month period is charged with an "offense." Four offenses in a year means dismissal. But if NUMMI is not perfect, even the dissidents say that the basic concept is good. No one wants to go back to the old GM pattern. Many are happy simply for the chance to make automobiles. As one worker said, "We got a second chance here, and we are trying to take advantage of it. Many people don't get a second chance" (Holusha, 1989, p. 1). GM was sufficiently impressed that it began to implement NUMMI techniques in other plants. Innovations such as self-managing teams that do their own quality audits led to a 21 percent reduction in costs and a substantial increase in quality at GM's plant in Lansing, Michigan (Hampton and Norman, 1987).

Efforts to transfer NUMMI's methods to other GM plants have not, however, always been successful. Specific techniques were sometimes implemented piecemeal in other plants, with predictably marginal results. Team decision making became a fad at GM, but often backfired because managers tended to dictate to the teams (Lee, 1988). Higashi told a *Wall Street Journal* reporter at one point that he was "afraid that the GM upper management does not understand the basic concept" (Schlesinger, 1987, p. 30).

NUMMI had one more problem. By 1989, Toyota could sell all the cars that it produced at NUMMI. GM had stopped producing its version of a Toyota and substituted a design of its own—the Geo Prizm. Unfortunately, GM had trouble selling this new line. Toyota increased its share of production to 60 percent, but the plant still operated below capacity. Some workers demonstrated their limited faith in GM management by voicing their hopes that Toyota would take responsibility for selling as well as making NUMMI's Chevrolets.

As the NUMMI case illustrates, successful applications of the human resource frame are usually not as idyllic as idealists might hope nor as soft as old-line managers often fear. The NUMMI experiment combined creative human resource management with demanding work standards to produce an automobile that was highly competitive in terms of both cost and quality. Such combinations are likely to become increasingly common in the future.

### Critiques of the Human Resource Frame

No sooner had human resource theorists begun to have a significant impact on management thinking than critics set out to question their ideas. Human resource theories have been criticized primarily on two grounds: that they are naive and that they are easily co-opted by power elites (Morrow and Thayer, 1977; Nord, 1974). The first criticism has appeared in several forms:

1. Human resource theorists hold a mistaken conception of human nature and seek to impose an academic, middle-class value system on everyone else.
2. These theorists ignore individual differences and the imperatives of organizational structure.
3. They are too optimistic about the possibility of integrating

individual and organizational needs, and they underplay issues of power, conflict, and scarcity in organizations (Perrow, 1986).

The initial criticism here is difficult to assess because it requires agreement about the nature of "human nature." Is Theory X more valid than Theory Y? It is possible to cite evidence in support of either view, and McGregor felt that either theory could become a self-fulfilling prophesy.

The criticism that human resource theorists ignore individual differences often rests on a misunderstanding of their work. Argyris and McGregor were both careful to acknowledge the existence and importance of individual differences, though neither of them made such differences central to their theories. Similarly, human resource theorists have not entirely ignored structure, though it has rarely been at the center of their concerns. Structural theorists often emphasize the ways that structure constrains choice. Human resource theorists tend to take the opposite tack and argue that choice can constrain structure. Thoroughgoing structuralists (for example, Perrow, 1970) often argue that structural imperatives impose very serious limits on the possibility of creating organizations significantly different from existing ones. Human resource theorists have usually preferred to think of structure as something that can and should be changed to meet human needs.

In their more glowing moods, human resource theorists may indeed become too optimistic about the possibilities for congruence between individual and system. In part, that may derive from their need for a positive myth. But even if integration of individual and organization is an as yet unrealized ideal, believing that such a thing is possible and worthwhile can energize efforts to go beyond the *status quo*.

In response to the second line of criticism, it is fair to say that human resource theorists have generally had little to say about power and the allocation of scarce resources. The classic works of Argyris, McGregor, and Likert devote much attention to concepts such as communication, feedback, and leadership but rarely mention power. In more recent human resource writing, power appears in optimistic and domesticated forms such as "empowerment" (Bennis and Nanus, 1985; Block, 1987) or "power in the service of others" (Greenleaf, 1973; Kouzes and Posner, 1987). Organizational politics, if mentioned at all, is usually viewed as a problem to be solved rather than as a natural and basic phenomenon in organizations.

This limited concern with power and politics is common among managers in the United States and elsewhere. By and large, human resource theorists have assumed that it is possible to make improvements that benefit both employer and employee. They have focused on improvements in organizational climate, management style, and management skills, not on radical changes in the distribution of power. They have rarely asked if there are fundamental differences in the interests of workers and management that are rooted in the larger institutional environment. Not surprisingly, their theories have often received a hospitable welcome in management circles, for they seem to promise to improve productivity and morale with no loss of management authority. Human resource theorists have seldom directly confronted the argument that organizations are instruments of domination (Morgan, 1986) and tools that serve their "masters" (Perrow, 1986). But power and the politics of scarcity are fundamental barriers to increasing the congruence between individual and organization, and human resource theorists will have to tackle that issue more directly than they have in the past.

### Summary

The human resource frame focuses on the fit between individual and organization. Human beings are viewed as having needs that energize their behavior. These include physiological needs, social needs, and needs for self-esteem and self-actualization. When the fit between the needs of an organization and the needs of its participants is good, both benefit: individuals find satisfaction and meaning in work, while the organization is able to make effective use of the talent and energy of its managers and workers. When there is a poor fit, the human resource frame predicts underutilization of human energy and talent, as well as frustration and psychological conflict for the individual. Individuals may become apathetic, put up resistance, or even attempt to sabotage or exploit the organization in return.

Large organizations increasingly face many of the problems predicted by the human resource frame, and more and more effort is being devoted to attempts to solve these problems. Job enrichment, participative management, self-managing teams, organizational democracy, organization development, and Theory Z all represent efforts in that direction.

The knowledge base in organizational behavior is still developing, and it is too early to make a conclusive determination of the validity of the human resource frame or of the solutions that it offers for the human problems that are found in all organizations. Although some of the currently popular "cures" for organizational ills may ultimately prove to be inadequate or misdirected, the need for such cures will continue, and it is likely that further research and experimentation will develop a more valid and comprehensive science of human resource management in organizations.

# Part Four

# THE
# POLITICAL
# FRAME

# 9

# *Power, Conflict, and Coalitions*

At sunrise on January 28, 1986, it was clear but very cold in Cape Canaveral—more like New Hampshire, where Christa McAuliffe was a high school teacher, than Florida. Curtains of ice greeted the ground crews as they inspected the support structures for Flight 51-L, the space shuttle *Challenger*. The temperature had plunged overnight to a record low of twenty-four degrees Fahrenheit (minus four degrees Celsius). The ice team removed as much as they could, and temperatures gradually warmed over the course of the morning. But it was still brisk at 8:30 A.M., and *Challenger*'s crew of seven astronauts noted the ice around them as they climbed into the shuttle. As McAuliffe, the first teacher in space, entered the ship, a NASA technician offered her an apple. She held the apple and beamed, then asked the technician to save it for her until she returned. At 11:38 A.M., *Challenger* lifted off. One minute later, there was a massive explosion in the booster rockets. Millions watched their television screens in horror as the shuttle and its crew were destroyed (Bell and Esch, 1987; McConnell, 1987; Marx, Stubbart, Traub, and Cavanaugh, 1987; Vaughn, 1990).

183

On the eve of the launch, an emergency teleconference had been called between the National Aeronautics and Space Administration (NASA) and the Morton Thiokol Corporation, the contractor that provided solid rocket motors for the shuttle. At the teleconference, a group of Thiokol engineers had pleaded with their superiors and with NASA to delay the launch. They feared that the unusually cold temperatures could cause a failure in synthetic rubber O-rings that sealed joints in the rocket motor. If the rings failed, the motor could blow up. The engineers recommended strongly that NASA wait for warmer weather (McConnell, 1987; Marx, Stubbart, Traub, and Cavanaugh, 1987; Bell and Esch, 1987; Vaughn, 1990). But Thiokol and NASA both faced strong pressures to get the shuttle in the air:

Thiokol had gained the lucrative sole source contract for the solid rocket boosters thirteen years earlier, during a bitterly disputed award process that veteran observers have characterized as a low point in squalid political intrigue. At the time of the award to then relatively small Thiokol Chemical Company in Brigham City, Utah, both the newly appointed chairman of the Senate Aeronautics and Space Science Committee, Democratic Senator Frank Moss, and the new NASA administrator, Dr. James Fletcher, were insiders in the tightly knit Utah political hierarchy. By summer 1985, however, Thiokol's monopoly position was under attack, and the corporation's executives were afraid to risk their billion-dollar contract by halting shuttle flight operations long enough to correct the faulty booster joint design [McConnell, 1987, p. 7].

Meanwhile, managers at NASA were experiencing pressures of their own. As part of their effort to build congressional support for the space program, NASA had promised that the shuttle would eventually pay for itself in cargo fees, like a boxcar in space. The projections of profitability were based on a very ambitious program: twelve flights in 1984, fourteen in 1985, and seventeen in 1986. In practice, NASA had fallen well behind schedule, with only five launches in 1984 and eight in 1985. The promise of "routine access to space" and flights that would eventually pay for themselves looked more and more dubious. With every flight costing the taxpayers about $100 million, NASA needed a lot of money from Congress, but the prospects were getting bleaker. NASA's credibility was eroding while the United States budget deficit was soaring (McConnell, 1987, pp. 28–29).

That was the context in which Thiokol's engineers recommended canceling the next day's launch. The response from NASA officials was swift and pointed. One NASA manager said he was "appalled" at the recommendation, and another said, "My God, Thiokol, when do you want me to launch? Next April?" (McConnell, 1987, p. 196). Thiokol asked for time to caucus. Thiokol's senior managers huddled and then decided, against the advice of their engineers, to recommend the launch. NASA accepted the recommendation, and launched Flight 51-L the next morning. The O-rings failed almost immediately, and the flight was doomed (McConnell, 1987; Marx, Stubbart, Traub, and Cavanaugh, 1987; Bell and Esch, 1987; Vaughn, 1990).

It is extremely disquieting to see political forces corrupting organizational decision making, even highly technical decisions that involve human lives. Why do such things happen? It is tempting to blame such tragedies on individual selfishness, myopia, or stupidity, but that explanation does not help very much. The key decision makers in the *Challenger* case were experienced, highly trained, and intelligent. If we tried to get better people, where would we find them? Even if we found them, how could we ensure that they, too, would not become politicized by the conditions in which they work?

Neither the structural frame nor the human resource frame focuses on the kinds of political issues that led to the *Challenger* disaster. Although there were structural and human resource problems in the space shuttle program, correcting them might not have prevented the tragedy. Neither the orderly, rational images of the structural frame nor the humane and collaborative images of the human resource frame fully capture the world of power and politics found in the *Challenger* incident.

From a structural perspective, organizations are guided by goals and policies set at the top. In the *Challenger* case we find a welter of goals, some inconsistent with one another. Some were set at the top (in the White House and in Congress), others were set by NASA administrators, and many were shaped by no one in particular—they gradually emerged like unwanted weeds from the political swamp.

The human resource frame emphasizes the malfunctions that result from the mismatch between the needs of organizations and the needs of individuals or from the strategies used to manage interpersonal and group dynamics. The mystery-mastery model discussed in Chapter Seven was functioning only too well in the NASA/Thiokol teleconference. But the human resource frame does not speak directly to the underlying political forces that set the stage for conflict and power plays, even though these same political forces confound organizations again and again.

In contrast, the political frame confronts these issues directly. It views organizations as "alive and screaming" political arenas that house a complex variety of individual and group interests. The following five propositions summarize the political perspective.

1. Organizations are *coalitions* composed of varied individuals and interest groups (for example, hierarchical levels, departments, professional groups, gender and ethnic subgroups).

2. There are *enduring differences* among individuals and groups in their values, preferences, beliefs, information, and perceptions of reality. Such differences change slowly, if at all.

3. Most of the important decisions in organizations involve the *allocation of scarce resources:* they are decisions about who gets what.

4. Because of scarce resources and enduring differences, *conflict* is central to organizational dynamics, and *power* is the most important resource.

5. Organizational goals and decisions emerge from bargaining, negotiation, and jockeying for position among members of different coalitions.

All these propositions come to life in the *Challenger* case. The space shuttle program was not something that NASA ran by itself. It was a very complex coalition that included NASA, the contractors, Congress, the White House, the military, the media, and even the American public. Consider, for example, why Christa McAuliffe was on the shuttle. There was scant substantive justification for putting a social science teacher in space; her fellow crew members had little need of her particular kind of expertise. But the American public had grown bored with astronauts who were white male test pilots. Human interest was good for NASA and Congress—it built public support for the space program. It was also good for the media, because it made for more interesting stories. Three years earlier, Dr. Sally Ride had generated excitement as the first female astronaut. Now, the idea of putting an ordinary citizen, a teacher, in space caught the imagination of the American people. Symbolically, Christa McAuliffe represented every American. When she flew, her fellow citizens flew with her.

The president, the press, the public, Congress, the contractors, and NASA were thus all part of the coalition that influenced decision making in the shuttle program. But, as in all coalitions, there were enduring differences in interests among the various coalition members. For example, NASA's interest in receiving funding competed with the public's interest in lower taxes, and the astronauts' interest in safety was at odds with the pressures on NASA and its contractors to maintain an ambitious schedule of space flights.

The political frame asserts that, in the face of enduring differences and scarce resources, conflict among members of a coalition is inevitable and power inevitably becomes a key resource. If resources are scarce, trade-offs have to be made. When there are enduring differences, the parties will disagree on how to reach agreement. Thus, on the eve of the *Challenger* launch, some of the parties in the coalition disagreed about how to balance technical and political concerns. How much risk was it worth to get the shuttle in the air?

The assumptions of the political frame define the sources of political behavior in organizations. They also predict when politics will be visible and dominant in organizations and when they will be invisible. A coalition forms in the first place because of interdependence among coalition members; they need each other, even though their interests may be only partly in harmony. The second assumption—enduring differences—suggests that politics will be more visible and dominant under conditions of diversity than of homogeneity. Agreement and harmony are much easier to achieve in a homogenous group or organization where everyone shares the same values, beliefs, and cultures.

The third characteristic—scarce resources—suggests that politics will be more salient and intense in difficult times. Many teachers and administrators in the American public schools look back to the 1960s as a golden age. School systems grew rapidly and were blessed with abundant resources. School administrators spent their time deciding which buildings to erect and which programs to initiate. The human resource frame became the dominant model for school management—until the 1970s, when the bottom fell out. Taxpayer protests and declining enrollments forced school districts to close schools and lay off teachers. Conflict mushroomed, and many school administrators succumbed to political forces that they could neither understand nor control.

A fourth key political issue is power—its distribution and exercise. Alderfer (1979) and Brown (1983) distinguish between overbounded and underbounded systems. In overbounded systems, power is highly concentrated, and the system is tightly regulated. In underbounded systems, power is diffuse, and the system is very loosely controlled. Overbounded systems regulate politics tightly. Underbounded systems are an open invitation to conflict and power games.

When power is concentrated at the top of a highly regulated system, politics does not disappear, but it is often forced underground. Until Gorbachev and *glasnost* emerged, it was common for westerners to view the Soviets as a vast, undifferentiated mass of people who all thought and felt the same way because they had been brainwashed by decades of government propaganda. The truth was otherwise, but even the so-called experts on Soviet affairs missed its significance (Alterman, 1989). No other nation is more ethnically diverse than the Soviet Union, and seven decades of Communist unity produced remarkably little cultural integration. Ethnic, political, philosophical, and religious differences simmered quietly beneath the surface so long as the Kremlin was able to maintain a tightly regulated society. *Glasnost* took the lid off, leading to a stunning outpouring of debate and dissent. The process was contagious, and Eastern Europe in 1989 was a continual source of surprise: a noncommunist government came to power in Poland, the Hungarian Communist party abandoned communism, the Berlin Wall came down, and the old order collapsed in Bulgaria, Czechoslovakia, and Romania.

A similar process with a tragic climax occurred in the democracy movement in China. A decade of economic reform encouraged increasing numbers of Chinese to test the limits of political liberalization. The diversity and discontent that had been driven underground in earlier years erupted everywhere. Because disagreement extended even to the top of the Chinese Communist hierarchy, the government response was hesitant and contradictory for more than a month (Kristoff, 1989). Conservatives, led by the venerable Deng Xiaoping, finally won the internal battle, and the crackdown in Beijing brought a brutal end to the democracy movement of 1989. But ending overt protest is very different from eliminating the underlying forces that produced the tumult in the first place. Many Chinese recalled the words of the great writer Lu Xun: "Lies written in ink cannot obscure a truth written in blood." The forces of protest went underground once again, to await another opportunity to surface in the future (Kristoff, 1989).

The final proposition of the political frame emphasizes that organizational goals arise not from fiat at the top, but from an ongoing process of negotiation and interaction among the key players in any system. The aftermath of Tiananmen Square in China provided one of many examples. Shortly after the crackdown, the Chinese Communist leadership announced a major purge to rid the party of the disloyal and the "capitalist roaders." Yet a year later, almost no one had been purged. Even prominent opponents of the crackdown had not yet been expelled, though a few found that their application for membership renewal was taking longer than usual. The fierce internal bargaining resulting from continuing divisions within the party severely limited the ability of the top leaders to implement their announced intentions.

The propositions of the political frame do not attribute politics to individual selfishness, myopia, or incompetence. They assert that interdependence, difference, scarcity, and power relations will inevitably produce political forces, regardless of the players. It is naive and romantic to hope that politics can be eliminated in organizations. Managers can, however, learn to understand and manage political processes.

## Organizations as Coalitions

Traditional views of organizations—both academic and common-sense views—assume that organizations have, or ought to have, clear and consistent goals. Generally, the goals are presumed to be established by those in authority. In business firms, the owners, or the top managers, are typically assumed to set the goal of maximizing profits. In public agencies, the assumption is usually that goals are set by the legislature and the executive to whom the agency is accountable. In a parliamentary system, for example, the goals of a ministry are presumably set by the chief administrator in ways that are consistent with the policies of the government in power. This view of goal setting is explicit in structural conceptions of management. The purpose of bureaucracy is to enhance rationality, but rationality is definable only if we have a reasonably clear sense of organizational objectives and tasks. A similar view is implicit in most human resource approaches.

The political frame, however, insists that organizational goals are set through negotiations among the members of coalitions. Different individuals and groups have different objectives and resources, and each attempts to bargain with other members or coalitions to influence goals and the decision-making process. Cyert and March (1963) explain the difference between structural and political views of organizational goals: "To what extent is it arbitrary, in conventional accounting, that we call wage payments 'costs' and dividend payments 'profit,' rather than the other way around? Why is it that in our quasi-genetic moments we are inclined to say that in the beginning there was a manager, and he recruited workers and capital? . . . The emphasis on the asymmetry has seriously confused the understanding of organizational goals. The confusion arises because ultimately it makes only slightly more sense to say that the goal of a business enterprise is to maximize profit than to say that its goal is to maximize the salary of Sam Smith, assistant to the janitor" (p. 30).

What Cyert and March are saying is something like this: Smith, the assistant janitor, Jones, the foreman, and Miller, the company president, are all members of a grand coalition, Miller Enterprises. All of them make demands on the coalition, and each bargains to get those demands met. Miller is in a more powerful position than Smith or Jones but she does not have a divine or inalienable right to determine the organizational goals. Her influence depends on how much power she mobilizes in comparison with the power of Smith and Jones and other members of the coalition.

There will be times when Smith, perhaps in combination with his colleagues in the union, will be able to mobilize more power than Miller. At those times, Smith and friends will leverage their own demands into the organization's goals. Miller, Jones, and Smith may all continue to believe that the goals are what Miller says they are (for example, "to make a fair profit while providing high-quality goods and services to customers and meeting our social responsibilities"). But Miller's goal statements are, at best, partial indications of the company's real objectives. They may, in fact, be mostly ceremonial. An analyst who compared Miller's public statements with the organization's actual pattern of decisions would probably conclude that the organization is irrational—it gives things that reduce profits or hamper efficiency to both workers and executives. From a political view, that is to be expected in a world of divergent interest groups, each doing its best to impose its own demands on the organizational agenda.

If political pressures on organizational goals are visible in private organizations, they are often blatant in the public sector. As we saw in the *Challenger* incident, public agencies typically operate amid a complex welter of constituencies, each making policy demands and using whatever resources it can muster to enforce those demands. The result, typically, is a confusing multiplicity of goals, many of which are in conflict with one another.

Universities, for example, are commonly assumed to have the primary goal of educating students. This assumption accounted for the puzzlement felt by an administrator at an elite university when the faculty resisted his suggestion for a more systematic approach to scheduling courses. He said, scratching his head, "I often get the feeling that the faculty seem to be scheduling classes for their own convenience." The administrator felt that this was a surprising and deviant practice, but then, he was relatively new to the university. After receiving more political lessons, he recognized that educating students is only one of many goals at a university and that each of these goals represents the interests of one or more of the university's major constituencies. Universities have to make a reasonable stab at educating students, because students and their allies often have power to enforce their demands on institutional policy. But faculty members are also powerful. Particularly in prestigious institutions, they are willing to use their power to ensure that class schedules do not unduly interfere with their research or, in some cases, their consulting. Is the university's goal education, or research, or the enhancement of faculty life-styles? From a political perspective, it is all the above and more.

### Power and Decision Making

In analyzing power, structural theorists emphasize authority: the legitimate, formal prerogative to make decisions that are binding on others. Managers make decisions that subordinates must accept. School principals make decisions for teachers, and teachers make decisions for students. Welfare workers make decisions for clients, and union leaders make decisions for their membership. The structural perspective emphasizes the primacy of authority as a mechanism for implementing organizational goals. Managers make rational decisions (optimal decisions consistent with the organization's purposes), monitor the actions of subordinates to make sure that the decisions are implemented, and evaluate how well subordinates carry out the directives.

Human resource theorists have typically placed little emphasis on power, though in recent years many of them have become enchanted with the notion of *empowerment* (Bennis and Nanus, 1985; Block, 1987). Unlike structuralists, human resource writers emphasize the limits and difficulties inherent in the exercise of authority. Since authority is primarily a one-way influence mechanism, it often impedes the integration of organizational and individual needs. When A can influence B, but not vice versa, there is a good chance that the relationship will be more satisfying for A than for B. Human resource theorists have tended to focus on forms of influence that enhance mutuality and collaboration. The implicit message is that participation, openness, and collaboration make power a nonissue.

The political frame views authority as only one among a number of other forms of power. It also acknowledges the existence and importance of human (and group) needs but focuses on situations of scarce resources and incompatible preferences where different needs collide. We can illustrate the difference between human resource and political perspectives by considering a case of policy conflict. Thus, a group of graduate students in a university department wants the university to become more democratic and responsive, while a group of faculty members in the same department insists that the university needs to tighten controls and standards. The human resource theorist is likely to ask: What are the needs and perspectives of each group? How can these two groups engage in a productive dialogue so that they can learn from one another, explore the differences in their positions, and find a solution that will integrate their different views? The human resource view assumes that the incompatibility of preferences can be reduced: that a win-win outcome is possible. The structural perspective assumes that some solutions are "better" than others—because they are based on better analysis or because they produce better shared outcomes—and that the parties can learn to recognize better solutions through rational exploration and open dialogue.

The political theorist is more likely to view divergent interests and conflict over scarce resources as an enduring fact of organizational life and is less likely to be optimistic about distinguishing among better and worse solutions. The question becomes, How does each group articulate its own preferences and mobilize power to get what it wants?

Gamson's (1968) analysis of political processes focuses on two major players in a social system: authorities and partisans. Authorities are defined essentially as the people who are entitled to make binding decisions. Gamson describes the relationship between authorities and partisans in this way: "Authorities are the recipients or targets of influence, and the agents or initiators of social control.

Potential partisans have the opposite roles—as agents or initiators of influence, and targets or recipients of social control" (p. 76).

As an example, parents often function as authorities, while children function as potential partisans in a family. Parents make binding decisions about such matters as who goes to bed when, when the television set can be turned on, and which child gets to use a particular toy. Parents initiate social control, and children are the targets or recipients of parental decisions. Precisely because the children are affected significantly by these decisions, they often attempt to exert influence on the decision makers. They will argue for a later bedtime or point out the unfairness of giving one child something that another does not have. They may try to split the authorities by getting something from one parent after the other has refused. They may form coalitions (with siblings, grandparents, and so on) in an attempt to strengthen their bargaining position.

The universal significance of the battle between authorities and partisans can be seen in the popular American comic strip "Calvin and Hobbes." Its hero, six-year-old Calvin, assures his mother that his stuffed tiger will eat her if she tries to put him to bed before nine. When his parents send him to bed without dinner, he telephones for delivery of a pizza with pepperoni. Dragged unwillingly through an art museum, Calvin imagines that he is a ferocious tyrannosaur, able to destroy people and paintings at will. His parents recognize that they are in constant danger of losing the battle for social control: his father muses about calling the orphanage, while his mother wishes that she had been blessed with a girl.

Social control is essential to those in formal positions because their authority depends on it. Officeholders retain authority only if the system remains viable. If partisan conflict becomes too powerful for the authorities to control, their positions are undermined. The process can be very swift, as events in Eastern Europe in 1989 illustrated. Established regimes had lost much of their legitimacy with the populace years earlier but held on through coercion and control of access to decision making. The senior *apparatchiki* had reason to hold on: their power and perquisites were tied to maintaining the "leading role" of the Communist party. As massive demonstrations erupted, the authorities faced an unnerving choice: they could use the police and army in hopes of preserving their power, or watch their power evaporate. Authorities in China and Romania chose the first course. That path led to bloodshed in both cases, but only the Chinese were able to quell the opposition—for a time. Elsewhere in Eastern Europe, the efforts of authorities to accommodate dissent were futile, and their power evaporated as swiftly as water in a desert.

The period of evaporation is heady but dangerous. The question is whether new authority can constitute itself quickly enough to avoid chaos. Authorities and partisans both have reason to fear a specter such as Lebanon represented in the 1980s—perpetual turmoil, with no authority able to bring partisan conflict under control. Still, when partisans are convinced that the existing authority is too evil or incompetent to continue, they often take that risk. Gamson (1968) and Baldridge (1971) both suggest that it depends on how much a given group of partisans trusts (or mistrusts) existing authority.

In the early years of the New Deal, the U.S. Supreme Court consistently invalidated major pieces of economic and social legislation that the Roosevelt administration was able to pass through Congress. Political conservatives were aghast when Roosevelt proposed to increase the size of the Court, a tactic that would have permitted him to appoint justices who were more likely to vote his way. In the 1930s, conservatives trusted the Court and wanted to protect its authority. Twenty years later, the tables were turned and a much more liberal Supreme Court attracted the wrath of political conservatives. They began to argue for curbing the power of a "runaway" Court, while liberals became staunch defenders of the Court's legitimacy. In the 1980s, the pendulum swung once again, as a succession of Republican presidents (Reagan and Bush) began to appoint justices of a more conservative cast.

These shifts in views of the Court illustrate Gamson's suggestion that partisans will trust authorities when they expect them to make "correct" decisions. When trust is high, potential partisans are unlikely to become mobilized; they will leave the authorities alone and even support them if they are attacked. But when trust is low and partisan groups expect the decisions of the authority to be bad, they will try to wrest power away—unless they see the authorities as too powerful to confront.

Even though partisans do not have authority, they do have a number of potential sources of power. A number of social scientists (French and Raven, 1959; Baldridge, 1971; Kanter, 1977) have tried to address the question, What must individuals and groups have in order to be powerful? The most significant forms of power include the following:

1. *Position power (authority).* Organizational positions, or roles, are associated with certain kinds and amounts of formal power. The higher an individual's position in an authority hierarchy, the more power that individual typically has.

2. *Information and expertise.* Power flows to those who have the information and know-how to solve important and vexing problems. For example, power flows to marketing experts in consumer products industries, to the faculty in elite universities, and to superstar conductors of symphony orchestras. Shifts in the environment may produce shifts in power. As the American health care industry experienced increasing financial and competitive pressures in the 1980s, power began to shift from the physicians (who were best at problems related to medical care) to managers (who were better at managing money and markets).

3. *Control of rewards.* People who can deliver jobs, money, political support, and other valued rewards can be extremely powerful. Political bosses in cities such as Chicago and New York kept themselves in power for years through their control of patronage, public services, and other rewards.

4. *Coercive power.* Coercive power rests on the ability to constrain, to block, to interfere, or to punish. A union's ability to walk out, students' ability to sit in, and an army's ability to clamp down are all examples of coercive power in action.

5. *Alliances and networks.* Getting things done in organizations involves working through a complex network of relationships among individuals and groups, and this is a lot easier to do if you have friends and allies. Kotter (1982) found that one of the key differences between more successful and less successful senior managers was the skill and attention they gave to building and cultivating their network of friends and allies. Less successful managers spent too little time building their networks and had much more difficulty getting things done.

6. *Access to and control of agendas.* Two of the by-products of networks and alliances are access to decision-making arenas and the ability to influence the agendas in those arenas. Many political systems, such as the *apartheid* system in South Africa, give some groups access to power while denying access to other groups. When decisions are made, the interests of those who have access are well represented, while the concerns and interests of absent parties are often distorted or ignored (Lukes, 1974; Brown, 1986).

7. *Control of meaning and symbols.* Elites and opinion leaders often have substantial ability to define and even impose the meanings and myths by which a group or an organization defines who they are, what they believe in, and what they value. Viewed positively, this is the capacity of leaders to provide meaning and hope. Viewed more cynically, this is the ability of elites to convince the powerless to accept and support social structures and decision-making processes that are not in their best interests (Brown, 1986). Several authors have observed that this can be a very subtle and unobtrusive form of power: when the powerless accept the myths promulgated by the powerful, conflict and power struggles may disappear (Brown, 1986; Frost, 1985; Gaventa, 1980).

8. *Personal power.* Individuals with charisma, political skills, verbal facility, or the capacity to articulate vision are powerful by virtue of their personal characteristics, in addition to whatever other power they may have.

The presence of multiple forms of power constrains the capacity of authorities to make decisions. People who rely solely on their authority often undermine their own power; they generate resistance and are outflanked, outmaneuvered, or overrun by individuals and groups who are more versatile in the exercise of power. Kotter (1985) argues that managerial jobs come with a built-in "power gap": the power conferred by a position is rarely enough to get the job done. Expertise, rewards, coercion, allies, and personal power all help to close the gap.

The existence of multiple power centers and multiple pressures helps to explain why so many administrators seem more powerful to their subordinates than to themselves. University presidents, for example, are often seen as exalted, remote, and very powerful figures by students and faculty. Yet one president remarked ruefully that his primary job seemed to be to provide "sex for the students, parking for the faculty, and football for the alumni." The remark was half facetious, but it reflects an important reality: it is costly for the president to make any decision, however correct and necessary, that produces rebellion in a major constituency. Students can rebel, faculty can boycott classes and make damaging statements in the press, and alumni can stop contributing to the university. The president's power lies particularly in *zones of indifference*—areas in which few people care deeply about what the president decides. On other issues, presidents are so heavily constrained by partisan pressures that it may be all they can do to keep conflict down to a manageable level so that the university can continue to function.

Of course, not all chief executives feel hemmed in by a welter of political forces. The political constraints on a decision maker will vary with the power of the decision maker and with the satisfaction or dissatisfaction of potential partisans. The chief executive who owns the company will feel fewer constraints than one who is watched closely by a majority shareholder. Individuals with expertise, strong track records, and high charisma are likely to have a great deal of latitude in making decisions. This is particularly true when things are going well and constituencies are basically satisfied. If an organization sets new profit records every year, it is unlikely that stockholders will besiege the management with complaints and demands for change. As many company presidents have learned, however, the first bad quarter can suddenly elicit a steady stream of letters and telephone calls from board members, stockholders, and financial analysts. After a series of management and marketing snafus, Apple Computer's board of directors chose to remove Steven Jobs as chief executive, even though he was the co-founder and the largest single stockholder of this highly successful company. The zone of indifference can expand or contract markedly, depending on how the organization is doing in the eyes of its major constituents.

## Conflict in Organizations

The structural perspective emphasizes social control and norms of rationality. From this point of view, conflict is a problem that interferes with the accomplishment of organizational purposes. Hierarchical conflict raises the possibility that the lower levels will ignore or subvert management directives. Conflict among major partisan groups can undermine an organization's effectiveness and the ability of its leadership to function. Such dangers are precisely why the structural perspective emphasizes the need for a hierarchy of authority. A basic function of authorities is to resolve conflict. If two individuals or departments cannot resolve a conflict between them, they take it to higher authorities who adjudicate the conflict and make a final decision that is consistent with the organization's goals.

From a political perspective, conflict is not necessarily a problem or a sign that something is amiss in an organization. Organizational resources are in short supply: there is not enough money to give everyone what they want, and there are too many jobs at the bottom and too few at the top. If one group controls the policy process, others may be frozen out. Individuals compete for jobs, titles, and prestige. Departments compete for resources and power. Interest groups vie for policy concessions. Under such conditions, conflict is natural and inevitable.

Environmental imperatives sometimes compel organizations to cope with increasing diversity, which often entails higher levels of conflict. This happened to American public schools in the 1970s and 1980s as increasing cultural diversity in the society forced them to cope with large numbers of highly vocal interest groups that were often in conflict both with school authorities and with one another.

Or consider the dilemma that confronted many large Japanese corporations in the late 1980s. Though firms such as Toyota and Matsushita had long had sales and production facilities overseas, the big decisions were still made by senior managers in Japan ("The Multinational, Eastern Style," 1989). As overseas operations grew, centralized decision making became more and more difficult. Changing conditions called for more autonomous units headed by local managers—European subsidiaries run by Europeans and American subsidiaries run by Americans. But that strategy carried an unavoidable price. More diversity meant less cultural homogeneity and more conflict, undermining a distinctive feature of Japanese firms. Europeans at the head of a European unit might respond more quickly and appropriately to local conditions, but they would also see things differently from the senior leadership in Japan.

Politically, conflict is not necessarily a bad thing. The focus in the political frame is not on the *resolution* of conflict (as is often the case in both the structural and human resource frames) but on the *strategy* and *tactics* of conflict. Since conflict is not going to go away, the question is how individuals and groups can make the best of it. It is important to note that conflict has benefits as well as costs: "A tranquil, harmonious organization may very well be an apathetic, uncreative, stagnant, inflexible, and unresponsive organization. Conflict challenges the status quo, stimulates interest and curiosity. It is the root of personal and social change, creativity, and innovation. Conflict encourages new ideas and approaches to problems, stimulating innovation" (Heffron, 1989, p. 185).

Brown (1983) and Heffron (1989) both note that there can be both too much and too little conflict in organizations and that intervention may be needed to increase or decrease conflict, depending on the situation. Conflict is particularly likely to occur at the boundaries, or interfaces, between different groups and units. *Horizontal conflict* occurs in the interface between different departments or divisions in an organization: between sales and production in manufacturing concerns, between different schools in the same city, between staff and line in public agencies. *Vertical conflict* occurs between different levels in a hierarchy: between teachers and principal in a school, between headquarters and divisions in a large corporation, or between students and the Chinese government in Tiananmen Square. *Cultural conflict* occurs between two groups with different values, traditions, beliefs, and life-styles: between blacks and whites in South Africa, between Catholics and Protestants in Northern Ireland, between Hindus and Sikhs in India. Cultural conflicts in the larger society are often imported into organizations, but organizations can create cultural conflicts of their own. The culture of management is different from the culture of blue-collar workers, and workers who become supervisors sometimes must struggle with the cultural adjustments required by their new role.

## Moral Mazes: The Politics of Getting Ahead

"Not long after the 'big purge' at Covenant Corporation, when 600 people were fired, the CEO spent $1 million for a 'Family Day' to 'bring everyone together.' The massive party was attended by over 14,000 people and featured clowns, sports idols, and booths complete with beanbag and ring tosses, foot and bus races, computer games, dice rolls, and, perhaps appropriately, mazes. In his letter to his 'Fellow Employees' following the event, the CEO said, 'I think Family Day made a very strong statement about the "family" of employees at Corporate Headquarters. And that is that we can accomplish whatever we set out to do if we work together; if we share the effort, we will share the rewards'" (Jackall, 1988, p. 37).

Jackall adds that "wise and ambitious managers resist the lulling platitudes of unity, though they invoke them with fervor, and look for the inevitable clash of interests beneath the bouncy, cheerful surface of corporate life" (p. 37). Beneath that surface is a world of circles and alliances, dominance and submission, conflict and self-interest, and, in Jackall's phrase, "moral mazes." Everyone understands that in most organizations, there are many jobs at the bottom and few at the top. Moving up in the organization inevitably involves competition for the scarce resource of promotion to bigger and better jobs. The preferred myth is that it is a free and fair competition in which those who perform better will always win, at least in the long run.

But assessing performance in managerial jobs is fraught with ambiguity. There are multiple criteria, and some criteria can be assessed only through the subjective judgments of observers (particularly bosses and other superiors). It is often hard to separate individuals' performance from the performance of those around them and from a host of environmental factors. Did the Thiokol engineers who fought to stop the launch of the shuttle *Challenger* deserve high grades because of their persistence and integrity or low grades because they failed to convince senior managers? When some of those same engineers "blew the whistle" and went public with criticisms of Thiokol, was that good performance or bad? Whistleblowers are regularly lauded by the press, yet punished or banished by their employers.

Managers frequently learn that getting ahead is a matter of their personal "credibility" and that such credibility comes from doing what is socially and politically correct in the context of their organization. That context reflects tacit forms of power that are deeply embedded in organizational patterns and structure (Frost, 1986). Jackall reports, for example, that in Covenant Corporation, a visit by the CEO to a plant meant spending $100,000 for new paint, along with $10,000 for a glossy book, complete with full-color photographs, describing the plant's achievements. Such expectations defined the rules of the game, and the game focused middle managers' attention on how to win rather than on the value of the game itself. Subtly and gradually, the organizational definition of the "right things" often weakens and undermines whatever values and moral principles managers bring with them to organizational life.

Getting ahead and making it to the top dominate the thinking of many managers and the social-political structure of many organizations (Dalton, 1959; Jackall, 1988; Ritti and Funkhouser, 1982). That being the case, there is clearly a need for both organizations and individuals to develop constructive and positive ways to master organizational politics. The question is not whether organizations will have politics, but what kind of politics. Will they be energizing or debilitating, hostile or constructive, devastating or creative? Jackall's view is pessimistic: "Bureaucracy breaks apart the ownership of property from its control, social independence from occupation, substance from appearances, action from responsibility, obligation from guilt, language from meaning, and notions of truth from reality. Most important, and at the bottom of all of these fractures, it breaks apart the older connection between the meaning of work and salvation. In the bureaucratic world, one's success, one's sign of election, no longer depends on an inscrutable God, but on the capriciousness of one's superiors and the market; and one achieves economic salvation to the extent that one pleases and submits to new gods, that is, one's bosses and the exigencies of an impersonal market" (Jackall, 1988, pp. 191-192). This is not a pretty picture, but it is accurate for many organizations and managers. More productive politics are possible but are not easy to implement. In the next chapter we will discuss some of the possibilities for doing so.

## Summary

The traditional view of organizations is that they are created and controlled by legitimate authorities, who set the goals, design the structure, hire and manage the employees, and seek to ensure that the organization functions in ways that are consistent with their objectives. The political frame offers a different perspective. Authorities control the power of position inherent in occupying an office, but they are only one among many contenders for other forms of power in the organization. Each contender has different preferences and beliefs. All contenders have access to various forms of power, and all compete for their share of scarce resources in a limited organizational pie.

The political perspective suggests that the goals, structure, and policies of an organization emerge from an ongoing process of bargaining and negotiating among the major interest groups. Sometimes, the legitimate authorities are the dominant members of the organizational coalition: this is likely to be the case in a small, entrepreneurial organization where the chief executive is also the owner. But large corporations are often controlled by senior management rather than by the stockholders or the board of directors. Government agencies may be controlled more by the permanent civil servants than by the political leaders at the top. The dominant group in a school district may be the teachers' union rather than the school board or the superintendent. In all such cases, naive, rational observers will feel that something is wrong. Like the puzzled university administrator who was surprised by faculty resistance to coordinated class schedules, they will feel that the wrong people are moving the organizational agenda in the wrong direction. But the political view suggests that the exercise of power is a natural part of an ongoing contest. Those who get and use power best will be winners.

There is no guarantee that those who gain power will use it wisely or justly. But it is *not* inevitable that power and politics are always demeaning and destructive. Constructive politics is a possibility, and a necessary possibility if we are to create institutions and societies that are both just and efficient.

# 10

# *The Manager as Politician*

The managers who decided to launch the space shuttle *Challenger* did not believe they were making a decision that would destroy the shuttle and kill seven astronauts. Everyone knew that there were risks, but there are *always* risks and judgments *always* have to be made about which risks are acceptable. Even in areas that are highly technical, momentous judgments can be distorted by political pressures. How can we try to prevent such catastrophes?

Many believe that the answer is simply to get politics out of management. Consider Benno Schmidt, whose leadership style as president of Yale University was described as "hard-nosed practicality doled out with a notable lack of levity" (Radin, 1989, p. 20). Criticized for being uncompromising and for not understanding the political dimension of his job, Schmidt's response was crisp: "I am not a politician. And I resist political measures of this job or this institution. In this job, the test of success is substance, not form, not posturing. I want to represent a different point of view: objectivity, principle as distinct from politics. I am resistant to a lot of the style and trappings people have come to associate with leadership of any sort in this society" (p. 20).

Though we wish Schmidt well (one of us is a Yale alumnus), we are skeptical about his philosophy of university leadership. Politics will not go away whenever the basic conditions of the political frame are present: enduring differences, scarce resources, and inter-dependence. Enduring differences mean that people will interpret events and situations differently and will often have difficulty agree-ing on what is important or even what is true. Scarce resources mean that no one can have everything that he or she wants and that decisions about who gets what must constantly be made. Interde-pendence means that people cannot simply ignore one another: they need each other's assistance, support, and resources. Under these conditions, attempts to eliminate politics drives them under the rug and into the closet, where they become even more counterproductive and unmanageable. We need instead to develop an image of positive politics and of the manager as constructive politician.

### Two Faces of Politics

McClelland (1975) describes two faces of power. The negative face is power as exploitation and personal dominance. The positive face is power as a means of creating visions and collective goals. Might there be two faces of politics as well? Everyone knows the negative face. The positive one is more elusive. Politicians and politics are widely scorned. What good can be said about a perspective that emphasizes power, conflict, bargaining, and self-interest? Consider the following case:

"'Doris Randall' was the new head of backwater purchasing department that she feared would join personnel and public rela-tions as the 'three Ps' of women's ghettoized job assignments in the electronics industry. But she eventually parlayed technical informa-tion from users of the department's services into an agreement from her boss to allow her to make the first wave of changes. No one in her position had ever had such close contacts with users before, and Randall found this a potent basis for reorganizing her unit into a set of user-oriented specialties" (Kanter, 1983, p. 219).

Doris Randall is a constructive politician. Starting from a weak position, she built a support base by establishing relation-ships with the people whose assistance she needed. She understood the essentials of effective leadership and management. Leaders and managers can never fully escape a fundamental dilemma: how to con-front the realities of diversity, scarcity, and self-interest, and still chan-nel human action in cooperative and socially valuable directions.

Kotter (1985) contends that too many managers are either naive or cynical. The naive see the world through rose-colored glasses;
they never want to believe that people are selfish, dishonest, or exploitative. The cynical believe the opposite: everyone is selfish, everything is political, and "get them before they get you" is the best guide
to conduct. Kotter believes that, in America, the naive outnumber the
cynical but that neither stance is effective: "Organizational excellence
. . . demands a sophisticated type of social skill: a leadership skill that
can mobilize people and accomplish important objectives despite dozens of obstacles; a skill that can pull people together for meaningful
purposes despite the thousands of forces that push us apart; a skill
that can keep our corporations and public institutions from descending into a mediocrity characterized by bureaucratic infighting, parochial politics, and vicious power struggles" (p. 11).

Kotter's view suggests that it is in the best interests of both
individual and organization for managers to be "benevolent politicians." For Kotter, this requires steering a course between naiveté
and cynicism: "Beyond the yellow brick road of naiveté and the
mugger's land of cynicism, there is a narrow path, poorly lighted,
hard to find, and even harder to stay on once found. People who
have the skill and the perseverance to take that path serve us in
countless ways. We need more of these people. Many more" (Kotter,
1985, p. xi).

What does that path look like? Why would anyone choose to
follow it? Kotter's answer is primarily pragmatic. The reason to
follow the path is that it works, both for the individual and for the
larger society. But staying on the path requires the ability both to
understand and diagnose diversity and complexity and to accumulate and use power effectively. Kotter believes that following such
a path is a moral undertaking, but his distinction between leadership and cynicism emphasizes results rather than ethics: leadership
produces collective action in the service of organizational goals,
while cynicism leads to parochial politics.

### Skills of the Manager as Politician

What political skills does a manager need? In a world of scarcity,
diversity, and conflict, the politically astute manager needs to de-

velop an agenda, build a base of support for that agenda, and learn how to manage relations with those who might support or resist the agenda. This requires understanding and skill in three major areas: (1) agenda setting (Kanter, 1983; Kotter, 1988; Smith, 1988); (2) networking and forming coalitions (Kanter, 1983; Kotter, 1982, 1985, 1988; Smith, 1988); and (3) bargaining and negotiating (Bellow and Moulton, 1978; Fisher and Ury, 1981; Lax and Sebenius, 1986).

*Agenda Setting.* Kanter (1983), in her study of internal entrepreneurs in American corporations, Kotter (1988), writing about effective corporate leaders, and Smith (1988), writing about effective U.S. presidents, all concluded that the first step in effective leadership is setting an agenda. In Kotter's view, effective leaders create an "agenda for change" that has two major elements: a *vision* of what can and should be, which considers the legitimate long-term interests of the parties involved, and a *strategy for achieving that vision,* which considers the relevant organizational and environmental forces. The agenda must provide a sense of direction while addressing the concerns of both the leader and other major stakeholders. The manager as politician needs to be familiar with the major stakeholders and understand their values, goals, and local agendas.

Kanter (1983) argues that "active listening to the information circulating in the neighborhood is really the first step in the generation of an innovative accomplishment" (p. 218). Only by knowing what others care about can you fashion your agenda in a way that will respond to their concerns: "While gathering information, entrepreneurs can also be 'planting seeds'—leaving the kernel of an idea behind and letting it germinate and blossom so that it begins to float around the system from many sources other than the innovator. Problem identification often precedes project definition, for there may be many conflicting views in the organization about the best method of reaching the goals. Discovering the basis for these conflicting perspectives while gathering hard technical data is critical at this stage" (p. 218).

A vision is inert without a strategy to make it happen. The strategy has to reflect a sound understanding of the major forces that work for and against the agenda. Smith (1988) makes this point about the American presidency: "In the grand scheme of American government, the paramount task and power of the president is to articulate the national purpose: to fix the nation's agenda. Of all the big games at the summit of American politics, the agenda game must be won first. The effectiveness of the presidency and the capacity of any president to lead depends on focusing the nation's political attention and its energies on two or three top priorities. From the standpoint of history, the flow of events seems to have immutable logic, but political reality is inherently chaotic: it contains no automatic agenda. Order must be imposed" (p. 333).

Almost no job has an automatic agenda. The bigger the job, the more difficult it is to wade through all the issues clamoring for attention and to bring order out of chaos. Contrary to Woody Allen's dictum, success in management requires a good deal more than just showing up. High office, even if the incumbent has great personal popularity, is no guarantee of success. Smith (1988) asserts that President Ronald Reagan was remarkably successful in his first year as president because he followed a classic strategy for winning the agenda game: "First impressions are critical. In the agenda game, a swift beginning is crucial for a new president to establish himself as leader—to show the nation that he will make a difference in people's lives. The first one hundred days are the vital test; in those weeks, the political community and the public measure a new president—to see whether he is active, dominant, sure, purposeful" (p. 334).

Reagan began with a vision but not a strategy. He was not gifted as a manager or strategist, though he had extraordinary ability to simplify complex issues and paint a picture in broad, symbolic brush strokes. Reagan's staff had painstakingly studied the first 100 days of his four predecessors. The staff concluded that it was essential in the early days to move with speed and focus. Pushing other agenda items to one side, they focused on two things: cutting taxes and cutting the federal budget. They also discovered a secret weapon in David Stockman, the only person in the Reagan White House who really understood the federal budget process. Stockman himself later admitted that he was astounded by the "low level of fiscal literacy" of Reagan and his key advisers (Smith, 1988, p. 354). According to Smith, "Stockman got a jump on everyone else for two reasons: he had an agenda and a legislative blueprint already prepared, and he understood the real levers of power. Two terms as a Michigan congressman plus a network of key Republican and Democratic connections had taught Stockman how to play the power game" (pp. 351–352). Reagan and his advisors had the vision. Stockman gave them the strategy.

*Networking and Coalition Building.* The *Challenger* disaster occurred even though engineers at both Morton Thiokol and NASA had been aware of the O-ring problem for a long time. They had tried to call it to their superiors' attention, mostly by writing memos. Six months before the *Challenger* accident, Roger Boisjoly, an engineer at Morton Thiokol, wrote a memo saying, "The result [of an O-ring failure] would be a catastrophe of the highest order—loss of human life" (Bell and Esch, 1987, p. 45). Two months later, another engineer at Thiokol wrote a memo that opened, "HELP! The seal task force is constantly being delayed by every possible means" (Bell and Esch, 1987, p. 45). That memo went on to detail the resistance that the task force was getting from other departments in the company.

A memo to your boss is sometimes an effective political strategy, but it more often is a sign of powerlessness and lack of political skill and sophistication. Kotter (1985) suggests four basic steps for dealing with the political dimensions in managerial work:

1.  Identify the relevant relationships (figure out who needs to be led).
2.  Assess who might resist cooperation, why, and how strongly (figuring out where the leadership challenges will be).
3.  Develop, wherever possible, relationships with those people to facilitate the communication, education, or negotiation processes needed to deal with resistance.
4.  When step three fails, carefully select and implement more subtle or more forceful methods.

The political frame emphasizes that no strategy will work without a power base. Managers always face a "power gap": managerial jobs never come with enough power to get the work done (Kotter, 1985). Managerial work can only be done with the cooperation of other people, often large numbers of people. Moving up the ladder brings more authority, but it also brings more dependence because the manager's success depends on the effort of large and diverse groups of people, sometimes numbering in the hundreds or thousands (Kotter, 1985, 1988). Rarely will those people provide their best efforts and fullest cooperation merely because they have been told to. If you want their assistance, it helps a great deal if they know you, like you, and see you as credible and competent.

The first task in building networks and coalitions is to figure out whose help you need. The second is to develop relationships with those people. You want them to be there when you need them. Kanter (1983) found that middle managers seeking to promote change or innovation in a corporation typically began by getting preliminary agreement for an initiative from their boss. They then moved into a phase of "preselling" or "making cheerleaders": "Peers, managers of related functions, stakeholders in the issue, potential collaborators, and sometimes even customers would be approached individually, in one-on-one meetings that gave people a chance to influence the project and the innovator the maximum opportunity to sell it. Seeing them alone and on their territory was important: the rule was to act as if each person were *the* most important one for the project's success" (p. 223).

Once you have cheerleaders, you can move on to "horse trading," that is, promising rewards in exchange for resources and support. This builds the resource base that lets you go to the next step of "securing blessings"—getting the necessary approvals and mandates from higher management (Kanter, 1983). Kanter found that the usual route to success at that stage was to identify the senior managers who had the most to say about the issue at hand, and develop a polished, formal presentation to get their support. The best presentations responded to both substantive and technical concerns, because senior managers typically cared about two questions: (1) Is it a good idea? (2) How will my constituents react to it? Once innovators got the blessing of higher management, they could go back to their boss to formalize the coalition and make specific plans for pursuing the project (Kanter, 1983).

The basic point is simple: as a manager, you need friends and allies to get things done. If you are trying to build relationships and get support from those friends and allies, you need to cultivate them. Hard-core rationalists and incurable romantics sometimes react with horror to such a picture. If what they want is right, why should they have to play political games to get it accepted? Like it or not, however, political dynamics are inevitable under conditions of ambiguity, diversity, and scarcity. Those are conditions that most managers, including the president of Yale, face every day.

Mistakes can be very costly. Smith (1988) reports a case in point. Thomas Wyman, the board chairman of the CBS television network, went to Washington in 1983 to lobby the U.S. attorney-general, Edwin Meese. An emergency at the White House forced Meese to miss the meeting, and Wyman was sent instead to the office of Craig Fuller, one of Meese's top advisers:

> "I know something about this issue," Fuller suggested, "Perhaps you'd like to discuss it with me."
>
> But Wyman waved him off, unaware of Fuller's actual role, and evidently regarding him a mere staff man.
>
> "No, I'd rather wait and talk to Meese," Wyman said.
>
> For nearly an hour, Wyman sat leafing through magazines in Fuller's office, making no effort to talk to Fuller, who kept working at his desk just a few feet away.
>
> Finally, Meese burst into Fuller's office, full of apologies that he simply wouldn't have time for a substantive talk. "Did you talk to Fuller?" he asked.
>
> Wyman shook his head.
>
> "You should have talked to Fuller," Meese said. "He's very important on this issue. He knows it better than any of the rest of us. He's writing a memo for the president on the pros and cons. You could have given him your side of the argument" [Smith, 1988, pp. xviii-xix].

Wyman missed an important opportunity because he failed to test his assumptions about who had power, who could help, and who could not.

***Bargaining and Negotiation.*** Bargaining is often thought to apply primarily to commercial, legal, and labor relations settings. From a political perspective, though, bargaining is central to decision making in organizations. The horse trading that Kanter describes as part of the coalition-building process is just one of many examples. Negotiation is called for whenever two or more parties have some interests in common and other interests in conflict. Labor and management both want an organization to do well enough to provide jobs for its employees but they often strongly disagree on how resources should be divided between management and workers. Engineers and top managers at Morton Thiokol had a common interest in the success of the shuttle program. They differed sharply on how to balance technical and political considerations in making hard decisions.

The fundamental dilemma in negotiations is the choice between "creating value and claiming value" (Lax and Sebenius, 1986):

> Value creators tend to believe that, above all, successful negotiators must be inventive and cooperative enough to devise an agreement that yields considerable gain to each party, relative to no-agreement possibilities. Some speak about the need for replacing the win-lose image of negotiation with win-win negotiation. In addition to information sharing and honest communication, the drive to create value can require ingenuity and may benefit from a variety of techniques and attitudes. The parties can treat the negotiation as solving a joint problem; they can organize brainstorming sessions to invent creative solutions to their problems [Lax and Sebenius, 1986, pp. 30-31].
>
> Value claimers, on the other hand, tend to see this drive for joint gain as naive and weak-minded. For them, negotiation is hard, tough bargaining. The object of negotiation is to convince the other guy that he wants what you have to offer much more than you want what he has; moreover, you have all the time in the world, while he is up against pressing deadlines. To "win" at negotiating—and thus make the other fellow "lose"— one must start high, concede slowly, exaggerate the value of concessions, minimize the benefits of the other's concessions, conceal information, argue forcibly on behalf of principles that imply favorable settlements, make commitments to accept only highly favorable agreements, and be willing to outwait the other fellow [Lax and Sebenius, 1986, p. 32].

One of the best-known "win-win" approaches to negotiation was developed by Fisher and Ury (1981) in their book, *Getting to Yes*. They argue that the basic problem in negotiations is that most people routinely engage in "positional bargaining": they take positions and then make concessions to reach agreement. Fisher and Ury give the example below of a conversation between a customer and the proprietor of a secondhand store (pp. 3–4):

*Customer:*  How much do you want for this brass dish?

*Shopkeeper:*  That is a beautiful antique, isn't it? I guess I could let it go for $75.

*Customer:*  Oh, come on, it's dented. I'll give you $15.

*Shopkeeper:*  Really! I might consider a serious offer, but $15 certainly isn't serious.

*Customer:*  Well, I could go to $20, but I would never pay anything like $75. Quote me a realistic price.

*Shopkeeper:*  You drive a hard bargain, young lady. $60 cash, right now.

*Customer:*  $25.

*Shopkeeper:*  It cost me a great deal more than that. Make me a *serious* offer.

*Customer:*  $37.50. That's the highest I'll go.

*Shopkeeper:*  Have you noticed the engraving on that dish? Next year pieces like that will be worth twice what you pay today.

Fisher and Ury argue that positional bargaining is inefficient and often produces poor outcomes: the parties, for example, may miss the opportunity to create an agreement that would benefit both of them. Fisher and Ury propose an approach to "principled bargaining" that is built around four strategies. The first is to "separate the people from the problem" (1981, pp. 3–4). The stress and tension of negotiations easily escalate into anger and personal attacks. The result is that negotiators sometimes want to defeat or hurt the other person at almost any cost. Since every negotiation involves both substance and relationships, the wise negotiator will "deal with the people as human beings and with the problem on its merits" (p. 40).

Fisher and Ury's second recommendation is to "focus on interests, not positions" (p. 11). If you get locked into a position, you might overlook other ways to achieve what you want. An example was the Camp David treaty between Israel and Egypt in 1978. The two sides were at an impasse for a long time over where to draw the boundary line between the two countries. Israel wanted to keep part of the Sinai, while Egypt wanted all of it back. Resolution became possible only when they looked at each other's underlying interests. Israel was concerned about security: no Egyptian tanks on their border. Egypt was concerned about sovereignty: the Sinai had been part of Egypt from the time of the Pharaohs. The parties agreed on a plan that gave all of the Sinai back to Egypt, while demilitarizing large parts of it (Fisher and Ury, 1981).

Fisher and Ury's third recommendation is to invent options for mutual gain, that is, to look continually for new possibilities that might bring advantages to both sides. Parties often consider only the first few alternatives that come to mind. But if they make the effort to generate more options, the chances of a better decision increase. The final recommendation is to "insist on objective criteria"—standards of fairness for both substance and procedures. When a school board and a teachers' union are at loggerheads over the size of the teachers' pay increase, the two sides can try to find objective criteria for a fair settlement, such as the rate of inflation or settlements in other districts. The classic example of looking for a fair procedure is two brothers deadlocked over how to divide a pie between them. They finally agreed that one would cut the pie into two pieces, and the other could choose the piece he wanted.

Fisher and Ury devote most of their attention to strategies for creating value, that is, how to find solutions that are better for both parties. They downplay the equally important question of claiming value—how negotiators can maximize their individual gains. In many ways, "win-win" bargaining is more consistent with a human resource than a political view of the world. By contrast, a bargaining tactics stance may better represent the political frame. A classic example is Schelling's (1960) essay on bargaining, which focuses particularly on the problem of how to make credible threats.

Suppose, for example, that I want to buy a house from you, and I am willing to pay $150,000 for it, although you do not necessarily know what my highest offer is. If I want to convince you that I am willing to pay only $125,000, how could I make my offer credible? Schelling notes that, contrary to a common assumption, I am not always better off in such a situation if I am stronger and have more resources. If you know that I am very wealthy, you might take my threat less seriously than if you know (or I can get you to believe) that it is barely possible for me to scrape up $125,000. Common sense also suggests that I should be better off if I have considerable freedom of action. Yet I may get a better price if I can convince you that my hands are tied—for example, that I am negotiating for a very stubborn buyer who will not go above $125,000, even if the house is worth more. Such examples suggest that the ideal situation for the bargainer is to have considerable resources and freedom to act but to be able to convince the other side that just the opposite is true. This gives us the following picture of the bargaining process:

1.  Bargaining is a mixed-motive game. Although both parties want an agreement, they have very different preferences about which agreement.
2.  Bargaining is a process of interdependent decisions, and what each party does affects the other. Each player wants, as much as possible, to be able to predict what the other will do while limiting the other's ability to do the same.
3.  The more player A can control player B's level of uncertainty, the more powerful A is.
4.  Bargaining primarily involves the judicious use of *threats* rather than sanctions. Players may threaten to use force, to go on strike, to break off negotiations, and so forth. In most cases, however, they much prefer not to have to carry out the threats.
5.  A critical bargaining skill is the ability to make threats credible. A threat will only work if your opponent believes you, and noncredible threats may even weaken your bargaining position.
6.  Calculation of the appropriate threat level is also critical. If I

"underthreaten," I may weaken my own position. If I "over-threaten," you may not believe me, may break off the negotiations, or may escalate your own threats.

Bellow and Moulton (1978) present a fascinating account of negotiations between lawyers for the U.S. Department of Justice and lawyers for then Vice-President Spiro Agnew. A legal case against Agnew developed by accident. A group of federal attorneys investigating local corruption in Baltimore County, Maryland, initially had no idea that the trail would lead them to the vice-president.

But Agnew himself made an early tactical error. Only a few weeks after the prosecutors began to subpoena witnesses, Agnew expressed concern about the investigation to the attorney general. Although the prosecutors had no reason to suspect Agnew at that point, they immediately became interested. If the vice-president was nervous, they wanted to know why.

The federal investigators then got a break. An attorney for William Fornoff, a potential defendant, came to the prosecutors and said, "I know you have A, B, and C, but what else do you have?" The prosecutors had nothing else but chose not to say so. They played a hunch—that an unknown case would be more threatening than a known one. They tried to control Fornoff's uncertainty and it worked. They insisted that they would make a deal only after Fornoff told them what he knew. He did, providing information that led the investigators to several of Agnew's political associates in Baltimore. They, in turn, provided evidence against Agnew.

When Agnew realized that some of his old friends were cooperating with the prosecutors, he sent his attorneys to negotiate. Both sides preferred to make a deal. The attorney general, Eliot Richardson, and Agnew both owed their jobs to the same man, President Richard Nixon. Richardson wanted Agnew out of office before something occurred that might permit him to become president. (Richardson's fear was justified: Nixon's resignation in the Watergate scandal would have made Agnew president.) Agnew wanted to avoid a trial and possible conviction. Both sides thus had reasons to avoid a trial, which would create uncertainties that neither side could control. The bargaining came down to three issues: whether

Agnew would resign as vice-president, how much Agnew would admit in court, and whether Agnew would go to jail. Initially, the prosecutors and Agnew's lawyers could not agree on any of the three questions.

During these negotiations, a newspaper broke the story that plea bargaining was under way. Someone in the prosecutor's office apparently leaked the information, perhaps to increase the pressure on Agnew. Agnew responded by promising that he would not resign, even if indicted. He was using a common tactic in adversarial bargaining: trying to convince the opponent that you have adopted an unchangeable position. He knew Richardson dreaded the possibility of a convicted felon in the office of the vice-president. The prosecution, meanwhile, kept much of its evidence secret—continuing to use the so-called black box technique to pressure Agnew.

In public, Agnew complained that he was being harassed and tried in the press. In private, he sent his attorneys to try again for a plea bargain. Most members of the prosecution wanted to hold out for a full public confession, if not a jail term. They reasoned that Agnew had to make a deal, but Agnew's attorneys refused to budge. Richardson finally agreed to settle for a resignation and minimal admissions in court. Richardson's decision was softer than his subordinates wanted, but he had little desire to bring an incumbent vice-president to trial. The deal was struck. Agnew resigned, appeared briefly in court, and made a nationwide television appearance in which he minimized any wrongdoing on his part.

We have now seen two dramatically different approaches to the question of bargaining—what Lax and Sebenius (1986) call "creating value" and "claiming value." But how does a manager choose between them? One approach is to ask how much opportunity is there for achieving a win-win solution, and if one will have to work with these people again. If everyone will be much better off with an agreement than without one, it makes sense to emphasize creating value. If the manager will have to work with the same people again in the future, it would be very dangerous to use value-claiming tactics that leave anger and mistrust in their wake. Managers who have a reputation for being manipulative and self-interested will have a hard time building the networks and coalitions that they need to be successful in the future.

Axelrod's (1980) research suggests that, when negotiators must work together over time, a strategy of "conditional openness" is most effective. This strategy tells the negotiator to start with open and collaborative behavior and to maintain this approach if the other party does too. If the other party becomes adversarial, however, the negotiator should respond in kind and remain adversarial until the opponent makes a collaborative move. It is, in effect, a friendly and forgiving version of tit for tat—do unto others exactly as they do unto you. In Axelrod's experimental research, this conditional openness strategy worked better than even the most fiendishly diabolical adversarial strategies (Axelrod, 1980).

One other criterion can be applied to the question of choosing collaborative or adversarial tactics, namely, what is the *ethical* thing to do? Bargainers often deliberately misrepresent their positions, even though few actions are more universally condemned than lying (Bok, 1978). This leads to a profoundly difficult question for the manager as politician: What actions are ethical and just?

## Morality and Politics

Block (1987), Burns (1978), and Lax and Sebenius (1986) all explore ethical issues in bargaining and organizational politics. Block's view rests on the assumption that individuals can empower themselves through an understanding of politics: "The cornerstone of this book is the idea that the process of organizational politics as we know it works against people taking responsibility. We empower ourselves by discovering a positive way of being political. The line between positive and negative politics is a tightrope we have to walk" (p. xiii).

Block argues that there is a bureaucratic cycle in organizations that often leaves individuals feeling vulnerable, powerless, and helpless. If we give too much power to the organization and to people around us, he says, we fear that power will be used against us, and we begin to develop indirect and manipulative strategies to protect ourselves. To escape the dilemma, managers need to support organizational structures, policies, and procedures that promote empowerment, and they must also make personal choices to empower themselves.

Block urges managers to build an "image of greatness" for their department or unit—an image of what the unit can contribute that is meaningful and worthwhile. "A vision is an expression of hope and idealism. The anxiety we feel means we are moving against the culture or working to recreate the culture, and that is what makes our vision a positive political act" (1987, p. 115).

Having created a vision, the manager needs to focus on building support for that vision. Block views this as a matter of negotiating agreement and trust. He suggests that managers need to differentiate between those with whom agreement and trust are initially high (allies and bedfellows) and those with whom they are low (adversaries and opponents). Adversaries, he says, are both the most difficult and the most interesting people to deal with. He argues that it is usually ineffective to pressure them and that the effective strategy is to "let go of them." He offers four steps for letting go: (1) tell them your vision of the organization, (2) state in a neutral way your best understanding of their position, (3) identify your own contribution to the problem, and (4) end the meeting by telling them what you plan to do but without making any demands on them.

To empower ourselves, Block argues, we have to believe that our well-being and survival are in our own hands, that we have an underlying purpose, and that we are committed to achieving that purpose *now*. Then, says Block, managers can choose between maintenance and greatness, caution and courage, and dependency and autonomy. Bureaucracy, in his view, nudges us in the direction of maintenance (holding on to what we already have), caution, and dependence.

Block recognizes that such a strategy might seem naively suicidal but argues that "war games in organizations lose their power when they are brought into the light of day" (p. 148). The political frame, however, questions that assumption. Block may be right in the case of political games that result merely from a misunderstanding or an unduly narrow understanding of one's self-interest. But in situations where resources really are scarce, and where there are real and durable differences in values and beliefs among different groups, bringing politics into the open may simply make everyone more tense and uncomfortable. Conflict may become more obvious and overt, but no more resolvable. Block's message about the importance of personal commitment to a vision for oneself and one's organization is important. Nevertheless, his view of politics disregards basic propositions of the political frame.

Burns's (1978) effort to develop a conception of positive politics is more complex. He considers examples as diverse and complex as Franklin Roosevelt and Adolph Hitler, Gandhi and Mao, Woodrow Wilson and Joan of Arc. He recognizes the reality of differences and conflict and argues that both conflict and power are central to the concept of leadership and management. Searching for firm moral footing in a world of cultural and ethical diversity, Burns turned to social science and specifically to the motivation theory of Maslow (1954) and the ethical theory of Kohlberg (1973). From Maslow he borrowed the idea of the hierarchy of motives (the needs hierarchy that we discussed in introducing the human resource frame in Chapter Eight). Moral leaders, he argued, appeal to higher levels on the need hierarchy.

From Kohlberg he adopted the idea of stages of moral reasoning. At the lowest stage, the "preconventional" level, moral judgments are based primarily on perceived consequences: an action is right if you are rewarded and wrong if you are punished. Kohlberg found preconventional reasoning primarily in children. In the next two stages—the "conventional" level—the emphasis is on conforming to authority and established rules. At the two highest stages—the "postconventional" level—ethical judgments rest on more general principles. At the fifth stage, ethical reasoning emphasizes the social contract and the greatest good for the greatest number. At the sixth and last stage, individuals base ethical judgments on universal and comprehensive moral principles.

Maslow and Kohlberg thus provided an ethical foundation on which Burns (1978) constructed a positive view of politics:

> Leaders are taskmasters and goal setters, but they and their
> followers share a particular space and time, a particular set of
> motivations and values. If they are to be effective in helping to
> mobilize and elevate their constituencies, leaders must be whole
> persons, persons with fully functioning capacities for thinking
> and feeling. The problem for them as educators, as leaders, is
> not to promote narrow, egocentric self-actualization, but to ex-

tend awareness of human needs and the means of gratifying them to improve the larger social situation for which educators or leaders have responsibility and over which they have power.

What does all this mean for the teaching of leadership as opposed to manipulation? "Teachers"—in whatever guise— treat students neither coercively nor instrumentally but as joint seekers of truth and of mutual actualization. They help students define moral values not by imposing their own moralities on them but by positing situations that pose moral choices and then encouraging conflict and debate. They seek to help students rise to higher stages of moral reasoning and hence to higher levels of principled judgment [pp. 448-449].

In other words, Burns argues that positive politics evolve when individuals choose actions that appeal to higher motives and higher stages of moral judgment.

For Lax and Sebenius (1986), ethical issues are inescapable for the manager as negotiator, and they provide a set of questions to help managers decide whether an action is ethical:

1.  Are you following rules that are understood and accepted? (In poker, for example, everyone understands that bluffing is part of the game.)
2.  Are you comfortable discussing and defending your action? Would you want your colleagues and friends to be aware of it? Your spouse, children, or parents? Would you be comfortable if it were on the front page of a major newspaper?
3.  Would you want someone to do it to you? To a member of your family?
4.  What if everyone acted that way? Would the resulting society be desirable? If you were designing an organization, would you want people to act that way? Would you teach your children to do it?
5.  Are there alternatives that rest on firmer ethical ground?

While these questions do not provide an ethical framework, they do embody several important principles of moral judgment:

1.  Mutuality—are all parties to a relationship operating under the same understanding about the rules of the game?
2.  Generality—does a specific action follow a principle of moral conduct that is applicable to all comparable situations?
3.  Caring—does this action show care for the legitimate interests of others?

These questions attempt to illuminate and clarify ethical and moral judgments. They raise issues that managers need to consider and that should be part of an ongoing conversation both in schools and at work about the moral dimension of management and leadership. Porter (1989) notes, however, that such a conversation is often absent or impoverished: "In a seminar with seventeen executives from nine corporations, we learned how the privatization of moral discourse in our society has created a deep sense of moral loneliness and moral illiteracy; how the absence of a common language prevents people from talking about and 'reading' the moral issues they face. We learned how the isolation of individuals—the taboo against talking about spiritual matters in the public sphere—robs people of courage, of the strength of heart to do what deep down they believe to be right. They think they are alone in facing these issues" (p. 2).

Organizations and societies may choose to banish moral discourse and to leave managers to face ethical issues alone, but they invite dreary and brutish political dynamics when they do so. In an increasingly pluralistic and secular world, the solution is not for organizations to impose a narrow ethical framework on their employees. Such an approach would not work and would not be desirable if it did. But organizations can take a moral stance. They can make it clear that they expect ethical behavior, and they can validate the importance of dialogue about the moral issues facing managers. Positive politics absent moral dialogue and a moral framework is as likely as successful farming without sunlight or water.

## Summary

The question is not whether organizations will have politics, but what kind of politics they will have. Politics can be and often is sordid and destructive. But politics can also be the vehicle for achieving noble purposes, and managers can be benevolent politicians. Organizational change and effectiveness depend on such managers. The constructive politician recognizes political realities in organizations and knows how to fashion an agenda, build a network of support, and negotiate effectively both with those who might advance and with those who might oppose the agenda. In the process, managers inevitably encounter a dilemma that is both practical and ethical—when to adopt strategies that are open and collaborative and when to choose tougher, more adversarial approaches. They will need to consider the potential for collaboration, the importance of long-term relationships, and most importantly, the values and ethical principles that they endorse.

# 11

# *Organizations as Political Arenas and Political Tools*

> Many have dreamed up republics and principalities which have never in truth been known to exist; the gulf between how one should live and how one does live is so wide that a man who neglects what is actually done for what should be done learns the way to self-destruction rather than self-preservation. The fact is that a man who wants to act virtuously in every way necessarily comes to grief among many who are not virtuous. Therefore if a prince wants to maintain his rule, he must learn how not to be virtuous, and to make use of this or that according to need [Machiavelli, (1514) 1961, p. 163].

Organizations are both political arenas and political tools. As arenas, they provide a setting for the ongoing interplay of interests and agendas among different individuals and groups. As tools, they are implements, often very powerful implements, for achieving the purposes of whoever is able to master them. The political frame sees the pursuit of self-interest and power as the basic process both within and between organizations. Organizational change, for example, is always political—it occurs when a particular individual or group is able to impose a particular agenda on the system. Individuals and groups may clothe their initiatives in a variety of ethical or technical disguises but do so to conceal their real purpose:

to redesign the world in the service of their interests. Remembering the Helen DeMarco case, consider some examples:

> A public agency recruits a group of analysts and computer experts who very quickly conclude that decision making in the agency needs to become more analytic, rational, and logical. They may be right, but they may also want to establish a niche in the agency for their own expertise and values.

> A new, young principal enters an elementary school and begins to urge the faculty to move away from traditional models of teaching toward "progressive, child-centered" approaches that "will better serve the children." While the principal is probably sincere, the new approaches may do more to express the principal's ideological commitments and needs than to improve the children's education.

A political view of organizations suggests that there is no such thing as permanent improvement: "happily ever after" exists only in fairy tales. In the real world, there are today's winners who may become tomorrow's losers. The ebb and flow of power both inside and outside the organization carries everything else with it. If the proportion of young people is declining relative to that of senior citizens, public schools will be in trouble unless they can create a market for lifelong learning. If college applicant pools are shrinking, colleges will have to pursue new students more aggressively. The power of students and admissions officers will increase, while that of the faculty will decline. When it became cheaper to produce television sets in Japan than in the United States, production and power moved across the Pacific. When it became cheaper to produce those sets in Thailand than in Japan, production and power shifted again.

The political perspective views change and stability in a paradoxical way, asserting both that organizations constantly change and that they never change. There is constant jockeying for position, and yesterday's elites may be tomorrow's also-rans. In organizations, as in football and chess, players come and go, but the game continues. The political frame says that in order to achieve results, you need power and you need to be prepared for conflict as a part of the process.

## Organizations as Arenas

From a political perspective, organizations, like other arenas, are designed and built to house contests. Arenas play an important role in determining what game will be played, who will be the contestants, and what interests will be pursued. From this perspective, every organizational process is political. Consider, for example, organizational design—the process of shaping and structuring organizations. Most approaches to organizational design, as seen earlier from the structural view, assume that the best design is the one that will contribute the most to achieving the organization's goals and strategy. Galbraith's (1973) theory of design, for example, is built around the problem of information: What information does an organization need to achieve its task? How much uncertainty is there in the information? How much communication is necessary in order for different parts of the organization to know what the other parts are doing? The theory argues that organizations operating in a highly uncertain environment will need a more flexible, less bureaucratic structure than those operating in more stable and predictable settings. Similar views appear in Lawrence and Lorsch (1967), Perrow (1970), and Mintzberg (1979).

Pfeffer (1978) has questioned the validity of structural perspectives and has offered an explicitly political conception as an alternative: "Since organizations are coalitions, and the different participants have varying interests and preferences, the critical question becomes not how organizations should be designed to maximize effectiveness, but rather, whose preferences and interests are to be served by the organization. . . . What is effective for students may be ineffective for administrators. What is effectiveness as defined by consumers may be ineffectiveness as defined by stockholders. The assessment of organizations is dependent upon one's preferences and one's perspective" (p. 223).

Pfeffer argues that, although the different groups in an organization may have conflicting preferences, they also have a shared interest in avoiding continuous conflict. So, the groups agree on ways of dividing up power and resources, and those divisions are reflected in the design of the organization. Organization structures are "the resolution, at a given time, of the contending claims for control, subject to the constraint that the structures permit the organization to survive" (p. 224).

As an example, Pfeffer looks at the process of participative management. Whereas human resource theory focuses on the use of participation to enhance fulfillment of individual needs, Pfeffer analyzes it as an example of co-optation, that is, a process whereby an organization gives something to individuals so as to induce them to ally themselves with organizational needs and purposes. If women in a university are vocal in demanding equality, the administration might create a "Committee on the Status of Women," schedule occasional meetings for the committee with top administrators, and provide it with a secretary and a research assistant. The administration might put highly vocal women on the committee and hope that they will focus their energies on the internal problems of the committee rather than on changing the university. If the strategy is successful, the administration can defuse a potential problem, while using the committee as public evidence of the university's commitment to equality and fairness. Similarly, when lower-level employees demand more influence, management can let them make decisions but make sure that it controls the information and the alternatives available to them.

Pfeffer does not argue that efficiency is never relevant to organizational design. The most powerful group in a coalition may have a stake in making the organization efficient. In such cases, it may appear that efficiency dominates design decisions, but in fact the appearance masks the political reality. If the top group becomes more concerned about its own rewards and perks than about the efficiency of the organization (a fairly common development in private and public organizations), then efficiency ceases to be the dominant factor.

Gamson's (1968) distinction between authorities and partisans implies two major sources of political initiatives: bottom-up initiatives that rely on the mobilization of interest groups to assert their agendas, and top-down initiatives that rely on authorities' capacity to influence subordinates. We will discuss examples of both to illustrate some of the basic processes of political action.

*Bottom-Up Political Action.* The battle over the existence, rights, and responsibilities of labor unions has been fought in the United States and Western Europe from the nineteenth century to the present. In some places, the battle is essentially over. Labor and management have long since made peace and developed relatively stable working relationships. In other countries, such as Poland and South Africa, the battle continues. A wildcat strike by coal miners in the Soviet Union in 1989 suggested that the process was beginning anew there.

Initially, the battle was a classic case of authorities versus partisans. Labor organizers relied primarily on bottom-up influence techniques—building group unity and staging demonstrations, walkouts, and sit-downs. Managers resisted with a variety of social control mechanisms, including legal restrictions, lawsuits, the discharge of union sympathizers, and the use of police or the military to quell strikers. Management insisted on its right to make binding decisions about conditions of employment and to negotiate individually with each employee. Unions insisted that such a relationship was both unequal and unjust and permitted arbitrary and exploitative behavior by management.

Over time, unions increasingly attempted to combine bottom-up with top-down initiatives. They mobilized political power to change the laws governing trade unions, with the result that the existence of unions is now firmly implanted in the legal systems of most developed nations. The rights of both unions and employers are now specified through an extensive body of law and regulation.

Throughout the battles over labor unions, both sides argued their position on grounds of justice and rationality. In America and Western Europe, employers argued that unions violated both property rights and individual freedom. In Poland in the 1980s, the government argued that the Solidarity Union was counterrevolutionary and seditious. Unions responded that workers had no freedom when they had no power. Although the battle was argued on rational and moral grounds, the political perspective suggests that power, not ideology, was the decisive factor. Alinsky's statement that people "speak on moral principles but act on power principles" (1971, p. 13) suggests that unions made gains because they had become strong enough to make their influence felt. When the auto workers had enough power to shut down the industry, management had to make concessions, regardless of the ideological merits of its position. In Poland, police and the military were brought in to quell worker unrest in 1956, 1970, 1980, and 1989. But when Poland's Communist leaders found that they could not make the economy work without the cooperation of Solidarity (whose membership included about one-fourth of the population), they finally gave up and invited Solidarity to participate in the government.

What enabled workers to obtain power? One answer points to a by-product of industrialization—the concentration of workers in large factories, often in large cities. The scale of the new factories and urban areas was so large as to dwarf the individual, creating an increased sense of powerlessness. But the fact that workers were concentrated in large numbers also provided the conditions under which organization became possible. A similar argument can be made about the conditions that sparked the civil rights movement in the United States in the 1960s. In the early part of the twentieth century, the majority of blacks lived in rural areas of the South. By 1960, however, a majority lived in cities and in the North. In that year, there were more than one million black residents of New York and almost as many in Chicago (Bell, 1976). It is difficult for blue-collar workers or black citizens to organize if they are scattered in small numbers across large areas. It is much easier if they are concentrated in large numbers in relatively few places. Industrialization and urbanization made it more necessary but also easier for both groups to organize.

The examples of trade unions and the civil rights movement provide several insights into the process by which political shifts come about in organizations and societies. In both cases, the precondition for change was a significant disruption in previous patterns. Trade unions developed in the context of the industrial revolution, rapid urbanization, and decline of the family farm. The civil rights movement came to the fore after a period of massive occupational and geographical shifts for black citizens. In each case, the arena was changing in ways that unfroze old patterns and created dissatisfaction for one group within the larger system. Both movements had elements of the classic pattern for revolution: a period of rising expectations followed by disappointment of those expectations.

In each case, the initial vehicle for bottom-up action was mobilizing and organizing—the formation of trade unions or of civil rights organizations. In both cases existing elites bitterly contested the legitimacy of such group activities and used coercive tactics to block them. Employers used lawsuits against trade unions but also relied on coercion and violence. The civil rights movement, particularly in its early stages, was subject to violent repressive efforts by whites. In both cases, the newly organized group made claims on the policy process and fought to have its rights embodied in law. Either movement might have failed had it been weaker or its opposition stronger. Each did, in fact, suffer many profound setbacks, but each was able to mobilize enough power to survive and make headway.

The two examples may be misleading in that, compared to many efforts at bottom-up change, they have been relatively successful. There is no accurate census of attempts to change from below, but many—perhaps most—such efforts fail. Even the most successful are only relatively so. Union busting still happens both in the United States and in other parts of the world. Discrimination on the basis of race or religion is still also found throughout the world.

For every successful bottom-up change effort, there are many efforts that fail, and many more efforts that are stillborn because no one thinks that they could succeed. The well-known difficulty of bottom-up political action leads many to believe that, if you want to get something done, you have to begin at the top. Yet research on top-down efforts is mostly a catalogue of failures, and the next section discusses the political problems inherent in such efforts.

*Political Barriers to Control from the Top.* Deal and Nutt (1980) conducted a revealing study of a group of local school districts that received funding from the U.S. Department of Education to develop experimental programs for improving the quality of education. A typical scenario for these projects included the following steps:

1.  The central administration learned of the federal funding program and investigated program guidelines.
2.  A small group of administrators met to develop a proposal for improving some aspect of the educational program. (The process was usually rushed and involved very few people, because time was short for meeting the proposal deadline.)
3.  When funding was approved, the administration announced with pride and enthusiasm that the district had been successful in a national competition and would receive substantial federal funding for a new project to improve instruction.
4.  The administration was startled and perplexed when teachers greeted the new proposal with resistance, criticism, and anger.
5.  The administration was caught in the middle between the teachers and the funding agency and came to view teacher resistance as a sign of defensiveness and unwillingness to change.
6.  The federally funded program became a political football that produced more disharmony, mistrust, and conflict than tangible improvement in the educational program.

The programs studied by Deal and Nutt represented examples of top-down change efforts under comparatively favorable circumstances. The districts were not in crisis, and the change effort received both financial support from and the blessing of the federal government. Yet the new initiatives set off political battles, and, in many cases, the administration found itself outgunned. In several districts, the teachers mobilized such intense community opposition to the project that the superintendent of schools was forced out of office.

In most instances, the administrators never anticipated the possibility of major political battles. Their proposal called for programs that they thought would be progressive, effective, and good for everyone. They rarely wondered about the risks involved in proposing changes that someone else was supposed to carry out. They assumed that most people would applaud their success in creating a new opportunity for the school system, and underestimated the possibility that the program would bring to the surface significant differences in political agendas between administrators and faculty.

The patterns described by Deal and Nutt can be seen repeatedly in attempts to achieve top-down change, including countless unsuccessful efforts at organizational improvement and change mounted by chief executives, frustrated managers, hopeful study teams, and high-status management consultants. In every case, the mistake was to assume that a combination of the right idea (as perceived by the proponent of the idea) and legitimate authority is the basic ingredient for a successful initiative. This assumption runs afoul of the political agendas and political power of the "low-erarchy"—the individuals and groups in middle- and lower-level positions in the organization who can devise a host of creative and maddening ways to resist, divert, undermine, or ignore change efforts.

### Organizations as Political Actors

All the factors that generate politics within organizations also exist in the relationships of organizations to one another and to the larger environment. Organizations have their own interests and compete with other contenders for a variety of scarce resources. Organizations have power, and significant organizations have significant power: "Not much moves and shakes in the world without them. The [world's] fifty biggest industrial companies employ 8.8 million people, more than the population of Sweden. They generated sales in 1987 of $1.5 trillion. Profits totaled $56 billion, nearly twice the gross national product of Ireland. These companies set the styles, invest the money, build the plants—sometimes altering the economies and ecologies of vast regions" (Farnham, 1989, p. 400).

Perrow (1986) argues that organizations serve their masters and that whoever controls a multibillion-dollar tool wields enormous power: "Bureaucracy is a tool, a social tool that legitimizes control of the many by the few, despite the formal apparatus of democracy, and this control has generated unregulated and unperceived social power. This power includes much more than just control of employees. As bureaucracies satisfy, delight, pollute, and satiate us with their output of goods and services, they also shape our ideas, our very way of conceiving of ourselves, control our life chances, and even define our humanity" (p. 5).

Perrow gives as an example the success of large pharmaceutical companies in persuading both government and the medical profession to protect the companies' profits. A major threat to the profit margins of drug companies is the sale of generic drugs—chemically equivalent drugs that sell at prices much lower than their brand name counterparts. In the United States, the industry trade association—an interorganizational coalition—persuaded most state legislatures to prohibit the sale of such drugs, ostensibly to protect consumers. The industry was also able to persuade the American Medical Association (AMA) to change a policy in its journals to permit drugs to be advertised by their brand names rather than their generic names. This was important because consumers normally buy whatever drug the doctor prescribes, and the drug companies wanted doctors to think in terms of brand names rather than chemical names. As a result of the policy shift, the AMA's advertising income tripled in seven years, and the manufacturers strengthened the position of their brands (Perrow, 1986).

The impulse to form coalitions is not unique to the private sector. In the late 1980s, for example, it was widely thought that American public schools could be improved by giving parents and students more choice about which schools children would attend. Proponents of choice plans reasoned that students would choose the schools that fit them best and that competition might have an invigorating effect on schools. But school boards and school administrators almost universally resisted the idea. Coalitions formed on both sides of the issue and sent lobbyists to state legislatures to argue their side of the case. Compared to giant corporations, public schools are relatively weak and vulnerable organizations, but even they are not simply passive creatures buffeted by their environment.

There has been a spirited debate among organization theorists about how much power organizations exercise over their environment and how much power their environment exercises over them. Proponents of the so-called population ecology view (Hannan and Freeman, 1977, 1989; McKelvey and Aldrich, 1983) argue that the environment has the same power over organizations that the natural environment has over species: it sustains those that are well adapted to their particular niche and selects out those that are maladapted. Supporters of the ecological view note that thousands of organizations are born and thousands die every year. Critics of the population ecology view respond that virtually all the births and deaths occur among infants. Large, mature organizations— whether public or private—almost never die. When *Fortune* publishes its annual list of the world's fifty largest corporations, no one is surprised to find that the top three are still General Motors, Exxon, and Royal Dutch/Shell.

The question of the relative power of organizations and their environment is more than a theoretical debate. It is critically important both to managers and to society. Do consumer marketing organizations create and control consumer tastes, or do they simply react to needs that are created by larger social forces? Perrow argues the first view, but many marketing experts take the second: "The marketing concept of management is based on the premise that over the longer term all businesses are born and survive or die because people (the market) either want them or don't want them. In short, the market creates, shapes, and defines the character of the demand for all classes of products and services. Almost needless to say, many managers tend to think that they can design goods and services and then create a demand for them. The marketing concept denies this proposition. Instead, the marketing concept emphasizes that the creative aspect of marketing is the discovery, definition, and fulfillment of what people want or need or which solves their life-style problems" (Marshall, 1984, p. 1).

Are large multinational corporations so powerful that they have become a law unto themselves, or are they strongly shaped by the need to respond to the people and cultures in the countries where they operated? The answer is some of both. Power relations are never static, and the power of even the most powerful corporations rises and falls. General Motors, the company that Billy Durant founded in 1906 and Alfred Sloan rebuilt in the 1920s, became the world's largest industrial corporation. Its resources and its power were and still are immense. Yet, for all its power, it was hard pressed in the 1970s and 1980s to convince American consumers to continue to buy its cars. Americans flocked to buy Volkswagens, Toyotas, and Volvos because they were unsatisfied with what GM was offering them. GM's size and financial strength were an enormous cush-ion—a lesser beast might not have survived all the marketing and management problems that afflicted the company in that period. But the trend was ominous, and GM's stakeholders began to mobilize:

"[In early 1987] Roger Smith went on a three-state odyssey to meet with some of GM's biggest shareholders. Angered at his ousting last year of dissident director H. Ross Perot with $700 mil-lion in 'hushmail,' they berated Smith for GM's meager profits, its falling market share, and its poor productivity despite $40 billion in new equipment since 1979. Why, they ask, is management paying itself big bonuses when much smaller Ford Motor Co. had over-taken GM in earnings? Unless Smith acted, some of them threatened to introduce a proposal at the shareholder's meeting critical of man-agement" (Nussbaum and Dobrzynski, 1987, p. 102).

A few weeks later, GM announced a number of major policy changes. The company agreed to buy back stock, cut capital spend-ing, cut inventories, and replace cash bonuses for managers with stock incentive plans linked to long-term performance. The insti-tutional shareholders then withdrew their proposal. General Mo-tors is still very large and very powerful, but the company and its many stakeholders have all paid a high price for its mistakes, mis-calculations, and inefficiencies. It has been able to exert substantial control over its environment, protecting itself in a variety of ways. Yet it still cannot get consumers in the United States, or anywhere else, to buy cars that they do not want, particularly if another com-pany offers them a more attractive alternative.

Over much of the present century, power in major corpora-tions tended to become more concentrated in the hands of manage-ment. As long as the economy and companies in general performed well, stakeholders had enough confidence in management not to raise serious questions. The myth of accountability—that managers are accountable both to the shareholders and the market—was ac-cepted at face value. As the U.S. economy started to falter in the 1970s, however, the situation began to change dramatically. And, by the late 1980s, *Business Week* could report that "the tight hold professional managers have on the corporation is slipping. Inves-tors are no longer passive. Outside directors are asserting themselves. Other stakeholders—from employees to communities—want a voice. The balance of power is beginning to shift. By any measure, the current crop of corporate managers has reigned over an era of unprecedented American economic decline. For at least a decade, America's standard of living has been eroding, its share of the world market shrinking, and its products retreating in the face of foreign competition. So it's no accident that the dominance of management is being challenged today" (Nussbaum and Dobrzynski, 1987, pp. 102-103).

Big institutional investors (who hold about one-third of all corporate shares in the United States), corporate raiders, concerned politicians, aggressive unions, environmental activists, consumer groups, and many others all began to take more and more active roles as power became more fluid and diffuse in an increasingly complex corporate environment. This battle is now a global one. Large multinational companies have enormous power, but they must also cope with the demands of governments, labor unions, and consumers the world over. As the world becomes a global village, this is the biggest political game in town.

### Conclusion: Strengths and Limits of the Political Frame

There are many who agree with Alinsky that "political realists see the world as it is: an arena of power politics moved primarily by perceived immediate self-interest" (1971, p. 13). For them, the political frame presents the only realistic portrayal of organizations. It captures a number of significant organizational dynamics that are absent or only implicit in the structural and human resource views. Indeed, neither of those two frames has attended nearly so explicitly to the organizational dynamics of conflict and power politics. The political frame says that power and politics are central to organizations and cannot be swept under the rug. This perspective represents an important antidote to the antiseptic rationality sometimes present in structural analysis, as well as to the excessive optimism that appears in some human resource discussions.

But the political perspective can be guilty of its own parochialism. Critics describe two major limitations in the frame:

1.  The political perspective is so thoroughly focused on politics
    that it underestimates the significance of both rational and col-
    laborative processes.
2.  The frame is normatively cynical and pessimistic. It overstates
    the inevitability of conflict and understates the potential for
    effective collaboration.

Both problems can be seen in Ritti and Funkhouser's (1982)
*The Ropes to Skip and the Ropes to Know.* The book is clearly and
entertainingly written and teaches through stories rather than long
lists of concepts—a rare feat for a textbook in organizational behavior. Ritti and Funkhouser purport to offer an inside view of how
organizations *really* function, as opposed to how they *pretend* to
function. The book's vignettes of life in the corporate world are
entertaining and much closer to the truth than the impersonal picture of organizational life that appears in many textbooks. But the
book presents a view of organizations in which rational decision
making is accidental and mostly indeterminate, substantive and
technical skills are of no particular significance, and belief in analysis or collaboration mostly shows naiveté. Political savvy, "impression management," and skill in using symbols are what counts.
*Doing* a good job is not that critical, but *appearing* to do a good
job is essential. Projects that aim to improve the quality of life in
organizations are, at best, harmless vehicles for the expression of
political agendas. At worst, they are manipulative nonsense.

Caplow's (1976) *How to Run Any Organization* expresses a
similar view in offering practical advice for the new heads of organizations. Among the many topics is the honeymoon period that
occurs right after a newcomer takes office. Should new leaders make
sweeping changes right away, or wait until they know the organization better? Caplow offers the following advice:

> The outsider following a strong predecessor must establish his
> authority at once, or he may never be able to do so. The im-
> munity offered by the honeymoon gives him a chance to dem-
> onstrate authority by introducing major changes before the old
> guard has a chance to begin the mutiny it will inevitably at-
> tempt. The only thing that limits his role as a new broom
> sweeping clean is his ignorance of the organization and the

danger that some of his innovations will have disastrous results. He can protect himself against this danger by emphasizing changes of style and general policy and avoiding projects
that require detailed implementation. His reign of terror, if he
conducts one at all, ought to be highly selective and limited to
a small number of potential opponents. The other key figures
in the organization, having been edified by these examples,
should be encouraged and supported in every possible way
[1976, p. 16].

In both the Ritti-Funkhouser and Caplow analyses, the task
of an organization and the needs of its members are mostly ignored
(except that individuals are expected to look out for their own
needs). Both books are thoroughly amoral: it is not important *what*
you are trying to accomplish. What counts is whether you play the
game well enough to win.

But, would Caplow hire an automobile mechanic or a surgeon on the basis of their political skills? Would Ritti and Funkhouser fly on an airplane whose pilots were trained primarily in
creating an *appearance* of competence? By the same token, would
organizations be viable if most of their members followed advice
*only* from the political frame? Could they get anything done? Even
if they could, would anyone want to be a part of such organizations?

The amorality that often characterizes political perspectives
raises questions of values. To what extent does the political perspective, even as it purports to be simply a description of reality, ratify
some of the least humane and most unsavory aspects of human
systems? Responding to criticism that the first edition of *The Ropes
to Skip and the Ropes to Know* seemed to advocate unethical behavior, Ritti argued that he saw nothing unethical about playing
hardball. Optimists who hope to work in a world of trust and altruism, he said, "are not going to see much altruism in [their]
colleagues" (Ritti and Funkhouser, 1982, p. v).

Argyris and Schön (1974) describe many of the same dynamics that are central to political perspectives. They note that most
individuals in organizations do behave as if " to maximize winning
and minimize losing" is one of their dominant values, even though
they often espouse a very different set of principles. Argyris and
Schön's data suggest that people often behave as they are repre-

sented in the political frame. But their data also contain some insights that suggest a counterpoint to this frame:

1.  Most people, most of the time, are unaware of the discrepancy between what they intend and what they do.
2.  Their behavior helps to create a world in which it is unlikely that they will become aware of the discrepancies.
3.  The result is that individuals are often prevented from learning about their own areas of ineffectiveness and persist in self-destructive, self-sealing cycles of behavior. Each new attempt to win often produces more losses.
4.  For the organization, the individual win-lose behaviors add up to massive problems of manageability and organizational learning and to massive frustrations and discontent for participants.

Argyris and Schön's data validate the accuracy of some important elements of the political frame but also raise significant questions about the completeness and the normative implications of the perspective. The political frame says some important things about organizations much more clearly than either the structural or the human resource frames. Yet it fails to discuss some equally significant issues that those frames capture. Each of the three has much to learn from the other, but no single theory has yet integrated the most important elements of all three.

# Part Five

# THE
# SYMBOLIC
# FRAME

# 12

# *Organizational Culture and Symbols*

To awestruck sightseers in the land of the business hierarch, the architectural grandeur is overpowering and impressive. Stately edifices dominate landscaped vistas of suburbia and mighty skyscrapers silhouette the profiles of major cities. Flowering gardens, soaring plazas, ample parking, vaulted lobbies, air conditioning, musical elevators, carpeted lounges, spacious dining rooms, and hundreds upon hundreds of linear offices bathed relentlessly in fluorescent brilliance dutifully impress gaping tourists.

But all this structural munificence does not divert the expert gamester who looks beyond the steel and concrete public visor of the corporate persona to identify the heraldic markings painted on the battle armor. Like the shields carried by knights of legend, the modern corporate building reeks with symbolism. Far from being a mere architectural wonder, every pane of glass, slab of marble, and foot of carpet performs a dual function in identifying the tournament site. The buildings are impersonal monuments to the power and wealth contained therein. Space itself, in both the exterior and interior layout, is weighted with abstract significance. Just as a heraldic seal reveals a great deal about the one using it, so spatial divisions reveal important information about the modern-day knights [Harragan, 1977, pp. 211–212].

243

The corporate temples that Harragan artfully describes are only one example of the symbols that permeate every facet of organizational life. The symbolic frame seeks to interpret and illuminate the basic issues of meaning and faith that make symbols so powerful in every aspect of the human experience, including life in organizations. This frame presents a world that departs significantly from traditional canons of organizational theories: rationality, certainty, and linearity. It is based on the following unconventional assumptions about the nature of organizations and human behavior:

1.  What is most important about any event is *not* what happened, but *what it means.*
2.  Events and meanings are loosely coupled: the same events can have very different meanings for different people because of differences in the schema that they use to interpret their experience.
3.  Many of the most significant events and processes in organizations are *ambiguous* or *uncertain*—it is often difficult or impossible to know what happened, why it happened, or what will happen next.
4.  The greater the ambiguity and uncertainty, the harder it is to use rational approaches to analysis, problem solving, and decision making.
5.  Faced with uncertainty and ambiguity, human beings create *symbols* to resolve confusion, increase predictability, and provide direction. (Events themselves may remain illogical, random, fluid, and meaningless, but human symbols make them seem otherwise.)
6.  Many organizational events and processes are important more for what they express than for what they produce: they are secular myths, rituals, ceremonies, and sagas that help people find meaning and order in their experience.

Symbolic phenomena are particularly visible in organizations with unclear goals and uncertain technologies. In such organizations, most things are ambiguous. Who has power? What is success? Why was a decision made? What are the goals? The answers are often veiled in a fog of uncertainty (Cohen and March, 1974). Serendipity is often more prominent than rationality in shaping organizational events and activities. Connections between causes and effects, goals and activities are as easily predicted from a table of random numbers or a crystal ball as from technical or systems logic. The symbolic frame is especially helpful in understanding the dynamics of legislatures, public agencies, educational organizations, religious orders, and even health care organizations. But the recognition that symbols are also important in corporations has spread rapidly in recent years.

The symbolic frame sees the rush of organizational life as more *fluid* than linear. Organizations function like complex, constantly changing, organic pinball machines. Decisions, actors, plans, and issues continuously carom through an elastic and ever changing labyrinth of cushions, barriers, and traps. Managers who turn to Peter Drucker's *The Effective Executive* for guidance might do better to study Lewis Carroll's *Through the Looking Glass*.

## Symbols and Initiation

To those with rational biases, the outlook of the symbolic frame may seem farfetched or bizarre. But those who have tried to manage or survive in organizations—particularly in the public and human services sectors—will find that the symbolic frame mirrors much of their experience. Effective, veteran managers typically find that the symbolic frame articulates the kind of wisdom that they have accumulated over the years. Newcomers, whether they know it or not, encounter powerful symbolic issues from the moment they enter an organization:

"The first problem faced by the new member is that of gaining entry into the men's hut—of gaining access to the basic organizational secrets. A key episode here is the rite of passage. This is more or less an affirmation to the individual of the fact that he has been accepted into the men's hut. And, as in the tribe, simply attaining puberty is not sufficient. There must be an accompanying trial and appropriate ritual to mark the event. The so-called primitives had the good sense to make these trials meaningful and direct. Upon attaining puberty you killed a lion and were circumcised.

After a little dancing and what not, you were admitted as a junior member and learned some secrets. The hut is a symbol of, and a medium for maintaining, the status quo and the good of the order" (Ritti and Funkhouser, 1982, p. 3).

Modern amenities such as central heating, flush toilets, and novocaine insulate us from many of the discomforts and uncertainties of earlier eras. It is tempting to believe that we are equally far beyond the primitive drives, sexism, and superstition that gave rise to institutions such as the men's hut. But consider the following stories from the U.S. Congress.

"Paul Tsongas attended his first meeting of the Senate Energy Committee in January 1979. . . . At the time, Tsongas had just finished a well-publicized race against Senator Edward Brooke, his name having thus appeared almost daily in the Washington newspapers for weeks. Taking his seat quietly at the far end of the table as befits a freshman, he listened intently as Chairman Henry Jackson welcomed everyone back for the new Congress and greeted the new members, including Senator 'Ton'gas.' Repeatedly stumbling over the name, Jackson drew ripples of laughter from the audience of lobbyists, staff, and press while Tsongas squirmed in the mandatory silence of freshmen" (Weatherford, 1985, pp. 32–33).

Henry ("Scoop") Jackson was no juvenile prankster; he was a savvy, powerful, and widely respected veteran of the Senate. He was simply welcoming Tsongas to the men's hut in a ritual that employed a verbal surrogate for ritual circumcision. It could have been worse—Tsongas had the advantage of being male. When women enter the men's hut, things can get even uglier: "One of the early female victims was a representative who was a serious feminist. Soon after arriving in Congress, she broke propriety by audaciously proposing an amendment to a military bill of Edward Hebert, Chief of the Defense Clan. When the amendment expectedly received only a single vote, she supposedly snapped at the aged committee chairman: 'I know the only reason my amendment failed is that I've got a vagina.' To which Hebert retorted: 'If you'd been using your vagina instead of your mouth, maybe you'd have gotten a few more votes'" (Weatherford, 1985, p. 35).

That last exchange seems particularly harsh, crass, offensive, and hostile, but its multiple meanings and various interpretations take us right to the heart of the symbolic frame. Readers might wonder why we did not choose a kinder and gentler anecdote, but this one is an extraordinary demonstration of how much can happen in a two-sentence, multilayered transaction. If we take the words literally, the parties are saying:

*Newcomer:*   Because of my physical characteristics as a woman, you are unwilling to accept me as a full member.

*Old-timer:*   If you would use your physical characteristics and offer your sexual favors to us, we *might* accept you.

That is an archetypal exchange in the relations between men and women. Symbolically it is attempted rape, deeply offensive to anyone committed to gender equality. It is emotionally explosive because men have at times communicated to women that their highest role is to be sexual servants. It also creates a very difficult dilemma for the newcomer, namely, how should she respond to this attack? If she lets him know how hurt and infuriated she is, that will only confirm the power of his comment. If she ignores it, then she lets him get away with a blatantly sexist comment. If she fights back, she will find the deck stacked against her. One strategy would be to reverse the attack. If, for example, she were to respond, Are you suggesting that the way for women to get votes in Congress is to sleep with other members? she is likely to turn the tables and create a dilemma for the old-timer. He has, indeed, suggested exactly that, but he cannot afford to admit it. If he did, his words would haunt him during his next reelection campaign.

Framed as an initiation ritual, the gender issue recedes, and we focus on the clash between a new arrival and an established veteran. Here the exchange is very similar to what Senator Tsongas experienced:

*Newcomer:*   I thought my performance deserved a better outcome.

*Old-timer:*   Kid, that's because you're wet behind the ears. You don't know the ropes and don't know your place. We know how to deal with uppity rookies around here. You had better pay a lot more attention to your elders.

Decoded this way, the exchange is a universal feature of initiation rituals, independent of time, place, or gender. The old timer
is reminding a rookie about how things work and who is in charge.
This interpretation adds to our understanding of the emotional
power of what he says, but there is still more going on. The exchange can also be interpreted as two-level negotiation about the
newcomer's role:

*Newcomer:* I expect that, as a woman, I will receive the same
rights and privileges as a man. Now that I'm here I expect full
membership.

*Old-timer:* *We'll* decide on your rights, and you won't get *any*
unless you shape up. There's a *price* for membership, and in your
case it's a high one.

The old-timer is communicating another universal and fundamentally important message: we are willing to accept you as one
of us *if* you are willing to pay the price. A family, group, organization, or society with cohesion and a sense of itself rarely offers free
admission to outsiders. The price is usually higher for people who
are somehow different or who question or threaten existing values,
norms, and patterns. Representatives of groups that have been excluded because of their gender, race, ethnicity, or religion cannot
become full-fledged members of a group or organization unless they
are initiated into the inner sanctum. The initiation may be bitterly
painful, and may raise poignant questions for the newcomer: What
price am I willing to pay to join this group? What is the difference
between legitimate adjustment to a new culture and sacrificing my
own values or identity? Why should I have to tolerate values or
practices that I see as wrong or unjust? Yet, only a weak culture will
accept newcomers with no initiation. The stronger a culture, the
stronger the message to newcomers that, "you are different and not
yet one of us." The initiation reinforces the existing culture at the
same time that it tests the newcomer's ability to become a member.
The sophisticated newcomer will attend carefully to those cultural
signals. The better a newcomer understands the new culture, the
better his or her chances of passing the initiation without compro-
mising personal value and beliefs.

Organizational Culture and Symbols249

The exchange can also be seen as a classic attempt by a
newcomer to reform the organization:

*Newcomer:* I know this place is hostile to women, and I expect
that to change.

*Old-timer:* If you want hostility, I'll show you hostility. Let me
remind you that we're in charge here, and we like this place the way
it is.

In a sense, both parties are playing a part. Newcomers are
expected to bring new ideas and perspectives. It is their *destiny* to
be agents of evolution and reform. Old-timers act as a force for
cohesion, stability, and the wisdom of the past. They are supposed
to pass on old values and practices. If the newcomers fully succumb
to the press of historical tradition, the organization risks stultifica-
tion and decay. If the old-timers fail to play their part, the organization risks chaos and disarray. The newcomer fared badly in the
first round, as newcomers often do. But there will be many more
rounds, and eventually the newcomer will become an old-timer. She
will most likely change and learn from the instruction of her elders,
but with persistence and skill she can leave her own imprint. Some
of her "revolutionary" ideas will come to be embodied in organizational rituals and transmitted as the wisdom of the past to fresh
faces in the decades ahead. By reframing the exchange as an initiation rite, rather than a sexual assault, the newcomer may discover
additional possibilities. She may then be able to make her point
while still allowing the acculturation process to bond newcomers
to the organization. As an example, a newly elected member of the
all-male board of a large corporation experienced a more subtle
form of a similar tactic. She learned that there were sexual innuen-
does and behind-the-scene suggestions about how she became a director. Determined to settle the matter, the new director called a
breakfast session of the directors at the annual meeting. During the
breakfast, someone asked about the agenda. "Well," she said, "the
prevailing rumor is that I'm sleeping with all of you, so I thought
we'd get together and talk about it." Faces first flushed and then
turned to smiles. The ensuing laughter indicated that the newcomer

had been accepted as a full-fledged member. She had made her point and passed the test at the same time.

## Culture and Rituals

Rituals, like other symbols, play a powerful, vital, and complex role in the life of any group or organization. They encode an enormous variety of meanings and messages into economical and emotionally powerful forms. They reflect and express an organization's *culture*—the pattern of beliefs, values, practices, and artifacts that define for its members who they are and how they do things. Culture is both product and process. As product, it embodies the accumulated wisdom of those who were members before we came. As process, it is continually renewed and re-created as new members are taught the old ways and eventually become teachers themselves.

Congress is a case in point because its functioning is so dependent on creating a sense of cohesion and solidarity among its members. The batch of new faces that arrives every other year makes it very difficult to maintain continuity and tradition. But, in one way or another, Congress has to create patterns and practices that are shared and publicly reinforced. Woodrow Wilson noted the complexity of the congressional process in 1880: "Like a vast picture, thronged with figures of equal prominence and crowded with elaborate and obtrusive details, Congress is hard to see satisfactorily and appreciatively at a single view and from a single standpoint. Its complicated forms and diversified structure confuse the vision and conceal the system which underlies its composition" (Weatherford, 1985, p. 19).

Structurally, Congress consists of a House of Representatives with 435 members, a Senate with 100 members, 5 delegates, the vice-president of the United States, and approximately 25,000 staff members. It houses almost 400 committees, each with a chairperson and some with budgets as large as $5 million. The two parties—Republican and Democratic—also have officers, committees, rooms, and staff members. Fifty state delegations have chairpersons and regular meetings. Staff officers include a doorkeeper, a sergeant at arms, a secretary, an architect, chaplains, and a parliamentarian.

The entire congressional body is governed by countless volumes of rules, formal precedents, and operating policies.

Of course, the primary function of Congress is to determine the laws of the United States. It was created to be a decision-making body. But Congress is also manifestly political. The initial price of membership is victory in a political campaign. Over food and wine, lobbyists bring special interests to the attention of the lawmakers. Coalitions form and reform as various issues make their way from the floor, to catacombs, cloakrooms, caucuses, offices, rest rooms, restaurants, and back again to official committees and eventually to formal floor votes. Deal making, bargaining, negotiation, and compromise have been brought to the level of art by those who make our policies and laws. Weatherford, however, uses another metaphor: "The congressional arena clamors in a primeval *bellum omnium in omnes* as one warrior struggles against another, as committee fights committee, and as the two chambers of Congress wage constant warfare on each other. In this glorious and glorified atmosphere, there are no losers, only victors and martyrs; even the defeated have the honor of falling on a heroic field surrounded by eulogies to their noble strength" (1985, p. 240).

Occasionally, the proceedings are interrupted by guerrillas who violate the rules of the game. The "terrible Hs" (Helms, Hatch, Humphrey, and Hayakawa), for example, at times played the role of renegades and rebels. But while rule breakers organized in gangs can disrupt the system, other members of Congress usually coalesce long enough to defeat, dispel, or co-opt the lawbreakers. Congress is an organization whose power and conflict are the stuff of everyday life, but both are governed by norms of dignity and civility.

The halls of Congress also are affected by a variety of human resource issues. Elected officials have needs, sometimes intrusive ones, as can be seen in the peccadilloes of Wilbur Mills, former chairman of the powerful House Appropriations Committee. Personal needs and interpersonal dynamics insinuate themselves into issues of national policy: Senator Lee Metcalf of Montana was believed to be a continuing source of problems for electric utilities because one of them had shut off his mother's power in midwinter in 1913 (Peters and Austin, 1985). Election to Congress does not place one's humanity on hold.

Elected officials also have to develop skills that will make them effective participants in the policy process. Thomas P. ("Tip") O'Neill served as speaker of the House for ten years and owed much of his success to his skill in maintaining genial, good-humored relationships with both allies and opponents. The ineptitude of Congress members less skilled than O'Neill is seldom revealed on the front pages of our newspapers. But their efforts do little to satisfy the needs of their constituents. They are the authors of policies that clog our system with unnecessary red tape. One way or another, the effectiveness of Congress is shaped by the needs and skills of its individual members.

While the structural, political, and human resource frames help, in Wilson's words, to "penetrate the system and focus our vision," they fall short of providing us with a full understanding of Congress. We need still another lens. The deeper mysteries of Congress are revealed only when we consider the U.S. Congress as a contemporary tribe. As such, it has much in common with the Sevante of Brazil, the Kawelka of New Guinea, or the Aztecs of Peru (Weatherford, 1985). Congressional hazing of new members provides just a glimpse of the rich existential underbelly of an extremely powerful and important organization.

Congress has powerful internal and external symbolic features. Its culture is a fascinating historical collection of myths, symbols, heroes and heroines, rituals, ceremonies, shamans, priests, stories, and storytellers. Its members sometimes come from families with a long lineage of congressional ancestry—for example, the Kennedys, Byrds, and Tunneys. Just as often, the congressional inheritance flows from elected officials to staffers or others in the official clan. Because members of Congress are heavily indoctrinated into the ways and traditions of the organization to which they are elected, the job of public service soon becomes an all-encompassing way of life.

The relationship of Congress to its external environment is also highly complex. From a symbolic view, policymaking is a modern ceremony, a dramatic reflection of cherished myths and values. Congressional activity and actions are important as expressive symbols rather than as instrumental outcomes. Like the ceremonies at the court of Versailles, or a Native American rain dance, congressional rituals and ceremony provide entertainment, hope, and a sense that the people have some control over what happens to them. They offer a drama in which Americans can witness the acting out of their nation's values and beliefs.

## Organizational Symbols

The symbolic frame forms a conceptual umbrella for ideas from a variety of disciplines. Symbols and symbolic phenomena have been studied in organization theory and sociology (Selznick, 1957; Blumer, 1969; Clark, 1972; Corwin, 1976; March and Olsen, 1976; Meyer and Rowan, 1978; Weick, 1976a; Davis and others, 1976), and political science (Dittmer, 1977; Edelman, 1971). Freud and Jung relied heavily on symbolic concepts in attempting to understand human behavior. Anthropologists have traditionally focused on symbols and their place in the culture and lives of human beings (Ortner, 1973). Symbolism relies on concepts from a variety of disciplines and the symbolic frame distills these diverse ideas into a lens for viewing life in collective settings.

The symbolic frame centers on the concepts of meaning, belief, and faith. Human beings have always found life bewildering. Events often cannot be explained: loved ones die before their time and evil people often are better off than those who are virtuous. Circumstances cannot always be controlled: tornadoes wipe out communities, and recessions put productive, established firms out of business. Contradictions often cannot be reconciled: good people do bad things and bad people do good ones. Dilemmas and paradoxes are everywhere: How can we keep the peace without building up an arsenal of weapons? How can we protect the lives and property of some citizens without impinging on the freedom of others? On a more prosaic level, how can we help people learn from evaluations that are threatening to them?

The symbolic frame assumes that organizations are full of questions that cannot be answered, problems that cannot be solved, and events that cannot be understood or managed. Whenever that is the case, humans will create and use symbols to bring meaning out of chaos, clarity out of confusion, and predictability out of mystery. *Myths* and other narrative forms such as *fairy tales* and *stories* provide explanations, reconcile contradictions, and resolve dilemmas (Cohen, 1969). *Metaphors* make confusion comprehensible (Ortony, A., 1974). *Scenarios* and *symbolic activities*—such as rituals and ceremonies—provide direction for action in uncharted and seemingly unchartable terrain (Ortner, 1973). Modern reincarnations of such symbolic figures as heroes, heroines, shamans, priests, and storytellers provide guides to and interpretations of what life in organizations really means. An organization's culture, moreover, is revealed and communicated most clearly through its symbols. The many McDonald's franchises are united as much by golden arches, core values, and the legend of Ray Kroc as by sophisticated control systems. Harvard professors may be remarkably free of structural limits, yet they are tightly constrained by rituals of teaching, the values associated with scholarship, and the myths and mystique of Harvard.

**Myths.** The term *myth* is often used pejoratively: "It's only a myth." "That's a myth, not fact." The implication is that there is no truth in myths. Myths may, in fact, communicate very significant truths, but it is important to understand the difference between myths and theories. Theories are subject to verification, that is, their validity can be tested. Myths arise to protect people from uncertainty, but they are not intended to be empirically testable: "Myth helps you put your mind in touch with this experience of being alive. It tells you what the experience is. Marriage for example. What is marriage? The myth tells you what it is. It's the reunion of the separated duad. You are now two in the world, but the recognition of the spiritual identity is what marriage is. It's different from a love affair. It has nothing to do with that. It's another mythological plane of experience." (Campbell, 1988, p. 6).

On another plane of human experience, myths serve several diverse functions: Myths explain. Myths express. Myths maintain solidarity and cohesion. Myths legitimize. Myths communicate unconscious wishes and conflicts. Myths mediate contradictions. Myths provide narrative to anchor the present in the past (Cohen, 1969).

Myths have two sides. On the negative side, they can blind us to new information and opportunities to learn. The myth that "authority must always equal responsibility" is still widely held by many managers, but the myth sets a standard that is both misleading and unrealistic. And consider many of the other myths that managers live by—the myth of planned organizational change, the myth of the need for change, the myth of organizational rationality, the myth of managerial control, the myth of the objective, neutral expert, and the myth of the one best way (Westerlund and Sjostrand, 1979). All of us have accepted one or more of these myths as true in our work with organizations as participants, managers, or consultants. Many of us still believe in them, even though we constantly encounter evidence that contradicts them. The uncertainty that would accompany the loss of our most cherished myths about organizations would be overwhelming. Myths keep us sane—but also dampen our curiosity, refract our images, and misdirect our attention.

Despite their potentially negative consequences, myths are necessary for establishing and maintaining meaning, solidarity, stability, and certainty. Manning describes the functions of myth in law enforcement agencies:

> [The police myth] alleviates social crises by providing a verbal explanation for causes, meanings, and consequences of events that might otherwise be considered inexplicable. . . . Because the actual probability that police action will occur to prevent, punish, or obviate the threat of crimes is low, the myth must be maintained. . . . The police myth sits apart from the actors in a drama of crime, gives them names and faces, and makes them subject to predictable scenarios with beginnings, middles, and ends. . . . Myths of police action concentrate public attention upon their force and conserving potential, even in times of rapid change . . . police myths freeze the organization in time and space, giving it a verified authority over the thing it opposes, and establish it in timeless Manichean *pas de deux* between the two poles of social life. Law enforcement is no longer seen as mere work, involving decisions, discretion, boredom and unpleasantries; it becomes a sort of creed [Manning, 1979, pp. 325-327].

All organizations have myths or sagas (Clark, 1972). But these myths or sagas vary in their strength and intensity (Baldridge,

1975). One of the distinctive characteristics of elite institutions—such as the U.S. Congress, IBM, Ivy League universities, or the Marine Corps—is the presence of strong myths and sagas: One family—535 Equals (some of whom are more equal than others); Respect for the individual; Veritas; and Semper Fidelis are shorthand for the myths that hold these institutions together and infuse daily activities with passion and meaning. The myths are shared widely and reinforced regularly. Educational organizations with strong sagas have a highly developed sense of mission, charismatic leaders at the helm, a committed cadre of influential faculty members, unique instructional programs, highly committed students, and a broad base of social support from alumni and other significant constituents in the environment (Clark, 1972). Reed, Anitoch, Swarthmore, and most exemplary high schools have strong, widely shared myths that are well known to the outside world. So do widely respected hospitals such as Massachusetts General and Beth Israel in Boston, Cedars of Lebanon in Los Angeles, and Virginia Mason in Seattle. The myths support claims of distinctiveness and transform a mere organization into a beloved institution (Clark, 1972).

A shared myth makes it easier to develop internal cohesion and a sense of direction and to maintain the confidence and support of external constituencies. At the same time, myths can be stubbornly resistant to change and can prevent an organization from adapting when conditions have changed dramatically. Consider the fate of AT&T. For a century, it pursued a goal of "universal service" in a noncompetitive environment. Forced to sever the national system from the local operating companies, the firm must now compete aggressively in a deregulated environment. But in changing it risks losing what made it successful.

*Stories and Fairy Tales.* Fairy tales are usually seen as providing entertainment and moral instruction for small children. Fairy tales comfort, reassure, and offer general directions and hope for the future. They also externalize inner conflicts and tensions (Bettelheim, 1977). Stories are often seen as the medium used by those who have nothing factual to offer—a professor, for example, may be accused of doing nothing more than telling "war stories." Such stories are often viewed as a source of entertainment rather than of truth or wisdom. Yet stories can also be used to convey information, morals, values, or myths vividly and convincingly (Mitroff and Kilmann, 1975). Many stories in organizations center on heroes and heroines. In Congress, for example, the legends of Senator Phillip Hart, Congresswoman Barbara Jordan, and Lewis Dascher live on through stories. Hart is remembered as the conscience of the Senate, Jordan as a politician who resigned at the height of her popularity, Dascher as the parliamentarian whose mastery of the rules of protocol made him "the image of Congress" (Weatherford, 1985). Stories and fairy tales both play an important, unappreciated role in modern organizations. Stories perpetuate values and update the historical exploits of heroes and heroines.

A very informative example of an organizational story comes from Procter & Gamble (Wilkins, 1976). As the story goes, some time before the turn of the century, Harley Procter—a son of one of the founders and an excellent salesman—concluded that the company's candle business would face difficulties because of an invention known as the electric light bulb. He was convinced that the company needed to emphasize its soap business. In church one Sunday morning, he experienced a revelation as he listened to the minister read about "ivory palaces" in the Forty-Fifth Psalm. He described this revelation to his very religious board of directors and was able to convince the board to give the company's "white" or "bath" soap a new name: Ivory. The board later approved a national advertising campaign, and Ivory soap became a household phrase.

The story has been used within Procter & Gamble to illustrate a number of important ideas and values—the revelation itself, the success of mass advertising, and the importance of science and honesty in establishing Ivory's composition as "99 and 44/100% Pure." The tale of Harley Procter also illustrates many of the functions that stories serve in organizations. Stories describe events in a way that listeners can easily remember. They summarize vividly, delete distracting details, and present clear, simple messages. They become organizational fairy tales that serve several roles:

1. Fairy tales often fulfill a wishful dream, as in the case of Harley Procter, whose ingenuity and faith built a great business. The memoirs of chief executives often bring that type of fairy tale to mind. Evil powers vainly try to cause the hero's downfall, but he

knows and does what is right, and his career takes on the aura of a dream come true. His power is great, and he uses it benignly.

2. The fairy tale entertains. The fairy tale's excitement is built on the great dangers that modern organizations can present. Just as fairy tale heroes overcome dragons and witches, Harley Procter overcame the threat of the light bulb. When one obstacle is surmounted, a new one will appear, but the courageous manager with the right theory can triumph over adversity and produce a happy ending: the true and correct organization takes form.

3. The fairy tale gives security. A veteran labor negotiator once described what he does by means of an image of a group of people huddled around a fire in a small clearing in the forest. Surrounding them were many unfriendly and hostile people. Periodically, a member of the group needed to go out and soothe the outsiders with a tale of the perfect future. Meanwhile, the group was sitting around the fire murmuring, "one cent, two cents, one cent, two cents." This gave them a sense of security.

4. The fairy tale gives knowledge. Many fairy tales are based on real events cast in colorful and robust terms. The story of Harley Procter reminds today's managers at Proctor & Gamble that faith, ingenuity, and good marketing can turn adversity into great opportunity.

5. The fairy tale is propaganda. It is easily accessible and easy to remember. Since it is enjoyable, it makes the message highly palatable. The story of Harley Procter's revelation takes Ivory soap beyond the realm of the mundane and the commercial: "99 and 44/100% Pure" takes on spiritual overtones and suggests that even God is on the side of Procter & Gamble (Westerlund and Sjostrand, 1979).

Stories are the medium for communicating an organization's central myth to insiders and outsiders. They establish and perpetuate organizational tradition. They are told and recalled in formal meetings and during informal coffee breaks. Stories are used to convey the meaning of the organization to outsiders and thereby gain their confidence and support. A story told by Kenneth Olsen, CEO of Digital Equipment Corporation, provides an excellent example of this:

> Digital is based here in New England, where we see everyday the places that have become famous because of the part they

played in the Revolutionary War. We all know that that war won our independence from the British, but there's another lesson to be learned from it.

The British came out here from Boston, marching in step, wearing their magnificent red coats, black hats, and boots. Their weapons were beautifully matched, and their battle techniques were well executed. When they arrived in Lexington, they found a bunch of farmers hiding behind rocks and trees carrying guns, throwing rocks, and wielding knives. The farmers seemed like a ragtag bunch, wearing all sorts of farming clothes and having no semblance of the order of the British Army.

Well, when the British Army attacked, they did so in formation: they moved in a line toward the farmers, firing and reloading as they had been taught so well to do. And the farmers, hiding behind rocks and trees, began to hit them as they stood out in their formations and bright red coats.

I think we have to remember that the war was won by being flexible, by being able to change what was being done if something seemed better. If we allow our formal plans and specifications to force us into rigid molds, we will lose the war too [O'Connell, 1983, p. 4].

Stories like this one infuse organizational myths into everyday decisions and policies. Stories legitimize existing practice. They let people know what is right and also indicate when things should change.

Stories and fairy tales help to address problems of morale, security, socialization, legitimacy, and communication. A good story provides a way of responding to an unpleasant "fact." One school administrator responded to questions about a new reading program by recounting stories of several children whose ability to read had increased dramatically. As evaluators talked to teachers, parents, and students, they repeatedly heard the same stories. Overall achievement scores became irrelevant in the face of these stories and the way in which they reinforced faith and belief in the program. Such stories can be used to communicate the success of a good program, but they can also be used to obscure the failure of a bad one. If reading scores decline significantly, a few dramatic success stories might be used to prevent anyone from taking a close look at the program's actual effectiveness. Like myths, stories and fairy tales are double-edged swords, but all are powerful means for maintaining collective meaning.

*Ritual and Ceremony.* Except in churches, fraternities, and sororities, ritual and ceremony often have negative connotations: "Citizen participation is only a ritual." "Our new president is more ceremony than substance." "Is this just going to be another ritual, or will we really do something?" Such statements carry the message that ritual and ceremony are empty, repetitive, inflexible, and useless. It is easy to cite examples of meaningless rituals, but doing so can obscure the meaningful role that rituals play in contemporary human affairs. A typical congressional day, for example, consists of a series of appearances in ritualized events:

> The normal work day of a member of Congress is spent making a series of cameo appearances in the various ritual arenas. Early in the morning he bangs the gavel calling a committee hearing to commence and, reading from a sheet, announces the subject, which is always of grave importance, and welcomes the visitors, who are always distinguished and dedicated experts. While the expert rambles on about this issue, the senator listens to an aide explaining about the upcoming meeting with a 4-H Club and at the same time signs a batch of documents thrust at him by his secretary. He then dashes over to the Senate floor, where he presents a one-minute oration on the need to increase widget exports to Third World countries, the national importance of the upcoming peach festival in his home state, and why he favors another round of disarmament talks as a way of solving the energy shortage. Having been delayed on the floor by a long line of other one-minute orators, he is late for another committee meeting that is supposed to mark up and report a bill. The amendment his staff drafted is not presented because the bells ring and the lights flash in the committee room, calling him back to the floor for a vote. Running out of the room with all the other senators, he asks if anyone knows what the vote might be on. Before they can decide, they are in the crowded hall in front of the chamber. Surrounded by lobbyists and by aides trying to find their masters, he barely catches a glimpse of his own legislative assistant pinned against a fluted column on the

far side of the room. Unable to get closer than twenty feet to one another, the aide gestures a set of prearranged signals to his boss telling how they need "to go on this one." Still not knowing the topic, he hurries into the chamber, registers his vote, and tries to get back to the subway before most of the other senators leave the chamber. Sitting with two other senators for the ride back to the office building, he asks if anyone knew what that vote was all about. One thinks it was a motion to table the motion to reconsider the addition of $5 million to build halfway houses for abused spouses. Another insists he heard something about a medal of honor commemorating John Wayne's heroic services to the American nation.

Even though our senator wants to return to the committee markup of the farm bill and propose his amendment, his aide tells him that he must go back to the original committee hearing because two teachers from his home state are about to testify as representatives of the huge and politically active State Educational Association. As he arrives back at the hearings, the teachers are almost finished, but he interrupts to welcome them, restate the importance of the grave subject and distinction of the witnesses, and to beg their forgiveness, for he has an appointment at the White House. The White House bill-signing ceremony is not for another four hours, but such excuses sound much better to hometown folks than telling them that he has a photograph appointment with the 4-H Club [Weatherford, 1985, pp. 206–208].

Historically, all human cultures have used ritual and ceremony to create order, clarity, and predictability, particularly in dealing with issues or problems that are too complex, mysterious, or random to be controlled in any other way. Indian rain dances and the Thanksgiving celebration of the Pilgrims both represent efforts to invoke supernatural assistance in the critical but unpredictable process of raising crops. Baptisms, bar mitzvahs, graduations, weddings, and anniversaries all serve to give meaning and direction to our lives.

We all create rituals to reduce uncertainty and anxiety. Anglers and ballplayers wear "lucky" shirts to help them catch a fish or win a game. Policeman have coffee with fellow officers before going on duty to control anxiety; they know that they will have little control over the situations that they will encounter in the course of their shift. Soldiers pray, send letters to loved ones, and engage in collective rituals before going into battle. Couples have rituals that bind them together and reduce anxiety—like the wife who fears the worst every time her husband takes a business trip and always hides a message somewhere in his suitcase before he leaves.

Rituals and ceremonies are as important to organizations and societies as they are to individuals, and serve four major roles: to socialize, to stabilize, to reduce anxieties and ambiguities, and to convey messages to external constituencies. A family, for example, uses rituals to bind its members together and to fuse past, present, and future into an understandable and comprehensible sense of family destiny: "A family's most intimate sense of itself grows out of years and years of doing the same things together over and over again. A family lives by its daily rituals, even if many of them are so taken for granted that, over time, they become invisible" (Simon, 1989, p. 30).

But rituals and ceremonies are as important to large corporations as they are to families. Several thousand people gather at the annual seminar of the Mary Kay Cosmetics company. They come to hear personal messages from Mary Kay, to applaud the achievements of star salespeople, to hear success stories from people who turned off television soap operas and took up careers, and to celebrate the symbols of their culture. The ceremony brings new members into the fold and helps to maintain uniformity among members of the Mary Kay family long after the seminar ends. It creates the pageant that makes the Mary Kay culture accessible to outsiders, particularly to consumers. Failure and obstacles disappear as they confront the "you can do it" spirit of the company symbolized by the bumblebee—a creature that, according to aerodynamics experts, should be unable to fly, but that, unaware of its limitations, flies anyway.

The exact distinction between ritual and ceremony is elusive. Ceremonies generally happen less frequently and are more grand and elaborate than rituals. In the U.S. Congress, however, ceremony is almost the order of the day:

> Ceremony operates best in a symbolically rich setting that calls
> for special seating arrangements, particular forms of dress, and

various ritual accoutrements such as crosses, thrones, flags, and masks. The full panoply of these objects marches around the congressional chamber in the process of legislation, but it is in the particular use of ritual language that the real nature of congressional ceremony emerges. Because of the sanctity of words, special speech forms are often used . . . to separate normal human interaction from interaction with particularly powerful beings such as gods or potentates. . . . Taboos on the use of personal names and certain pronouns reach an inordinate level in the American Congress, where neither the words *I* nor *you* are proper. Nor can the legislators address one another directly by name, as in "Edward Kennedy," "Ted," or even the more formal "Senator Kennedy." A simple phrase such as "I would like to ask you" becomes "Mr. President, the Senator from Texas would like to ask the Senator from California" [Weatherford, 1985, pp. 189–190].

Ceremony is also evident in other matters of national importance. In the United States, political conventions select candidates, even though in recent years there has been little suspense about the outcome. For several months, competing candidates for the presidency trade clichés and exchange epithets. The same pageantry unfolds each election year. In fact, the rhetoric and spontaneous demonstrations often seem staged, the campaigning is often repetitious and superficial, and the act of voting often seems disconnected from the main drama. But the process of electing a president is an important ceremony. It provides a sense of social involvement. It is an outlet for the expression of both discontent and enthusiasm and provides live drama for people to watch and enjoy. It gives millions of people a sense of participation in an exciting adventure. It draws attention to common social ties and to the importance of accepting the candidate who eventually wins (Edelman, 1977). It provides an opportunity for candidates to reassure the public that there are clear answers to our most important questions and clear solutions to our most difficult problems.

Even in nations with different political processes, elections have important symbolic meanings. Mexico has been dominated by the PRI (the Institutional Revolutionary Party) since 1929, and PRI candidates virtually always win. But that does not prevent candidates from campaigning relentlessly to communicate the image that "I am of the people." People gather in droves to hear the speeches, and there are banners everywhere. The voting process in remote villages unfolds through a ritual like the following (Vogt and Abel, 1977):

1. A crowd gathers and voting booths are set up.

2. A group of literate residents carefully count all the ballots to see that the number equals exactly the official count of voters on the town list.

3. As people watch, an official marks ten ballots with an X for the PRI while one of the literate residents checks off ten names from the list.

4. Another official marks another ten (and so on).

5. Work parties form to deal with the remaining ballots. Two or three literate men mark X on the ballots. Another group folds the ballots. A third group carries the ballots to the ballot box. Another man puts the ballots in the slot.

6. The process continues until all the ballots are filled out and all the names are checked off.

7. An official signs a paper—fifteen copies—noting that the polls opened at 8 A.M. and closed at 5 P.M. and that there were no irregularities in voting.

8. The ballot boxes are collected by other officials and the voting booths are taken down.

The voting process does much more than elect candidates. The campaign gives everyone a chance to come out for the candidate, declare his or her political position, and bargain with a system that is temporarily flexible. Voting is seen as if it were a transaction with the gods: "Here is our political support, our offerings to you, now in exchange we want a new bridge built across the river and the roof of the schoolhouse repaired" (Vogt and Abel, 1977, p. 187).

Despite the cultural differences between the electoral systems in Mexico and the United States, both may be viewed primarily as collective ritual, ceremony, and "a parade of abstract symbols, yet a parade which our experience teaches us to be a benevolent or malevolent force that can be close to omnipotent" (Edelman, 1977, p. 5).

Elections illustrate many of the basic characteristics of rituals and ceremonies. They are repetitious and occur at fixed intervals (such as the four-year cycle for presidential elections). They involve various kinds of stylized behavior. They are staged (political conventions, for example), and they follow a predictable order. They have explicit purposes (such as the democratic selection of candidates), but they also convey both explicit and implicit symbolic messages. They explain, make things comprehensible, and provide meaning (for example, when a challenger explains how current problems have been created by the incumbent). They provide connections and order—elections reassure us of both continuity and predictability in the political process. They provide a bridge between order and chaos. Even though the problems appear to be getting worse, we can select a new candidate who promises to make things better. Rituals both mirror our ideas and shape them: elections mirror a cultural belief in democracy and shape our beliefs about current political problems and solutions.

Rituals are not confined to politics—they play an equally significant role in other organizations. Rituals can communicate meaning from one individual to another, or from an organization to its environment. Some organizational events are clearly ceremonial, such as retirement dinners and welcoming speeches for new employees. But many significant rituals are rarely viewed as such, because they are typically assumed to be rational and instrumental activities. Consider the following examples:

1. Performance appraisals rarely produce learning or useful information about employee performance, yet most organizations persist in conducting them every year.

2. Regular meetings of committees often produce few if any discernible outcomes but do give members another opportunity to make the same speeches and to debate the same perennial issues.

3. Management training programs often produce little visible improvement in managers' skills, but they do socialize participants into the management culture, and they certify the graduates as having special status.

4. Tests and interviews for hiring new employees often produce data of doubtful validity, but they may bolster the self-confidence of those who are hired and allow those who are not to feel that they were treated fairly.

The persistence of processes that never accomplish what they are supposed to is one indication of the need for ritual and ceremony in organizations. They provide order and meaning that help to bind an organization together. If the rituals are properly conducted and attuned to the myths that people value, they can fire the imagination and deepen the beliefs of participants. But if they are out of touch with real needs, they can become cold, empty forms that people resent and avoid. Rituals and ceremonies can release creativity and transform or create meanings, myths, and strategies. They can also cement the *status quo* and block adaptation and learning. As with other symbols, they can cut both ways.

*Metaphor, Humor, and Play.* A symbol is something that stands for something else—often something that is much deeper and more complex than the symbol itself. Metaphors, humor, and play all illustrate the important "as if" quality that symbols have. They provide ways of grappling with issues that are too complex, mysterious, or threatening to deal with more directly.

Metaphors can also be used to make the strange familiar and the familiar strange or to place the self and others on a social continuum. One candidate calls his opponent a jellyfish, and the opponent responds by calling him a barracuda. A new chief executive justifies her reorganization as "cleaning up the mess" that her predecessor left. Others in the organization view it simply as an attempt by an outsider to put a feather in her career cap. Metaphors compress complicated issues into understandable images, and they can affect our attitudes, evaluations, and actions. A college president who sees the university as a factory will probably establish very different policies from a president who sees the university as a craft guild or a shopping center. Consultants who see themselves as organizational physicians are likely to be different from consultants who see themselves as salesmen or shaman.

Humor also serves important "as if" functions. Hansot (1979) argues that it is less important to ask why people are humorous in organizations than to ask why they are so serious. She argues that humor plays a number of important functions in organizations. Humor integrates, expresses skepticism, contributes to flexibility and adaptiveness, and indicates status. Humor is a classic device for distancing, but it can also be used to socialize, include, and convey membership. Humor can establish solidarity and promote face-saving. Most important, humor is a way of illuminating and breaking frames to indicate that any single definition of a situation is arbitrary.

To illustrate the role of humor in reframing organizational events, consider a story about the late Marcus Foster when he was superintendent of schools in Oakland, California. A panicked high school principal called Foster to ask for help: "Twenty-five armed Black Panthers are standing outside my office!" Foster responded immediately, "Think of them as pink panthers," and hung up the phone. The humor in the idea of "pink panthers" enabled the principal to handle the situation brilliantly.

Play and humor are linked and can serve some of the same functions. In most work settings, play and work are sharply distinguished: play is what people do when they are not working. The only images of "play" in common organizational use connote aggression, competition, and struggle ("we've got to beat them at their own game"; "we dropped the ball on that one"; "the ball is in his court now") rather than relaxation and fun.

If play is viewed as a state of mind (Bateson, 1972; Goffman, 1974), any activity can be done playfully. Play permits relaxing the rules in order to explore alternatives. It encourages experimentation, flexibility, and adaptiveness. March (1976) suggests five guidelines for organizational play:

1. Treat goals as hypotheses.
2. Treat intuition as real.
3. Treat hypocrisy as transition.
4. Treat memory as an enemy.
5. Treat experience as a theory.

## Organizations as Cultures

Applying the term *culture* to organizations is not a new idea. Several decades ago Arnold (1938) and Barnard (1938) moved us below the conscious level of organizations to capture a deeper, more powerful force in everyday life. Selznick (1957) and others continued the tradition, but their work failed to capture the full attention of modern theorists or managers, who for many years continued to emphasize the rational properties of organizations. But all that has changed in recent years as a result of a full-scale revival of interest in symbolic ideas. The concept of culture now occupies a powerful place in both academic and managerial discourse.

What culture is and what role it plays in organizations are hotly contested questions. Some agree that organizations have cultures; others prefer to think that organizations are cultures. Definitions of culture range from formal to commonsense ones. Schein (1985, p. 9), for example, defines culture as "a pattern of basic assumptions—invented, discovered, or developed by a given group as it learns to cope with its problems of external adaptation and integration—that has worked well enough to be considered valid and, therefore has to be taught to new members as the correct way to perceive, think, and feel in relation to their problems." Bower (1966) defines culture more succinctly as "the way we do things around here."

There are also different views of the relationship between culture and leadership. Some argue that leaders are shaped by culture, while others believe that, at least under some conditions, leaders can shape culture. Those who believe that leaders can make a difference disagree as to whether symbolic leadership is more often empowering or manipulative. There is still another controversy surrounding the relationship between culture and performance. Some argue that organizations with strong cultures outperform those that rely on policies, rules, or other more obtrusive forms of coordination and motivation. Others reverse the causal relationship: cohesive cultures result from organizational success. Still others point out that cohesive cultures produce better performance only if the cultural patterns fit the demands of the marketplace.

Our view is that every organization develops distinctive beliefs and patterns over time. Many of these patterns and assumptions are unconscious or taken for granted. They are reflected in myths, fairy tales, stories, rituals, ceremonies, and other symbolic forms. Managers who understand the power of symbols have a better chance of influencing their organizations than do those who focus only on other frames.

From a symbolic perspective, meaning, rather than others defined by Maslow, is the most basic human need. Managers who take the time to understand symbolic forms and activities and then go on to encourage their use can help create an effective organization if what the organization stands for is isomorphic with the challenges of the environment or marketplace.

Consider two contrasting examples: Scandinavian Air System (SAS) and Eastern Airlines. Peters and Austin (1985) commented, "One of the most remarkable turnarounds we've ever observed was crafted by Jan Carlzon of (SAS). In the middle of the 1981–83 recession that clobbered most airlines, Carlzon's company went from losing $10 million a year to making $70 million a year on over $2 billion in sales" (p. xxi). When Carlzon became chief executive of SAS, he set out to make it the European business traveler's favorite airline by giving every front-line employee both the opportunity and the responsibility to provide the best possible service for every passenger. Carlzon emphasized that the average SAS passenger came into contact with five SAS employees and that each of those contacts was a "moment of truth." SAS, he said, was no more and no less than fifty million such moments of truth a year.

Eastern Airlines figures in a very different story. Under the leadership of the legendary Eddie Rickenbacker, Eastern became one of the most successful airlines in the world, but over time it failed to adapt to the dramatic changes in the airline industry. Its culture gradually disintegrated, and Eastern entered a long period of declining earnings and increasing hostility between labor and management. The climax came in 1988 when the nearly bankrupt airline was acquired by Frank Lorenzo's Texas Air Corporation. Lorenzo was an aggressive entrepreneur who had entered the airline industry in 1972 with the acquisition of Texas International Airlines. Texas Air at the time was a small regional airline with an outdated fleet and a $7 million negative net worth (Weinberg, 1984). Through a combination of cost cutting, aggressive marketing, creative financing, and tough bargaining with unions, Lorenzo was able to acquire Continental Airlines, New York Air, and People Express Airlines. With the addition of Eastern, Texas Air's combined holdings became, for a time, the largest in the United States airline industry. But Eastern turned out to be very difficult to digest

(Weiner, 1990). Eastern's employees, still loyal to their image of the "old" Eastern, wanted a leader committed to rebuilding the airline's culture of pride and excellence. They got instead a strategy based on cutting costs and selling off assets. Lorenzo consistently managed to alienate his employees (Davis, 1987), and to turn himself into a negative symbol. An influential congressman likened Lorenzo to a nineteenth-century robber baron, and one veteran Eastern pilot said, "We put our heart and soul into this airline, and Frank Lorenzo has pulled that heart and soul out" (Butterfield, 1989, p. 19). When Eastern's machinists went on strike, pilots and flight attendants honored the picket lines, and the airline was virtually shut down (Butterfield, 1989; Weiner, 1990).

When an organization plunges into a crisis of confidence like the one at Eastern Airlines, it needs someone more like Jan Carlzon than Frank Lorenzo, someone who recognizes the power of symbol and culture in building spirit and confidence. Even Frank Lorenzo finally came to that conclusion. In August 1990, Lorenzo announced that he was quitting the airline industry and selling his holdings to Jan Carlzon's SAS (Weiner, 1990, p. D-8). Carlzon said in an interview that Lorenzo's departure was crucial: "Without that in the picture, we wouldn't have done it" (Weiner, 1990, p. A-1).

### Summary

The symbolic frame emphasizes the tribal aspect of contemporary organizations. Traditional views emphasize organizational reality and objectivity. The symbolic frame counterposes a set of concepts that emphasize the complexity and ambiguity of organizational phenomena, as well as the ways in which symbols mediate the meaning of organizational events and activities. Myths and stories give drama, cohesiveness, clarity, and direction to events that would otherwise be confusing and mysterious. Rituals and ceremonies provide ways of taking meaningful action in the face of ambiguity, unpredictability, and threat. Metaphors, humor, and play allow individuals and organizations to escape from the tyranny of facts and logic, to view organizations and their own participation in them as if they were something new and different from their appearance, and to find creative alternatives to existing choices. In *Feast of Fools,* Cox (1969, p. 13) summarizes the importance of symbolism in modern life: "Our links to yesterday and tomorrow depend also on the aesthetic, emotional, and symbolic aspects of human life—on saga, play, and celebration. Without festival and fantasy, man would not really be a historical being at all."

# 13

# *The Organization as Theater*

Theatre as an activity, as a staging of reality, depends on the ability of the audience to frame what they experience as theatre. It depends precisely on the audience recognizing, being aware, that they are an audience; they are witnesses to, not participants in, a performance. It depends further on a distinction between actors and the parts they play—characters may die on stage, but actors will live to take a bow. Finally, theatre depends on a recognition that performances play with reality in such a way as to turn the taken-for-granted into a plausible appearance [Mangham and Overington, 1987, p. 49].

Managers and organization theorists usually assume a linear, cause-effect connection between activities and outcomes. Decisions solve problems. Evaluations separate effective from ineffective programs and people. Leaders make things happen. Administrators administer. Structures coordinate activity. Planning shapes the future. The environment affects decision making, and decisions shape the environment. Such statements seem so obvious that they are rarely questioned.

Yet, these "obvious" connections often fail in the everyday world. Decisions may not decide anything (March and Olsen, 1976). Evaluations rarely accomplish what they are supposed to (Dornbusch and Scott, 1975). Structures may have little to do with activities (Cohen, Deal, Meyer, and Scott, 1979; Weick, 1976a). Things make leaders happen instead of the other way around (Edelman, 1977). Change efforts reinforce the *status quo* (Baldridge and Deal, 1975; Deal and Ross, 1977). Planning produces no plans or produces plans that have no effect on the future.

The development in the United States of the Polaris Missile System was heralded as an example of government activity at its best. One of its distinctive characteristics was the introduction of modern management techniques—such as PERT charts and Program Planning and Budgeting System (PPBS)—into the public sector. Those techniques were reflected in several structural forms, such as specialist roles, technical divisions, management meetings, and a Special Projects Office. Since Polaris turned out to be a highly successful project, it was easy to conclude that the modern management techniques were a major causal factor of this success. The admiral in charge of the project received a plaque recognizing his contribution in bringing modern management techniques to the U.S. Navy. A visiting team of British experts recommended PERT to the British Admiralty.

However, a later study of the Polaris project suggested a different interpretation of what really happened. The activities of the specialists were in fact only loosely coupled to other aspects of the project. The technical division produced plans and charts that were largely ignored. The management meetings served two primary purposes: they were arenas that the admiral used to publicly chide poor performers, and they were revival meetings that reinforced the religious fervor around the Polaris project. The Special Projects Office served as a briefing area in which members of Congress and other visiting dignitaries were informed about the progress of Polaris through an impressive series of diagrams and charts that had little to do with the actual status of the project. The team from the British navy apparently surmised this on their visit and therefore recommended a similar approach (Sapolsky, 1972).

Although the structural forms may not have served their ostensible purposes, they helped to foster a myth that maintained strong external support for the Polaris project and kept its critics at bay. The myth provided breathing space so that people could do their work on the basis of informal coordination, and it helped to

keep their spirits and self-confidence high. The development of the
Polaris missile demonstrates the power of theatre—for audiences
both inside and outside the organization.

The idea that there can be activities without results casts
doubt on a substantial proportion of human endeavor. At first
glance, such a heresy might seem wholly negative—undermining
the hope and morale of those who want to make a contribution to
their organizations. The symbolic frame does argue that cause-and-
effect relationships are often elusive or absent, but it offers a hopeful
interpretation of this phenomenon. Organizational structures, activities, and events are more than simply instrumental. They are
part of the organizational theatre, an ongoing expressive drama that
entertains, creates meaning, and portrays the organization to itself.
Geertz observed of Balinese pageants, "The carefully scripted, assid-
uously enacted ritualism of court culture was, once more, 'not
merely the drapery of political order, but its substance'" (Mangham
and Overington, 1987, p. 39).

Internal theater also plays to an audience outside the organization. It signals to the outside world that all is well. If management is making decisions, if plans are being formulated, if new
units are being created in response to new problems, if sophisticated
evaluation and control systems are in place, then the organization
must be well managed and worthy of support. Getting the drama
right is particularly critical in sectors where outputs are ambiguous
and hard to measure, but good theater also is important even in
highly technical organizations.

Theatre plays a role in a variety of situations. When external
constituencies question the worth of existing practices, organizations promise reform and stage a drama called *Change*. If consumers complain about the quality of its current products, the
organization creates a consumer affairs department and promises
tighter quality standards. If the government questions the fairness
of its personnel practices, the organization hires an affirmative action officer. If the organization is experiencing a crisis, a new leader
is brought in who promises to make substantive changes. An example of this occurred during the crises that rocked Poland beginning
in 1980: "Poland's new Communist party leader, Stanislaw Kania,
last night promised more democracy and pledged the party would

work to regain the confidence of the disquieted Poles. In his first speech as national leader Kania promised less ceremony and more substance and called on the Poles to rally around the party after a summer of labor and political turmoil" (Soderlind, 1980, p. 1).

From the vantage point of the symbolic frame, organizational structures, activities, and events are secular theatre. They express our fears, joys, and expectations. They arouse our emotions and kindle our spirit. They reduce our uncertainty and soothe our bewilderment. They provide a shared basis for understanding events and for moving ahead.

### Structure as Theater

In earlier chapters, organizational structure was depicted as a network of interdependent roles and units coordinated through a variety of horizontal and vertical linkages. Since structure needs to be responsive to organizational purposes, the shape of an organization is determined by its goals, technologies, and environment (Woodward, 1970; Perrow, 1979; Lawrence and Lorsch, 1967). An alternative view is that structure is like stage design: an arrangement of space, lighting, props, and costumes to make the organizational drama vivid and credible to its audience. The dramatic perspective suggests that, at least in most organizations, structure may not have much to do with task and technology after all.

The symbolic view suggests a number of noninstrumental purposes that structure can serve. One purpose is to express the prevailing values and myths of the society. In many organizations, goals are multiple and elusive, the technology is underdeveloped, the linkages between means and ends are poorly understood, and effectiveness is almost impossible to determine. Schools, churches, mental health clinics, personnel departments, and management consulting firms all share these characteristics. One way for such organizations to achieve legitimacy is to maintain an appearance that conforms to the way society *thinks* they should look. The setting and costumes should be appropriate. Churches should have a building, religious artifacts, and a properly attired member of the clergy. Mental health clinics should have waiting rooms, uniformed nurses, and certified mental health professionals.

A study of elementary schools found no relationship between the structure of a school district and classroom instruction. The policies, efforts, and activities of administrators and specialists had little or no impact on how teachers taught. The research suggested that school districts had three major levels of personnel—central administrators, building administrators, and teachers—whose activities were mostly independent of one another. Other research on schools—both public and private—shows similar patterns (Abramowitz, Tenenbaum, Deal, and Stackhouse, 1978). Structure and activity seem to be unrelated to each other, and both are loosely linked with the environment.

Meyer and Rowan (1978) apply symbolic logic to the role of structure in public schools. They argue that a school will have difficulty sustaining public support unless it gives the right answer to three questions: First, does it offer appropriate topics (for example, third-grade English, American history)? Second, are the topics taught to age-graded students by certified teachers? Third, does the school look like a school (with classrooms, a gymnasium, a library, and a flag near the front door)? If the school is an institution of higher education its worth is likely to be measured by the size and beauty of its campus, the number of books in its library, its faculty-student ratio, and the number of professors who received Ph.D. degrees from high-prestige institutions.

Kamens (1977) applies this theme to higher education. First, the major function of colleges and universities is symbolic—to redefine students as graduates possessing special qualities or skills; second, the legitimacy of the transformation must be negotiated with important constituencies; third, this is done through legitimizing myths about the quality of education that are validated by the structural characteristics or appearance of the institution.

The appropriate structural form, in Kamens's view, depends on two major features of an institution: whether it is elite or nonelite and whether it allocates students to a specific corporate group in the society. Each type of institution will espouse a different myth and will dramatize different aspects of its structure. Size, complexity, formal curriculum, admissions procedures, and demographics all vary according to the symbolic messages that the institution attempts to communicate. The main considerations are having the right actors, a suitable script, and an appropriate stage. Elite schools, for example, will dramatize selectivity ("we will only accept one out of ten of the highly qualified candidates"); develop an attractive residential campus ("the residential experience is an essential feature of our total curriculum"); advertise a high ratio of faculty to students ("this provides for ongoing contact and dialogue between individual students and the many dedicated, outstanding faculty members"); develop a curriculum that restrains specialization ("we seek to educate the whole person, rather than to train narrow specialists").

If an institution or its environment changes, then some adaptation will be necessary for the institutional persona to mirror those shifts. A new audience may require a revision in actors, script, or setting. Since legitimacy and worth are judged by correspondence between structural characteristics and prevailing myths, organizations are frequently obliged to alter their appearance to produce consonance. In this view, organizational structures are built out of "blocks" of contemporary myth, a reason why universities adopt core curricula or new programs in cognitive psychology.

Another purpose of organizational structure is to convey a "modern" appearance, that is, to communicate to external audiences that this is not a horse-and-buggy operation, but one that is fully up-to-date. A modern drama must reflect contemporary issues and dilemmas. In response to legal and social pressures, business organizations create affirmative action policies and roles, even though their hiring practices may change very little. As economics becomes increasingly fashionable, banks hire sophisticated economists, but place them in departments well away from the mainstream of decision making. As laws are passed mandating education for children with special needs, schools hire psychologists and learning-disabilities specialists who are featured prominently but who then perform functions that classroom teachers rarely see or understand. In response to criticism of their antiquated management methods, universities adopt sophisticated control systems that produce elaborate printouts but have little effect on operations. Legislatures pass laws on occupational safety, and factories create safety units that post signs that are mostly ignored.

The new structures reflect legal and social expectations and represent a bid for acceptance and support from relevant constituencies. An organization that does not have an affirmative action program signals that it is out of step with prevailing expectations. Nonconformity invites questions, criticism, and inspection. At the same time, it is much easier to appoint an affirmative action officer than to change hiring practices that are deeply embedded in both individual beliefs and organizational culture. Since the presence of the affirmative action officer is much more visible than any given hiring decision, the new role may successfully signal to those outside the organization that a change has occurred, even if the change is only pro forma.

In government, administrative agencies often serve the same symbolic functions. Agencies are created to encapsulate existing ambivalence or conflicts. Conflict between shippers and railroads led to formation of the Interstate Commerce Commission. Conflict between labor and management produced the National Labor Relations Board. Conflict between consumers and producers of food and drugs resulted in the Food and Drug Administration. Concern over pollution led to the Environmental Protection Agency. Yet such agencies often serve mostly political and symbolic functions (Edelman, 1977).

Politically, regulatory agencies are often "captured" by those whom they are supposed to regulate. Major drug companies are far more effective than the public in lobbying and influencing decisions about drug safety. In practice, agencies legitimize elite values, reassure the public that they are zealously protecting its interests, and struggle for continuing funding from the legislature. They reduce tension and uncertainty and increase the public's sense of confidence and security (Edelman, 1977).

From a symbolic perspective, organizations are judged not so much by their actions as by their appearance. The right formal structure provides a ceremonial stage for enacting the correct drama of the day for the appropriate audience. The drama provides reassurance, fosters belief in the purposes of the organization, cultivates and maintains the faith of the audience, and so forth. Structures may do little to coordinate activity or establish relationships among organizational participants, but they do provide internal symbols that help participants to cope, find meaning, and play their role in the drama without reading the wrong lines, upstaging the lead actors, or confusing a tragedy with a comedy.

## Organizational Process as Theater

Structurally administrative and technical processes are the basic tools that organizations use to get work done. These processes include formal meetings, evaluation systems, accounting systems, management information systems, and labor negotiations. Technical processes vary with the task to be achieved. In industrial organizations, workers assemble parts into a salable product or conduct operations that result in a batch of something (such as petroleum or industrial chemicals). In what we might call people-processing organizations, a variety of technical activities can be observed. Professors give lectures to provide students with knowledge and wisdom that will help them in later life. Physicians diagnose illnesses and prescribe treatments to help people get well. Social workers write case reports to identify and remedy conditions that entrap individuals in a cycle of poverty.

People who work in organizations spend much of their time engaged in such processes. To justify the way they spend their time and to maintain a sense of self-worth, they (and others) must believe that the processes work and produce the intended outcomes. But effort does not always lead to effectiveness, and organizational processes often fail to produce what they are supposed to. Many meetings make no decisions, solve no problems, and lead only to a need for more meetings. Conflict is often ignored rather than resolved or managed (Deal and Nutt, 1980). Planning produces documents that no one uses.

Even at the technical core, particularly in people-processing organizations, there is considerable slippage between processes and intended outcomes. Graduates often wonder why the things they learned at the university seem irrelevant or counterproductive in their new work setting. Patients wonder why symptoms linger after medication and treatment. Poor people see that the same problems persist despite the best efforts of social workers. However, even processes that produce no results may still play a vital role in the organizational drama. They serve as scripts and stage markings that provide opportunities for self-expression, forums for airing grievances, and arenas for negotiating new understandings and meanings.

*Meetings.* According to March and Olsen (1976), meetings serve as "garbage cans" into which problems are dumped. At any moment in an organization, there are participants looking for places to expend time and energy, problems looking for solutions, and solutions looking for problems. A scheduled meeting attracts all three, and the outcome of the meeting depends on a complicated interplay among the inputs that happened to arrive: Who came? What problems, concerns, or needs did they bring with them? What solutions or suggestions did they have to offer? Meanwhile, the meeting soaks up excess time and energy. It provides an opportunity for new myths to be created and old ones to be renegotiated. It helps individuals become clearer about their role in the organizational drama and to practice and polish their lines.

A faculty meeting in a distinguished university exemplifies the garbage can logic. The agenda outlined three topics for a two-hour meeting: (1) whether to accept $300,000 to support an annual award for an outstanding woman educator; (2) whether to begin a new doctoral program; (3) whether to approve a new core curriculum in the school's largest department. The discussion of the $300,000 gift lasted one hour and thirty minutes and covered the following issues: sexism, longstanding conflicts between the social sciences and the professions, minority rights, academic freedom, excellence in the university, institutional autonomy, faculty integrity, and declining enrollments. The discussion produced a committee to explore the issue further. In contrast, the discussion of the new doctoral program lasted twenty minutes, and the program was approved unanimously. The discussion about the core curriculum lasted barely ten minutes. The chairman of the committee that developed the new curriculum gave a brief speech and answered one question. The curriculum was also approved unanimously.

The first item on the agenda—the award for a woman educator—elicited the same old topics, problems, and solutions that were carried by the same faculty members from meeting to meeting. The other two items came late in the meeting after some faculty members had already left and resulted in unanimous decisions with little debate or deliberation. Many of the important functions of garbage cans can be easily seen in the discussion of the first time. Older professors had an opportunity to deliver thoughtful speeches, and younger faculty members had a chance to offer new perspectives. The rights of women and minorities were highlighted and reinforced. Academic freedom and institutional autonomy were reaffirmed. The faculty members reminded themselves of the school's excellence. The diversity of the faculty was publicly displayed. A new committee gave vocal individuals an additional opportunity to render service. The school's history and ideology were recreated and reinforced.

Garbage cans are particularly likely to form around issues that are emotionally powerful and symbolically visible, but technically fuzzy. Normally, a discussion of organizational mission is likely to attract a much larger and more diverse set of inputs than a conversation about cost-accounting procedures. Examples of garbage cans in the organizational literature include studies of reorganization (Olsen, 1976b), the choice of a new chief administrator (Olsen, 1976a), and conflict over desegregation (Weiner, 1976). Garbage cans may not produce rational discourse or effective problem solving, but they serve symbolic functions that help to prevent individual and organizational disintegration.

*Planning.* This is an administrative process that has become increasingly prominent as a sign of good management. An organization that does not plan is thought to be reactive, shortsighted, and rudderless. Planning has become a ceremony that an organization must conduct periodically if it wants to maintain its legitimacy. A plan is a badge of honor that organizations wear conspicuously and with pride.

Cohen and March (1974) identify four major functions that plans serve in universities:

1. Plans are symbols. Academic organizations provide few "real" pieces of feedback data. They have nothing analogous to profit or sales figures. How are we doing? Where are we going? An organization that is failing can announce that it has established a plan to revitalize itself. An institution that does not have a nuclear

reactor, or an economics department, can announce a plan to get one, and may see its stock soar past that of rival institutions.

2. Plans become games. In an organization whose goals and technology are unclear, plans and the insistence on plans become an administrative test of will. If a department wants a new program badly enough, it will spend a substantial amount of effort to justify the expenditure by fitting it into a plan. If an administrator wishes to avoid saying yes to everything but has no basis for saying no to anything, asking the department to submit a plan is a way to test its commitment.

3. Plans become excuses for interaction. As several students of planning have noted, benefits come more from the process than from the plan itself. The development of a plan forces some discussion and may induce some interest in and commitment to relatively low priorities in departments and schools. Occasionally, that interaction yields positive results. But rarely does it yield an accurate forecast. As people engage in discussions of the future, they may modify each other's views about what should be done today, but their conclusions about next year are likely to be altered in the interim by changes in personnel, political climate, foundation policy, or student demand.

4. Plans become advertisements. What is frequently called a "plan" by a university is really an investment brochure. It is an attempt to persuade private and public donors of the attractiveness of the institution. Such plans are characterized by glossy photographs, by *ex cathedra* pronouncements of excellence, and by the absence of relevant information.

When they surveyed college presidents, Cohen and March (1974, p. 113) asked about the linkage between plans and current decisions. The responses fell into four main categories:

> "Yes, we have a plan. It is used in capital project and physical location decisions."

> "Yes, we have a plan. Here it is. It was made during the administration of our last president. We are working on a new one."

"No, we do not have a plan. We should. We are working on one."

"I think there's a plan around here someplace. Miss Jones, do we have a copy of our comprehensive, ten-year plan?"

A study of a large-scale planning project in a suburban school district (Edelfson, Johnson, and Stromquist, 1977) provides another illustration of the symbolic importance of planning. Project Redesign was a five-year planning effort, supported by federal funds, that involved a significant proportion of the district's professionals and citizens in creating a means for the school district to meet the challenges of the 1980s.

The plan produced no major decisions or changes in the district. But it did provide participants with the chance to participate and interact, which they liked. It provided a garbage can that attracted a variety of problems, solutions, and conflicts that might have caused more difficulty if they had surfaced in some other arena. It provided the district with another opportunity to present itself as a model district. It renewed faith in the virtues of participation, the merits of grass-roots democracy, the value of good ideas, and the efficacy of modern planning techniques.

*Evaluation.* Assessing the value of people, departments, and programs is a major activity in almost all organizations. Evaluation efforts often consume substantial time and effort and result in lengthy reports that are then presented with considerable ceremony in formal meetings. Universities convene visiting committees to evaluate schools or departments. The federal government mandates evaluations of many of its programs. Social service agencies commission studies or program audits when important problems or issues arise. Yet the results typically disappear into the recesses of people's minds or the shelves of administrators' offices.

Organizations need to undertake evaluations if they are to be viewed as responsible, serious, and well managed, even though the results of evaluations are rarely used for decision making. Evaluations are used for other purposes. Evaluation data can be used as a weapon in political battles or as justification for decisions that would have been made in any event (Weiss, 1980). Evaluation fosters belief, confidence, and support from external constituencies and benefactors.

In public organizations, Floden and Weiner (1978, p. 17) argue, "[e]valuation is a ritual whose function is to calm the anxieties of the citizenry and to perpetuate an image of government rationality, efficiency, and accountability. The very act of requiring and commissioning evaluations may create the impression that government is seriously committed to the pursuit of publicly espoused goals, such as increasing student achievement or reducing malnutrition. Evaluations lend credence to this image even when programs are created to appease interest groups."

The picture of a committed government serves two functions. First, it improves the image of public officials. In both democratic and authoritarian systems, political leaders must appear to be confident, efficacious, and in control if they hope to produce any changes (Arnold, 1938; Ellul, 1965). The impression of government rationality also promotes a feeling of security in the citizenry. Societal problems are often magnified by the media to the point where a crisis seems imminent. The threat of crisis leads to a widespread sense of helplessness and hopelessness. Evaluations serve to combat this feeling by fostering the belief that the government is acting on everyone's behalf to find solutions to pressing problems. The publicity given to these efforts reduces the level of public anxiety, whether or not evaluations produce useful information. Evaluations may also serve as a means for reducing complex social problems to a choice between relatively well-defined alternatives. The reduction of apparent complexity acts both to make the problems seem more manageable and to give citizens the sense that they have a firm understanding of the issues involved (Ellul, 1965).

The evaluation process often takes the form of high drama. Prestigious evaluators are hired, and the process receives considerable publicity. Participants wear "costumes" that are more formal than normal dress. New roles are enacted: evaluators ask penetrating questions, and respondents give answers that portray the world as it is supposed to be. The results are often presented dramatically, especially when they are favorable. Negative results, in contrast, are often couched in vacuous language with high-sounding recommendations that no one is likely to take very seriously. All attempts to solve the problems disappear after the ceremony is concluded.

Occasionally, an evaluator blows the whistle by producing a highly critical report. The drama then becomes a tragedy that is often injurious to both parties. In the United States, a widely publicized report on public education (the Coleman Report) argued the thesis that "schools don't make a difference." The report and the subsequent debate undermined public confidence in the schools at the same time as it raised questions about the cohesion and maturity of the social sciences.

Evaluation persists primarily because it serves significant symbolic purposes. Without it, we would worry about the efficiency and effectiveness of activities. Evaluation produces magic numbers to help us believe that things are working. An evaluation shows that organizations take goals seriously. It demonstrates that an organization cares about its performance and wants to improve itself. Evaluations provide opportunities for participants to share their opinions and to have them publicly heard and recognized. Evaluation results help people relabel old practices, provide opportunities for adventure outside the normal routine, and foster new beliefs (Rallis, 1980).

*Collective Bargaining.* This is the most common process for resolving conflicts and achieving workable agreements between labor and management. Through a combination of persuasion and muscle flexing, the two sides reach an agreement on wages and working conditions. But collective bargaining can also be viewed as a drama: "A young executive took the helm of a firm with the intention of eliminating the bickering and conflict between management and labor. He commissioned a study of the company's wage structure and went to the bargaining table to present his offer. He informed the union representatives what he had done, and offered them more than they had expected to get. The astonished union leaders berated the executive for undermining the process of collective bargaining and asked for another five cents an hour beyond his offer" (Blum, 1961, pp. 63-64).

The story supports the symbolic interpretation of collective bargaining as drama. When some actors fail to follow the script, others become angry because they cannot deliver their lines. The drama is played to an audience, and it represents a struggle designed to convince each side that the ending was the result of a heroic battle. The drama, if well acted, conveys the message that the two opponents fought hard and persistently for what they believed was right (Blum, 1961). It conceals the reality that, in many cases, the actors knew in advance exactly how the play would end.

*Power.* This is usually seen as an attribute that individuals or systems possess—an attribute based on the resources that they are able to control. Power is discussed as if it were real, that is, it is seen as something that can be seized, exercised, or redistributed. But power, like many other organizational phenomena, is often ambiguous. It is not always easy to determine who has power in a given organization. How one goes about getting power is often unclear. It is sometimes even hard to know when power is being exercised.

From a symbolic perspective, individuals have power if others believe that they do. Such beliefs are encouraged by events or outcomes that become linked to particular individuals. The unemployment rate improves, and incumbents take credit. A firm becomes more profitable, and we attribute its success to the chief executive. A new program is started at a time when things are getting better anyway, and the program gets credit.

The belief that certain individuals are powerful is often based on observing their interactions. Individuals with formal status who talk a lot, who belong to many committees, and who feel close to the action are likely to be perceived as having power. But there may be little relationship between those characteristics and the ability to get what one wants. The relationship may be negative. Those who are dissatisfied with an organization may plunge into all sorts of activities in an attempt to change it and still have no impact (Enderud, 1976).

Myths of leadership generally attribute power to individuals. Individuals cause important events to occur. Whether things are going well or badly, we like to think that we can legitimately hold someone responsible. Cohen and March (1974) have this to say about college presidents: "Presidents negotiate with their audiences on the interpretations of their power. As a result, during recent years of campus troubles, many college presidents sought to emphasize the limitations of presidential control. During the more glorious days of conspicuous success, they solicited a recognition of their responsibility for events. This is likely to lead to popular impressions of strong presidents during good times and weak presidents during bad times. Persons who are primarily exposed to the symbolic presidency (for example, outsiders) will tend to exaggerate the power of the presidency. Those people who have tried to accomplish something in the institution with presidential support (for example, educational reforms) will tend to underestimate presidential power or presidential will" (pp. 198–199).

Edelman (1977) makes a similar point: "Leaders lead, followers follow, and organizations prosper. While this logic is pervasive, it is somewhat misleading. Marching one step ahead of a crowd moving in a particular direction may define realistically the connection between leadership and followership. Successful leadership is having followers who believe in the leader. By believing, people are encouraged to link positive events with leadership behaviors. George Gallup once remarked, 'People tend to judge a man by his goals, by what he is trying to do, and not necessarily by what he accomplishes or how well he succeeds' " (p. 73).

The effectiveness of leaders is judged on the basis of their style and their ability to cope. It also helps if they have the opportunity to participate in well-publicized but noncontroversial activities and to figure in dramatic performances that emphasize the traits popularly associated with leadership—traits such as forcefulness, responsibility, courage, and decency. The assumption that leaders can make a real difference is reassuring but often fallacious. Cohen and March (1974) compare the college president to the driver of a skidding automobile: "The marginal judgments he makes, his skill, and his luck will probably make some difference to the life prospects of his riders. As a result, his responsibilities are heavy. But whether he is convicted of manslaughter or receives a medal for heroism is largely outside his control" (p. 203).

Leadership, therefore, is less a matter of action than of appearance. And when leaders do make a difference in a more proactive sense, it is usually by enriching and updating the script for the

organizational drama—by constructing new myths that alter beliefs
and generate faith among members of their audience.

## Summary

In a world of chaos, ambiguity, and uncertainty, individuals search
for order, predictability, and meaning. Rather than admit that the
ambiguity may not be resolvable or the uncertainty reducible, individuals and societies create symbolic solutions. Organizational
structure and processes then serve as theater: they become dramatic
performances that promote cohesion inside organizations and bond
organizations to their environment.

The symbolic frame introduces and elaborates concepts that
in the past were rarely applied to organizations. These concepts
sharply redefine organizational dynamics and have significant implications for managing and changing organizations. Historically,
theories of management and organization have focused on instrumental issues. We see problems, try to develop and implement solutions, and then ask, What did we accomplish? Often, the answer
is nothing or not much, and we find ourselves repeating the old saw
that the more things change, the more they remain the same. Such
a message is disheartening and disillusioning. It produces a sense of
helplessness and a belief that things will never improve significantly.

The symbolic frame sounds a more hopeful note. For a variety of reasons, we have decided to reframe our organization. It may
be that we are restless, frustrated, or feel the need to renew our faith
in the organization. We therefore enact a new play called *Change*.
At the end of the pageant, we can ask three questions:

1. What was expressed?
2. What was attracted?
3. What was legitimized?

The answers are often enormously uplifting. The drama allows us to resolve contradictions and envision a solution to our
problems. Old conflicts, new blood, borrowed expertise, and vital
issues are attracted into the arena of change where they combine and
begin to produce new myths and beliefs. Change becomes exciting,

uplifting, and vital. The message is heartening and spiritually invigorating. There is always hope. The world is always different. Each day is potentially more exciting and full of meaning than the next. If not, we can change the symbols, revise the drama, develop new myths, or dance.

# 14

# *Organizational Culture in Action*

How does the symbolic frame apply to organizations and small groups? What general principles do managers need to observe in building or shaping a meaningful culture? Every group or organization needs to attend to symbols and symbolic activity, and one highly successful group of engineers has demonstrated how to go about doing this.

In the 1970s a small group of Data General engineers created a new thirty-two-bit computer in record time. With fewer resources and less support, the Eagle Group outperformed all other divisions at Data General and developed a product that could compete with Digital Equipment's VAX, which at that time represented the state-of-the-art in computer technology. In *The Soul of a New Machine*, Kidder (1981) documented the group's deeds and accomplishments, noting that "more than two dozen people worked on [the project] over time, without any real hope of material rewards, for a year and a half; and afterward most of them felt glad . . . [that they] had created 4,096 lines of microcode, which fit into a volume about eight inches thick; diagnostic programs amounting to thousands of lines of code; over 200,000 lines of system software; several hundred pages of flow charts; about 240 pages of schematics; hundreds and hundreds of engineering changes from the debugging; twenty hours of videotape to describe the new machine; and now a couple of functioning computers in blue-and-white cases, plus orders for many more on the way" (pp. 275–276).

## Sources of Eagle Group's Success?

Why did this group succeed when so many groups of engineers—or of educators, physicians, executives, or graduate students—start out with high hopes but eventually fail? Did the individuals of the Eagle project bring extraordinary talent to it? Not really. While each was highly skilled, there were equally talented engineers working on other Data General projects. Were team members always treated with dignity and respect? Quite the contrary. As one engineer noted, "no one ever pats anyone on the back" (Kidder, 1981, p. 179). Instead, the group experienced what they called mushroom management: "Put 'em in the dark, feed 'em shit, and watch 'em grow" (p. 109). For over a year, group members jeopardized their health, their families, and their careers: "I'm flat out by definition. I'm a mess. It's terrible. . . . It's a lot of fun" (p. 119).

Were financial rewards a motivating factor? One engineer echoed the sentiments of his colleagues, "I don't work for money" (p. 61). Nor were they motivated by fame. Their heroic efforts were rewarded neither by formal appreciation nor by official applause. The group quietly dissolved shortly after completing the new computer, and most members of the team moved unrecognized to other parts of Data General—or to other companies.

Perhaps it was the group's structure that accounted for its success. Were its members pursuing well-defined and laudable goals? The group leader, Tom West, offered the following precept: "Not everything worth doing is worth doing well" (p. 119). Pushed to translate his maxim, he elaborated, "If you can do a quick-and-dirty job and it works, do it" (p. 119). Did the group have an especially clear and well-coordinated set of roles and relationships? According to Kidder, it kept no charts, graphs, or organization tables that meant anything. One of the group's engineers put it even more graphically: "The whole management structure—anyone in the Harvard Business School would have barfed" (p. 116).

Maybe the political frame can help unravel the secret of the group's phenomenal performance. Perhaps its members were motivated more by power than by money: "There's a big high in here somewhere for me that I don't fully understand . . . some of it's a new power trip. . . . The reason I work is because I win" (p. 179). They were encouraged to circumvent the formal structure to advance the group's interests: "If you can't get what you need from some manager at your level in another department, go to his boss—that's the way to get things done" (p. 191). Group members were also unusually direct and confrontational: "Feeling sorely provoked, [David] Peck one day said to this engineer, 'You're an asshole.' Ordered by his boss to apologize, Peck went to the man he had insulted, acting sheepish and said, 'I'm sorry you're an asshole'" (p. 224).

The group was highly competitive with others in the company: "There's a thing you learn at Data General, if you work here for any period of time . . . that nothing ever happens unless you push it" (p. 111). They also competed with one another. Their "tube wars" provide a typical example: "One day [Carl] Alsing [head of Microkids] came back from lunch and went to work on his terminal. Everything looked right, all his files seemed to be in place—until he tried to do something with them. Then, to his surprise, he found that all of them were vacant. 'It was like opening a filing cabinet and finding all the drawers empty. They were dummy files. It took me an hour to find the real ones. So now I can never be sure, when I log on the system, that what I see is real.' Alsing struck back. He created an encrypted file and tantalized the team, 'There's erotic writing in there and if you can find it, you can read it'" (p. 107).

Here we begin to encounter the secrets of the group's success. The tube wars—and other exchanges among group members—were more than games. The exchanges were a form of play that released tension, created bonds, and contributed to group spirit. Their performance was the result of "webs of voluntary mutual responsibility, the product of many 'signings-up' [that] held them together" (p. 120). A shared and cohesive culture, rather than a clear structure, fulfilled needs, or a negotiated political order provided the invisible force that gave the group its drive: "Control seemed to be nowhere and everywhere at once. It was an almost intangible commodity, passed from hand to hand down the hierarchy of the group, and everyone got some. [Tom] West gave Alsing responsibility for getting the microcode done on time. Retaining ultimate authority, Alsing let Holland assume almost complete technical command; and after establishing general rules and keeping an eye on them, Holland gave each Microkid virtual reign over a portion of the code" (p. 159).

## Leading Principles

From the Eagle Group's experience we can distill several important tenets of the symbolic frame that apply to any group:

*How Someone Becomes a Group Member Is Important.* Joining a group is more than a rational decision. It is nearly always a mutual choice that is enriched by some form of ritual. In the Eagle Group the decision to become a member was called signing up (Kidder, 1981, p. 66):

> "It's gonna be tough," says Alsing. "If we hired you, you'd be working with a bunch of cynics and egotists and it'd be hard to keep up with them."
> "That doesn't scare me," says the recruit.
> "There's a lot of fast people in this group," Alsing goes on. "It's gonna be a real hard job with a lot of long hours, and I mean *long* hours."
> "No," says the recruit, in words more or less like these. "That's what I want to do, get in on the ground floor of a new architecture. I want to do a big machine. I want to be where the action is."
> "Well," says Alsing, pulling a long face. "We can only let in the best of this year's graduates. We've already let in some awfully fast people. We'll have to let you know."
> (We tell him that we only let in the best. Then we let him in.)
> "I don't know," said Alsing, after it was all done. "It was kind of like recruiting for a suicide mission. You're gonna die, but you're gonna die in glory."

This was the ritual of signing up. Through the ritual, an engineer became part of a special effort and agreed to forsake family, friends, and health to accomplish the impossible. Signing up was a sacred declaration: "I want to do this job and I'll give it my heart and soul" (Kidder, 1981, p. 63).

***Diversity Gives a Team a Competitive Advantage.*** While nearly all the group's members were engineers, each had a unique talent and style. Tom West, the group's official leader, was by reputation a highly talented technical debugger. He was also aloof and unapproachable—the Prince of Darkness. Wallach, the group's computer architect, was a highly creative maverick. According to Kidder (1981, p. 75), before accepting West's invitation to join the group, he went to de Castro, the president of Data General:

"Okay," says Wallach, "What the fuck do you want?"

"I want a thirty-two-bit Eclipse," says de Castro.

"Are you sure? If we can do this, you won't cancel it on us? You'll leave us alone?"

"That's what I want, a thirty-two-bit Eclipse and no mode bit."

Wallach signed up, and his love of literature, stories, and verse provided a literary substructure for the technical architecture of the new machine. Alsing, the group's microcode expert, was as warm and approachable as West was cold and remote. He headed the Microkids, the group of young engineers who programmed the new machine. Ed Rasala, Alsing's counterpart, "Lieutenant of Hardware," headed the Hardy Boys, the group's hardware design team. If Alsing was a creative genius, Rasala was a hyperactive, risk-taking, and detail-oriented mechanic. "I may not be the smartest designer in the world, a CPU giant, but I'm dumb enough to stick with it to the end" (p. 142).

Diversity among the group's top engineers was institutionalized in specialized functions. West buffered the team from upper-management interference and served as a group "devil." Wallach created the original design. Alsing and the Microkids created "a symbolic language that would fuse the physical machine with the programs and tell it what to do" (p. 60). Rasala and the Hardy Boys built the machine's actual circuitry. Understandably, there was tension among these diverse individuals and groups. But harnessing the resulting energy galvanized the different parts into a working team: "Guyer's a mechanic, he likes to fix things. Holberger gets an esoteric notion of an idea and then starts implementing it. Holberger gets a thrill out of making it work, but also out of inventing it. Guyer's more of a craftsman. Guyer can build it and refine it and he works for the pleasure of getting the last bug out of it" (p. 198).

"Microkids and Hardy Boys are arguing. A Microkid wants the hardware to perform a certain function. A Hardy Boy tells him, 'No way—I already did my design for microcode to do that.' They make a deal: 'I'll encode this for you, if you'll do this other function in hardware.' 'All right' " (p. 116).

*Example Rather Than Command Holds a Group Together.* Wallach's design provided some coordination among Eagle's autonomous individuals and groups. Very little was accomplished through rules. The group had rules but "never explicitly [played] by those rules" (p. 113). De Castro, Data General's CEO, was referred to as a distant god. "De Castro's down here only as a presence . . . yet as a presence, he's an iron hand" (p. 269). De Castro's maxim was, "I guess the only good strategy is one that no one else understands" (p. 113).

West, the group's official leader, rarely interfered with the actual work, nor was he highly visible in the laboratory. One Sunday morning in January, however, when the team was supposed to be resting, a Hardy Boy happened to come by the lab and found West sitting in front of one of the prototypes. The next Sunday, West did not return, and after that they rarely saw him in the lab. For a long time he did not even hint that he might again put his own hands inside the machine.

West's contribution to the project was causing trouble for the engineers and making mundane events and issues appear to be special. "He created . . . a seemingly endless series of 'brushfires,' and got his staff charged up about putting them out. He was always finding romance and excitement in the seemingly ordinary" (p. 275).

The other members of the group's formal leadership followed de Castro and West in creating ambiguity, encouraging inventiveness, and leading by example. Heroes of the moment provided inspiration and direction. Subtle and implicit signals rather than concrete and explicit guidelines or decisions held the group together and directed it toward a common goal.

*A Specialized Language Fosters Cohesion and Commitment.* Every group develops words, phrases, and metaphors unique to its circumstances. A specialized language both reflects and shapes a group's culture. A common language allows group members to communicate easily, with minimal misunderstandings. To the members of the Eagle group, for example, a *kludge* was something to be avoided—perhaps a machine with a loose wire held together with adhesive tape; a *canard* was anything false; *fundamentals* were the source of enlightened thinking; and the word *realistically* typically prefaced flights of fantasy. "Give me a *core dump*" meant tell me your thoughts. A *stack overflow* meant that an engineer's memory compartments were too full; a *one-stack-deep* mind indicated shallow thinking. "Eagle" provided a label for the project, while "Hardy Boys" and "Microkids" gave identity to the major subgroups. The two prototype computers were named Woodstock and Trixie.

A shared language binds a group together and is a visible sign of membership. It also sets a group apart from outsiders and reinforces the group's unique values and beliefs. Asked about the Eagle group's headquarters, Tom West observed, "It's like a cattle yard. What goes on here is not part of the real world." Asked for an explanation, West remarked, "Mmmmmmmmm, the language is different" (p. 50).

*Stories Carry History and Values, While Reinforcing Group Identity.* In high-performing organizations and groups, stories keep traditions alive and provide examples to guide everyday behavior. The subtle and powerful influence of Eagle's leaders—some of whom remained distant and remote—often had its source in stories about them. Tom West's reputation as a "troublemaker" and "excitement-junkie" was conveyed through stories about the computer wars of the mid seventies. Kidder (1981, p. 44) quotes Alsing as saying:

> West's never unprepared in any kind of meeting. He doesn't
> talk fast or raise his voice. He conveys—it's not enthusiasm

exactly, it's the intensity of someone who's weathering a storm and showing us the way out. He's saying, "Look, we gotta move this way." Then once he gets the VP's to say it sounds good, Tom goes to some of the software people and some of his own people. "The bosses are signed up for this," he tells them. "Can I get you signed up to do your part?" He goes around and hits people one at a time, gets 'em enthused. They say, "Ahhh, it sounds like you're just gonna put a bag on the side of the Eclipse," and Tom'll give 'em his little grin and say, "It's more than that, we're really gonna build this fucker and it's gonna be fast as greased lightning." He tells them, "We're gonna do it by April."

A story about Wallach emphasized another element in Eagle's cultural glue, namely, irreverent disdain for superiors, which reinforced the group's sense of ground-level creativity and independence: "Wallach had decided to 'play with the turkey's (an executive) mind.' For a week, everytime he ran into this man, Wallach would smile at him. The following week, however, whenever Wallach encountered the man, he would make himself look sad. Finally, the executive could stand it no longer and asked for an explanation—which was what Wallach had been waiting for. 'Steve, how come you're so happy when you see me sometimes, and then sometimes you look like you wish I wasn't there?'

" 'I don't know,' said Wallach, 'I'm very moody.'

" 'Then,' recalled Wallach, 'I went into my office, closed the door, and got hysterical' " (Kidder, 1981, p. 73).

Stories about the dogged persistence and creativity of group members created an atmosphere that encouraged others to go beyond themselves. As they neared completion, a debugging problem threatened the entire project. Veres, one of the engineers, worked day and night, with others, to locate the error:

A few hours later, Holberger [Hardy Boys—Rasala's Lieutenant] drives into Westborough. The sun is in his eyes this morning, and he wonders in a detached way where it will be hitting his windshield when they finish this job. Debugging Eagle has the feel of a career in itself. Holberger isn't thinking about any one problem, but about all the various problems at once, as he walks into the lab. What greets him there surprises him. He

shows it by smiling wryly. A great heap of paper lies on the
floor, a continuous sheet of computer paper streaming out of
the carriage at [the] system console. Stretched out, the sheet
would run across the room and back again several times. You
could fit a fairly detailed description of American history . . .
on it. Veres sits in the midst of this chaos, the picture of the
scholar. He's examined it all. He turns to Holberger. "I found
it," he says [Kidder, 1981, p. 207].

*Humor and Play Reduce Tension and Encourage Creativity.*
Groups often focus single-mindedly on the task at hand and dis-
courage any activity not related to work. Seriousness replaces god-
liness as a desired virtue. But effective groups encourage both play
and humor. Surgical teams and cockpit crews, among other groups,
have learned that joking and playful banter are an essential source
of invention and team spirit. Humor releases tension and helps to
resolve the issues that arise from day-to-day routines as well as from
sudden emergencies.

Play among the members of the Eagle project was an essential part of group life: "Alsing figured that before the Microkids did
anything else, they must learn how to manipulate Trixie [the com-
puter]. He didn't want simply to give them a stack of manuals and
say 'Figure it out.' So he made up a game. As the Microkids arrived,
in ones and twos, during the summer of 1978, he told each of them
to figure how to write a certain kind of program in Trixie's assembly language. This program must fetch and print out the contents
of a certain file, stored inside the computer. 'So they learned the way
around the system and they were very pleased,' said Alsing. 'But
when they came to the file finally, they found that access to it was
denied them'" (pp. 105–106).

Through the resulting play, the Microkids learned to use the
computer, coalesced into a team, and learned their way around their
new environment. They also learned that creativity was valued by
their leader.

Humor provided a continuous thread as the team struggled
to accomplish its formidable task. The humor often stretched the
boundaries of good taste, but that, too, was part of the group's
identity:

[Alsing] drew his chair up to his terminal and typed a few letters—a short code that put him in touch with Trixie, which was the machine reserved for the use of his microcoding team. "We've anthropomorphized Trixie to a ridiculous extent," he said.

He typed, WHO.

On the dark-blue screen of the cathode-ray tube, with alacrity, an answer appeared: CARL.

WHERE, typed Alsing.

IN THE ROAD, WHERE ELSE! Trixie replied.

HOW.

ERROR, read the message on the screen.

"Oh, yeah, I forgot," said Alsing, and he typed, PLEASE HOW.

THAT'S FOR US TO KNOW AND YOU TO FIND OUT.

Alsing seemed satisfied with that, and he typed, WHEN.

RIGHT FUCKING NOW, wrote the machine.

WHY, wrote Alsing.

BECAUSE WE LIKE TO CARL [Kidder, 1981, pp. 90–91].

Throughout the year and a half it took to build their new machine, the engineers of the Eagle Project relied on play and humor as a source of relaxation, stimulation, and renewal.

*Ritual and Ceremony Lift Spirits and Reinforce Values.* Ritual and ceremony are expressive activities. As parentheses on an ordinary workday, they enclose a special form of human behavior. What occurs on the surface of such activities is not nearly so important as the deeper meanings that are communicated. Ritual and ceremony provide opportunities for reinforcing values and bonding individuals to the organization and to one another. Despite stereotypes of engineers as narrowly task focused, the Eagle Group was very aware of the importance of symbolic activity, and the leadership encouraged ritual and ceremony from the project's beginning.

Rasala, head of the Hardy Boys, for example, established a rule requiring that changes in the boards of the prototype be updated each morning. This activity allowed efforts to be coordinated in a formal way. More important, the daily updating provided an occasion for informal communication, bantering, and gaining a sense of the whole. The engineers, however, disliked the daily procedure, so Rasala changed it to once a week—on Saturday. He made it a point to always be there himself for the updating:

"Above all, Rasala wanted around him engineers who took an interest in the entire computer, not just in the parts that they had designed. He said that was what was needed to get Eagle out the door on time. He wanted the Hardy Boys to bind into a real team, and he spoke with evident frustration of engineers who were reluctant to work on boards that someone else had designed, who felt comfortable only when working on their own" (Kidder, 1981, p. 150).

Eagle's leaders met regularly. But their meetings focused more on symbolic issues than on substance and decisions: "Steve Wallach, Carl Alsing, and Ed Rasala looked forward to their collective weekly meetings with West. He held them in his office on Fridays at 3:00 P.M. They'd do some business, West would tell them the latest company gossip, and, like Alsing at his own meetings with subordinates, West might submit to what Alsing called 'zingers from his troops.' 'We could be in a lot of trouble here,' West might say, referring to some current problem. And Wallach or Rasala would reply, 'You mean *you* could be in a lot of trouble, right, Tom?' It was Friday, they were going home soon, and relaxing, they could half forget that they would be coming back to work tomorrow" (p. 132).

At Alsing's urging, West made himself available to anyone who wished to talk informally to him: "At that transitional evening hour, before hurrying away toward his farmhouse, West would leave his door ajar, like an invitation, and leaning back, his hands fallen still, he would entertain most any visitor" (p. 133).

In addition to the recurring rituals, the Eagle group held periodic ceremonies to raise spirits and reinforce the common direction. Alsing instigated a ceremony toward the end of the project to provide a burst of renewed energy for the final push. The festivities called attention to the values of creativity, hard work, and teamwork: As their first favorite pretext for a party, they used a presentation of the Honorary Microder Awards that Alsing and the Microcoder Team had instituted. Not to be outdone, the Hardy Boys cooked up the PAL Awards, the first of which they gave to the Eclipse Group's own "CPU," after work, at a local establishment called the Cain Ridge Saloon. The citation read as follows:

### Honorary Pal Award

In recognition of unsolicited contributions to the advancement of Eclipse hardware above and beyond the normal call of duty, we hereby convey unto you our thanks and congratulations on achieving this "high" honor.

The same values and spirit are reinforced over and over again in a continued cycle of celebratory events:

Chuck Holland handed out his own special awards to each member of the Microteam, the Under Extraordinary Pressure Awards. They looked like diplomas. There was one for Neal Firth, "Who gave us a computer before the hardware guys did," and one to Betty Shanahan, "for putting up with a bunch of creepy guys." Having dispensed the Honorary Microcode Awards to almost every possible candidate, the Microteam instituted the All-Nighter Award. The first of these to Jim Guyer, the citation ingeniously inserted under the clear plastic coating of an insulated coffee cup.

*Informal Cultural Players Make Contributions Disproportionate to Their Formal Roles.* Alsing was the main organizer and instigator of parties. He was also the conscience of Eagle and a confidant of nearly everyone: "For a time, when he was still in college, Alsing had wanted to become a psychologist. He adopted that sort of role now. Although he did keep track of his team's technical progress, he acted most visibly as the social director of the Microteam, and often of the entire Eclipse Group. Fairly early in the project, Chuck Holland had complained, 'Alsing's hard to be a manager for, because he goes around you a lot and tells your people to do something else.' But Holland also conceded, 'The good thing about him is that you can go and talk to him. He's more of a regular guy than most managers'" (p. 105).

Every group or organization has a "priest" or "priestess" who ministers to spiritual needs. Informally, these people hear confessions, give blessings, maintain traditions, encourage ceremonies, and intercede in matters of gravest importance. Alsing did all these and, like the tribal priest, was a counterpart and interpreter of the intentions of the chief:

> West warned him several times "if you get too close to the people who work for you, Alsing, you're gonna get burned." But West didn't interfere, and soon he stopped issuing warnings.
>
> One evening while alone with West in West's office, Alsing said: "Tom, the kids think you're an ogre. You didn't even say hello to them."
>
> West smiled and replied. "You're doing fine, Alsing" [Kidder, 1981, p. 118].

Rosemarie Seale's duties also expanded well beyond those of a typical secretary. If Alsing was the priest, she was the mother superior: "To Rosemarie, the Eagle project was like a gift. She had so much to do every day: budgets to prepare, battles to fight with one department or another, mail to sort when the mailroom was untimely moved, phones to answer, documents to prepare, paychecks to find and deliver on time, the newcomers to attend to ('Would they have a place to sit—and the conditions weren't the best, you know—and would they have a pencil?'). Each day brought another small administrative crisis. 'I was doing something important,' she said" (pp. 57–58).

In any group, a network of informal players deals with human issues outside formal channels. In the Eagle Project, their efforts were encouraged, appreciated, and rewarded outside the formal chain of command; they helped keep the project on track.

**Soul Is the Secret of Success.** The symbolic side of the Eagle Group was the real secret of its success. Its soul, or culture, created a new machine: "Ninety-eight percent of the thrill comes from knowing that the thing you designed works, and works almost the way you expected it would. If that happens, part of *you* is in that machine" (p. 273).

All members of the Eagle Group put something of themselves into the computer. Individual efforts went well beyond the "job" and were supported by a way of life that encouraged each person to commit himself or herself to doing something of significance. This commitment was elicited through the ritual of signing up and then maintained and accentuated by shared diversity, exceptional leaders, a common language, stories, rituals, ceremonies, play, and humor. In the best sense of the word, the Eagle Group was a team, and their efforts were knitted together by a cohesive culture. Symbolic elements were crucial to the group's success.

The experience of the Eagle Group is not unusual. Many executives are beginning to realize that there is more to developing a successful organization than meeting needs, designing roles and systems, or dealing with conflicts. The U.S. Air Force, in the aftermath of the Vietnam War, embarked on a vigorous effort to reaffirm its traditions and rebuild its culture. It adopted a new motto, "Cohesion Is a Principle of War," and developed Project Warrior, which emphasized the deeds of both living and dead heroes. Rituals were revitalized and reinforced. For example, the Air Force instituted a "re-blueing" ceremony to encourage recommitment to its values.

Countless other organizations have taken similar steps. Facing intense foreign competition and a severe profit squeeze, Ford Motor Company set out in the 1980s to build a culture committed to the principle that Quality Is Job One. Mitsubishi Corporation, with over 25,000 products ranging from "noodles to space satellites" (Lifson and Takagi, 1981), used an elaborate entrance ceremony for newly hired employees as part of its effort to reinforce a corporate culture that stressed professionalism, cooperation, and entrepreneurship.

## Strengths and Limits of the Symbolic Frame

Of the four organizational perspectives, the symbolic is the newest, least developed, and least mapped. It is therefore too early to make a definitive evaluation of it. Very few empirical investigations have employed symbolic theories of organization as a conceptual base. It is already clear, however, that investigations of symbolic phenomena are unlikely to employ so-called rigorous social science research methods. Easily quantified questionnaires and highly structured experimental investigations are ill suited to the subtle shades of meaning and affect that are so critical in symbolic analysis. If symbolic perspectives grow and prosper (as we believe they will), they are likely to produce a revival of interest in traditional fieldwork methods from anthropology and sociology and to deepen the current emphasis on qualitative methods and ethnography.

Symbolic perspectives have already made a significant conceptual contribution to the study of organizations, and that contribution is likely to grow. They question traditional views that the "substantive" is somehow better or more rational than the merely "symbolic." They suggest that if we try to banish ritual, ceremony, and myth from organizations, we may destroy them rather than improve them. Symbolic perspectives ask that we reexamine many organizational phenomena that have traditionally been viewed as dysfunctional or ineffective, because those activities may in fact be very functional in terms of their symbolic or expressive purposes.

No conceptual perspective is completely value neutral, and symbolic perspectives raise a knotty question about the two faces of symbols. One face is symbol as camouflage and distortion. Symbols can serve dishonest, cynical, or repressive functions. The myth that a certified teacher is a good teacher may protect incompetence and insulate educational institutions from needed changes. The other face is symbol as embodiment and expression of meaning. Human beings live in a world that is fundamentally ambiguous and uncertain. An earthquake, a fire, or a sudden reversal in the business cycle can destroy even the most careful and thoughtful of lives or institutions. Again, no amount of rationality or resources can provide completely satisfactory insurance against uncertainty, anomie, and meaninglessness. For these reasons, we develop rituals that provide order and predictability. We create sagas that reassure us about the worthy past of our institutions, as well as myths that give us something to believe in. Both faces of symbol are significant, and both are easy to find in existing organizations. The recognition and exploration of that duality may be one of the most significant contributions that the symbolic analysis of organizations can make.

Structural and political views often focus on the immutability of existing organizational structures and processes. Structural views stress the deterministic forces of goals and technology. Political views emphasize the immutable forces of scarce resources and intransigent interests. Symbolic views suggest a different perspective: the "facts" of the social world are the facts that humans have chosen to construct. That view can become a basis for optimism about the possibilities of organizational change: "We all create worlds. The more we are able to create worlds that are morally cogent and politically viable, the more we are able, as workers and citizens, to manage or to resist" (Brown, 1978, p. 378).

# Part Six

# Improving Leadership Practice

# 15

# *Integrating Organizational Theories*

Each of the four frames—structural, human resource, political, and symbolic—illuminates a different slice of life in organizations, but, for the most part, these different perspectives are used independently of one another by theorists as well as by practitioners. Theorists generally emphasize a single approach and defend it against all challengers, and practicing managers typically prefer to use only one frame. Indeed, many would-be leaders move from company to company or agency to agency in search of a situation that conforms to their idea of how things should be organized.

Incomplete maps in either research or practice limit our ability to understand and manage organizations. They make it hard to explain variations and fluctuations in data from different organizations. The inability to consider multiple perspectives continually undermines efforts to manage or change organizations. Important new technologies fail because of inadequate attention to retraining the workers who must implement the new methods. Sophisticated training outcomes disappear when people with new skills find themselves back in the same old roles facing the same pressures as before. Efforts to empower lower-level participants run afoul of traditional authority patterns, and cultural changes are derailed by entrenched political interests. If there is a lesson here, it is that complex realities require complex approaches. Integrating the

309

frames into a multidimensional theory and a comprehensive approach to management is a needed next step.

## Integrating the Frames in Theory

The division of organization theory into mutually competitive camps and the commitment of members of each camp to a single perspective are captured in a morality tale from Beer (1981):

> Here we are in the countryside, surrounded by all the intricate, multicolored, everchanging complexities of the natural environment. A specialist comes along to the fallen tree trunk on which we are sitting. "Can you understand it all, then?" he asks. No, we agree, it is all a great mystery. "What you need," says the specialist, "is a pair of my truth spectacles." We buy them for a small sum—though it is more than they are worth because (did we but know it?) the truth spectacles are simply dark, red-tinted glasses.
>
> "What do you see?" asks the specialist. We tell him that we see everything is red. What is more, we cannot any longer see a lot of complicated details that we saw before. "Exactly! That is our triumph," says the specialist. "What you are seeing is the truth that underlies all the confusion. The world is *really* red. And the rules that govern it are *actually* quite simple" [p. 187].

The problem is seldom that the one true theory is lost among a crowd of false pretenders. Usually, the problem is that there are several valid perspectives, each of which is interesting and significant but able to arrive at only part of the truth. For example, much time and energy have been invested in trying to demonstrate that "micro is more important than macro" or "organizational behavior is superior to organization theory." ("Micro" and organizational behavior refer to work on individual and group behavior in organizations. "Macro" and organization theory refer to studies of total organizations as systems.) The micro–macro dichotomy, in particularly, oversimplifies the problem and suggests that one or the other approach must be correct.

We have focused primarily on work in organizational theory

and behavior that falls fairly neatly into one of the four frames. But we have also noted that some work makes use of conceptions from more than one of the four major lenses. Although such work is still in the minority, it is increasing rapidly. Six or seven years ago, we could identify no examples of work that contained concepts from all four frames and very few that included more than two. More recently, however, we have found three examples that make significant use of all four (Table 2).

Our argument for conceptual pluralism (Bolman and Deal, 1984) is echoed in an increasing range of organizational research

Table 2. Examples of Multiple-Frame Research.

| Perspectives | Authors | Salient Concepts |
|---|---|---|
| Structural and human resource | Lawrence and Lorsch (1967) | Differentiation and integration |
| Structural and political | Cyert and March (1963) | Sequential attention to goals |
| Human resource and political | Alderfer and Smith (1990) | Embedded intergroups |
| Human resource and symbolic | Argyris and Schön (1978) | Theories for action |
| Human resource and symbolic | Bennis and Nanus (1985) | Empowerment, vision |
| Political and symbolic | Cohen and March (1974) | Organized anarchy |
| Structural, human resource, and political | Kanter (1977) | Opportunity, power, numbers |
| Structural, human resource, and political | Kotter (1982) | Agendas, relationships, networks |
| Four frames | Kanter (1983) | Segmentation, empowerment, power skills, culture |
| Four frames | Perrow (1986) | Bureaucracy, human relations, institutional school, power |
| Four frames | Birnbaum (1988) | Collegial, bureaucratic, political, anarchic |

and theory. A particularly stimulating example is Morgan (1986), who identifies eight different images or metaphors for organizations. Of those eight, one is structural ("organization as machine"), two are political ("organization as political system" and "organization as instrument of domination"), two are symbolic ("organization as culture" and "organization as flux and transformation"), and one is cybernetic ("organization as brain"). His other images intermingle elements from more than one frame. Morgan includes the human resource frame as a minor item in the image of the organization as an organism and devotes far more attention to adversarial than to consensual models of organizations. Curiously, Morgan produced a subsequent work aimed at senior managers (Morgan, 1988) in which political images largely vanish—conflict, power, and politics all disappear from the index, and structural, human resource, and symbolic concepts become dominant. Morgan (1986) tends to view organizations as snakepits; Morgan (1988) sees organizations more as flower gardens.

The relative scarcity of work guided by multiple perspectives makes organization research an unproductively fractionated endeavor. Singular approaches oversimplify the complexity of human organizations. The following propositions summarize our view of where the field is, and where it needs to go:

*Pluralism slows research by impeding communication among different perspectives.* Differentiation, as Lawrence and Lorsch (1967) argued, produces problems of integration. When people choose different theoretical camps, they impede communication because either they do not try to communicate (for example, scholars read only the literature that conforms to their own theoretical predilections) or they misunderstand one another when they do try.

To illustrate the first problem, consider two works that say very similar things, in different languages, with little apparent recognition of their complementarity. Argyris and Schön (1974, 1978) argue that individuals and organizations are often ineffective not because they fail to do what they intend to do but because they are unaware of the discrepancy. Their "theory of action" prevents them from learning. Argyris and Schön's conceptions of "espoused theory" and "theory-in use" combine elements from both human resource and the symbolic perspectives. Beer (1981), in a stimulating essay on the equifinality of death, also argues that systems fail to do what they are supposed to do. Their models of reality lack "requisite variety" and simultaneously prevent recognition of their own errors. Beer uses systems theory and cybernetics to say something remarkably parallel to what Argyris and Schön are saying. But would he agree with their prescriptions for improving organizational learning? It is difficult to be sure because of the very different language used in each theory. There may be instructive parallels between "requisite variety" (Beer) and "single-loop learning" (Argyris and Schön), but translation problems impede the effort to tease them out.

An example of the second problem—misunderstanding—appears in a published dialogue between Salancik and Pfeffer (1977, 1978) and Alderfer (1977a). Salancik and Pfeffer (1977) presented a critique of need-satisfaction theories. Alderfer (1977a), a need-satisfaction theorist, responded with a critique of Salancik and Pfeffer. They, in turn, responded with a further critique of need satisfaction and a proposal for "social information processing" theories (Salancik and Pfeffer, 1978). The theories that Alderfer defends are central to the human resource perspective. Social construction of reality, which Salancik and Pfeffer defend, is central to the symbolic perspective. There is significant validity to both views, and they are more complementary than conflicting. But in the heat of debate, the common ground was lost. Alderfer (1977a) misinterprets Salancik and Pfeffer's conception of "redefining the situation" as being equivalent to "defensive coping" (p. 666). In effect, he takes a symbolic concept and translates it into a human resource concept (in this case, a concept from psychoanalytic theory), but the translation radically alters the meaning.

Conversely, Salancik and Pfeffer (1977) while implicitly arguing that human beings have a need for social acceptance nevertheless make a sweeping attack on the concept of psychological needs (1978). Needs shape how individuals interpret situations, but interpretations also influence which needs are elicited. Hungry people focus on cues related to food but may shift to other needs if they believe no food is available. The concepts of "need" and "interpretation of the situation" are so interconnected that neither can be studied adequately without considering the other. But that will not happen as long as scholars on both sides treat the issues as a win-lose proposition.

*Each theoretical perspective has a unique, comparative advantage.* Each of the four frames describes a set of phenomena that are present in any human system, but each is likely to be more salient and illuminating in some circumstances than in others. Some phenomena are simply more visible or prominent under certain conditions and more likely to recede into the background under others. Table 3 presents a set of hypothesized linkages between the four perspectives and major contextual variables. The table suggests, for example, that structural ideas will be particularly salient and helpful in organizations with clear goals, adequate information systems, well-developed technologies, and stable authority. When employees have high leverage (so that organizations have to work harder to keep them on the job and productive) and when their morale and motivation are problematic, human resource issues are likely to be very prominent. Political processes are likely to stand out when resources are scarce or declining, goals and values are in conflict, diversity is high, and the distribution of power is unstable or diffuse. Finally, symbolic issues are likely to be of particular importance when ambiguity and uncertainty are high, information is weak, and diverse cultures are colliding with one another.

We are not suggesting that each frame is valid only under certain conditions. Symbolic processes, for example, are not irrelevant under conditions of consensus and certainty. But they are much less obvious when everyone is clear about the job to be done and agrees with everyone else on the best way to do it. It is important for theorists to be aware of the range of conditions that they are implicitly assuming. Salancik and Pfeffer (1978), for example, found that students rated a boring task as more interesting when they were underpaid than when they were overpaid. They use that evidence to prove that the concept of redefinition of the situation is more useful than the concept of need satisfaction in predicting job satisfaction. But, since the study did not compare a boring task with an interesting one, it failed to directly examine the human resource proposition that some tasks are more responsive to human needs than are others.

**Table 3. Salience of Frames.**

| *Frame* | *Conditions for Salience* |
|---|---|
| Structural | Goals and information clear; cause-effect relations well understood; strong technologies and information systems; low conflict, low ambiguity, and low uncertainty; stable legitimate authority. |
| Human resource | Employee leverage high or increasing; employee morale and motivation low or declining; resources relatively abundant or increasing; low or moderate conflict and uncertainty; diversity low or moderate. |
| Political | Resources scarce or declining; goal and value conflict; diversity high or increasing; distribution of power diffuse or unstable. |
| Symbolic | Goals and information unclear and ambiguous; cause-effect relations poorly understood; weak technologies and information systems; cultural diversity. |

*Each perspective enacts a different image of organization.* Pondy and Mitroff (1979) describe what they see as a troublesome paradox: "What we teach now to practitioners will create the very phenomena that we have available to study in the future" (p. 28). Their statement is valid but not really paradoxical, and it articulates a truth now being recognized by all the social sciences. Any science of human behavior is a science of the artificial. It attempts to understand and explain the worlds that human beings and human cultures have chosen to create. In the social sciences, there is no final distinction between valid prediction and self-fulfilling prophesy. Consider the model of the relationship between organization theories and organizational phenomena shown in Figure 13.

Traditional social science models assume that the significant causal direction is from the phenomena to the theory. This presupposes that there is an objective reality independent of human theories—truth exists and quietly waits for us to find it. Symbolic perspectives imply the opposite—reality is a product of our theories, and truth is a figment of our imaginations. Taken alone, each view oversimplifies and misleads. Neither organizations nor human beings are infinitely malleable, and some stubborn realities resist our

**Figure 13. Relationships Between Theories and Phenomena.**

most determined efforts to change them. But it is also true that students can be taught to believe a variety of different theories and that organizations are undoubtedly influenced by the theories of participants.

As scientists and as managers, our theories and methods influence both the world that we see and the world that we enact. Any perspective can be self-fulfilling. Organizational research is likely to remain dull and directionless if we continue to do no more than defend our own intellectual preferences. More exciting and creative possibilities will emerge if we begin to work at the boundaries of our knowledge.

*Each perspective contains ingredients that are essential to an integrative science of organizations.* The structural approach reminds us that most human beings and human institutions, regardless of what they do in practice, are *intentionally and subjectively* rational—they are usually trying to get on with the job as *they* understand it. Structuralists correctly insist on the crucial importance of structure and context in influencing the premises on which people make choices.

The human resource frame reminds us that the participants in human systems are indeed human beings, with all their exquisite complexity. Individuals have needs and feelings, along with ideas, conscious wills, and primordial ids, a capacity to learn as well as to avoid learning, and abilities and deficiencies. This perspective reminds us that human beings are adaptable but not infinitely so— they persist in behaving like people, and organizations have to come to grips with that fact.

The political frame correctly asserts that resources are always scarce and that individuals and groups will continue to fight over how those resources should be allocated. Conflict may sometimes result from misunderstandings, deficiencies in skill, or hostile intentions. Often, though, it is deeply entrenched in an organization.

The two p's about which we are so often ambivalent—power and politics—will not go away and cannot be ignored.

The symbolic frame reminds us of the enormous extent to which reality is socially constructed and symbolically mediated. "Meaning" is what is most important about any human event, but meaning is not an objective given; it is arrived at through one belief system or another. In situations where multiple cultures intersect and the important issues or tasks are fraught with ambiguity, symbolic processes can be a central part of the science of organization.

## Systems Theories

There are two intellectual traditions that cut across the structural, human resource, political, and symbolic perspectives: Von Bertalanffy's (1949) general theory of systems and Wiener's (1967) conception of cybernetics as the science of control and communication in animals and machines. Von Bertalanffy wanted to develop a general theory of systems that would cut across disciplines and systems, so that the theory would be applicable to the cell, the person, the group, the organization, and the society. The general systems approach has spawned efforts such as Miller's (1978) attempt to develop a general theory of living systems and Boulding's (1977) admittedly ambitious proposal to develop a "general theory of practically everything." Combining ideas from systems theory and cybernetics leads to a fifth frame that can be represented in the following propositions:

1. A system is a set of interacting and interrelated parts.
2. Human organizations are appropriately viewed as open systems. Their boundaries are permeable, and they are continually engaged in importing, transforming, and exporting matter, energy, information, and people.
3. Human organizations are capable of negative entropy; that is, they can survive and grow, rather than decay and die, if they are able to work out a mutually beneficial relationship with their environment. The organization, for example, provides goods or services in return for the resources it needs to survive and prosper.

4.  Systems are arranged hierarchically, so that every system is a supersystem for systems contained within it and a subsystem for systems containing it. (A classroom is a supersystem for teacher and students but a subsystem for the school, and so on up and down the hierarchy.)

5.  A system is more than the sum of its parts: its properties emerge from the relationship among its parts and from the system's relationship to its environment.

6.  Organizations tend to maintain steady states, that is, states of dynamic equilibrium in which diverse forces are approximately balanced. Such steady states have the property of ultra-stability: the more that a system is threatened with disequilibrium, the more resources it will marshall to maintain or restore its balance.

7.  To maintain a steady state, open systems need adaptive processes, including feedback loops, that enable the systems to sense relevant changes in the internal or external environment and to adjust their properties accordingly.

Cybernetic views are particularly helpful in understanding how organizations maintain steady states—how a college, for example, maintains essentially the same structure, activities, and processes over a period of many years. According to Birnbaum's (1988) cybernetic view, managers are very much like a collection of semiautonomous thermostats. Each thermostat monitors temperature at a certain location and takes action whenever things get too hot or too cold. If applications cool off, the admissions staff increases its recruiting efforts. If the additional recruiting brings in weaker students, the faculty will increase its complaints about the admissions office. Feeling the heat from the faculty, the admissions staff will develop initiatives to find "quality" applicants. Birnbaum notes that such a system often requires very little coordination or even leadership from the top. If the college president just leaves them alone, the mutual adjustment processes of the individual thermostats will often do an effective job of keeping the system working smoothly.

Systems theory points to certain issues as worthy of study. Organization-environment linkages are critical in organization theory, and systems theory has undoubtedly played a major role in drawing attention to that interface. Systems theory also highlights the importance of boundary-spanning processes and roles (see, for example, Kahn and others, 1964; Leifer and Huber, 1977; Tushman, 1977). Systems theory searches for isomorphisms: if we understand a particular dynamic in small groups, it is worth investigating whether parallel phenomena operate at the level of smaller and larger systems.

Its generality and its significant, although nonspecific, heuristic value make systems theory a candidate to become a more general theory of organizations. But there is little evidence that theorists are eager to use systems concepts and terms to reconceptualize their views. For example, Perrow's (1986) incisive analysis of the state of organization theory virtually ignores systems theory. Perhaps one problem is that because it aspires to encompass *all* systems, systems theory has not developed concepts that are specific to *human* systems. Attractively systematic and general, the approach lacks much of the richness found in the four frames.

## Summary

Historically, much of the theory and research on organizations has been dominated by one frame or another. It has become increasingly apparent that such single-frame approaches severely limit our ability to understand and manage organizations. The trend toward more comprehensive, multiframe approaches is rapidly gathering steam and promises a challenging and exciting future for organizational science.

# 16

# *Integrating Frames for Effective Practice*

In previous chapters, we have focused primarily on examining each of the frames independently. Our goal has been to demonstrate the logic and subtleties of each frame and to help managers and leaders acquire artistry in using the frames for both diagnosis and action. In this chapter, however, we will consider the frames in combination. How do you decide which frame to use? How can you integrate the different frames? We begin by examining what the world of the manager is really like. We then consider what happens in that world when different people employ different frames. Next, we provide a set of questions and guidelines to use in thinking through which frames are likely to be most important and helpful in different situations. Finally, we examine the practices of successful managers and organizations to see whether they employ multiple perspectives and, if so, how they employ them.

### Life as Managers Know It

Much of the prevailing mythology depicts managers as rational actors who spend most of their time planning, organizing, coordinating, and controlling the activities of subordinates. Periodicals, books, and business schools often present the modern manager as an unruffled individual who wears a three-piece suit, has a well-organized desk, and makes decisions with the help of loyal subordinates and sophisticated information systems. The manager develops strategic plans and communicates them through a well-defined structure to produce predictable and effective responses. It is an attractive picture, but it is mostly misleading fantasy.

Social scientists (Mintzberg, 1973; Kotter, 1982) have provided a glimpse of what managerial life is really like. It is a hectic existence. Managers spend most of their time shifting rapidly from one meeting or encounter to another. Each encounter presents a different blend of challenges. Kotter spent months observing senior managers and rarely found them *making* a decision. Instead of being made, decisions *emerged* from a fluid and sometimes confusing series of conversations, meetings, and memos. Managers often have sophisticated information systems that ensure an overload of detail about what happened last month or last year, yet fail to answer the far more important question: What is likely to happen tomorrow? Information systems offer surprisingly little help in deciding what to do next. For such decisions, managers operate mostly on the basis of intuition, hunches, and the kind of judgment that they have derived from long-term experience in their organization. They are far too busy to spend time thinking or reading; they get most of their information orally—in meetings or over the telephone. They are hassled priests, modern muddlers, and corporate wheeler-dealers.

How does one reconcile the actual work of managers with the epic imagery? What does the discrepancy mean to people who often feel deep down that what they really do has little relation to what they should be doing? What happens if managers aspire to an unattainable ideal? One common consequence is frustration and feelings of inadequacy: There must be something wrong with me! Managers believe that they should be rational and in control, yet they often find themselves confused and bewildered. They believe that they are supposed to plan, organize, delegate, and control, yet they find themselves constantly meeting, muddling, and playing catch-up. They want to see themselves as problem solvers and decision makers, but the problems are often so ill-defined and the decisions so murky that they often find today's decision in yester-

day's action or get swept into decisions by the ongoing flow of
events.

## Across the Frames: Organizations as Multiple Realities

Organizations are full of managers who see one or two frames as
right and all others as wrong. They see their preferred frames as
useful, while the others are superficial, unrealistic, or repellent.
Their commonsense personal theories are well defined and well
defended. When a frame confirms their predictions, they happily
embrace its message. When it challenges their core assumptions,
they deny or attack it.

But all organizations contain multiple realities, and every
event can be interpreted in a number of ways. Table 4 examines a
number of organizational processes through each of the frames. As
the table shows, any event can serve multiple purposes. The outcome of planning, for example, may be a specific set of objectives.
But as Edelfson, Johnson, and Stromquist (1977) pointed out in
their study of a major planning project in a school district (Project
Redesign in Palo Alto, California), planning also creates arenas for
airing conflict and can become a sacred occasion to renegotiate
symbolic meanings. The main benefit of the project was not the
final plan. More important, the process generated satisfaction
among participants, led to the formation of new coalitions, and
clothed educational efforts in the district in new imagery and
symbols.

The simultaneous existence of multiple realities often leads
to misunderstanding and conflict when different individuals use
different perspectives to frame the same event. Consider, for example, a meeting once called by a hospital administrator to make an
important decision. The chief technician viewed the meeting as an
opportunity for expressing feelings and building relationships, the
director of nursing saw it as an opportunity to gain power vis-a-vis
physicians, and the medical director looked upon it as another occasion for reaffirming the hospital's distinctive approach to medical
care. The meeting was cacophonous.

The same issues are illustrated in the following case:

Table 4. Four Interpretations of Organizational Processes.

| Process | Structural Frame | Human Resource Frame | Political Frame | Symbolic Frame |
|---|---|---|---|---|
| Planning | Strategies to set objectives and coordinate resources | Gatherings to promote participation | Arenas to air conflicts and realign power | Ritual to signal responsibility, produce symbols, negotiate meanings |
| Decision making | Rational sequence to produce right decision | Open process to produce commitment | Opportunity to gain or exercise power | Ritual to provide comfort and support until decision happens |
| Reorganizing | Realign roles and responsibilities to fit tasks and environment | Maintain a balance between human needs and formal roles | Redistribute power and form new coalitions | Maintain an image of accountability and responsiveness; negotiate new social order |
| Evaluating | Way to distribute rewards or penalties and control performance | Process for helping individuals grow and improve | Opportunity to exercise power | Occasion to play roles in shared ritual |
| Approaching conflict | Maintain organizational goals by having authorities resolve conflict | Develop relationships by having individual confront conflict | Develop power by bargaining, forcing, or manipulating others to win | Develop shared values and use conflict to negotiate meaning |
| Goal setting | Keep organization headed in the right direction | Keep people involved and communication open | Provide opportunity for individuals and groups to make interests known | Develop symbols and shared values |
| Communication | Transmit facts and information | Exchange information, needs, and feelings | Vehicles for influencing or manipulating others | Telling stories |
| Meetings | Formal occasions for making decisions | Informal occasions for involvement, sharing feelings | Competitive occasions to win points | Sacred occasions to celebrate and transform the culture |
| Motivation | Economic incentives | Growth and self-actualization | Coercion, manipulation, and seduction | Symbols and celebrations |

Dr. Gregory O'Keefe found himself the focus of a fierce battle between 1,200 year-around residents of Vinalhaven, Maine (an island fishing community), and the National Health Service Corps (NHSC), which pays his salary and is insisting he take a promotion to an administrator's desk in Rockville, Maryland.

O'Keefe doesn't want to go, and his patients don't want him to either. The islanders are so upset that, much to the surprise of NHSC officials, they have enlisted the aid of Sen. William Cohen (R-Maine) and U.S. Health and Human Services Secretary Margaret Heckler to keep him here.

It's certainly not the prestige or glamour of the job that is holding O'Keefe, who drives the town's only ambulance and, as often as twice a week, takes critically ill patients to mainland hospitals via an emergency ferry run or a Coast Guard cutter, private plane, or even a lobster boat.

Apparently unyielding in their insistence that O'Keefe accept the promotion or resign, NHSC officials seemed startled last week by the spate of protests from angry islanders, which prompted nationwide media attention and inquiries from the Maine congressional delegation. NHSC says it probably would not replace O'Keefe on the island, which, in the agency's view, is now able to support a private medical practice.

Cohen described himself as "frustrated by the lack of responsiveness of lower-level bureaucrats. . . ." But to the NHSC, O'Keefe is a foot soldier in a military organization of more than 1,600 physicians assigned to isolated, medically needy communities. And he's had the audacity to question the orders of a superior officer.

"It's like a soldier who wanted to stay at Ft. Myers and jumped on TV and called the Defense Secretary a rat for wanting him to move," Shirley Barth, press officer for the federal Public Health Service, said in a telephone interview Thursday [Goodman, 1983, p. 1].

The NHSC officials apparently had trouble seeing beyond the structural frame—they had a task to do and a structure for achieving it; the opposition was illegitimate. O'Keefe saw it in human resource terms—he believed the work that he was doing was meaningful and satisfying and the islanders needed him. For Senator Cohen, it was a political issue—could minor bureaucrats be allowed to abuse their power in a way that was insensitive and harmful to the welfare of his constituents? For the hardy residents of Vinalhaven, O'Keefe was a heroic figure of mythic dimensions: "If he gets one night's sleep out of twenty, he's lucky, but he's always up there smiling and working" (Goodman, 1983, p. 1). The islanders were full of stories about O'Keefe's humility, skill, dedication, wit, confidence, and spirit of caring.

With everyone using different frames, confusion and conflict were predictable. The inability of NHSC officials to understand and acknowledge the existence of other frames illustrates the costs of clinging to a single view of a situation. In their minds, they were doing exactly what they were supposed to do. But to everyone else they became another symbol of mindless bureaucracy.

This example again shows the need for integrating the four frames. In many situations the hardest thing to understand is why other people are reacting the way they are. Whenever others' actions seem to make no sense, it is worth asking whether you and they are using different frames. Even if their frame is inappropriate or misguided, it helps to know what it is. It makes sense to them; their frame—not yours—determines how they will act.

## Matching Frames to Situations

For different times and different situations, one perspective may be more important than others. At a critical strategic crossroads, a rational process that focuses on gathering information and carrying out analyses may be exactly what an organization needs. At other times, developing commitment or building a power base may be more critical. In times of great stress, such as AT&T experienced after divesting its regional operating companies, decision-making processes may become a form of ritual that provides comfort and support. Choosing a frame, and understanding the frames that others are using, involves a combination of analysis, intuition, and artistry. We cannot supply the intuition or the artistry, but Table 5 provides questions that can facilitate analysis and stimulate intuition. It suggests the conditions under which each frame is likely to be a significant determinant of effectiveness. We will therefore consider each of these questions in some detail; we begin with the question of commitment.

**Table 5. Choosing a Frame.**

| Question | Structural Frame | Human Resource Frame | Political Frame | Symbolic Frame |
|---|---|---|---|---|
| How important are commitment and motivation? | Unimportant | Important | ? | Important |
| How important is the technical quality of the decision? | Important | ? | Unimportant | Unimportant |
| How much ambiguity and uncertainty is present? | Low to moderate | Moderate | Moderate to high | High |
| How scarce are resources? | Moderately scarce | Moderately abundant to abundant | Scarce (or getting scarcer) | Scarce to abundant |
| How much conflict and diversity is present? | Low to moderate | Moderate | Moderate to high | Moderate to high |
| Are we working top down or bottom up? | Top down | Top down | Bottom up | Top down or bottom up |

*How important are commitment and motivation?* Both of these are important when two conditions are present: (1) successful performance depends on the efforts and skills of individuals and (2) the degree to which the individuals in question are motivated and committed is problematic. For example, successful implementation of a new curriculum in a school district is heavily dependent on how the teachers feel about the curriculum, and it is well known that teachers can be very successful in resisting a teaching innovation that they do not like. In such situations, managers would need to ask what they can do to ensure motivation. They might employ strategies of support and participation from the human resource frame, or they might try to link the new curriculum to important symbols and meanings in the culture of the district. The chart shows a question mark for the political frame on this issue because the political frame could help or hurt, depending on how it is used.

An attempt to use political coercion to gain cooperation is likely to be counterproductive, but negotiation with the teachers to try to reach an agreement acceptable to all parties might be effective.

Consider another issue—the use of kidney-dialysis machines. The machines are life saving for those who need them. The problem is that, like many other sophisticated medical technologies, they are very expensive and there are not always enough of them to go around. The agonizing question becomes whose life will be saved. Here, the issue of commitment is overwhelming, but there is virtually no chance of getting someone who needs such a machine to take no for an answer. At best, the human resource frame may help in a small way to reduce the pain and agony of making a decision.

*How important is the technical quality of the decision?* In some cases, any decision that is acceptable to the major constituents will be satisfactory. In others, making the *right* decision is critical. At first glance, it may seem hard to believe that the technical quality of a decision could ever be *unimportant,* but that is often true of decisions that involve distributing a scarce resource. As an example, consider the college that found itself embroiled in a three-month battle over the choice of a commencement speaker. The faculty was pushing for an individual with strong academic credentials, while the students' candidate had recently been the subject of a major motion picture. The college president concluded that she would be quite happy with any commencement speaker who was acceptable to both groups.

If it is a question of a curriculum change in public schools, technical quality and motivation are both important, and the problem is finding an appropriate balance between them. A superb curriculum will fail if teachers undercut it, but a poor curriculum implemented with energy and gusto will not be much better. An effective change process will need to consider both structure and people. In the case of kidney dialysis, designing the machines and deciding when they are medically appropriate are technical decisions. Deciding how to allocate the machines when there are not enough to go around is a political issue. The skills and concerns of the manager as politician then become central. He or she must have mastered the arts of agenda setting, networking, and negotiation and must also have a firm understanding of his or her own value system.

Where technical quality is important, the structural frame is likely to be particularly useful, but the human resource frame might also be relevant if it helped to elicit the kind of effort and energy that produces high performance. The political and symbolic frames are less likely to be salient for the goal of technical quality.

*How much ambiguity and uncertainty is involved?* Some situations are much more ambiguous than others. Ambiguity is relatively low when the assumptions of the structural frame are met, that is, goals are reasonably clear, the technology is well understood, and people's behavior is mostly rational. As ambiguity increases, however, the political and symbolic frames become increasingly relevant. The political frame assumes that individuals generally act rationally in pursuit of their self-interests but that the resulting battles among individuals and interest groups may be confused and chaotic. The symbolic frame assumes that symbols are a way of creating a perception of order, meaning, and "truth" in situations that are too complex, uncertain, or mysterious to be susceptible to rational analysis.

The conditions of clear goals and well-understood technology fit the design and manufacture of dialysis machines, but not their distribution. Thus, we can expect that the structural frame will work well for the first problem, but the political and symbolic frames will take precedence in the second. Curriculum changes also present conditions of significant ambiguity, though not so overwhelming as in the case of dialysis. Here, politics and symbols will be important, though there is more opportunity to mix them with elements of the structural and human resource frames.

*How scarce are key resources?* The human resource frame fits situations of relative abundance because its basically optimistic assumptions about human capacity for growth and collaboration are most likely to be valid in firms that are profitable and growing or in public agencies that are strongly supported and well funded. At the other extreme, the political frame is particularly appropriate when resources are extremely tight. In those conditions, self-interest and self-protection are likely to give rise to the power plays and conflicts that are central to the political frame.

The structural frame is likely to fit situations in the middle. The idea of structure implies limits on available options, which in turn implies conditions of moderate scarcity. Extreme scarcity often fosters levels of conflict that exceed the capacity of existing authority systems. Since symbols seem to play a part in every culture and every social class—from the very poor to the very wealthy—the symbolic frame may be appropriate across a wide range of situations, including both extreme scarcity and great abundance of resources.

In the allocation of dialysis machines, or whenever treatment is unavailable to someone whose life depends on it, scarcity is a critical issue. Though we might wish it were otherwise, that scarcity makes it inevitable that decisions will be heavily political. In the case of curriculum change, the situation varies with the circumstances. With good times and sensitive leaders, resources may be abundant and politics largely invisible. In more difficult circumstances, curriculum change can easily evoke major political battles.

*How much conflict exists around this issue?* Since high conflict tends to undermine authority and existing institutions, the structural frame is likely to work best when conflict is low enough to be contained within existing structures. The human resource frame is appropriate to situations of moderate conflict. It postulates conflict between individual and organization and suggests ways to manage and reduce that conflict. Beyond a certain point, though, conflict may become so intense that it exceeds the capacity of human resource options to deal with it, as in the case of decisions about allocating dialysis machines. In those situations, the political and symbolic frames are most likely to be useful.

*Are you operating top down or bottom up?* The structural frame assumes that revising the structure is the primary solution to organizational problems, and the option of structural change is open primarily to people with authority, who can make changes from the top down. Similarly, the human resource frame has developed a series of approaches to organizational improvement that usually require change or support from the top in order to be successful. The political frame, in contrast, is particularly appropriate for change from the bottom up. Bottom-up change agents rarely have much authority and need to find other bases of power. The kidney-dialysis situation creates different roles for decision makers and those who will be affected by their decisions. Decision makers, such as physicians and medical administrators, work top down and have an incentive to rely on the structural frame. Their lives are made easier if they can develop structures and policies that will transform the decision from a personal one to an institutional one. But patients and their families will be working from the bottom up, and the political frame is the obvious choice for them. A similar dynamic often occurs in curriculum change. School administrators, working top down, present the need for change in rational and structural terms. They are often stunned and resentful when teachers, working bottom up, turn to political strategies.

The questions in Table 5 will not substitute for judgment and intuition in choosing a frame, but they can help to guide and augment those processes. For example, consider once again the Helen Demarco case in Chapter Two. Her boss, Paul Osborne, had a plan for major organizational change. Helen thought the plan was a mistake but did not feel that she could directly oppose her boss. What should she do? The issue of commitment and motivation was important, both in terms of her lack of commitment to Osborne's plan and her concern about finding a solution that Osborne would accept. That suggests that she might have been able to use the human resource frame, but there is no evidence that she considered such an option. Demarco felt that the technical quality of the plan was important but that she could not influence Osborne's judgment on the technical issues. Ambiguity played a significant role in the case. The technical problem may or may not have been ambiguous, but the more important problem of influencing Osborne created substantial uncertainty for Demarco. On the last three questions in Table 5, Demarco's situation obviously fits the political frame: resources were scarce, conflict was high, and she was trying to influence decisions from the bottom up. The case is a poor candidate for the structural frame, and Demarco might have an uphill battle if she used a human resource approach. The tide in the Demarco case was toward politics and symbols, and she chose to go with the flow.

The questions in Table 5 cannot be followed mechanically to the one correct answer for every situation. In some cases, the questions might tell you to use the same frame that you and everyone else have always used. If the old frame shows signs of inadequacy, however, it may be time to try a new perspective. In still other cases, the analysis might lead you toward a perspective completely different from any now found in your organization. You may discover an exciting and creative new option, but you will have to face the problem of how to communicate your discovery to those who see a different reality.

### Effective Managers and Organizations

Is effectiveness really related to the ability to use multiple frames? If so, how are the frames combined and integrated in practice? We will compare three influential explorations of managerial and organizational effectiveness with our argument about the need for multiple perspectives. One focuses on organizational excellence (Peters and Waterman, 1982), a second emphasizes the characteristics of effective senior managers in the private sector (Kotter, 1982), and a third investigates determinants of effectiveness among senior administrators in the U.S. government (Lynn, 1987).

Peters and Waterman's *In Search of Excellence* explored the question of what high-performing corporations have in common. They studied more than sixty large companies in six major industries: high technology (for example, DEC and IBM), consumer products (such as Eastman Kodak and Procter & Gamble), manufacturing (3M and Caterpillar, Inc.), service (McDonald's and Delta Air Lines), project management (Bechtel Group and Boeing), and natural resources (Exxon and Du Pont). The companies were chosen on the basis of both objective performance indicators, such as long-term growth and profitability, and the judgments of knowledgeable observers.

The companies were not wholly representative of American businesses. More than two-thirds of them were in high technology or consumer goods. A number of industries were either underrepresented or not included at all (banks, insurance companies, manufacturers of durable consumer goods). Companies in slow, mature industries had little chance of making the list (there were no railroads, steel companies, utilities, or coal-mining firms).

Peters and Waterman based their study on interviews, observations, and literature about the companies, and their book is really a series of stories and anecdotes about how high-performing companies manage to be effective. In Table 6 we list eight characteristics that they found in nearly all these companies, and in what follows we will discuss each of those characteristics in terms of their connections to the structural, human resource, political, and symbolic frames.

A *bias for action* means that effective companies do not get bogged down in endless paperwork and bureaucratic entanglements. When unsure, they conduct a quick, limited experiment rather than a two-year research project. Their approach is to act first, and learn from the results. A proclivity for action is an antidote to the constraining and dulling effects of the "dead hand of structure," and to the pervasiveness of uncertainty and ambiguity. Requiring a full justification before doing anything is a powerful way to ensure that nothing new or different ever gets done.

The characteristic of *close to the customer* fits under the human resource frame if we view customers as a part of an organization's human resources. At all levels of high-performing companies, close customer contact is an obsession. They treat customers exactly the way the human resource frame says to treat people—understand and respond to their needs.

Effective companies encourage and reward *autonomy and entrepreneurship*. In large companies, innovation is often stifled by bureaucracy. Employees fear making mistakes. Excellent companies encourage risks and tolerate occasional failures. Their methods combine structural and human resource approaches. Structurally the companies are highly decentralized and are broken down often into large numbers of relatively independent subunits. Communications, norms, and incentive systems are designed to provide protection, rewards, and security to risk-taking innovators.

*Productivity through people* restates a central premise of the human resource frame. While Peters and Waterman acknowledge that most companies give lip service to "people," excellent companies really mean it. Excellent companies consistently show concern for their people. Their in-house language underscores the importance of individuals, the organization views itself as an extended

**Table 6. Frames and Characteristics of High-Performing Companies.**

| Characteristic | Related Frames |
| --- | --- |
| 1. Bias for action | Structural, symbolic |
| 2. Close to the customer | Human resource |
| 3. Autonomy and entrepreneurship | Human resource, structural |
| 4. Productivity through people | Human resource, symbolic |
| 5. Hands-on, value-driven | Symbolic |
| 6. Stick to the knitting | Structural, human resource, symbolic |
| 7. Simple form, lean staff | Structural |
| 8. Simultaneous loose/tight properties | Structural, symbolic |

*Source:* Adapted from Peters and Waterman, 1982.

family, the chain of command is relatively informal, and the training and socialization of employees are ongoing and intensive.

Of *hands-on, value-driven,* Peters and Waterman (1982) say: "[If] we were asked for one all-purpose bit of advice for management [we] might be tempted to reply, 'Figure out your value system. Decide what your company *stands for*'" (p. 279).

Each excellent company "is clear on what it stands for and takes the process of value shaping seriously" (p. 280). Values are rarely transmitted formally or in writing. Rather, values move through an organization in the form of "stories, myths, legends and metaphors" (p. 282)—all central to the symbolic frame. "The excellent companies are unashamed collectors and tellers of stories, of legends and myths in support of their basic beliefs. Frito-Lay tells service stories. Johnson & Johnson tells quality stories. 3M tells innovation stories" (p. 282).

*Stick to the knitting* means that successful corporations explicitly avoid becoming conglomerates. IBM stays out of the toothpaste business, and Procter & Gamble doesn't try to sell computers. The excellent companies usually grow by developing new businesses closely related to what they do best. They rarely participate in the merger mania that periodically sweeps Wall Street. They seem to know that the acquisition of unrelated businesses creates three problems. The first is a structural issue: more diversity means that it will be more difficult to link and coordinate the different businesses. Second is a human resource issue—senior managers of the acquirer believe that they know how to run the new business, even though they don't. Acquired firms that were profitable are often mismanaged and ruined by the well-meaning attempts of new owners to make the subsidiary fit the corporate mold. Finally, there is a cultural problem. The symbols and cultural glue that work in one industry are rarely transferable to another. Procter & Gamble's marketing-driven culture and 3M's technology-driven culture have both been very successful. A merger of the two would undoubtedly mean tribal warfare.

*Simple form, lean staff* is a structural rule of thumb. As organizations get bigger, the formal structure tends to get more and more complicated. Organization charts become too large and complicated to fit on anything other than a very large wall. Even small decisions are routed through dozens of departments and meetings to ensure that all bases are covered. Excellent companies generally try to minimize these trends. A prototypical example is Johnson & Johnson, a $5 billion company that is split into some 150 different "companies." These divisions are members of one of eight product groups. The corporate staff is relatively small, and each of the divisions is buffered from excessive intrusions by corporate staffers. In many other successful companies the same rule is followed: keep headquarters relatively small and split the company into loosely coupled, manageable chunks. This strategy reduces complexity and increases flexibility for each of the separate units. Each unit can accomplish its individual mission without paying unnecessary attention to what other units are doing.

The final characteristic of excellent companies—*simultaneous loose/tight properties*—is a capstone tendency. According to Peters and Waterman, the high performers are able to have it both ways. They combine high levels of central control with substantial decentralization, autonomy, and entrepreneurship. They maintain control mostly through values and culture rather than relying on procedures and systems. A widely shared culture of relatively homogeneous people (most 3M managers are chemical engineers while most Procter & Gamble managers came up through marketing) means that nearly everyone is committed to the basic mission of the company. Under these conditions, a company can afford to give substantial leeway to both individuals and units.

If these eight properties work for the companies that Peters and Waterman studied, will they work for others? Don't count on it. The eight properties include every frame but one—political. Do effective organizations eliminate politics? Or did Peters and Waterman overlook a powerful force that might frustrate or even defeat other organizations that try to emulate their model of excellence?

Recall that their sample included only companies with strong records of sustained growth and profitability. When resources are relatively abundant, political dynamics are less likely to be prominent. Growth and profitability yield many new, high-level jobs and usually mean that resources will be plentiful. Organizational slack can be used to forestall conflict. Recall, too, that strong cultures produce homogeneity rather than pluralism. For many reasons, almost everyone in the companies studied by Peters and Waterman shared similar values, beliefs, and myths. Unifying cultures reduce conflicts and political strife.

By definition, the Peters and Waterman sample excluded companies that had not been doing well—those where resources were tighter and conflict was higher. Their sample also excluded public organizations that are, inevitably, embedded in and responsible to the political processes of government. While the excellent companies were "close to the customer," none was dependent on the whims of congressional committees for its annual budget.

Even in successful companies, it is likely that power and conflict are more important than the Peters and Waterman analysis suggests. If you ask any manager, What makes your organization successful? he or she will rarely refer to political conflicts or cliques or to people who are jockeying for position. Even if they exist, company politics are typically kept in the closet—secrets known to every insider but rarely put on public display.

Peters and Waterman's "lessons from American's best-run companies" capture important elements of the structural, human resource, and symbolic frames, but the absence of political considerations is troubling. What would happen, for example, if one of their "excellent" companies encountered a weakening or a reversal in the business cycle? The political frame suggests that resources would become scarcer, conflict would increase, and political dynamics would become more prominent. In fact, that happened to several of the companies that Peters and Waterman studied. DEC encountered such a period during the recession of 1982–1983, and newspapers were soon describing conflicts among top management and noting the departure of several senior executives. Moreover, any sophisticated public-sector manager knows that politics have to be addressed. They cannot simply be ignored or made to disappear.

Kotter (1982) took a different approach from that of Peters and Waterman. Instead of focusing on excellent companies, he focused on successful managers. Over a five-year period (from 1976 to 1981), he studied fifteen general managers. His sample included "individuals who hold positions with some multifunctional responsibility for a business" (Kotter, 1982, p. 2). Kotter's managers averaged $150,000 in annual salary in 1978 and ran organizations with at least several hundred employees. Some managed organizations with more than 10,000 employees and annual budgets over $1 billion.

Complexity, uncertainty, and dependence were the most striking features of the general managers' jobs. They regularly dealt with an enormously diverse and complicated set of issues and problems, yet the information that they needed most was often hard to get. Their effectiveness depended on the cooperation of a large network—hundreds or even thousands of people in a variety of roles both inside and outside the organization. "As a result of these demands, the typical [general manager] faced significant obstacles both in figuring out what to do and in getting things done" (Kotter, 1982, p. 122). Table 7 lists, by frame, the six major challenges or dilemmas that Kotter found to characterize management jobs.

This table shows striking parallels across the four frames. General managers need to set a general direction or agenda for their organization. But it is not always easy to determine the right goals for an organization, and this means that agenda setting is just as much an act of faith as it is a rational process. Allocating scarce resources combines both structural and political considerations—deciding where resources will best further the mission of the organization, while simultaneously finding ways to satisfy important constituents. Keeping on top of a very large and complicated set of

Table 7. Frames Relevant to Challenges in General Managers' Jobs.

| Challenge | Relevent Frame |
|---|---|
| Set goals and policies under conditions of uncertainty | Structural, symbolic |
| Achieve "delicate balance" in allocating scarce resources across different businesses or functions | Structural, political |
| Keep on top of a large, complex set of activities | Structural, human resource |
| Get support from bosses | Human resource, political |
| Get support from corporate staff and other constituents | Human resource, political |
| Motivate, coordinate, and control large, diverse group of subordinates | Structural, human resource |

activities required not only an effective chain of command but also an effective informal network of people who could provide key information. The support and resources of three groups were essential: superiors, subordinates, and other key stakeholders (including corporate staffs, customers, and suppliers). Successful general managers were notable for their interpersonal skills and comfort with the use of power—basic tools of the human resource and political frames, respectively.

Kotter found many differences among the general managers. Some were genially charismatic while others were icily efficient. Many worked long hours at a frenetic pace; some had a much more leisurely approach. Some spent much of their time responding to the crisis of the moment; others were able to devote the bulk of their attention to long-term mission and strategy. Some of these differences were attributable to different backgrounds and personal characteristics; many were attributable to differences in their jobs. But there were also numerous similarities. For example, all the general managers had spent most of their careers in the same industry, often in the same company. A major component of the general managers' success—despite their belief in the transferability of their skills— derived from their long-term experience and extensive knowledge of a specific organization.

Kotter also found significant similarities among the more

successful general managers. These arose from three basic tasks of the job: setting an agenda, building a network, and using the network to get things done. Successful general managers were more aggressive in setting agendas and building networks. Their success depended on the efforts and cooperation of hundreds or even thousands of other people. Hence, they needed to set agendas that others could understand and support, and they needed to have strong networks in place.

"[These] effective executives did not approach their jobs by planning, organizing, motivating, and controlling in a very formal sense. Instead, they relied on more continuous, more informal, and more subtle methods to cope with their large and complex job demands. The most important products of their approach were agendas and networks, not formal plans and organizational charts. . . . They typically spend the vast majority of their time with other people, discussing a wide variety of topics. [They] asked numerous questions, yet they rarely could be seen making big decisions. These conversations often included a considerable amount of joking and non-work-related issues. . . . The [general managers] rarely gave orders, but often tried to influence others. Their time was seldom planned in advance in any detail and was usually characterized by varied and disjointed conversations" (Kotter, 1982, p. 126). Kotter acknowledges that, on the surface, the general managers' behavior does not seem very "professional"—at least in the light of current mythology about good management. But he argues that such behavior is the necessary response to the diversity, complexity, and uncertainty that senior managers face.

Lynn (1987) studied five agency heads who worked for the U.S. government during the Reagan administration. All attempted to achieve significant change in their agencies with varying success. Lynn set out to determine what made the difference. Lynn concluded that success depended on four factors: personality, skills and experience, the design for change, and the favorability of the situation. Personality, as Lynn describes it, has to do with an executive's flexibility and capacity to develop positive relationships with constituents and subordinates. For example, Raymond Peck was rated as ineffective as director of the National Highway and Safety Administration, even though he faced a favorable environment. He was widely viewed as "combative, cocky, suspicious, and hard to pin down" (Lynn, 1987, p. 259). In contrast, Mark Fowler did relatively well as chairman of the Federal Communications Commission. He was seen as an "inflexible idealogue," but was often forgiven because of his "folksy, outgoing, buoyant, and optimistic personality" (Lynn, 1987, p. 257).

Lynn's skills variable includes structural elements like planning and organizing, and a large dose of political skill and sophistication: "Building legislative support, negotiating, and identifying changing positions and interests" (Lynn, 1987, p. 248). The most effective of the five executives, in Lynn's assessment, was Ford B. Ford, assistant secretary of labor with responsibility for the relatively obscure Mining Health and Safety Administration. Lynn rated Ford strong in personality and skills and strongest in terms of his strategy for change. Ford studied his agency carefully and concluded that it needed to change both its strategy and its criteria for success. MHSA had measured its effectiveness in terms of things that were easy to count (such as the number of citations issued and penalties collected). Ford wanted to focus more directly on the goal of reducing accidents and injuries. To achieve that goal, he saw a need to move the agency away from its excessively adversarial relationship with the industry that it regulated. He implemented a reorganization that moved more authority and autonomy to local managers, and altered the performance criteria for inspectors to emphasize injury reduction rather than number of inspections. His changes created significant discontent among the inspectors, but Ford had built a strong base of support both with the industry and with his own district managers. Ultimately, the organization moved toward "Ford's central strategic premise that mine managers, workers, and inspectors should be partners in promoting mine safety" (Lynn, 1987, p. 261). Lynn concluded that the quality of an executive's strategy was the paramount factor in determining success; his argument parallels Kotter's emphasis on the challenge of setting an agenda under conditions of conflict and uncertainty.

Comparing the three different studies reveals both similarities and differences. All three give roughly equal emphasis to structural and human resource considerations. Kotter and Lynn put much greater emphasis on political issues and less emphasis on symbolic issues than do Peters and Waterman. It comes as no surprise that Lynn found political skills to be critical for political appointees in government, but differences in sector cannot account for the differences between the other two studies, since both focused on the private sector. Differences in how the studies were conducted might have played a significant role. Peters and Waterman's research consisted mostly of informal interviews and casual observations. Kotter's research was the most intensive and systematic: he interviewed each general manager for several hours, and observed all over several full work days. While a senior manager might not mention politics in a single interview, it would be much harder to keep it secret while in full view over the course of several days. It is not surprising that issues of power, dependence, and scarce resources were much more prominent in Kotter's more intensive study.

Only a few of Kotter's managers actively managed their organizations' culture. The others did not—including most of the less outstanding general managers. There may be two reasons for this. Compared to the Peters and Waterman sample, these general managers came from a broader range of companies. Many of these were not companies known for their robust cultures. Moreover, most of the general managers were not chief executives. They had responsibility for a major unit within a larger corporation. For this reason, they may have operated within the context of a culture that was largely defined and managed by their superiors. In sum, each of the studies emphasized three frames, but omitted a fourth. Peters and Waterman, focusing on successful companies, omitted the political frame but put heavy emphasis on symbolic issues. Kotter and Lynn, in their studies of senior executives, omitted the symbolic frame but emphasized politics. For one reason or another, each study screened out an important dimension of managing complex organizations that another included. As experienced managers know, what you don't see often bites you.

In recent years, a new line of research on managers' frame preferences has provided additional data on how frame preferences influence leadership effectiveness. Bensimon (1988, 1989) studied college presidents and found that multiframe presidents were viewed as more effective than single-frame presidents. (More than a third of the presidents used only one frame, while only a quarter relied on more than two.) Single-frame presidents tended to be less experienced and to rely on the structural or human resource frames. Bensimon found that presidents who relied solely on the structural frame were particularly likely to be seen as ineffective leaders. Wimpelberg (1987) found similar results in a study of eighteen principals of elementary schools in Louisiana. Wimpelberg's study paired nine effective and nine less effective schools. Data from interviews with the school principals suggested that principals of ineffective schools usually relied almost entirely on the structural frame, while principals in effective schools used multiple frames. For example, when asked about hiring teachers, principals in less effective schools talked about the standard procedures (for example, how vacancies are posted and how the central office sends candidates for interviews), while more effective principals talked about "playing the system" to get the teachers they needed.

Bensimon also found that presidents thought they relied on more frames than their colleagues saw them use. They were particularly likely to rate themselves higher than they were rated by colleagues on the human resource and symbolic frames. Only half of the presidents who saw themselves as symbolic leaders were perceived as symbolic by others on their campus. Bolman (1989) found similar results in a group of European managers from a multinational corporation. These managers rated themselves higher on the human resource and symbolic frames than did their colleagues, but lower on the structural and symbolic. Bensimon (1988), Bolman (1989), and Wimpelberg (1987) all found that individuals who relied primarily on the structural frame were particularly likely to be viewed as ineffective leaders.

## Summary

The image of firm control and crisp rationality often attributed to managers has little relevance to the messy world of complexity, conflict, and uncertainty that they typically inhabit. They need multiple frames to survive. They need to understand that any event or process can serve multiple purposes and that different participants are often operating in different frames. They need to consider important organizational variables that help to assess which frames are likely to be salient and which are likely to be effective in any given situation. Among the key variables are motivation, technical constraints, uncertainty, scarcity, conflict, and whether an individual is operating top down or bottom up.

Several lines of recent research support the view that effective leaders and effective organizations rely on multiple frames. Studies of effective corporations, of individuals in senior management roles, and of educational administrators all point to the need for multiple perspectives.

# 17

# *Choosing a Frame: The Power of Scenarios*

Meryl Streep, like other great actors and actresses, shows an extraordinary capacity to lose herself in a role and *become* the character whom she plays, whether an Australian mother accused of killing her child, or a Polish mother interned in a Nazi concentration camp. Changing the script changes her: who she is, how she appears, what she does. Few of us have the dramatic skill and versatility of a Streep or a Laurence Olivier, but most of us *can* alter what we do by choosing to follow different scenarios. We have been learning how to do this all our lives. Students use different scenarios for meetings with professors than for discussions with peers. Managers follow different scenarios with bosses than with subordinates. Both men and women tend to employ different scenarios with members of the same sex than with members of the opposite sex.

Each of the four frames generates a different set of strategies for responding to managerial challenges, and those differences can be translated into alternative scenarios. Just as the same actor can have a totally different effect when playing two different scripts, managers can enhance their flexibility and freedom by writing scenarios for themselves that include elements from different frames. To illustrate that process, we will use the frames to generate scenarios for four different leadership styles and apply those styles to a case, Robert F. Kennedy High School.

## ROBERT F. KENNEDY HIGH SCHOOL

On July 15, 1970, David King became principal of the Robert
F. Kennedy High School, the newest of the six high schools in
Great Ridge, Illinois. The school had opened in the fall of 1968
amid national acclaim for being one of the first schools in the
country to be designed and constructed for the "house system"
concept. Kennedy High's organization was broken down into
four "houses," each of which contained 300 students, a faculty
of 18, and a housemaster. The Kennedy complex was specially
designed so that each house was in a separate building connected to the "core facilities"* and other houses by an enclosed
outside passageway. Each house had its own entrance, classrooms, toilets, conference rooms, and housemaster's office.

King knew that Kennedy High was not intended to be
an ordinary school when it was first conceived. It had been
hailed as a major innovation in inner-city education, and a
Chicago television station had made a documentary about it in
1968. Kennedy High had opened with a carefully selected staff
of teachers, many of whom were chosen from other Great Ridge
schools and at least a dozen of whom had been specially recruited from out of state. Indeed, King knew his faculty included graduates from several elite East and West Coast
schools, such as Stanford, Yale, and Princeton, as well as several of the very best Midwestern schools. Even the racial mix
of students had been carefully balanced so that blacks, whites,
and Puerto Ricans each comprised a third of the student body
(although King also knew—perhaps better than its planners—
that Kennedy's students were drawn from the toughest and
poorest areas of the city). The building itself was also widely
admired for its beauty and functionality and had won several
national architectural awards.

Despite these careful and elaborate preparations, Kennedy High School was in serious difficulty by July of 1970. It

*The core facilities included the cafeteria, nurse's room, guidance offices,
the boys' and girls' gyms, the offices, the shops, and the auditorium.

had been racked by violence the preceding year, having been twice closed by student disturbances and once by a teacher walkout. It was also widely reported (although King did not know for sure) that achievement scores of its ninth- and tenth-grade students had actually declined during the last two years, while no significant improvement could be found in the scores of the eleventh- and twelfth-graders' tests. Thus, the Kennedy High School for which King was taking over as principal had fallen far short of its planners' hopes and expectations.

### David King

David King was born and raised in Great Ridge, Illinois. His father was one of the city's first black principals, and thus King was not only familiar with the city but with its school system as well. After two years of military service, King decided to follow his father's footsteps and went to Great Ridge State Teachers College, from which he received his B.Ed. in 1955 and his M.Ed. in 1960. King was certified in elementary and secondary school administration, English, and physical education. King had taught English and coached in a predominantly black middle school until 1960, when he was asked to become the school's assistant principal. He remained in that post until 1965, when he was asked to take over the George Thibeault Middle School, a large middle school of 900 pupils which at the time was reputed to be the most "difficult" middle school in the city. While at Thibeault, King gained a citywide reputation for being a gifted and popular administrator and was credited with changing Thibeault from the worst middle school in the system to one of the best. He had been very effective in building community support, recruiting new faculty, and raising academic standards. He was also credited with turning out basketball and baseball teams which had won state and county middle-school championships. King knew that he had been selected for the Kennedy job over several more senior candidates because of his ability to handle tough situations. The superintendent had made that clear when he told King why he had been selected for the job.

The superintendent had also told him that he would need every bit of skill and luck he could muster. King knew of the formidable credentials of Jack Weis, his predecessor at

Kennedy High. Weis, a white, had been the superintendent of a small, local township school system before becoming Kennedy's first principal. He had also written a book on the "house system" concept, as well as a second book on inner-city education. Weis had earned a Ph.D. from the University of Chicago and a divinity degree from Harvard. Yet, despite his impressive background and obvious ability, Weis had resigned in disillusionment and was described by many as a "broken man." In fact, King remembered seeing the physical change which Weis had undergone over that two-year period. Weis's appearance had become progressively more fatigued and strained until he developed what appeared to be permanent black rings under his eyes and a perpetual stoop. King remembered how he had pitied the man and wondered how Weis could find the job worth the obvious personal toll it was taking on him.

### History of the School

1968–1969: The school's troubles began to manifest themselves in the school's first year of operation. Rumors of conflicts between the housemasters and the six subject-area department heads were widespread throughout the system by the middle of the first year. The conflicts stemmed from differences in interpretations of curriculum policy on required learning and course content. In response to these conflicts, Dr. Weis had instituted a "free market" policy by which subject-area department heads were supposed to convince housemasters of why they should offer certain courses, while housemasters were supposed to convince department heads of which teachers they wanted assigned to their houses and why they wanted those teachers. Many observers in the school system felt that this policy exacerbated the conflicts.

To add to this climate of conflict, a teacher was assaulted in her classroom in February of 1969. The beating frightened many of the staff, particularly some of the older teachers. A delegation of eight teachers asked Weis to hire security guards a week after the assault. The request precipitated a debate within the faculty about the desirability of having guards in the school. One group felt that the guards would instill a sense of safety within the school and thus promote a better learning climate, while the other group felt that the presence of guards in the school would be repressive and would destroy the sense of community and trust which was developing within the school. Dr. Weis refused the request for security guards because he believed that symbolically they would represent everything the school was trying to change. In April a second teacher was robbed and beaten in her classroom after school hours and the debate was rekindled, except that this time a group of Spanish-speaking parents threatened to boycott the school unless better security measures were instituted. Again, Dr. Weis refused the request for security guards.

1969–1970: The second year of the school's existence was even more troubled than the first. Because of cutbacks ordered during the summer of 1969, Dr. Weis was not able to replace eight teachers who resigned during the summer, and it was no longer possible for each house to staff all of its courses with its own faculty. Dr. Weis therefore instituted a "flexible staffing" policy whereby some teachers were asked to teach a course outside of their assigned house and students in the eleventh and twelfth grades were able to take some elective and required courses in other houses. During this period, Chauncey Carver, one of the housemasters, publicly attacked the move as a step toward destroying the house system. In a letter to the *Great Ridge Times,* he accused the board of education of trying to subvert the house concept by cutting back funds.

The debate over the flexible staffing policy was heightened when two of the other housemasters joined a group of faculty and department chairmen in opposing Chauncey Carver's criticisms. This group argued that the individual house faculties of fifteen to eighteen teachers could never offer their students the breadth of courses that a schoolwide faculty of sixty-five to seventy teachers could offer and that interhouse cross-registration should be encouraged for that reason.

Further expansion of a cross-registration or flexible staffing policy was halted, however, because of difficulties encountered in the scheduling of classes in the fall of 1969. Several errors were found in the master schedule which had been pre-planned during the preceding summer. Various schedule difficulties persisted until November of 1969, when the vice-principal responsible for the scheduling of classes resigned. Mr. Burtram Perkins, a Kennedy housemaster who had formerly planned the schedule at Central High, assumed the scheduling function in addition to his duties as housemaster. The scheduling activity took most of Perkins' time until February.

Security again became an issue when three sophomores were assaulted because they refused to give up their lunch money during a "shakedown." It was believed that the assailants were from outside the school and were not students. Several teachers approached Dr. Weis and asked him to request security guards from the board of education. Again, Dr. Weis declined, but he asked Bill Smith, a vice-principal at the school, to secure all doors except for the entrances to each of the four houses, the main entrance to the school, and the cafeteria. This move appeared to reduce the number of outsiders in the school.

In May of 1970 a disturbance occurred in the cafeteria which appeared to grow out of a fight between two boys. The fight spread and resulted in considerable damage to the school, including the breaking of classroom windows and desks. The disturbance was severe enough for Dr. Weis to close the school. A number of teachers and students reported that outsiders were involved in the fight and in damaging the classrooms. Several students were taken to the hospital for minor injuries, but all were released. A similar disturbance occurred two weeks later, and again the school was closed. The board of education then ordered a temporary detail of municipal police to the school despite Dr. Weis's advice to the contrary. In protest to the assignment of the police detail, thirty of Kennedy's sixty-eight teachers staged a walkout, which was joined by over half the student body. The police detail was removed from the school, and an agreement was worked out by an ad hoc subcommittee of the board of education with informal representatives of teachers who were for and against assigning a police detail. The compromise called for the temporary stationing of a police cruiser near the school.

### King's First Week at Kennedy High

Mr. King arrived at Kennedy High on Monday, July 15th, and spent most of his first week individually interviewing the school's key administrators (see page 351 for a listing of Kennedy's administrative staff as of July 15th). He also had a meeting with all of his administrators and department heads on

Friday of that week. Mr. King's purpose in these meetings was to familiarize himself with the school, its problems, and its key people.

His first interview was with Bill Smith, who was one of his vice-principals. Mr. Smith was black and had worked as a counselor and as a vice-principal of a middle school prior to coming to Kennedy. King knew that Smith had a reputation for being a tough disciplinarian and was very much disliked among many of the younger faculty and students. However, King had also heard from several teachers, whose judgment he respected, that Smith had been instrumental in keeping the school from "blowing apart" the preceding year. It became clear early in the interview that Smith felt that more stringent steps were needed to keep outsiders from wandering into the buildings. In particular, Smith urged King to consider locking all of the school's thirty doors except for the front entrance so that everyone would enter and leave through one set of doors only. Smith also told him that many of the teachers and pupils had become fearful of living and working in the building and that "no learning will ever begin to take place until we make it so people don't have to be afraid anymore." At the end of the interview, Smith told King that he had been approached by a nearby school system to become its director of counseling but that he had not yet made up his mind. He said that he was committed enough to Kennedy High that he did not want to leave but that his decision depended on how hopeful he felt about its future.

As King talked with others, he discovered that the "door question" was one of considerable controversy within the faculty and that feelings ran high, both in favor of the idea of locking all the doors and against it. Two of the housemasters in particular, Chauncey Carver, a black, and Frank Czepak, a white, were strongly against closing the house entrances. The two men felt that such an action would symbolically reduce house "autonomy" and the feeling of distinctness that was a central aspect of the house concept.

Chauncey Carver, master of "C" House, was particularly vehement on this issue as well as on the question of whether students of one house should be allowed to take classes in another house. Carver said that the flexible staffing program introduced the preceding year had nearly destroyed the house concept and that he, Carver, would resign if King intended to expand the cross-house enrollment of students. Carver also complained about what he described as "interference" from department heads in his teachers' autonomy.

Carver appeared to be an outstanding housemaster from everything that King had heard about him—even from his many enemies. Carver had an abrasive personality but seemed to have the best-operating house in the school and was well liked by most of his teachers and pupils. His program also appeared to be the most innovative of all. However, it was also the program which was most frequently attacked by the department heads for lacking substance and not covering the requirements outlined in the system's curriculum guide. Even with these criticisms, King imagined how much easier it would be if he had four housemasters like Chauncey Carver.

During his interviews with the other three housemasters, King discovered that they all felt infringed upon by the department heads but that only Carver and Czepak were strongly against "locking the doors" and that two other housemasters actively favored cross-house course enrollments. King's fourth interview was with Burtram Perkins, who was also a housemaster. Perkins was a black in his late forties who had been an assistant to the principal of Central High before coming to Kennedy. Perkins spent most of the interview discussing how schedule pressures could be relieved. Perkins was currently involved in developing the schedule for the 1970–1971 school year until a vice-principal was appointed to perform that job (Kennedy High had allocations for two vice-principals and two assistants in addition to the housemasters. See page 351).

Two pieces of information concerning Perkins came to King's attention during his first week there. The first was that several teachers were circulating a letter requesting Perkins' removal as a housemaster because they felt he could not control the house or direct the faculty. This surprised King because he had heard that Perkins was widely respected within the faculty and had earned a reputation for supporting high academic standards and for working tirelessly with new teachers. However, as King inquired further, he discovered that Perkins was greatly liked within the faculty but was also generally recognized as a poor housemaster. The second piece of information concerned how Perkins' house compared with the others. Al-

---

**Administrative Organization**
**Robert F. Kennedy High School**
**Great Ridge, Illinois**

---

| | |
|---|---|
| Principal: | David King, 42 (black)<br>B.Ed., M.Ed., Great Ridge State<br>College |
| Vice-Principal: | William Smith, 44 (black)<br>B.Ed., Breakwater State College<br>M.Ed., (Counseling) Great<br>Ridge State College |
| Vice-Principal: | vacant—to be filled |
| Housemaster, A House: | Burtram Perkins, 47 (black)<br>B.S., M.Ed., Univ. of Illinois |
| Housemaster, B House: | Frank Czepak, 36 (white)<br>B.S., Univ. of Illinois<br>M.Ed., Great Ridge State<br>College |
| Housemaster, C House: | Chauncey Carver, 32 (black)<br>A.B., Wesleyan Univ.<br>B.F.A., Pratt Institute<br>M.A.T., Yale University |
| Housemaster, D House: | John Bonavota, 26 (white)<br>B.Ed., Great Ridge State College<br>M.Ed., Ohio State University |
| Assistant to the Principal: | vacant—to be filled |
| Assistant to the Principal:<br>(for Community Affairs) | vacant—to be filled |

---

though students had been randomly assigned to each house, Perkins' house had the largest absence rate and the greatest number of disciplinary problems in the school. Smith had also told him that Perkins' dropout rate for 1969-1970 was three times that of any other house.

While King was in the process of interviewing his staff, he was called on by Mr. David Crimmins, chairman of the history department. Crimmins was a native of Great Ridge, white, and in his late forties. Crimmins was scheduled for an appointment the following week but asked King if he could see him immediately. Crimmins said he wanted to talk with King because he had heard that a letter was being circulated asking for Perkins' removal and he wanted to present the other side of the argument. Crimmins became very emotional during the conversation and said that Perkins was viewed by many of the teachers and department chairmen as the only housemaster who was making an effort to maintain high academic standards and that his transfer would be seen as a blow to those concerned with quality education. He also described in detail Perkins' devotion and commitment to the school and the fact that Perkins was the only administrator with the ability to straighten out the schedule and that he had done this in addition to all of his other duties. Crimmins ended by saying that if Perkins were transferred, he, Crimmins, would personally write a letter to the regional accreditation council telling them how badly standards had sunk at Kennedy. King assured him that it would not be necessary to take such a drastic measure and that a cooperative resolution would be found. King was aware of the accreditation review that Kennedy High faced the following April, and he did not wish to complicate the process unnecessarily in any way.

Within twenty minutes of Crimmins' departure, King was visited by a young white teacher named Tim Shea who said that he had heard that Crimmins had come in to see him. Shea said that he was one of the teachers who organized the movement to get rid of Perkins. Shea said that he liked and admired Perkins very much because of his devotion to the school but that Perkins' house was so disorganized and discipline so bad that it was nearly impossible to do any good teaching. Shea added that it was "a shame to lock the school up when stronger leadership is all that's needed."

King's impressions of his administrators generally matched what he had heard about them before arriving at the school. Carver seemed to be a very bright, innovative, and charismatic leader whose mere presence generated excitement. Czepak seemed to be a highly competent, though not very imaginative, administrator who had earned the respect of his faculty and students. Bonavota, who was only twenty-six, seemed very bright and earnest but unseasoned and unsure of himself. King felt that with a little guidance and training Bonavota might have the greatest promise of all. At the moment, however, he appeared to be a very uncertain and somewhat confused person who had difficulty simply coping. Perkins seemed to be a very sincere and devoted person who had a good mind for administrative details but an almost total incapacity for leadership.

King knew that he would have the opportunity to make several administrative appointments because of the three vacancies which existed. Indeed, should Smith resign as vice-principal, King would be in the position of filling both vice-principalships. He knew that his recommendations for these positions would carry a great deal of weight with the central office. The only constraint that King felt in making these appointments was the need to achieve some kind of racial balance among the Kennedy administrative group. With his own appointment as principal, the number of black administrators exceeded the number of white administrators by a ratio of two to one, and as yet Kennedy did not have a single Puerto Rican administrator even though a third of its pupils had Spanish surnames.

### The Friday Afternoon Meeting

In contrast to the individual interviews, King was surprised to find how quiet and conflict-free these same people were in the staff meeting that he called on Friday. He was amazed at how slow, polite, and friendly the conversation appeared to be among people who had so vehemently expressed negative opinions of each other in private. After about forty-five minutes of discussion about the upcoming accreditation review, King broached the subject of housemaster–department head relations. The ensuing silence was finally broken by a joke which Czepak made about the uselessness of discussing that topic. King probed further by asking whether everyone was happy with the current practices. Crimmins suggested that this was a topic that might be better discussed in a smaller group. Everyone in the room seemed to agree with Crimmins except for Betsy Dula, a young white woman in her late twenties who was chairman of the English department. She said that one of the problems with the school was that no one was willing to tackle tough issues until they exploded. She said that relations between housemasters and department heads were terrible and it made her job very difficult. She then attacked Chauncey Carver for impeding her evaluation of a nontenured teacher in Carver's house. The two argued for several minutes about the teacher and the quality of the experimental sophomore English course that the teacher was giving. Finally, Carver, who by now was quite angry, coldly warned Mrs. Dula that he would "break her neck" if she stepped into his house again. King intervened in an attempt to cool both their tempers, and the meeting ended shortly thereafter.

The following morning, Mrs. Dula called King at home and told him that unless Chauncey Carver publicly apologized for his threat, she would file a grievance with the teachers' union and take it to court if necessary. King assured Mrs. Dula that he would talk with Carver on Monday. King then called Eleanor Debbs, one of the school's math teachers whom he had known well for many years and whose judgment he respected. Mrs. Debbs was a close friend of both Carver and Mrs. Dula and was also vice-president of the city's teachers' union. He learned from her that both had been long-term adversaries but that she felt both were excellent professionals.

She also reported that Mrs. Dula would be a formidable opponent and could muster considerable support among the faculty. Mrs. Debbs, who was herself black, feared that a confrontation between Dula and Carver might create tensions along race lines within the school even though both Dula and Carver were generally quite popular with students of all races. Mrs. Debbs strongly urged King not to let the matter drop. Mrs. Debbs also told him that she had overheard Bill Smith, the vice-principal, say at a party the preceding night that he felt that King didn't have either the stomach or the forcefulness necessary to survive at Kennedy. Smith further stated that the only reason he was staying was that he did not expect King to last the year. Should that prove to be the case, Smith felt that he would be appointed principal.

David King, the new principal of Kennedy High School, faces a formidable set of leadership problems. The school is in disarray. The previous principal left "a broken man." The staff is fiercely divided. How might reframing help David King face these problems? We will begin by using each frame to generate a scenario. By *scenario,* we do not mean a detailed set of instructions about what to say and do. We use the term instead to refer to a philosophy and a set of orienting assumptions. Those assumptions provide a framework to guide action and stimulate improvisation.

In seminars and classes, we give students and managers the following instructions: "Assume that you are David King. It is Sunday, and you have completed your first week at RFK. You promised Betsy Dula that you would have a talk on Monday with Chauncey Carver. How will you approach your meeting with Mr. Carver?" We then ask small groups to choose one of their members to role-play David King in the meeting with Chauncey Carver. We assign each group a scenario, keyed to one of the four frames. (The rest of the group observes the group role play and comments on it at the end.)

Exhibit 2 contains a scenario for a structural leader. It is a generic scenario that could be applied to almost any situation that a manager might encounter, including the situation facing David King. The scenario provides only a brief and general description of the structural orientation, but we have found that most managers can use it to develop an approach that is broadly consistent with the scenario. At the same time, there are great differences among different individuals and groups in how they implement the scenario and how well their approaches work. For every frame, including the structural frame, we have seen both brilliant and dreadful approaches to the role of David King. Consider the following example.

**Exhibit 2. A Structural Scenario.**

The fundamental responsibility of managers and leaders is to clarify organizational goals, attend to the relationship between structure and environment, and develop a structure that is clear and appropriate to the goals, the task, and the environment. Without such a structure, people become unsure what they are supposed to be doing. The result is confusion, frustration, and conflict. In an effective organization, individuals are clear about their responsibilities and their contribution. Policies, linkages, and lines of authority are clear. When an organization has the right structure, and people understand it, the organization can achieve its goals and individuals can be effective in their roles.

The job of a leader is to focus on task, facts, and logic, not personality and emotions. Most "people" problems really stem from structural flaws rather than from flaws in individuals. Structural leaders are not necessarily authoritarian, and do not necessarily solve every problem by issuing orders (though that will sometimes be appropriate). Instead, they try to design and implement a process or structure appropriate to the problem and the circumstances.

[King calls the meeting in his office. He is seated behind his desk working on some papers when Carver arrives.]

*King:*   Chauncey, thanks for coming by. I wanted to talk to you about some of the ideas I'm developing about how to work on the problems at Robert F. Kennedy. I'd like to get the benefit of your thinking.

*Carver:*   Sure.

*King:*   It seems to me that we have some serious organizational problems, particularly around the role of the housemaster and the department chair. One of the first tasks we need to work on is how to clarify that role relationship and reduce the kind of conflict that we've been having.

*Carver:*   The problem is that the department chairs don't understand the house concept. Their minds are still in a traditional high school.

*King:*   We need to reexamine the role of the department head and the housemaster. Both have to be clear about their own jobs, and how they should interface with each other.

*Carver:*   I'm pretty clear about my job.

*King:*   We'll see. The main thing I wanted to talk about is the incident that occurred in Friday's meeting between you and Betsy Dula. Of course you agree that your response to Betsy was not a professional way to talk to a colleague?

*Carver:*   No. I thought the way she attacked me in a public meeting was unprofessional.

*King:*   That's not the issue. I expect you to apologize to her. We need to create a climate where the professionals can work together.

*Carver:*   She attacks me and I'm supposed to apologize to her? The answer is no!

In this example, David King opened with a discussion of structural issues, but then made an abrupt transition to the exchange between Dula and Carver. Like many managers, King tended to assume that structural leaders are autocratic, even though the scenario cautions against such an interpretation. It is not surprising that his attempt to force an apology from Carver generates resistance and polarizes the discussion. King has now backed himself into a corner. If he continues to try to force the issue, he risks making a powerful enemy, but if he backs down he could be seen as weak. King did not recognize that an apology is not a structural solution to an organizational problem; it is a personal solution to an interpersonal problem.

Another, more sophisticated example of a structural approach to the situation appears in the following role play:

[King again calls Carver into his office.]

*King:* Thanks for coming over, Chauncey. I hope that you can help me deal with some of the organizational problems that I think the school needs to solve.

*Carver:* Like what?

*King:* The basic issue is how to make the house system work. One piece of that is how do we coordinate the work of the houses with the work of the academic departments. The exchange in Friday's meeting between you and Betsy Dula seems to me to be part of a larger problem of linking the houses and the departments.

*Carver:* The real question is whether we're committed to the house system.

*King:* If we get the house system to work, people will be committed. I think we need a process to look at how we do that, including the relationships between housemasters and department chairs.

*Carver:* What do you have in mind?

*King:* I'd like to set up a special task force to look at the structure of the house system. I plan to chair the task force myself. We need someone on the group who can represent the house perspective, and I hope you will be willing to serve.

*Carver:* Who else will be on it?

*King:* Right now, I'm thinking about one other housemaster, the assistant principal, and two department chairs, including Betsy Dula.

*Carver:*  You want Betsy and me on the same task force?

*King:*  Yes, but to make that work, I think we need a process for resolving the dispute between the two of you. Betsy has threatened to file a grievance over your statement about breaking her neck. I don't think that would be helpful for you or the school. What I think we need is a meeting between the two of you, which I would chair as a neutral third party, to discuss the differences between you.

*Carver:*  What do you have in mind for the meeting?

*King:*  How about if I talk to both of you before the meeting and develop an agenda that we all agree on?

*Carver:*  O.K. If Betsy's willing, I'm willing.

The second "structural" David King tenaciously stayed on a structural path. He framed the conflict between Carver and Dula as part of larger structural issues and used the conversation with Carver to set up both a task force to work on the structure of the school and a meeting to try to resolve the personal conflict. Though Carver did not respond with much enthusiasm, he did agree to take the next step.

Exhibit 3 describes a David King who focuses on human resource considerations. The human resource scenario, like the structural one, can be acted out well or badly. Ineffective human resource leaders tend to be too cautious and wishy-washy. Consider the following example:

[King drops by Carver's office and asks if he has a minute to talk. Carver says O.K.]

*King:*  I dropped by to let you know how much I value the contribution that you've been making to the school. You've been doing a great job in House C.

*Carver:*  Thanks.

*King:*  I'm worried about that interchange on Friday, though.

### Exhibit 3. A Human Resource Scenario.

---

People are the heart of any organization. When people feel the organization is responsive to their needs and supportive of their goals, leaders can count on their commitment and loyalty. Administrators who are authoritarian or insensitive, who don't communicate effectively, or who don't care about their people can never be effective leaders. The human resource leader works on behalf of both the organization and its people, seeking to serve the best interests of both.

The job of the leader is support and empowerment. Support takes a variety of forms: letting people know that you are concerned about them, listening to find out about their aspirations and goals, and communicating personal warmth and openness. A leader empowers people through participation and openness and through making sure that they have the autonomy and the resources that they need to do their jobs well. Human resource leaders emphasize honest, two-way communication as a way to identify issues and resolve differences. They are willing to confront others when it is appropriate, but they try to do so in a spirit of openness and caring.

---

*Carver:*  What interchange?

*King:*  Between you and Betsy.

*Carver:*  She and I have disagreed before. It's no big deal.

*King:*  Well, don't you feel that we should do something?

*Carver:*  About what?

*King:*  To make Betsy feel better.

*Carver:*  Making Betsy feel better is not my job.

*King:*  Well, maybe you should talk to Betsy.

*Carver:*  I don't have anything to say to Betsy.

Observers felt that David King was so determined to be pleasant and nonthreatening that he never dealt with the real issues. Carver reported feeling puzzled about what King was trying to communicate. A more effective human resource scenario can be seen in the following conversation:

[King sets up an informal meeting in Carver's office.]

*King:*  Chauncey, I really appreciate your finding time to meet on such short notice. You are a key person in this school, and I called this meeting because I really need your help.

*Carver:*    What kind of help are you looking for?

*King:*    Here's what I'm concerned about. Betsy called me yesterday, and she's very upset about the exchange you and she had in Friday's meeting. She threatened to file a grievance unless she got a public apology from you.

*Carver:*    There's no way I'm going to apologize to her! She should consider apologizing to me.

*King:*    Why?

*Carver:*    She attacked me in that meeting.

*King:*    She did criticize you, but you threatened to break her neck.

*Carver:*    That wasn't really a physical threat. I was angry at the time.

*King:*    I can understand you were angry, but how would Betsy know for sure that the threat wasn't real?

*Carver:*    She knows me better than that.

*King:*    That's not what she's saying. This kind of tension between two people who are leaders in the school is bad for all of us. How should we resolve it?

*Carver:*    Maybe I need to talk to Betsy.

*King:*    I agree, and I'd like to join you for that conversation.

      Observers of the above scenario felt that King was supportive, but also very firm and clear. They were impressed by the fact that Carver himself suggested meeting with Dula.

      On the one hand, the human resource scenario usually does not generate significant anger or conflict. King opens the conversation in a friendly spirit and frequently wins agreement from Carver to take a step toward resolving the dispute with Dula. On the other hand, the scenario often leads King to focus almost entirely on the personal issue between Carver and Dula rather than on the larger organizational issues.

Exhibit 4 presents the political view of organizations and leadership. Some David Kings interpret the political frame as an invitation to strong-arm subordinates, as in the following example:

[King calls Carver to his office.]

*King:*   Chauncey, come on in. I've just come from a meeting with the superintendent and the chairman of the school board, and they told me that I should do whatever it takes to get this school back in order. I'm ready to do that.

[King pauses. Carver says nothing.]

*King:*   I expect you to fix the problem with Betsy Dula.

*Carver:*   What problem?

*King:*   You threatened her physically in Friday's meeting. She wants an apology. I suggest you apologize before any more damage is done.

*Carver:*   Why should I apologize? In the first place, she attacked me in a public meeting. In the second place, you were the one who brought up the issue of relations between the housemasters and the

**Exhibit 4. A Political Scenario.**

---

Managers have to recognize political reality and know how to deal with it. Inside and outside any organization, there are always a variety of different interest groups, each with its own agenda. There are not enough resources to give everyone what he or she wants, and there is always going to be conflict.

The job of leaders is to recognize the major constituencies, develop ties to their leadership, and manage conflict as productively as possible. Above all, they need to build power bases and use power carefully. They cannot give every group everything it wants, although they can try to create arenas for negotiating differences and coming up with reasonable compromises. They also have to work hard at articulating what everyone in their organizations has in common. They must tell the people in their organizations that it is a waste of time to fight each other when there are plenty of enemies outside that they can all fight together. Groups that fail to work well together internally tend to get trounced by outsiders who have their own agendas.

---

department chairs. Frank warned you that it wouldn't be productive. Maybe you should apologize to both of us.

*King:*   Mr. Carver, I am not asking if you *want* to apologize. I am telling you that you are going to apologize!

*Carver:*   [With slow, icy calm:] Mr. King, as a professional educator, I expect my colleagues to treat me with respect. Until you're ready to do that, I don't think this meeting will be very productive. [Carver walks out.]

Observers were split on King's effectiveness in this role play. Many applauded King's opening statement because it made it clear to Carver that King was now in charge. Many also praised King for employing a firm and decisive approach to the Dula issue. But others felt that King was too heavy-handed and particularly criticized his persistence in strong-arming Carver, even after it was clear that such a tactic would not work.

Politically sophisticated approaches are usually more subtle and more attuned to others' interests. A meeting between Carver and such a David King went as follows:

[King drops in on Carver in Carver's office.]

*King:*   Chauncey, have you got a couple of minutes?

*Carver:*   Sure, what's up?

*King:*   We have a problem, and I'd like to get your input. Have you talked to Betsy Dula since Friday's meeting?

*Carver:*   No. Why?

*King:*   She called me yesterday, and she was steaming. Remember when you told her you'd break her neck if she came in your house?

*Carver:*   Well, yes, but . . .

*King:*   How did you think she reacted?

*Carver:*   She didn't like it, but I didn't like her jumping on me in that meeting.

*King:*   Understood. Anyway, she says she's ready to go all the way on this one: file a grievance, make it a public battle, the whole thing. What'll it mean if she does that?

*Carver:* She may be bluffing. We've had battles before. I think she'll calm down.

*King:* I'm worried about what if she doesn't. I know you want to save the house system, and I'd like to help you do it. But the school is under a lot of pressure from the parents and the board. We've got accreditation coming up. How's it going to play in the newspapers if we have a major public battle between two administrators—particularly when a black man threatened to attack a white woman?

*Carver:* You're right, we don't need that.

*King:* What's it going to take to get this one calmed down?

*Carver:* Maybe I need to talk to Betsy.

*King:* That's a good idea. I wonder if it would also be good if I'm there when you talk to her, just in case things get a little hot.

*Carver:* Yeah, I guess that's O.K.

In this example, the political David King is mindful of the political dynamics both in and outside the school. He wants Carver to work on solving the problem with Dula but moves in gradually, never appearing to take sides or to push Carver into a corner. Observers of this David King felt that he was extremely skillful in maneuvering Carver, although some people wondered if he could use the same approach repeatedly. Would people begin to wonder where he really stood, and whether he could be trusted?

Exhibit 5 presents the symbolic frame scenario—a scenario that emphasizes personal charisma and explicit attention to symbols and to organizational culture. Symbolic leadership is particularly dependent on the skill and art of the individual. When symbolic role plays go awry, the results can be as embarrassing as a bad soap opera. When they go well, they can be transforming. The following symbolic role play shows some of the things that can go wrong:

**Exhibit 5. A Symbolic Scenario.**

Symbolic managers believe that the most important part of a leader's job is inspiration—giving people something that they can believe in. People will give their loyalty to an organization that has a unique identity and makes them feel that what they do is really important. Effective symbolic leaders are passionate about making their organizations the best of their kind and communicate that passion to others. They use dramatic, visible symbols that give people a sense of the organizational mission. They are visible and energetic. They create slogans, tell stories, hold rallies, give awards, appear where they are least expected, and manage by wandering around.

Symbolic leaders are sensitive to an organization's history and culture. They seek to use the best in an organization's traditions and values as a base for building a culture that provides cohesiveness and meaning. They articulate a vision that communicates the organization's unique capabilities and mission.

---

*King:* Chauncey, you and I both know that we're in this together—both fighting for the same cause.

*Carver:* What cause?

*King:* It's what the flag in front of the school represents—the future of America. Keeping this country great.

*Carver:* You can worry about that. My job is to make sure that our kids get an education.

*King:* Sure, but that's a means to doing something that we all care about as Americans.

*Carver:* Are you talking about old-fashioned American values like racism and oppression?

*King:* [Obviously startled.] No, uh, no. But you know what I mean, Chauncey. We all have to work together. It's like Benjamin Franklin said. We must hang together, or we'll all hang separately.

*Carver:* David, I don't know what you're talking about.

*David:* Sure you do, Chauncey. It's like, when I was a kid, the Fourth of July was my favorite holiday.

*Carver:* I like fireworks, too, but what's that got to do with the school?

David King in this role play fell into one of the most common traps for symbolic leaders: he made the wrong assumptions about the symbols that would speak to Chauncey Carver. Even when Chauncey made that clear, David still persisted in a call to patriotism that was inappropriate for his audience.

Nevertheless, leaders who understand the symbols and meanings that are central for their audience can be extremely effective. In the following example, a participant in a management program who described herself as completely uncharismatic used the following approach:

*King:* [With enthusiasm] Chauncey! Hey, come on in. It's great that we can get together! You know, you're one of the real leaders in this school. We're going to need that kind of leadership as we work to make this the best high school in Great Ridge. Can I count on you to provide some of the leadership we need?

*Carver:* I'll do what I can.

*King:* I knew I could count on you, because I know that you're as excited as I am about the potential in this school!

*Chauncey:* Well, yeah, but this school's got a lot of problems.

*King:* Sure, we've got problems, and we have to do something about them. But you could spend all your time worrying about problems and never get around to the important thing—what kind of school do we all want to build here? Do we want it to be one more worn-out urban high school, or do we want a place that's special, that really shows what you can do when everyone really works at it? This may sound corny, but I never forget what Dr. King said. "I have a dream!" That's how I feel about this school, and I want everyone to share in that dream.

*Carver:* I'm with you, but we have a lot of people here who don't really believe in the house system. They really want to tear down what we've been trying to build.

*King:* Chauncey, there's some conflict here, there's some disagreement, but that's part of the excitement. Take that meeting Friday, that was really exciting! Sure, you and Betsy had a tug-of-war, but what it showed me is that you both care about the school, and you're both willing to stand up and fight for what you believe in. If you and I and Betsy and the whole staff really care about making this school a real lighthouse, we can do it. We'll have some battles along the way, but that's how we learn.

Observers were impressed by this David King's enthusiasm and optimism, and even Carver felt more hopeful than he had before the meeting. At the same time, observers wondered whether King was too caught up in symbols and the big picture and thus might find it very difficult to solve more pressing matters such as Dula's grievance.

As the examples illustrate, the different scenarios produce significant differences in David King's approach to Chauncey Carver, as well as in Carver's response to him. No one of the scenarios is consistently more effective than the others, and all four of the frames can be implemented well or badly. We have used these scenarios with a number of students and practicing managers. Few individuals are equally comfortable with all four, but many are surprised that they are better than they anticipated in playing scenarios that initially felt unfamiliar or alien to their sense of themselves. They discover new possibilities and capacities that they did not previously know that they possessed.

Watching all four role plays has often been a powerful experience for individuals who approach the class believing that "there's only one way to deal with someone like Carver." Seeing four different David Kings helps to show that there are always multiple possibilities and that each of the frames can generate new and promising options.

## Summary

The frames can be used as scenarios, that is, as guidelines for managing and leading organizations. Each frame provides a distinctive framework for action, and each is likely to lead to different results, even when applied to the same situation. All of us know how to play different roles in different situations, and we can use those capacities to become more effective managers and leaders.

How well a scenario will work depends on both the situation and the skill of the person who applies it. Each of the scenarios can be applied well or badly, depending on the skill and artistry of the individual. Most people feel more comfortable and confident with some of the scenarios than with others, but many are also surprised to learn that they can discover new possibilities and expand their own leadership effectiveness by practicing and applying scenarios outside their usual range of behavior.

# 18

# Reframing Change: Training and Realignment

Warren Bennis provides a stunning account of the typical complexities of organizational change in describing his administrative experiences in Buffalo in the late 1960s:

> On December 19, 1966, I received a phone call from an assistant to President Martin Meyerson . . . at the State University of New York at Buffalo. The assistant began the conversation with almost sinful empathy: "I bet you don't know what's going on here at Buffalo, do you?" I allowed that I did not, and he proceeded to describe an academic New Jerusalem of unlimited money, a new $650-million campus, bold organizational ideas, a visionary president, a supportive chancellor and governor, the number of new faculty and administrators to be recruited, the romance of taking a mediocre upstate college and creating—well—the Berkeley of the East. Would I consider taking part in the effort? I was smitten by the verve, the *chutzpa*—and by the thought of having a hand in the transformation. SUNY at Buffalo had been a relatively unnoticed local college founded by the thirteenth U.S. president, Millard Fillmore, "His Accidency." It had gained an uneven distinction between 1930 and 1962, the year it became part of the University of New York [Bennis, 1973, pp. 112–113].

At the time, New York's public system of higher education was coming under heavy criticism, and Governor Nelson Rockefeller wanted New York's state university to be as good as anyone's, including that of archrival California. New York had therefore lured Meyerson from Berkeley to help turn the dream into a reality (Bennis, 1973). Meyerson arrived with a monumental plan to transform Buffalo. The plan included (1) restructuring all the departments into seven new faculties; (2) building thirty small colleges on a new campus to provide a more intimate experience for students; and (3) establishing action-research centers, as well as councils on international studies, urban studies, and higher education studies. Within two months, the faculty senate approved the plan.

Bennis was attracted by Meyerson's concept. He liked the emphasis on decentralization and flexibility and the commitment to raising the self-esteem of the campus and the community. Meyerson also assured him that all the necessary resources would be forthcoming. Bennis accepted the offer to become the university's provost. "I was sold on the man and his conceptual vision. The timing seemed perfect, the new organizational design would go into effect on the same day my term of office was to begin. I arrived at Buffalo in the fall of 1967, and during 1967–68 I recruited nine new chairmen and two deans for the faculty and changed about 90 percent of the leadership structure in the social sciences area. The faculty gained forty-five new full-time teachers. I spent almost three-fourths of my first year in recruiting" (Bennis, 1973, pp. 119–120).

"Buffalo raided Harvard, Yale, and Princeton. Each new appointment increased enthusiasm, generated new ideas, and escalated the Meyerson optimism. The tiny, crowded campus barely contained the excitement. Intellectual communities formed and flourished" (p. 125).

For a while, the miracle seemed on track and moving ahead at full steam. The new faculty were eager and highly motivated, and the academic quality of the students improved markedly: "For one year, Buffalo was an academic Camelot. The provosts met around the president's conference table to work miracles." But Bennis also began to experience some doubts: "Occasionally I got signals that not everyone on campus took us quite as seriously as we took ourselves. One morning I found a Batman cape on my coatrack. The anonymous critic had a point: the atmosphere was a bit heavy with omnipotent fantasy" (Bennis, 1973, p. 126). The signals of trouble in paradise began to increase. There were rumors that course cards for College A, a unit dedicated to self-study and self-evaluation, were being sold and bartered and that students who did little work were rewarding themselves with *A's*. "Why do you think they call it College A?" one student asked.

> There were other rumblings in paradise. The centers were not doing well. We learned that it is easier to break down barriers than to build bridges. For example, the Center for Higher Education did not generate new programs or attract faculty and students as planned. The Center for International Studies began to publish a newsletter—the only substantial sign of its new status. The Center for Urban Studies undertook a series of much-needed but thoroughly conventional programs in Buffalo's inner city.
>
> In one form or another all the faculties had problems. Many departments raised questions about the new faculty structure. I felt that the many individual accomplishments, the promising new programs, [and] the appointment of a particularly good teacher or administrator did not add up to a significantly changed university. We were not consolidating our gains, and I feared that they might somehow slip away. These feelings were eventually confirmed. Camelot lasted barely a thousand days [pp. 127–128].

Bennis tells a familiar story of hopeful beginnings, a turbulent middle, and a depressing ending. In the Buffalo case, the effort was triggered by shifts in the larger environment. Environmental forces led to the creation of a new vision for SUNY at Buffalo. Meyerson and his colleagues concentrated their efforts on recruiting and restructuring but seemed to underestimate the power of the political and cultural dynamics that were inevitably triggered. The Buffalo experience illustrates a seemingly ironclad law, that is, a change conceived from one or two perspectives will soon generate other, unintended changes. Change agents who look through only one or two lenses misread or miss entirely the unanticipated consequences of their actions. They continue down the same path without noticing the signs warning them that they are no longer headed where they want to go.

### Accelerating External Pressure

*The Turbulent World of Modern Organizations.* If the changes now rocking our environment were temporary, the slow, uncertain pace at which organizations are being revamped would matter less. But the reverse is true. Powerful forces in the environment are pressing on public and private organizations throughout the world. Rather than abating, the pressure on organizations to alter existing policies, patterns, and practices are likely to increase. Table 8 provides examples of several major external forces that are seriously threatening the *status quo*.

*Globalization.* Internationalization and globalization are ungainly terms for a set of powerful forces now affecting both corporations and governments around the world. Market pressures create both opportunities and threats. Corporations see the possibility of new markets or fear that they will lag competitively if they fail to internationalize. But reaching out to new international markets immediately creates structural issues. Should a company organize by country, by product line, or by both? How should it allocate decision making between headquarters and regions? How can it ensure effective communications among units that are separated by thousands of miles and multiple time zones? Doing business globally means hiring people from different nations and cultures. These people bring different attitudes toward work (and toward life) and present new challenges for training and personnel departments. Politically, globalization creates new possibilities for conflict. How much authority will be centralized at the parent headquarters, and how much will be allocated to regional offices? Will the senior management be largely national or multinational? At the branch offices of an international firm headquartered in Japan, will Japanese managers still run things, or will power shift to local managers? Symbolically, there is the problem of adjusting to a variety of languages and cultures, allowing for enough variety to respond

**Table 8. Environmental Pressures for Change.**

| Force | Problems Within Each Frame | | | |
|---|---|---|---|---|
| | Structural | Human Resource | Political | Symbolic |
| Globalization | Size, complexity, communications problems | Wider differences in attitudes, needs, skills | Conflict between different regions and between central office and regions | How to build cohesiveness and common purpose in the face of cultural differences |
| Information technology | Decentralization, downsizing | Develop new skills | Power shifts from central functions to operating units | Meaning of work in high-technology environments |
| Deregulation | Structural shifts to respond to environmental change | Change in needed attitudes and skills | Internal and external power shifts (for example, consumer more important, government less important) | Redefinition of culture and mission |
| Demographic changes | Units to respond to changing populations (training, affirmative action) | Changing work force, more varied needs, new training requirements | Conflict between newcomers and old-timers | Old-timers feel sense of loss, newcomers feel alienation |

to local conditions while at the same time building a sense of "one company" with a shared mission and set of values.

*Information Technology.* The explosion in information technology is a major contribution to the push for globalization. Technologies such as electronic mail and the fax machine make it much simpler to do business anywhere in the world. New technologies are also a force for change in their own right. They create pressures to decentralize, which has both structural and political implications. Gorbachev's *perestroika* is, in part, a response to the rapid advent of new technologies such as microcomputers. As noted in an earlier chapter, the mainframe computer of the 1960s was compatible with Soviet tendencies toward central planning. But that same centralized planning style became a hindrance in the fast-paced, high-technology world of the 1980s. Russian society needed to find ways to move decision making downward and to make room for entrepreneurship. This inevitably involved a political shift and was strongly resisted by party officials and central bureaucrats whose power was threatened. Restructuring also had powerful implications for crucial skills: central planners needed to become more collaborative and less authoritarian. Thousands of lower-level managers had to learn how to function in a world that presented both more opportunities and higher risks. Finally, the changes raised fundamental symbolic questions about communist ideology. The new techniques and management philosophies sounded suspiciously like capitalism and had to be defended under labels such as "socialist realism."

*Deregulation.* In the 1980s, deregulation and privatization became popular trends in many nations. A salient example was the move to deregulate airlines in the United States. In theory, deregulation increases both flexibility and competition. It also increases new investment opportunities. Structurally, this requires much stronger and more sophisticated marketing units. These, in turn, imply a need for new skills in marketing and customer relations. One highly visible example is the growth of frequent-flyer programs, which require both new units and new employees. Politically, deregulation shifts power—marketing and finance become much more powerful, operations and human resource management become less so. In the regulated era, the airlines were almost guaranteed a profit, as long as they got airplanes in the air. As a result, the threat of a strike usually brought quick concessions from airline management. They knew they could recoup their costs, and there was little risk that a lower-cost competitor would emerge. In the deregulated environment, however, the airlines had to ask their pilots and flight attendants for "give-backs." The shift from a service to a marketing emphasis also creates issues around culture and mission. Airline managers, for example, often must struggle to find ways to convince employees to give up old practices and values and adapt to the new realities.

*Demographic Shifts.* Population changes affect organizations around the world. In the Soviet Union, ethnic Russians are apprehensive because other groups are growing at a more rapid rate than they are. Jews in Israel and whites in the United States face a similar reality. Japan has attracted increasing numbers of non-Japanese immigrants, who come to take jobs that most Japanese no longer want. But the new populations raise difficult questions for a nation that is proud of its cohesive culture.

Such shifts have implications for both government and industry. Governments need to create new units to deal with new issues: immigration, economic integration, education, and social services, to name a few. Profound human resource issues arise in introducing people with different cultures and different orientations to education and work. Such shifts inevitably produce conflicts. In a number of communities in the United States in the 1980s, English speakers responded to the rapid increase in the Hispanic population by pushing for laws that would make English the official language. In all these examples, the trend is toward a more diverse and multicultural population. Such changes create both a sense of loss for members of the previously dominant groups and feelings of alienation or oppression among the emerging groups. The clash of cultures often weakens the old cultural glue and creates profound challenges for symbolic leadership: how to find coherence, shared values, and a common mission in the midst of pluralism.

The interconnections among the frames illustrated in Table 8 are always present in a significant change process. In his account of one situation at Buffalo, Bennis was able to identify many of those issues with great clarity and eloquence. The more difficult challenge for managers and leaders is to identify them in advance. When we plan change, we need to learn from the experience of those who have gone before us. To do this, we must be willing to reexamine our current assumptions about change. In this and the following chapter, we show that each of the four frames has important lessons for managing change.

### Change and the Frames

In examining scores of major organizational change efforts, we have repeatedly observed managers or leaders whose strategies are limited, and we have often come across change agents who are wedded to one or two frames. One common strategy is either to import new people or to try to change existing people. Over and over, however, the new blood is either rejected or assimilated so completely that it disappears in the stream of old roles and relationships. A second strategy is to redesign the structure of the organization, only to find that people are either unable or unwilling to carry out their new responsibilities. Roles are then informally redesigned to fit what people used to do rather than what they are now supposed to do.

Restructuring, recruiting, and retraining can be powerful levers for change. But creating new roles and developing new skills need to be done in concert. Retraining people without revising roles or revamping roles without reeducating people almost never works. If managers anticipated the skills required for new roles and vice versa, their ability to change organizations would improve significantly.

Even if managers were to take into account the connection between skills and structure, however, change would still be difficult, as the Buffalo case reminds us. Change affects more than roles and skills. It alters power relationships and undermines existing agreements and pacts. Most important, it intrudes upon deeply rooted symbolic agreements and ritual behavior. Below the surface, the social tapestry begins to unravel, threatening the organization's collective unconscious and existential character. Adding political and symbolic elements to an already complicated mix of people and structure can create a potentially explosive situation.

If we think of change as a four-dimensional process, each frame suggests a different view of the major issues. Those issues are summarized in the propositions in Exhibit 6. The human resource frame focuses on needs and skills, the structural frame on alignment and clarity, the political frame on conflict and arenas, and the symbolic frame on loss of meaning. In this chapter, we will develop the structural and human resource frames; in the next, we will move toward a more integrative approach to change by including political and symbolic views.

### Change and Training

It sounds simplistic to argue that investments in change must be matched with collateral investments in training. But many changes have faltered because managers have been unwilling to spend as much time and money on human resources as on technology. In many organizations, for example, human resource departments are simply afterthoughts that no one takes seriously.

On a microlevel, it is easy to observe the fallacies of such thinking. In one large U.S. firm, for example, top management decided to purchase state-of-the-art technology. This investment was expected to cut in half the time between a customer order and delivery of a product. Such speed would provide a decisive advantage over key competitors. The strategy was crafted during hours of careful analysis by the executives. The new technology was launched with the appropriate fanfare. The CEO assured a delighted sales force that it would now have a competitive edge. After the initial euphoria, however, the sales force realized that its old methods of filling customer orders were obsolete. Years of experience were suddenly useless. Even the oldest and most accomplished salespeople had become virtual neophytes. The management team informed the CEO that the sales force had become concerned about its ability to use the new technology. His response was: "Then get someone in human resources to throw something together. You know, what's-her-name, the person we just hired as vice-president of human resources." A year later, the new technology was perform-

Exhibit 6. Reframing Organizational Change.

---

Human Resource:
>  Change causes people to feel incompetent, needy, and powerless. Developing new skills, creating opportunities for involvement, and providing psychological support are essential.

Structural:
>  Change alters the clarity and stability of roles and relationships, creating confusion and chaos. This requires attention to realigning and renegotiating formal patterns and policies.

Political:
>  Change generates conflict and creates winners and losers. Avoiding or smoothing over those issues drives conflict underground. Managing change effectively requires the creation of arenas where issues can be negotiated.

Symbolic:
>  Change creates loss of meaning and purpose. People form attachments to symbols and symbolic activity. When the attachments are severed, they experience difficulty in letting go. Existential wounds require symbolic healing.

---

ing far short of even the most pessimistic projections. The needed training never materialized. The company's window of opportunity was lost to the competition.

As a counter example, the tax division of a major accounting firm, Arthur Andersen & Company, recently launched a major change effort. For years the division had operated successfully by following the traditional, conservative mind-set of the tax profession. Clients called with questions. The typical answer was: "Yes, you can do that" or "No, you can't." The new approach asked the tax accountants to become more proactive. Rather than simply provide an answer, they were asked to probe behind a client's question to find out why the client was raising the issue. This new approach was designed to obtain a more complex view of the problem and to link the client with more comprehensive services of Arthur Andersen & Company. It was a win-win situation: savings for the client and more business for Arthur Andersen & Company.

Unlike many organizations, Arthur Andersen & Company places a premium on training and education. Its corporate school offers a variety of state-of-the-art courses. Anticipating the importance of training in making the new approach successful, the firm appointed an educational task force. The task force developed a prototype two-day course with intensive regional follow-up and coaching from partners who had mastered the method. The group spent several months designing the course and then brought in outside experts to critique the plan. The first pilot course convened partners from Arthur Andersen & Company offices worldwide. Care was taken to include partners who were opposed to the changes as well as those who saw the competitive advantage of the new approach. The course instructors were widely respected tax partners.

Because the course provided ample opportunities for people to examine and debate one another's assumptions, as well as learn new skills, it was immensely successful. Arthur Andersen & Company invested thousands of dollars in the prototype and pilot programs and hundreds of thousands more in training its partners and associates worldwide. The company realized the importance of investing heavily in training to make sure that its people supported the change and could do what the new approach required.

From a human resource perspective, people have good reason to resist change. No one enjoys the feeling of being incompetent or powerless. Changes in practices, procedures, or routine patterns undercut people's ability to perform their work with confidence and success. If they are told to make changes that they do not understand, moreover, they may wind up feeling puzzled and powerless.

Change also makes people feel in need of support. If we return for a moment to Maslow's (1954) hierarchy, which we discussed in Chapter Six, we can easily see why. Think of a surgeon who, for years, has performed an operating room procedure successfully. But advances in the technology for this procedure replace the scalpel with a laser. A self-actualized physician may quickly regress and begin to wonder about her abilities. Not feeling secure with the new procedure the physician starts to think about the income she may lose and to worry about her mortgage and her ability to provide for her family. Deep down, she comes to doubt her ability to go on with her life. She is at a point where she needs significant psychological support. A safety net could be created by setting up a program for physicians in similar circumstances. Colleagues can provide support and reassurance to each other as they share feelings and discuss ways to cope with a challenging transition. The following case shows a similar transition challenge.

Rosemary Devens decided early in her adolescence that she wanted to be a pastor, but her Protestant denomination had been reluctant to accept the ordination of women. Initially, she received little encouragement from family or friends. She persisted. By the time she completed college and divinity school, the denomination had shifted its stance and was encouraging women to become pastors. After graduate school, Rosemary spent a year as an intern in a large church. The minister of the church, Peter Escher, was a supportive mentor, and Rosemary's internship was a challenging but exhilarating experience.

Devens was puzzled, though, that some of her efforts to provide leadership to church activities did not work as well as she hoped. Escher had assigned her to work with a committee to examine the church's religious education program, and Rosemary took on the task with zest. Initially, the committee members seemed as enthusiastic as she was, but gradually attendance and motivation seemed to slump. She asked Escher for his advice, and he suggested that perhaps she should "just give it time."

During the internship she participated in a series of workshops sponsored by the denomination for interns and their supervisors. The workshop faculty included both experienced ministers and behavioral science consultants. The workshops were eye-openers for Rosemary, because she heard things about her interpersonal style that no one had ever told her. She was particularly stunned when one fellow intern told her, "If you're the same way in a church that you are in this group, I wouldn't want to work for you. You're too demanding, and too insistent that things go your way."

She talked to Peter, and he confirmed that church

members sometimes had the same perceptions of Rosemary: they admired her energy and commitment, but sometimes found her too impatient and insistent that her own views were right. "I'm confident that you're going to be a very successful minister," Peter said, "but when you go into your own church, there's the risk that people might think that you want to take over their church." Rosemary began to reflect on why she was impatient. Partly, she concluded, it was her commitment to her work, but part of it was her anxiety about whether she really had what it takes to be a good minister. "I think I've been assuming that people won't respect me unless I prove that I always have the right answer," she said to Escher.

Back at the church, Rosemary met with the members of the religious education committee. She told them about the feedback that she had received, and asked how it fit with their views. One member responded, "I think you're being too hard on yourself. I really enjoy working with you." But another said, "I enjoy working with you too, but I'm glad you brought this up. I sometimes feel that you want to do everything yourself, and you don't really need us to help you." The conversation continued for more than an hour. For Rosemary, it was one of the most difficult, but most valuable moments in her ministry.

A year later, when Rosemary became the minister of a small, suburban church, she remembered that lesson well. On a number of occasions, she told parishioners that she cared so much about the work of the church, that she might sometimes seem too impatient and demanding. "If you see me doing that, tell me," she said. Her ministry at that church was an enormous success.

As the case demonstrates, the combination of training, mentoring, open communications, and outside consultation helped Rosemary and her parishioners address critical problems. Change creates feelings of incompetence and insecurity. Training, psychological support, and participation are ways to increase the probability that needed improvements will succeed. Unless people have the skills and confidence to do what change requires, they will resist the change or even sabotage it, while awaiting the return of the good old days.

### Change and Realignment

Individual skills and confidence are not the only important issues in organizational change. Structural problems regularly block efforts to bring about change through training and recruitment. One school system, for example, created a policy requiring its principals to assume a more active role in supervising instruction. The principals were trained in classroom observation methods, as well as in procedures for conducting follow-up conferences with teachers. But morale problems and complaints about the principals soon began to surface. No one had thought to consider how changes in the principals' roles might affect the roles of teachers. Nor had anyone thought to question existing agreements about authority. Was it legitimate for principals to spend so much time in classrooms or to make wide-ranging suggestions about ways to improve teaching? Most important, no one had anticipated who would handle the administrative duties for which the principals no longer had time. As a result, supplies were often late, parents came to feel neglected, and discipline began to deteriorate. By the middle of the year, there was a noticeable change in the behavior of the principals. Most had reverted to their prior, laissez-faire approach to supervision.

The formal structure of an organization provides clarity, predictability, and security. Formal roles prescribe duties and outline how work is to be performed. Policies and standard operating procedures synchronize various efforts into coordinated actions. The formal distribution of authority lets everyone know who is in charge, when, and over what. But change undermines these structural arrangements, creating ambiguity, confusion, and distrust. People no longer know what they are expected to do or what they can expect from others. Everyone thinks someone else is in charge when, in fact, no one really is.

Because of changes in its external environment, a hospital was experiencing high levels of employee turnover and absenteeism, difficulty in recruiting nurses, and poor communication and low morale among staff members. There were also rumors that a union might be organized. The hospital administrator called in an outside consultant, and his report eventually confirmed that the hospital had several structural problems:

> One set of problems was related to top management and the functioning of the executive committee. Members of the executive committee seemed to be confused about their roles and the degree of decision-making authority they had. Many shared the perception that all of the important decisions were made (prior to meetings) by Rettew [the hospital administrator]. Many also perceived that major decisions were made behind closed doors, and that Rettew often made "side deals" with different individuals, promising them special favors or rewards in return for support at the committee meetings. People at this level felt manipulated, confused, and dissatisfied.
>
> Major problems also existed in the nursing service. The director of nursing seemed to be patterning her managerial style after that of Rettew. . . . Nursing supervisors and head nurses felt that they had no authority, while staff nurses complained about a lack of direction and openness by the nursing administration. The structure of the organization was unclear. Nurses were unaware of what their jobs were, whom they should report to, and how decisions were made [McLennan, 1989, p. 231].

Problems such as these typically accompany change in hospitals and other organizations. People no longer know what their duties are, how to relate to others, or who has the authority to make decisions. The structural benefits of clarity, predictability, and rationality are replaced with confusion, loss of control, and the belief that politics rather than policies are now governing everyday behavior. To counter such problems, those implementing changes must anticipate the structural issues that may arise and work to realign roles and relationships. In some situations, this can be done informally. In others, new structural arrangements need to be negotiated in a more formal way.

Deal and Ross (1977) describe how the formal structure of a small school district was renegotiated following a series of changes that had left the district administrator facing many of the same problems as those of the aforementioned hospital. The district had been troubled persistently with conflicts, misunderstandings, and mistrust among various individuals and groups. As the superintendent observed, "The climate was uptight, people were stepping on each others' toes, and there was a pervasive lack of trust among teachers, principals, and the district office staff." Earlier, a consultant with a human resource orientation had tried to frame the problem in interpersonal terms. But as people began to confront one another, the difficulties seemed to intensify. According to the superintendent, "The consultant produced more problems, rather than helping to solve anything." The creation of a new role—resource teacher—in each school further intensified the difficulties that everyone was experiencing. The final straw was a particularly acrimonious meeting of the entire administrative group. At 5:00 P.M., only one item on a lengthy agenda had been covered. The group disbanded, vowing to meet again—only when absolutely necessary. Everyone had decided it would be simpler to just go it alone. In effect, each person or subgroup decided to operate independently of others.

The superintendent then decided to retain a new consultant, this time someone with a strong structural orientation. This consultant used an exhaustive process to identify the kinds of perceptions that people had of their work roles and relationships. He focused on task-specific role differentiation and auxiliary relationships. The administrative groups first identified their major tasks, which included goal setting, conducting evaluations, budgeting, testing, taking attendance, working with community groups, and designing the curriculum. These tasks formed the rows of a matrix, while the columns were made up of the various roles or role groups of the district—board, superintendent, principals, resource teachers, and so on. Each person was then asked to fill in the matrix using a language similar to RACI (discussed earlier) designed to highlight formal responsibilities and relationships:

1.  General responsibility, or overseer
2.  Operating responsibility, or task manager
3.  Specific responsibility, or subtask specialist
4.  Must be consulted
5.  May be consulted

6.  Must be notified
7.  Must approve

As the groups began to pool their individual perceptions, several issues became apparent. First, it was not clear where decisions should be made or even where they were being made. Often, the district office assumed that the principals were making decisions that the principals assumed were being made at the district office. Occasionally, both groups claimed decision-making rights in the same area. Second, roles were confused and overlapping. In important instructional areas no one claimed authority or responsibility. In other areas, everyone saw himself or herself as a prime actor, thus creating duplication and conflict. For the most part, both individuals and groups were uncertain what they were supposed to be doing or how their efforts were related to those of others. The language of the process provided a specific way to pinpoint the structural difficulties and to renegotiate formal work arrangements. Once each group had worked out its roles, meetings were held between the different groups. Eventually, a series of meetings with all the administrators helped everyone involved reach consensus on the district's new formal roles and relationships. Many of the initial problems were resolved, and the group continued to meet periodically to review and revise its structural configuration.

### Summary

Any major organizational change generates four kinds of issues. First, it will have an effect on individuals' needs to feel effective, valued, and in control. Second, it will require new kinds of structural alignment with the organization. Third, the change will cause conflict among those who will benefit and those who will not benefit from it. And, finally, the change will result in loss of meaning for some members of the organization. The problem of individual needs, skills, and attitudes requires careful attention to issues of training, support, and involvement. The issue of structural alignment requires attention to reshaping the organizational structure. We will consider the other two issues in the following chapter.

# 19

# *Reframing Change: Conflict and Loss*

In the previous chapter, we saw a hospital that faced a series of structural problems that were never resolved, even with the assistance of outside consultants. Meetings between the consulting team and executive committee generated disagreement and conflict. The director of nursing walked into a meeting armed with a book on hospital administration. She attacked the consulting team and claimed that their approach was irrelevant to hospitals.

When the consultants produced their final report, the executive committee balked at letting the staff see it. They feared that the report was a bombshell that other groups would use as a weapon. Several meetings were held to discuss the consultant's findings, but attendance was limited and discussion was constrained by a rumor that anyone who spoke up would "pay for it later." The study was tabled, and many of the hospital's top nurses left for jobs elsewhere. Needed structural realignments were undermined by hospital politics.

The scenario at that hospital is not unusual. Changing an organization invariably creates conflict among existing groups. Change creates winners and losers. Some individuals and groups support the changes, others are dead set against them. Usually, conflicts are smoothed over and left to smoulder beneath the surface.

Occasionally, however, the issues burst into the open as a result of specific circumstances and events.

A case in point comes from an effort funded by the U.S. government to improve rural schools in America. The Experimental Schools Project provided money for making comprehensive changes in the schools. It also carefully documented the experience of each participating district over a five-year period. The first year—the planning period—was free of conflict. But as the plans were put into action, hidden issues boiled to the surface. This example from a school district in the Northwest illustrates a common pattern.

> In the high school, a teacher evaluator explained the evaluation process while emphasizing the elaborate precautions to insure the raters would be unable to connect specific evaluations with specific teachers. He also passed out copies of the checklist used to evaluate the [evaluation forms]. Because of the tension the subject aroused, he joked that teachers could use the list to "grade" their own [forms]. He got a few laughs; he got more laughs when he encouraged teachers to read the evaluation plan by suggesting, "If you have fifteen minutes to spare and are really bored, you should read this section." When another teacher pointed out that her anonymity could not be maintained because she was the only teacher in her subject, the whole room broke into laughter, followed by nervous and derisive questions and more laughter.
>
> When the superintendent got up to speak, shortly afterwards, he was furious. He cautioned teachers for making light of the teacher evaluators who, he said, were trying to protect the staff. Several times he repeated that because teachers did not support the [Experimental School Project] they did not care for students. "Your attitude," he concluded, "is damn the children and full speed ahead!" He then rushed out of the room.
>
> The superintendent's speech put the high school in turmoil. The woman who questioned the confidentiality of the procedure was in tears. Most teachers were incensed at the superintendent's outburst, and a couple said they came close to quitting. As word of the event spread through the system, it caused reverberations in other buildings as well [Firestone, 1977, pp. 174–175].

After this heated exchange, the conflict between the administration and teachers intensified. The school board became involved and, as a result of rumors that he was to be fired, the school superintendent found that his authority has been considerably reduced.

Such a sequence is predictable. As changes begin to emerge, various camps form. For the most part, conflicts are avoided or smoothed over until they erupt in divisive battles. Coercive power is used to determine who will win. Most often, proponents of the *status quo* win and the change agents lose.

From a political perspective, conflict is a natural part of life in organizations. Like other political issues, conflict is best dealt with through processes of negotiation and bargaining in which settlements and agreements can be worked out. If it is ignored until it becomes explosive, the disputes are settled in street fights much like the one that took place in the school district. Street fights have no rules and anything goes. People get hurt and scars are created that can last for years.

The political alternative to the street fight is the *arena*. Arenas provide rules, referees, and spectators, and they create opportunities to turn divisive issues into shared agreements. Through bargaining, the participants can reach a compromise between the *status quo* and the innovative ideals. Both winners and losers are rewarded. This process of adapting new ideas to existing structures is an essential ingredient in successful change.

Mason and Mitroff (1981) and Mitroff (1983) describe a process to help managers make policy decisions under conditions of uncertainty and conflict. It may be, for example, that different factions have formed, each with its own idea of what is happening and what should be done. The process involves articulating and discussing the different assumptions of the various groups.

Mitroff gives the example of a drug company facing competitive pressure from generic substitutes for its branded, prescription drug. Management had split into three different factions: one group wanted to raise the price of the drug, one wanted to lower it, and one wanted to keep it the same while cutting internal costs (Mitroff, 1983). Each group collected information, constructed models, and developed reports showing that its solution was the correct one. The process became a frustrating spiral. Mitroff intervened to get each group to indicate who were the major stakeholders and what assumptions each group made about those stakeholders. It turned out that everyone agreed that the most critical stakeholders were physicians, who prescribed the drug. Each group made different assumptions about how physicians would respond to a price change. But no one really knew. The three groups finally agreed to implement a price increase in selected markets to test their assumptions about physician responses.

The intervention worked by altering the arena and creating a more productive set of rules. Similarly, the school districts that created arenas for the resolution of conflict were the most successful in bringing about comprehensive change. In the school district cited above, the teachers reacted to administrative coercion with their own power strategy: "Community members initiated a group called 'Concerned Citizens for Education' in response to a phone call from one teacher who noted that 'parents should be worried about what the [administrators] are doing to their children.' The superintendent became increasingly occupied with responding to demands and concerns of the community group. Over time, the group joined in a coalition with teachers to defeat several of the superintendent's supporters on the school board and to elect members who were more supportive of their interests. The turnover in board membership reduced the administrators' power and authority, making it necessary to rely more and more on bargaining and negotiation strategies to promote the intended change" (Deal and Nutt, 1980, p. 29).

Changing an organization creates division and conflict among competing interest groups. Successful change requires the ability to frame issues, build coalitions, and establish arenas in which issues can be negotiated into workable pacts. As one insightful corporate executive remarked: "We need to confront (not duck) and face up to disagreements and differences of opinions and conflicting objectives. . . . All of us must make sure—day in and day out—that conflicts are aired and resolved before they lead to internecine war."

## Change and Loss

Competition and conflict are not new issues at PepsiCo. In the early 1980s, the Cola wars—a battle between Coke and Pepsi—had reached a fever pitch. The Pepsi Challenge—a head-to-head taste test—was making an inroad on Coca-Cola's market share. In blind tests, even avowed Coke drinkers preferred Pepsi's taste. In a Coke counter challenge, held at Coke's corporate headquarters in Atlanta, Pepsi again won by a slight margin. Later, Pepsi stunned the industry by signing Michael Jackson to a $5 million celebrity advertising campaign. Coke's executives were getting nervous. Coca-Cola struck back with one of the most important announcements in the company's ninety-nine-year history. Old Coke was to be replaced with new Coke.

> Shortly before 11:00 A.M. (on Tuesday, April 23, 1985), the doors of the Vivian Beaumont Theater at Lincoln Center opened to two hundred newspaper, magazine, and TV reporters. The stage was aglow with red. Three huge screens, each solid red and inscribed with the company logo, rose behind the podium and a table draped in red. The lights were low; the music began. "We are. We will always be. Coca-Cola. All-American history." As the patriotic song filled the theater, slides of Americana flashed on the center screen—families and kids, Eisenhower and JFK, the Grand Canyon and wheat fields, the Beatles and Bruce Springsteen, cowboys, athletes, the Statue of Liberty—and interspersed throughout, old commercials for Coke. Robert Goizueta [CEO of Coca-Cola] came to the podium. He first congratulated the reporters for their ingenuity in already having reported what he was about to say. And then he boasted, "The best has been made even better." Sidestepping the years of laboratory research that had gone into the program, Goizueta claimed that in the process of concocting Diet Coke, the company flavor chemists had "discovered" a new formula. And research had shown that consumers preferred this new one to old Coke. Management could then do one of two things: nothing, or "buy the world a new Coke." Goizueta announced that the taste-test results made management's decisions "one of the easiest ever made" [Oliver, 1986, p. 132].

The rest is history. Coke drinkers rejected the new product. Some felt betrayed, and many were outraged: "Duane Larson took down his collection of Coke bottles and outside of his restaurant

hung a sign, 'They don't make Coke anymore.' . . . Dennis Over-
street of Beverly Hills hoarded 500 cases of old Coke and advertised
them for $30 a case. He is almost sold out. . . . San Francisco *Ex-
aminer* columnist Bill Mandel called it 'Coke for wimps.' . . . Finally, Guy Mullins exclaimed, 'When they took old Coke off the
market, they violated my freedom of choice—baseball, hamburgers,
Coke—they're all the fabric of America'" (Morganthau, 1985,
pp. 32-33).

Even bottlers and other employees of Coca-Cola were aghast:
"By June the anger and resentment of the public was disrupting the
personal lives of Coke employees, from the top executives to the
company secretaries. Friends and acquaintances were quick to attack, and once proud employees now shrank from displaying to the
world any association with the Coca-Cola company" (Oliver, 1986,
pp. 166-167).

Coca-Cola rebounded with Classic Coke, but the damage was
already done. What led Coke's executives into such a quagmire?
Several factors were at work. Pepsi was gaining market share. As the
newly appointed CEO of Coca-Cola, Goizueta was determined to
modernize the company. A previous innovation, Diet Coke, had
been a huge success. Most important, Coca-Cola's founder, Robert
Woodruff, had just passed away. On his deathbed, he reportedly
gave Goizueta his blessing for the new recipe.

In their zeal to compete with Pepsi, Coke's executives had
overlooked a central tenet of the symbolic frame. The meaning of
an object or event can be far more powerful than the reality. To
many people, old Coke was a piece of Americana. It was linked to
cherished memories.

The executives of Coca-Cola underestimated the symbolic
meaning of their own core product. Symbols create meaning. When
a symbol is destroyed or vanishes, people experience emotions that
are almost identical to those felt at the passing of a spouse, child,
old friend, or pet. Unknowingly, when the executives of Coke introduced new Coke, they announced the death of an important
American symbol.

When a relative or close friend dies, we feel a deep sense of
loss. Unconsciously, we have the same feelings when a computer
replaces old procedures, a logo is changed after a merger, or a new

leader replaces another. Because the events take place in an organization rather than a family, the feelings of loss are often denied or attributed to other causes. But nearly any significant change in an organization triggers two conflicting responses. The first is to keep things as they were, to replay the past. The second is to ignore the loss and rush pell-mell into the future. Individuals or groups in organizations can get stuck in either response or bog down in vacillating between the two. Nurses in one hospital's intensive care unit were caught in the loss cycle for ten years following their move from an old ward. An executive of AT&T, four years after divestiture, remarked: "Some mornings I feel like I can set the world on fire. Other mornings I can hardly get out of bed to face another day." The experience of loss is an unavoidable by-product of change. Many executives and employees in today's businesses, hospitals, schools, universities, public agencies, and military organizations are caught in an endless cycle of unresolved grief. The bad news is that unless their wounds heal, morale and productivity will continue to suffer. The good news is that something can be done to help people let go of old ways and accept new programs, technologies, leaders, or symbols.

In our personal lives, the pathway from loss to healing is often prescribed. Every culture outlines a sequence for transition rituals following a significant loss. This is almost always a collective experience in which pain is expressed, felt, and juxtaposed against humor and hope. In many societies, the sequence of ritual steps involves a wake, a funeral, a period of mourning, and a commemoration.

### Rites of Mourning

From a symbolic perspective, transition rituals must accompany significant organizational change. In the military, for example, the change of command ceremony is formally scripted. A wake is held for the outgoing commander, and the torch is passed publicly to the new commander in full ceremony. After a period of time the old commander's face or name is displayed in a picture or plaque on the wall of the unit.

The following cases provide examples of how rites of mourn-

ing can lead to healing and help people let go of the past so that
they can invest in the future.

> Judge Green's decision to break up AT&T brought an
> end to a century-old tradition of high-quality, universal
> telephone service. The divestiture was unparalleled in
> its magnitude and left in its wake divorces, suicide, al-
> cohol abuse, and thousands of wounded people whose
> lives had been tied for generations to "Ma Bell." A
> Long Lines Division of the company produced a short
> film clip entitled "Farewell Ma Bell." The film was in-
> troduced as part of a large occasion to mark the depar-
> ture of several employees. The film featured themes of
> farewell from a number of popular songs: "I'll Be See-
> ing You in All the Old Familiar Places," "Are You
> Lonesome Tonight?" "Bye-Bye, Baby," "Doesn't Any-
> body Ever Stay in One Place Anymore?" "A Love Affair
> Is a Wondrous Thing," "Good Night, Good Night,"
> and "One of These Days You'll Miss Me, Honey." The
> tape circulated informally in the company, because it
> helped people to recognize and share their grief. It typi-
> cally brought tears to the eyes of everyone in the group.
> The integration of humor and nostalgia, love and sad-
> ness, helped people begin to heal.

A group of physicians in a large medical center changed
its privately held practice to a publicly held corporation. For nearly a year after the change, nurses and staff
noted a significant change in the physicians. Their morale deteriorated, their behavior became more erratic,
and they seemed to be impossible to work with. At a
management retreat, a senior orthopedic surgeon responded to the wholesale criticism of physicians.
Through a voice choked with tears, he said, "None of
you have any idea of what we are going through." His
remarks brought the real issue to the attention of everyone—especially the physicians themselves.
    A retreat was arranged for all two hundred physi-

cians. The key event of the two days was a dinner featuring skits, songs, and poetry. Many of the physicians who were most upset about the change were featured in the program. The interplay of sadness and satire recognized the transition, and let the physicians express their loss and move on as employees, rather than owners, of their practice.

In 1989, Fulton County School system in Atlanta, Georgia, closed twenty-three schools. They accomplished this highly difficult task with little of the turmoil that typically overwhelms efforts to terminate programs, divisions, or units. They succeeded, in part, because they encouraged each school to provide opportunities for teachers, students, administrators, parents, and others to share their grief, let go, and move on. One elementary school, for example, invited the entire community, as well as graduates and retirees, to attend the closing ceremony. The principal gave a speech, students read poems, and teachers, alumni, and others shared memories from the school's rich history. As the ceremony drew to a close, the custodial staff wrapped the entire school with a large red ribbon. The next day a crew demolished the brick building. Later, each person who attended the closing event received a brick tied with a red ribbon. With the brick came a picture of the school, adorned with the ribbon, and a videotape, taken from a helicopter, that showed the custodians wrapping the school for its last picture.

When the chief financial officer of a large U.S. corporation retired, he stipulated that there would be no fanfare surrounding his departure. On his last day, he simply cleaned out his desk and left. Sometime later, however, his wife called the president of the company to report that her husband was having a difficult time. In turn, the president informed her that the morale and productivity of the administrative and finance group had also

deteriorated. Together, they arranged for a belated
going-away party. The CFO had always eaten lunch in
the dining room at corporate headquarters. He perennially complained about the lack of space for private
luncheons. The president decided to build a small private dining room and name it in the CFO's honor.
When the room was completed, the president set up a
party. The CFO's wife arranged for him to return to the
company dining room for a bogus luncheon appointment. Instead, he found himself at a surprise party, during which the new room was dedicated. The party
completed a process that had been left unfinished when
he left the company. Productivity increased in the financial division, and the CFO found a new zest in retirement. Once a month, he returned to the dining room
for lunch with his former colleagues.

Each of these examples illustrates the importance of transition rituals in change processes, whether the changes involve people, programs, units, or entire companies. Symbolic events initiate
a sequence of ritualistic steps that allow people to let go of the past,
deal with the present, and move into a meaningful future. The form
of these transition rites will vary from place to place. But unless
people recognize their loss, they will vacillate between hanging on
to the past and plunging into a meaningless future. The loss of
attachment even to negative symbols or harmful symbolic activities
needs to be marked by some form of expressive event.

Owen (1987) vividly documents the symbolic issues involved
in change in his description of events at Delta Corporation. It is a
familiar scenario. An entrepreneur named Harry invented a product
that created a high enough demand to support a company of 3,500
people. Although the initial public stock offering was successful,
the company was soon to experience soaring costs, flattened sales,
and a decrease in creativity and new products. Faced with stockholder dissatisfaction and charges of mismanagement, Harry passed
the torch to a new leader.

Harry's replacement was very clear about her vision for
Delta. She wanted "engineers who could fly." But her vision was

juxtaposed against a history of "going downhill." And, elsewhere in the company, various groups were governed by an even more complicated array of stories.

Each of these stories represented a different theme in Delta Corporation. The stories within the finance division exemplified the new breed of executives brought in after Harry's departure. "The Killing of '82" told about a financial vice-president who sold so many of the tax losses incurred under Harry's management that he managed to make a profit for the company. The "Cash Flow Kid" was a new arrival in middle management whose expertise in managing cash flow garnered a solid return on short-term deposits. "In Praise of Wilbur," a story at the operating level of the finance group, was actually about an in-house computer.

As one might expect, the stories in the research and development division were notably different. At the executive level, Old Harry stories extolled the creative accomplishments of the former CEO. Middle management stories focused on the Golden Fleece award given monthly behind the scenes to the researcher who had developed the idea with the least bottom-line potential. Two stories were commonly shared among those "on the benches." Serendipity Sam was the researcher who accumulated the most Golden Fleece awards and whose exploits continued the legend of excitement and innovation from Harry's regime. The Leper Colony was the nest of Harry's contemporaries who had chosen, or been pushed into, a state of semiretirement.

The production side of Delta also had its stories. "Making the Quota" exemplified an executive value that put numbers over quality. "Reuben" was a tale of a politically sensitive supervisor whose ability to cover himself and impress his superiors led to a series of promotions. On the shop floor, most of the stories focused on The Zebra, a local bar where people gathered after hours. Those who met there formed a tight cabal in opposition to their superiors.

Rather than having a companywide story, Delta Corporation was a collection of independent cells, each with its own story. Across the levels and divisions the stories clustered into two competing themes: the management orientation of the new arrivals and the innovative traditions of the company.

The new CEO recognized the importance of blending old

and new into a company where "engineers could fly." She summoned thirty-five people from across the company to a management retreat. Her strategy surprised everyone: "She opened with some stories of the early days, describing the intensity of Old Harry and the Garage Gang (now known as the Leper Colony). She even had one of the early models of Harry's machine out on a table. Most people had never seen one. It looked rather primitive, but during the coffee break, members of the Leper Colony surrounded the ancient artifact, and began swapping tales of the blind alleys, the late nights, and the breakthroughs. That dusty old machine became a magnet. Young shop floor folks went up and touched it, sort of snickering as they compared this prototype with the sleek creations they were manufacturing now. But even as they snickered, they stopped to listen as the Leper Colony recounted tales of accomplishment. It may have been just a 'prototype,' but that's where it all began" (Owen, 1987, p. 172).

After coffee break, the CEO divided the group into several subgroups to share their hopes for the company. When the participants returned, their chairs had been rearranged into a circle with Old Harry's prototype in the center. With everyone now facing one another, the CEO led a discussion, linking the stories from the various subgroups. Serendipity Sam's report came in an exalted torrent of technical jargon. The members of the Leper Colony quickly jumped in to add details and elaborate on the theme. Before long, they and Sam were engaged in an animated conversation:

> The noise level was fierce, but the rest of the group was being left out. Taking Sam by the hand, the CEO led him to the center of the circle right next to the old prototype. There it was, the old and the new—the past, present, and potential. She whispered in Sam's ear that he ought to take a deep breath and start over in words of one syllable. He did so, and in ways less than elegant, the concept emerged. He guessed about applications, competitors, market shares, and before the long the old VP for finance was drawn in. No longer was he thinking about selling [tax] losses, but rather thinking out loud about how he was going to develop the capital to support the new project. The group from the shop floor forgot about the Zebra and began to spin a likely tale as to how they might transform the assembly

lines in order to make Sam's new machine. Even the Golden
Fleece crowd became excited, telling each other how they always knew that Serendipity Sam could pull it off. They con-
veniently forgot that Sam had been the recipient of a record
number of their awards, to say nothing of the fact that this new
idea had emerged in spite of all their rules [Owen, 1987,
pp. 173-174].

In one intense event, part of the past was buried, yet its spirit
was resurrected and revised to fit the new set of circumstances. The
disparaging themes and stories were merged into a company where
"engineers could fly" in a profitable way.

### Integrating the Change Perspectives

Four issues are salient in collective reactions to change:

1. Change causes people to feel incompetent, needy, and powerless.
2. Change creates confusion and unpredictability throughout an
   organization.
3. Change generates conflict.
4. Change creates loss.

As managers deal with these issues they need to consider four
strategies: (1) training and support for employees, (2) realigning
formal roles and relationships, (3) establishing arenas, and (4) providing transition rituals. Unless each issue is matched with an appropriate response, the intended changes will fail—or backfire.
Failure to consider one or more of these issues is a chief cause of
our inability to change organizations.

Hank Cotton's experience at Cherry Creek High School demonstrates the importance of a multiframe change strategy (Deal and
Peterson, 1990):

When Hank Cotton arrived at Cherry Creek, he found a
situation much like many American public schools in
the 1970s. His predecessor, in the innovative 1960s, had
liberalized the school's authority structure. Requirements and rules were relaxed. Students were given an

array of educational options, and were permitted to
leave the grounds anytime they were not in class.
Teachers offered or canceled classes when they wished.
Sanctions for missing class were enforced erratically.

This policy of freedom and permissiveness had
educational benefits, but it also had costs. Courses pro-
liferated, student attendance weakened, and discipline
deteriorated. Community concerns about academic
achievement and drug use on campus found their way
to the school board. A new superintendent eventually
hired Cotton as Cherry Creek High School's new principal. Cotton's initial strategy was a blend of structure
and politics. Structurally, he installed new policies and
realigned his role by reassuming the authority his
predecessor had relinquished. A policy on absenteeism
outlined specific sanctions for missing class. Over two
hundred students were suspended shortly after the policy was put in place. A new parking policy prohibited
students from parking illegally on the lawn. One of the
first cars towed belonged to the son of a school board
member. Cotton publicly reaffirmed the importance of
rationality and consistency: "All students will be treated
equally, no matter who [their] parents are" (p. 64). A
new system for evaluating teachers was developed to
help standardize instructional approaches while providing adequate freedom for teachers. To counter the proliferation of courses, Cotton asked the social sciences
department to redesign the curriculum and eliminate
many of the school's seventy electives. He argued that
the principal had the right to initiate curricular change,
and the school board supported him. He further extended his authority by appointing department chairs,
rather than accepting the choice of each respective
faculty.

Obviously, Cotton's first year at Cherry Creek
was not a smooth one. The social sciences department
filed a grievance. Over half the faculty signed a petition
protesting the changes. As Cotton noted, "If the

teachers had been able to vote on whether to retain me that first year, I would have been out" (p. 65). His actions divided the community. While many parents and residents were supportive of the improvements in order and discipline, the parents of the suspended students and the board member whose son's car was towed were just as vocal in their opposition. Though Cotton had exercised his authority, his power base was shaky at best.

But Cotton seemed to understand that authority is only one form of power. He worked hard to bolster his allies and to co-opt or neutralize his opponents. Cultivating his supporters was not so hard. Cotton began with a cadre of teachers and parents who saw the need for more order and direction. Cherry Creek is centered in an upper-middle-class community where natural interest groups formed around student achievement and traditional instructional patterns. He actively courted the support of parents through personal phone calls to explain and justify new policies and procedures. He met regularly with parent groups and with the parent senate, student senate, and faculty senate.

His encouragement of parental interest brought as many as 1,000 people to PTA meetings. He eliminated many responsibilities that teachers hated, such as hall duty, cafeteria, study hall supervision, and sign-out sheets. Cotton treated every encounter as an opportunity for give-and-take. Open conflict at Cherry Creek became a natural and expected part of everyday life, over time. The opening of a new high school in the district provided a graceful way out for teachers who continued to resist the new regime. Thereafter Cotton actively recruited teachers who supported his idea of what the school might become.

Even before the acute problems were resolved, Hank Cotton focused on human resource and symbolic issues at the high school. He used both the school's regular budget and a special foundation that he created to fund conferences, special projects, and paid summer work. Through such opportunities he was able to recognize excellent teaching and help teachers develop new skills and ideas. Teachers whose classroom performance needed improvement were coached, retrained, and encouraged to attend seminars and college courses. Teachers who failed to measure up were transferred or encouraged to seek employment elsewhere.

Cotton himself attended seminars, institutes, and executive development programs to improve his leadership skills. His emphasis on learning let others know that self-improvement was an expected virtue, not a weakness. Students also were encouraged to grow socially as well as intellectually. Their social development was placed on a par with scholastic achievement. The school's campus remained open, and the authority of student government was expanded so that students could learn responsibility and earn recognition outside the classroom.

From the beginning, the culture and history of the school received Cotton's special attention. Rather than offer a new direction, he reaffirmed the school's historic commitment to achievement and academic success. He used every meeting and encounter to articulate and reinforce old values that had been eclipsed by the 1960s emphasis on innovation, equality, and autonomy. He modeled the school's academic ethics by visibly carrying and publicly reading novels, histories, and philosophical treatises. In memoranda, he quoted liberally from classic literature and history. He wrote lucidly about his ideas and visions of what Cherry Creek High could be. He told stories about innovation, hard work, and the many ways that teachers made a difference in the lives of students.

Cotton revitalized the school's rituals and ceremonies. Students were again required to wear caps and gowns at graduation. He often changed to a dark suit and tie to preside over athletic and scholastic awards events. Bumper stickers announced, "Let the tradition continue . . . as the legend lives on . . ." (p. 76). When the district developed a phrase, "Onward to Excellence," Cotton commissioned a neon poster for the high school: "Beyond Excellence to Greatness" (p. 77).

Over a five-year period, Cherry Creek High School evolved from an organization in trouble to one of the best schools in the district. Absenteeism is minimal, vandalism is nearly nonexistent, students regularly succeed in scholarship and extracurricular activities. Graduates who do honors work in college credit the school for giving them a solid preparation.

### Summary

Issues of alignment, needs, conflict, and loss invariably accompany efforts to change organizations. In the previous chapter, we discussed ways to understand and manage the issues of structural alignment and human needs. In this chapter, we turned to conflict and loss.

Change usually benefits some people more than others: it creates winners and losers, which is bound to produce conflict. Change agents often underestimate the opposition or drive conflict underground. Attention to the political dimensions of change implies recognizing competing interests and creating arenas with rules, roles, and referees to provide conflicting individuals and groups with an opportunity to air and negotiate their differences.

Change also produces loss, particularly for those who are the targets rather than the initiators of change. Old patterns, familiar routines, and taken-for-granted meanings are all disrupted by organizational change. The deeper the loss, the more important it is to create rituals of transition—opportunities to both celebrate and mourn the past and help people evolve new structures of meaning.

It is not the case that organizations never change. There is always something new underfoot or in the air. The problem is that many of the changes occur haphazardly and not by virtue of managerial decision or plan. Much of the literature on organizational change emphasizes the issues of planning, of human resistance, and using leverage from the top of the hierarchy to get those at lower levels to behave differently. Changes then fail because those at the top overemphasize rationality and underestimate the power of lower-level participants to resist.

A fully effective change process requires attention to all four issues: structure, needs, conflict, and loss. Changes in one frame inevitably reverberate through the others, and the frame that is ignored is very likely to be the one that distorts or undermines the effort.

# 20

# Reframing Leadership

Leadership is offered as a solution for most of the problems of organizations everywhere. Schools will work, we are told, if principals provide strong instructional leadership. Around the world, middle managers say that their organizations would thrive if only senior management provided strategy, vision, and "real leadership." Though the call for leadership is universal, there is much less clarity about what the term means: "For many—perhaps for most—Americans, leadership is a word that has risen above normal workaday usage as a conveyer of meaning and has become a kind of incantation. We feel that if we repeat it often enough with sufficient ardor, we shall ease our sense of having lost our way, our sense of things unaccomplished, of duties unfulfilled" (Gardner, 1986, p. 1).

## The Idea of Leadership

In almost every culture, the oldest literature includes sagas that recount the deeds of heroic leaders: "Essentially, it might be said there is but one archetypal mythic hero whose life has been replicated in many lands by many, many people. A legendary hero is usually the founder of something—the founder of a new age, the founder of a new religion, the founder of a new city, the founder of a new way of life. In order to found something new, one has to leave the old and go in quest of the seed idea, a germinal idea that will have the potentiality of bringing forth that new thing" (Campbell, 1988, p. 136).

The English word *leader* is more than a thousand years old, little changed from its Anglo-Saxon root *laedare*, which meant to lead people on a journey. An unquestioned, widely shared canon of common sense holds that leadership is a very good thing and that we need more of it—at least, more of the right kind. Yet, there is much confusion and disagreement about what leadership really means. Despite tens of thousands of pages written about it, leadership remains an elusive concept. Social science research on leadership has provided few generalizations that are reliable and even fewer that are interesting.

Why is the concept of leadership so elusive? To begin to answer that question, we might ask why leadership has always been vital in every culture and every historical period. The need for leadership derives ultimately from the uncertainties and dangers built into the human condition. Minute by minute, day by day, and year by year, we all experience the need to know what to think, feel, and do. In situations that are clear and familiar, the decisions are easy. In more confusing, uncertain, and threatening situations, however, human beings often need help. Leaders are one source of help. They help us feel less fearful and more confident. They help us find attractive and plausible versions of what to think, feel, and do. They help us to see possibilities and discover resources. Therein lie both the power and the risk of leadership. Leadership, like love, carries risks of both dependence and disappointment. We may look to leaders when we might do better to look to ourselves. We may follow false prophets. But it makes no more sense to reject leadership altogether than to shun all forms of intimacy. We need to approach both with a combination of hope and wisdom.

Sennett (1980, p. 197) writes, "Authority is not a thing; it is a search for solidity and security in the strength of others which seems to be like a thing." The same is true of leadership. It is not a thing. It exists only in relationships and only in the imagination and perception of the parties to a relationship. Inevitably, it means different things to different people, but the list of meanings is not boundless. When managers are asked the question, What is leadership? they typically provide three or four basic answers. Each of those answers is limited, but each helps us construct a more adequate conception of what leadership is.

The first and most prevalent commonsense conception is that leadership is the ability to get others to do what you want. Because it equates leadership with power, this definition covers both too much and too little. It is too broad because it covers such things as the naked exercise of force, a very different thing from leadership. It is too limited because it omits much of the art and poetry of leadership: values, visions, and leadership as relationship.

A second lay definition is that leaders motivate people to get things done. It is true that leaders influence more by persuasion and example than by force and seduction. "Getting things done" adds the important idea that leadership is to be judged by its products. But still missing is the question of purpose and value: How do we assess the results that leadership produces?

A third commonsense definition is that leaders provide a vision. This adds the elements of meaning, purpose, and mission that were missing in the previous definitions, but it suggests that the vision is the solitary creation of the leader. It also neglects to ask if anyone likes or supports the leader's vision.

A fourth lay definition, popular among participative managers and helping professionals, is that leadership is *really* facilitation. It is participative and democratic and helps constituents find their own way. The task of a leader is not to get what he or she wants but to *empower* people to do what *they* want. This has the merit of countering the idea that leaders act and followers react, that leaders are powerful and followers are dependent. At the same time, it risks turning leaders into weathervanes who simply turn whichever way the wind is blowing.

These views of leadership are only a sample of the many lay images of leadership. Exhibit 7 gives a spectrum of definitions of leadership provided by scholars and by leaders themselves. The variety in the definitions shows that the concept is diffuse and controversial. Yet the idea has survived for centuries, and almost everyone thinks that it is important. To begin to clarify the concept, we need to identify its basic elements and to distinguish leadership from the related ideas of power, authority, and management.

**Exhibit 7. Conceptions of Leadership.**

"Leadership is any attempt to influence the behavior of another individual or group" (Paul Hersey in *The Situational Leader*).

"Managers do things right. Leaders do the right thing" (Warren Bennis and Burt Nanus in *Leaders: Strategies for Taking Charge*).

"Leadership is the ability to decide what is to be done and then get others to want to do it" (Dwight D. Eisenhower).

"Leadership is the process of moving a group in some direction through mostly noncoercive means. Effective leadership is leadership that produces movement in the long-term best interests of the group" (John Kotter in *The Leadership Factor*).

"Leadership is the process of persuasion or example by which an individual (or leadership team) induces a group to pursue objectives held by the leader or shared by the leader and his or her followers" (John Gardner in *On Leadership*).

"Leadership over human beings is exercised when persons with certain motives and purposes mobilize, in competition or conflict with others, institutional, political, psychological, and other resources so as to arouse, engage, and satisfy the motives of followers" (James MacGregor Burns in *Leadership*).

"Leadership is a particular kind of ethical, social practice that emerges when persons in communities, grounded in hope, are grasped by inauthentic situations and courageously act in concert with followers to make those situations authentic" (Robert Terry in "Leadership—A Preview of a Seventh View").

Most images of leadership suggest that leaders get things done and get people to do things: leaders are powerful. Yet many examples of power fall outside our image of leadership. Armed robbers, extortionists, bullies, traffic cops, and prison guards have certain kinds of power but are rarely thought of as leaders. Implicitly, we expect a leader to influence through noncoercive means, to produce some degree of cooperative effort, and to pursue goals that transcend his or her own narrow self-interest.

Leadership is also distinct from authority, though leaders may possess authority and authorities may be leaders. The concept of authority is as controversial as that of leadership, but much social science thinking about the concept begins with the work of Max Weber. Weber (1947) linked authority to legitimacy. People voluntarily obey authority because they believe it is legitimate, and will cease to obey if they perceive that authority has lost its legitimacy. Weber distinguished three major forms of authority:

1. Traditional—we obey a particular custom or official because our ancestors did.
2. Legal-rational—we obey people who hold certain offices, such as school principals, because we believe that they have the right to make decisions, a right based on the premise that the system will work better if we do so.
3. Charismatic—we obey a particular person because of an "uncommon and extraordinary devotion of a group of followers to the sacredness or the heroic force or the exemplariness of an individual and the order revealed or created by him" (Weber, 1947, pp. 358–359).

The notions of legitimacy and voluntary obedience suggest that there are strong links between authority and leadership. A leader cannot lead without legitimacy, and the obedience that leaders get is primarily voluntary rather than forced. Yet there are important distinctions between the two concepts. Authority refers to the phenomenon of voluntary obedience, including many examples (such as obedience to law) that fall outside the domain of leadership. As Gardner (1989) put it, "The meter maid has authority, but not necessarily leadership" (p. 7).

Leadership is also different from management, though the two are often confused. One may be a leader without being a manager, and many managers could not "lead a squad of seven-year-olds to the ice cream counter" (Gardner, 1989, p. 2). The fact that managers are *expected* to lead makes it more likely that they will. But many teachers will attest vehemently that, if anyone in their school is providing leadership, "it sure isn't the principal."

It is easy to nod agreement to the appealing phrase offered by Bennis and Nanus (1985) that "managers do things right, and leaders do the right thing" (p. 21). We soon realize, however, that while this aphorism captures a crucial distinction, there is more. Gardner (1989) argues against contrasting leadership and management too sharply because of the risk that leaders "end up looking like a cross between Napoleon and the Pied Piper, and managers like unimaginative clods" (p. 3). He suggests several dimensions for distinguishing leadership from management. Leaders think longer-term, they look beyond their unit to the larger world, they reach and influence constituents beyond their immediate jurisdictions, they emphasize vision and renewal, and they have the political skills to cope with the challenging requirements of multiple constituencies.

It is hard to imagine an outstanding manager who is not also a leader. But it is misleading and elitist to imagine that leadership is provided *only* by people in high positions. Such a view leads us to ask too much of too few. It encourages senior managers to take more responsibility than they can discharge. For example, we cannot expect school administrators to produce major improvements in education without significant help from teachers, students, parents, and school boards. In schools and elsewhere, it is important to help administrators lead more effectively but equally important to elicit leadership from others. We need *more* leaders as well as *better* leadership.

## Unheroic Leadership

We should ask of leaders neither more nor less than they can provide. Popular images of John Wayne, Bruce Lee, and Sylvester Stallone provide a distorted and romanticized view of how leaders function. Murphy (1988) wisely calls for recognition of the unheroic side of leadership. We need to recognize that leadership is always situational and relational and that leaders are often not the most potent force for change or improvement. We offer three propositions that may provide a more realistic view of leadership.

*Leadership and Context.* Traditional notions of the solitary, heroic leader have led us to focus too much on the actors and too little on the stage on which they play their parts. We often overemphasize the influence of individuals and underemphasize the significance of context. Against the assumption that "leaders make things happen," it is important to counterpose the proposition that "things make leaders happen." That proposition is reflected in the diagram in Figure 14.

Figure 14. Things Make Leaders Happen.

Organizational context influences both what leaders must do and what they can do. The requirements for leadership differ depending on whether an organization is public or private, large or small, wealthy or poor. In the late 1980s, the leadership problems facing Roger Smith at General Motors—which could produce far more cars than it could sell—were very different from those facing Vladimir Yamnikov, the chief executive of the Stolichnaya vodka distillery in Moscow, which could sell more vodka than it could produce. Smith's problem was how to align GM with its markets; Yamnikov's was to persuade central bureaucrats to provide the raw materials that he needed to increase production (Lohr, 1989). No single formula for leadership is possible or advisable for the great range of situations that potential leaders encounter.

*Leadership as Relationship.* The heroic image of leadership conveys the notion that leadership is largely a one-way process: leaders lead and followers follow. Such a view blinds us to the reality that leadership fundamentally involves a relationship between leaders and their constituents. Two-way influence between leaders and constituents adds an additional element of complexity to the model as shown in Figure 15.

Leaders are not independent actors, nor is the relationship between leaders and those whom they lead a static one. The relationship is interactional; leaders both shape and are shaped by their constitutents. Cleveland (1985) notes that leaders often promote a new idea or initiative only *after* large numbers of their constituents already favor it. It is important to distinguish carefully here between leaders and leadership. Leadership is not simply a matter of what a leader does but of what occurs in the relationship between a leader and others. The actions of leaders generate responses from others

Figure 15. Two-Way Influence Between Leaders and Constituents.

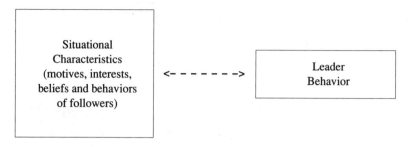

that, in turn, affect leaders' capacity for taking further initiatives (Murphy, 1985).

***Leadership and Position.*** It is common to equate leadership with high position and, for example, to regard the terms *school leadership* and *school administration* as synonymous. Although we look to administrators for leadership, it is both elitist and unrealistic to look *only* to them (Barth, 1988). The assumption that leadership is solely the job of administrators relegates everyone else to the passive role of follower. At the same time, it encourages managers to try to do everything and to take on more responsibility than they can ever adequately discharge.

One can have power and authority without being a leader. Administrators are leaders only to the extent that others grant them cooperation and see them as leaders. Conversely, one can be a leader without holding a position of formal authority. Leadership is not a zero-sum commodity. There are opportunities for leadership by participants in a variety of roles, and good organizations are likely to be those that encourage leadership from many quarters (Kanter, 1983; Barnes and Krieger, 1986).

Leadership, then, is a relationship between leaders and their constituents. It is a subtle process of mutual influence that fuses thought, feeling, and action to produce collective effort in the service of the purposes and values of *both* the leader and the led. Single-frame managers are unlikely to understand and attend to the intricacies of the process. Several studies noted earlier (Bensimon, 1988, 1989; Wimpelberg, 1987) support the idea that leaders need multiple frames, but the literature on managerial leadership often oversimplifies the issues and offers advice that can easily lead managers into error and disappointment.

### What Do We Know About Good Leadership?

Perhaps the two most widely accepted propositions about leadership are that all good leaders must have the "right stuff"—qualities such as vision, strength, and commitment—and that good leadership is situational, that is, what works in one setting will not necessarily work in a different one. An example of the first proposition is the belief that for a school to be successful, it must be headed by a strong and visionary instructional leader. An example of the second proposition is the view widely held by managers that "it takes a different kind of person to lead when you're growing and adding staff than when you're cutting budgets and laying people off."

Despite the apparent tension between "one-best-way" and "contingency" views of leadership, both are right. Several studies have found similar characteristics among unusually effective leaders across a variety of sectors and situations. Another body of research has identified situational variables that critically influence the kind of leadership that will work under different conditions.

*One Best Way.* The last decade has spawned a series of studies of "good leadership" in organizations, particularly in the private sector (Bennis and Nanus, 198 ; Clifford and Cavanagh, 1985; Conger, 1989; Kotter, 1982, 1988; 1 uzes and Posner, 1987; Levinson and Rosenthal, 1984; Maccob) 1981; Peters and Austin, 1985; Vaill, 1982). All have been qualitative studies of organizational leaders, mostly corporate executives. The methodology in these reports has varied from the recording of casual impressions to the use of systematic interviews and observation.

Vision is the only characteristic of effective leadership that is universal in these reports. Effective leaders help to establish a vision, to set standards for performance, and to create a focus and direction for organizational efforts.

No other characteristic is universal, but several appear repeatedly. One that is explicit in some (Clifford and Cavanagh, 1985;

Kouzes and Posner, 1987; Peters and Austin, 1985) and implicit in most of the others is the ability to communicate a vision effectively to others, often through the use of symbols. Another characteristic mentioned in many studies is commitment or passion (Clifford and Cavanagh, 1985; Vaill, 1982; Peters and Austin, 1985). Good leaders care deeply about the work of their organization. They believe that nothing in life is more important than doing that task well, and they communicate that belief to others. Still a third frequently mentioned characteristic is the ability to inspire trust and build relationships (Kotter, 1988; Maccoby, 1981; Bennis and Nanus, 1985). Kouzes and Posner (1987) found that honesty came first on the list of traits that managers said they most admired in a leader.

Beyond the ability to establish and communicate a vision and the capacity to inspire trust, consensus breaks down. The studies cited above, along with extensive reviews of the literature on leadership (Bass, 1981; Hollander, 1978; Gardner, 1987), provide a long list of attributes associated with effective leadership: risk taking, flexibility, self-confidence, interpersonal skills, task competence, intelligence, decisiveness, understanding of followers, and courage, to name only a few.

*Contingency Theories.* The dearth of attributes consistently found in effective leaders reinforces the argument that leadership varies with the situation. The qualities of leadership that first-level supervisors need are different from those found in chief executives. The public and private sectors require different kinds of leadership. And the leadership qualities required of the president of the United States differ from those required of the president of the Soviet Union. The kind of leadership needed for skilled and highly motivated followers may not work for followers who are alienated and unskilled.

Several writers have offered situational theories of leadership (Fiedler, 1967; Fiedler and Chemers, 1974; Hersey, 1984; Hersey and Blanchard, 1977; Reddin, 1970; Vroom and Yetton, 1973), but those theories are limited in their conceptualization of leadership and lack strong empirical support. The theories usually fail to distinguish between leadership and management, and they typically assume that the domain of leadership is limited to the relationships between managers and their immediate subordinates. Burns (1978), Gardner (1986), and Kotter (1985) argue persuasively that leaders need skill in managing relationships with all significant stakeholders, including superiors, peers, and external constituents. Contingency theories are a major area for further research. Almost everyone believes that widely varying circumstances require different forms of leadership, but research into the truth of that assumption is still sparse.

## Thin Books with Thin Advice

Despite the limited evidence for one-best-way and contingency views, both are very popular in how-to books on managerial leadership. It would, of course, be comforting to have a simple set of leadership principles that would always work. Many writers have tried to provide such comfort. Two examples point up the pitfalls of this approach.

*Managerial Grid.* One model of leadership popularized through scores of books, articles, and training programs is the Managerial Grid (Blake and Mouton, 1969, 1985). The Managerial Grid rests on the proposition that there are two fundamental dimensions that determine a leader's effectiveness: concern for task and concern for people. The model assumes that all approaches to leadership can be arrayed on a two-dimensional grid such as the one in Figure 16. Theoretically, the grid contains eighty-one cells, though Blake and Mouton emphasize only five of those possibilities:

> 1,1: the manager who has little concern for task or people and is simply going through the motions
> 1,9: the friendly manager who is concerned about people but has little concern for task
> 9,1: the hard-driving taskmaster
> 5,5: the compromising manager who tries to balance task and people
> 9,9: the ideal manager who integrates task and people and produces outstanding performance

**Figure 16. Managerial Grid Model.**

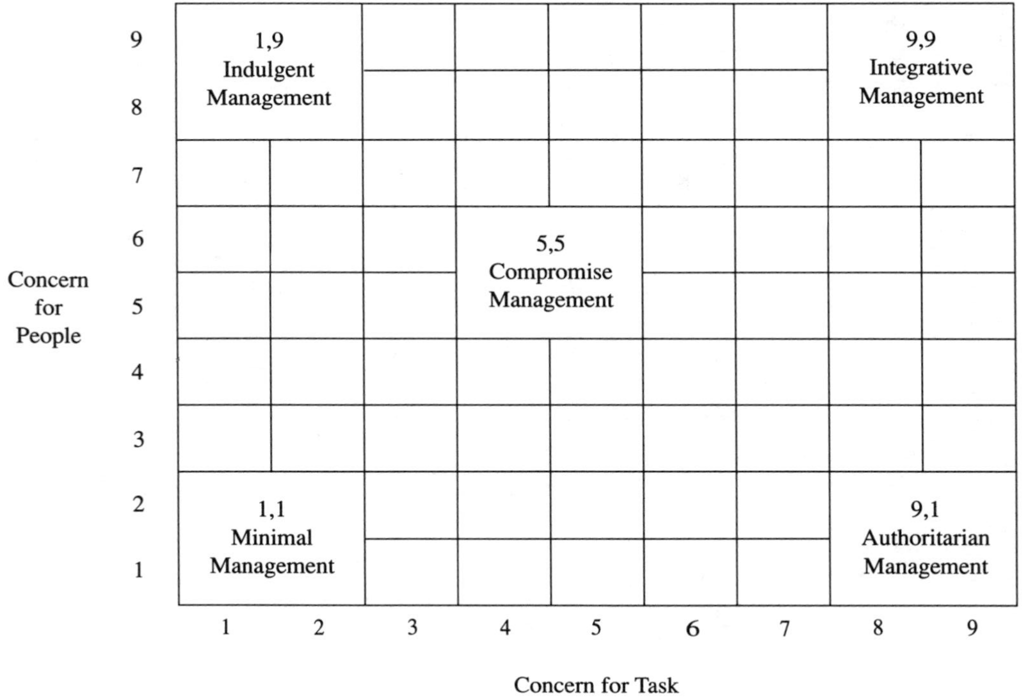

Concern for People

| 9 | 1,9 Indulgent Management | | | | | | | 9,9 Integrative Management |
|---|---|---|---|---|---|---|---|---|
| 8 | | | | | | | | |
| 7 | | | | | | | | |
| 6 | | | | | | | | |
| 5 | | | 5,5 Compromise Management | | | | | |
| 4 | | | | | | | | |
| 3 | | | | | | | | |
| 2 | 1,1 Minimal Management | | | | | | | 9,1 Authoritarian Management |
| 1 | | | | | | | | |

1    2    3    4    5    6    7    8    9

Concern for Task

*Source:* Adapted from Blake and Mouton, 1985.

Blake and Mouton have argued forcefully that the integrative, 9,9 style is the one best way to lead (Blake and Mouton, 1982). They give the following example (p. 26) of how a 9,9 leader would deal with a receptionist who is starting her first day on the job:

*Boss:* This is your first day. It's likely to be a little tough. How do you feel?

*Subordinate:* I'm all thumbs. I don't know what to do.

*Boss:* Then that's a good place to begin. That's where we start setting goals. What is your understanding of this job?

*Subordinate:* Well, I'm to be the receptionist. I've never had any experience with that.

*Boss:* Let's look at what a receptionist does.

*Subordinate:* For one, answer the phone.

*Boss:* Yes, what else?

*Subordinate:* Greet visitors, type some.

*Boss:* Anything else?

*Subordinate:* I suppose I might be expected to run errands.

*Boss:* Maybe. That's a good overview of the whole job. Let's talk about those things, one at a time. Telephone answering is our first contact with our clients. Let's talk about goals for answering the phone.

*Subordinate:* What goals? What's that got to do with answering the telephone?

*Boss:* Let me ask you a question. How do you feel when you telephone someone and the phone rings twenty times and there is no answer?

*Subordinate:* I don't like it.

*Boss:* I don't like to be kept waiting either. Can we set an objective for prompt answering?

*Subordinate:* Maybe I can answer it within the first several rings. I can experiment with it to see if I can get it down to three rings.

Blake and Mouton present the dialogue to show that a 9,9 style, participation, and two-way discussion work even with new and inexperienced subordinates. Obviously, most of us would prefer the 9,9 boss in the dialogue to an insensitive, heavy-handed lout. But granted the attractive features of the 9,9 model, does it provide an adequate conception of leadership?

One important limitation of the Managerial Grid is its implicit assumption that the essence of leadership is an interpersonal relationship between managers and their direct subordinates. Blake and Mouton's 9,9 dialogue falls mostly within the human resource frame. Nevertheless, it does contain some contradictions. Blake and Mouton extol the benefits of mutuality, but the dialogue shows mostly one-way influence from the boss to the subordinate. It thus provides ammunition for critics who argue that the human resource frame has more to do with skillful manipulation than with genuine integration of the needs of individuals and organizations.

For the most part, the Managerial Grid theory has little to say about the structural, political, and symbolic dimensions of organizations. The theory assumes that all a leader has to do is integrate concern for task with concern for people to be effective across the full range of leadership situations. But what if the structure of the organization has become unwieldy and inappropriate? What if there are major political conflicts? What if the organization's culture is empty and threadbare?

The grid approach also gives little attention to any constituents except direct subordinates. The theory might be very helpful to a new principal trying to decide what to say in her first meeting with faculty members. But what would it tell Roger Smith to do with the thousands of workers who would lose their jobs if General Motors closed more plants? Should he meet with them in small groups and ask them how they feel about being laid off? How could it help Vladimir Yamnikov deal with crusty central planners who jealously guard their traditional bases of power?

Finally, the Managerial Grid lacks concepts for dealing with variations in situations. It holds that 9,9 is a leadership style for all situations and all seasons. While Blake and Mouton (1982) defend that view vigorously, it has become the most heavily criticized element of their theory, and several contingency models have attempted to address this shortcoming. One of the most popular is the so-called situational leadership model developed by Hersey and Blanchard (1977) and Hersey (1984).

*Situational Leadership.* The cover of Hersey's 1984 book modestly promises, "Increase your productivity and profit through America's most influential leadership program, used by over one million managers in more than five hundred top companies." Can all these managers and top companies be wrong? We fear so, if they take the model too seriously. The problem is not with the idea that leadership is situational but with the significant limitations found in the Hersey-Blanchard model.

Their model uses the two basic dimensions of leadership in the Managerial Grid: tasks and people. Hersey (1984) defines task behavior as "the extent to which the leader engages in spelling out the duties and responsibilities of an individual or group" (p. 31). Relationship behavior is defined as "the extent to which the leader engages in two-way or multiway communication" (p. 32). It includes "listening, encouraging, facilitating, providing clarification, and giving socioemotional support" (p. 32). Their definition of task behavior is thus narrowly structural, and their definition of relationship behavior encompasses only a small slice of the human resource frame.

Hersey combines task and people into a two-by-two chart like Figure 17 which illustrates four possible "leadership styles": *telling* (high task and low relationship), *selling* (high task and high relationship), *participating* (low task and high relationship), and *delegating* (low task and low relationship).

When should a manager use each style? The model says that it depends on subordinates' "maturity" (Hersey and Blanchard, 1977) or "readiness level" (Hersey, 1984). Hersey defines readiness in terms of two characteristics of subordinates: their attitudes (how much do they *want* to do a good job) and their skills (do they have the skills to do the job well). The model distinguishes four levels of readiness among subordinates and argues that different styles are appropriate for different situations.

For subordinates at the lowest level (unable and unwilling to do a good job), the appropriate management style is "telling": such

**Figure 17. Situational Leadership Model.**

| | |
|---|---|
| *High Relationship - Low Task:* | *High Relationship - High Task:* |
| **Leadership Through Participation** | **Leadership Through Selling** |
| Use when followers are "able" but "unwilling" or "insecure." | Use when followers are "unable" but "willing" or "motivated." |
| *Low Relationship - Low Task:* | *Low Relationship - High Task:* |
| **Leadership Through Delegation** | **Leadership Through Telling** |
| Use when followers are "able" and "willing" or "motivated." | Use when followers are "unable" and "unwilling" or "insecure." |

*Source:* Adapted from Hersey, 1984.

people need to be directed by the boss. At the next higher level (willing but unable), subordinates want to do the job but lack the necessary skills. The model says that leaders need to "sell" in these situations, that is, explain their decisions and provide subordinates an opportunity for clarification. At the next level, when subordinates are able but unwilling, the leader should use "participating" to increase motivation. He or she does this by sharing ideas and discussing issues with subordinates. At the highest level, with subordinates who are both able and willing, the leader should simply delegate: the subordinates will do their jobs well without leader input.

At first glance, the model seems sensible enough. Indeed, why else would so many "top companies" train their supervisors to be situational leaders? What could be wrong with a model that says leaders should vary their behavior in response to different levels of readiness among their subordinates? In fact, there is considerable reason to believe that the model is wrong and little evidence to suggest that it is right (Hambleton and Gumpert, 1982; Graeff, 1983). If, for example, managers provide unwilling-unable subordinates high direction and low support, what would cause their motivation to improve enough for them to move on to the next level? The manager of a design team in a computer company told us with regret, "I treated my group with a 'telling' management style and found in fact that they became both less able and less willing."

The situational model fails to distinguish between support for a person and support for specific actions. Hersey (1984) claims that high support to subordinates who are unable and unwilling would reward poor performance. Does that mean that when children are unmotivated and unskilled, parents and teachers should provide high direction and low support until the kids shape up? Blake and Mouton, like many experts on both parenting and teaching, would argue that high direction and *high* support would make much more sense.

Similar questions can be raised about all the propositions in the model. Hersey and Blanchard oversimplify the options available to leaders and the range of situations that leaders encounter. They provide a situational model that neglects all but a few situational variables. The model makes no distinction among different organizational levels, different industries, different sectors, or different cultures.

The Hersey-Blanchard theory also neglects the problem of the Pygmalion effect. As seen earlier theories do more than influence our views of reality. They also become self-fulfilling prophesies. McGregor (1960) made the same argument about Theory X: if managers believe that their subordinates are unwilling to carry out their duties, they are likely to direct and try to control them, which will tend to intensify their unwillingness. Hersey and Blanchard do not discuss how managers should test their perceptions of subordinates' motivation and ability. Implicitly, they assume that managers' perceptions are usually reliable. They focus entirely on how managers should influence subordinates and ignore the importance of influence in the other direction.

Dealing with people is a perennially perplexing aspect of managing. Managers are always looking for ideas to make the job easier. Many introductory textbooks in organizational behavior include an uncritical discussion of the Hersey-Blanchard theory (usually with a footnote acknowledging that there is little evidence to show that the theory is correct). The Hersey-Blanchard model is comforting for managers because it promises to make their lives less perplexing and confusing. The promise is illusory, but this model, like many others, has come to serve as a secular religion for managers. True believers will defend their faith with fervor, as the following case illustrates:

> A major corporation was developing a new management training program for a group of some 2,000 technical managers. A task force with representatives from two divisions in the company came together to decide what should be taught. The representatives from division A had participated in Managerial Grid seminars. They knew in their hearts that the grid was the one best way and that it should be the foundation of the seminar. The managers in division B had attended situational management seminars, and their faith in the situational model was equally unshakable.
>
> Initially, the two sides engaged in polite talk and rational argument. When that failed, the conversation gradually became more heated. Eventually, the group found itself hopelessly deadlocked. An outside consultant came in to mediate the dispute. He listened while the representatives from each division reviewed the conversation. The consultant then said to the group, "I'm impressed by the passion on both sides. I'm curious about one thing. If you all believe so deeply in these models and if it makes a difference which models someone learns, why can't I see any difference in the behavior of the two groups?" Stunned silence fell over the room. Finally one member said, "You know, I think

he's right. We don't use the damn models, we just
preach them." That was the end of the impasse.

## Summary

Though leadership is widely accepted as a cure for organizational
ills, it is also widely misunderstood. Many views of leadership fail
to recognize that it is relational and contextual and that it is not
simply a matter of wielding power or occupying a certain position.
Inadequate ideas about leadership often result in oversimplified
advice to managers. Currently popular models of "leadership,"
such as the Managerial Grid and the Hersey-Blanchard situational
model, neglect many of the most critical challenges that leaders face.

We need to reframe leadership to move beyond the impasses
created by oversimplified models. In the next two chapters, we will
look at leadership through each of the four frames and discuss how
each frame represents a distinctive and significant contribution to
an integrative view of leadership.

# 21

# *Leaders as Architects and Catalysts*

Each of the frames offers a different perspective on what leadership is and how it operates in organizations. Each can result in either effective or ineffective conceptions of leadership (Table 9). In this chapter, we will look at the skills and processes associated with effective leadership in the structural and human resource frames. We will also present a set of heuristics (rules of thumb) that are consistent with the practice of successful leaders who use each frame.

### Architects or Tyrants: Structural Leadership

The idea of structural leadership often evokes images of petty tyrants and rigid bureaucrats who never met a rule that they didn't like. In contrast to the other frames, however, there is almost no literature on structural leadership. Partly, this is because structural theorists are often suspicious of the concept of leadership. Perrow (1970), for example, argues that "apparent leadership problems are often problems of organizational structure" (p.10). Hall (1987) emphasizes that leadership is heavily constrained by structure and environment, and writes that "for most organizations in most circumstances, changing leadership is little more than a cosmetic treatment" (p. 149). Hall adds: "Why is leadership romanticized?

422

**Table 9. Reframing Leadership.**

| Effective Leadership | Structural | Human Resource | Political | Symbolic |
|---|---|---|---|---|
| Leadership is: | Social architect | Catalyst, servant | Advocate | Prophet or Poet |
| Leadership process: | Analysis, design | Support, empowerment | Advocacy, coalition building | Inspiration, framing experience |
| *Ineffective Leadership* | *Structural* | *Human Resource* | *Political* | *Symbolic* |
| Leadership is: | Petty tyrant | Wimp, pushover | Con artist, hustler | Fanatic, fool |
| Leadership process: | Management by detail and fiat | Management by abdication | Management by fraud, manipulation | Management by mirage, smoke, and mirrors |

Leadership seems to be an extremely easy solution to whatever problems are ailing an organization. Looking to new leadership can mask such issues as inappropriate structural arrangements, power distributions that block effective actions, lack of resources, archaic procedures, and other more basic organizational problems. With all this, one might wonder, why study leadership, and why have there been so many studies in the past? The fact is that in certain situations leadership is important, even critical. The situations, however, occur much more infrequently and are much more constrained than most treatises on leadership consider" (p. 150).

The message is that leadership is neither very important nor very basic. Hall and other structural writers have detailed their arguments about the structural constraints on leadership (Hall, 1987; Perrow, 1986) but have rarely looked at the other side of the coin: leadership as a variable in determining structure. In fact, structural leadership may be extremely powerful and enduring, even if it is more subtle, and less obviously heroic, than some other forms of leadership, as the career of Alfred P. Sloan, Jr., so vividly illustrates.

Sloan became president of General Motors in 1923 and was a dominant force in the corporation for thirty-three years, until his retirement in 1956. Sloan was a brilliant social architect, and the structure and strategy that he established in GM made it the world's largest corporation. Sloan has been described as "the George Washington of the GM culture" (Lee, 1988, p. 42), even though "Sloan's genius was not in inspirational leadership, but in organizational structures" (p. 43).

At the turn of the century, there were some thirty manufacturers of automobiles in the United States, and in 1899 they produced a grand total of about six hundred cars. Most of those carmakers stumbled shortly after leaving the starting gate, and two late entries, the Ford Motor Company (founded by Henry Ford in 1903) and GM (founded by William Durant in 1908) quickly became the front-runners in the race to dominate the American automobile industry. Henry Ford's single-minded determination to build a car that everyone could afford had given Ford a commanding lead by the time Sloan became president of General Motors.

Under GM's founder, Billy Durant, GM's divisions had operated as independent fiefdoms. Cost got out of control, and a slump in car sales in 1920 created a financial crisis. Chevrolet lost $5 million in 1921, and only Du Pont money and Buick's profitability kept GM afloat (Sloan, 1965). In Sloan's first year, matters got worse instead of better. Market share dropped from 20 percent to 17 percent, while Ford's increased to 55 percent. But Sloan had begun several years earlier to develop a new strategy for GM. Henry Ford still clung to the same vision that had made his company so successful—a single, low-priced, mass-market car. Ford was famous for saying that his customers could have any color they wanted, as long as it was black. The Model T was reliable and cheap, but Ford sold essentially the same automobile for almost twenty years. In the early years of the auto industry, customers would buy anything with four wheels and a motor, and Ford saw no great need for creature comforts like windows in the Model T. Sloan surmised that consumers would pay a little more for such amenities as protection from rain and snow. The strategy worked, and Chevrolet began to nibble away at Ford's market. By 1928, Ford sales dropped so precipitously that Henry Ford took the dramatic step of closing his River Rouge plant for a year in order to retool. General Motors took the lead in the great auto race for the first time since 1908. For the next sixty years, no one sold more cars than General Motors.

In addition to selling the right cars, Sloan believed that GM had to have the right structure. Like many other large American corporations at the time, GM was structured essentially as a holding company—a loose combination of previously independent firms. Durant had built GM by buying everything in sight, but his free-wheeling leadership style had also created serious problems: "GM did not have adequate knowledge or control of the individual operating divisions. It was management by crony, with the divisions operating on a horse-trading basis. The main thing to note here is that no one had the needed information or the needed control over the divisions. The divisions continued to spend lavishly, and their requests for additional funds were met. The minutes of the Executive and Finance committees in late 1919 and early 1920 show continued massive overruns on appropriations" (Sloan, 1965, pp. 27–29).

Sloan recognized that GM needed a better structural form. The major alternative at the time was a functionally organized, centralized organization, but Sloan felt that such a structure would be wrong for GM. Instead, he set out to create one of the world's first decentralized organizations. He replaced Durant's minimal headquarters with a larger central office. Heading the corporation was a small executive committee, supported by large financial and advisory staffs. The basic idea was simple: centralize planning and resource allocation but decentralize operating decisions. In large, centralized organizations, top management tends to become preoccupied with day-to-day operating decisions. Sloan's plan called for the operating divisions to make most of the operating decisions while top management focused on long-range strategy and on the allocation of resources to carry it out. The job of the central staff was to ensure that top management had the information and control systems needed to do that job.

By the late 1920s, Sloan headed an organization that had both better cars and a more versatile structure than Ford. Henry Ford still dominated his centralized, functional organization, and his company was poorly positioned to compete with GM's multiple divisions, each of which focused on a different car in a different price range. Sloan's structural leadership made GM one of the first major

corporations to implement a structural form that eventually came
to be the dominant form for large industrial corporations:

> With the creation of a general office consisting of general ex-
> ecutives and a large financial and advisory staff and with the
> calibration of product flow and day-to-day operating activities
> to forecast demand, the basic organizational structure and ad-
> ministrative procedures of the modern industrial enterprise
> were virtually completed. Although they developed many vari-
> ations and although in very recent years they have been occa-
> sionally mixed into a matrix form, only two basic organiza-
> tional structures have been used for the management of large
> industrial enterprises. One is the centralized, functional depart-
> mentalized type perfected by General Electric and Du Pont be-
> fore World War I. The other is the multidivisional, decentral-
> ized structure initially developed at General Motors and also at
> Du Pont in the 1920s. The first has been used primarily by
> companies producing a single line of goods for one major
> product or regional market, the second by those manufacturing
> several lines for a number of product and regional markets
> [Chandler, 1977, p. 463].

In the 1980s, GM found itself with another structural leader,
Roger Smith, but the results that he achieved were less satisfying.
Like Sloan, Smith ascended to the top job at a difficult time. In
1980, Smith's first year as GM's chief executive, all the American
automakers lost money. For GM it was the first loss since 1921.
Smith knew that GM had serious competitive problems, and he
wanted to build a strategy to make it "the world's first 21st century
corporation" (Lee, 1988, p. 16). The essence of Smith's view was
structural and technological. He restructured all the vehicle operations, and spent billions of dollars on his vision of a corporation
of computerized, paperless offices and robotized assembly plants.
The changes were dramatic and far-reaching, but success was problematic: "[Smith's] tenure has been a tragic era in General Motors
history. No GM chairman has disrupted as many lives without com-
mensurate rewards, has spent as much money without returns, or
has alienated so many along the way. An endless string of public
relations and internal relations insensitivities has confused his organization and complicated the attainment of its goals. Few em-

ployees believe that [Smith] is in the least concerned with their well-being, and even fewer below executive row anticipate any measure of respect, or reward, for their contributions. No GM chief executive's motives have ever been as universally questioned or his decisions as thoroughly mistrusted" (Lee, 1988, pp. 286–287).

Smith and Sloan were equally uncharismatic. Sloan was a somber, quiet engineer who habitually looked as if he were sucking a lemon. Smith's leadership aura was not helped by his blotchy complexion and squeaky voice. Neither had much sensitivity to human resource or symbolic issues in organizations. Why, then, was Sloan's structural contribution so durable, and Smith's so problematic? The answer comes down to how well each implemented a structural mode of leadership. If leaders who rely primarily on the structural frame are successful, it is not because of their ability to inspire but because they have the right answer for their organization and are able to get their answer accepted and implemented. We discuss below the characteristics of effective structural leadership.

*Structural leaders do their homework.* Sloan had several advantages when he took over leadership at GM. He was a brilliant engineer who had grown up in the auto industry. Before coming to GM, he had been the chief executive of an auto accessories company, where he implemented a divisional structure. When GM bought Sloan's firm, Sloan came into the parent corporation as a vice-president and board member. From the time he started working for Durant in 1916, he devoted much of his energy to studying GM's structural problems. Sloan also believed strongly in information and research; he pioneered in the development of better information systems internally and better market research externally. Moreover, Sloan was not a loner. He was an early convert to group decision making and created a committee structure to make the major decisions at GM.

Roger Smith had spent his entire career with General Motors, but most of his jobs had been in the finance department. His closest brush with a manufacturing job was in a nonautomotive division, where his most notable accomplishment was to sell off two money-losing divisions, one of which was Frigidaire (Lee, 1988). Much of Smith's vision for a new General Motors involved changes in production technology, an area where he had little experience or expertise.

*Structural leaders develop a new model of the relationship of structure, strategy, and environment for their organization.* Sloan's structural vision for General Motors was intimately tied to a view of the market for automobiles and to a strategy for reaching that market. He foresaw a growing market, continual improvement in automobiles, and increasingly discriminating consumers. In the face of Henry Ford's stubborn attachment to producing the same car year after year, Sloan introduced the idea of the "price pyramid" and the annual model change. The price pyramid called for a different car for every pocketbook; inexpensive Chevrolets at the bottom of the pyramid, Buicks and Oldsmobiles in the middle, and high-priced Cadillacs at the top. Every year, there was a new model of each car. Automotive technology in the 1920s was evolving almost as fast as microcomputer technology in the 1980s, and the annual model change became a fundamental concept in the industry. Sloan had faith in the virtues of decentralization, and the structure that he created let Chevrolet's managers concentrate on developing a high-volume, low-cost car for the mass market, while Cadillac developed luxury vehicles for the rich.

For a variety of reasons, GM began to move away from Sloan's concepts in the 1960s. Some of the reasons were purely defensive. Fearing a government effort to break up the corporation, GM began to reduce the independence of the car divisions and to centralize design and engineering. Increasingly, the car divisions became marketing groups that had to sell whatever cars the corporation gave them. In the early 1980s, the corporation was giving them "look-alike cars." It was sometimes hard to tell the difference between a Chevrolet and a Cadillac, and many consumers became confused and angry.

Smith implemented a reorganization in the 1980s that was billed as a move back toward decentralization. He reorganized the car operations into two product divisions: one for big cars (Cadillac-Buick-Oldsmobile) and one for small cars (Chevrolet and Pontiac). But engineering and design were consolidated rather than decentralized, and Smith's promise to move decisions downward was abruptly reversed when costs began to rise. When GM executives asked, "When will we get the authority to do the job?" Smith's response was, "Frankly, the results we've seen so far don't warrant additional responsibility" (Lee, 1988, pp. 119–120).

Smith's vision for GM always focused more on costs and technology than on marketing. GM's primary competitive problem, as he saw it, was high costs, caused primarily by blue-collar wages. Well before Smith arrived, GM had begun to develop plant-floor programs to improve worker participation, but Smith saw technology, not human resource management, as the wave of the future. Ironically, one of Smith's best investments was a joint venture with Toyota at the NUMMI plant in Fremont, California. "With only a fraction of the money invested in GM's heavily robotized plants, Fremont is more efficient and produces better-quality cars than any plant in the GM system" (Hampton and Norman, 1987, p. 102).

*Structural leaders focus on implementation.* The right answer helps only if it can be implemented. Structural leaders sometimes fail because they miscalculate the difficulty of putting their design in place. They often underestimate the resistance that it will generate, and they take few steps to build a base of support for their innovations. In short, they are often undone by human resource, political, and symbolic considerations.

Although Sloan showed little understanding of human resource issues, he knew intuitively that it was important to get understanding and acceptance from his management for major policy decisions. He did that by continually asking for advice and by establishing committees and task forces to address every major issue. When a new problem came up, Sloan's custom was to write a memo to senior managers, ask for their ideas, and create a committee to discuss and implement a solution.

*Effective structural leaders continually experiment, evaluate, and adapt.* Sloan continually tinkered with GM's structure and strategy and encouraged other managers to do likewise. The Depression produced a drop of 72 percent in sales at GM between 1929 and 1932, but the company adapted to hard times so adroitly that it increased its market share and made money every year. Sloan briefly centralized operations to meet survival needs in the Depression but moved back to decentralization once the industry began to recover. In the 1980s, Smith spent billions on his campaign to modernize the corporation and cut costs, yet GM lost market share every year and continued to be the highest-cost producer in the industry.

"Much of the advanced technology that GM acquired at such high cost hindered rather than improved productivity. Runaway robots started welding doors shut at the new Detroit-Hamtramck Cadillac plant. If the once-mighty GM cannot find a way to reverse its slide, the next decade might be the company's last" ("On a Clear Day . . . ," 1989, p. 77). In August 1990, the challenge of reversing GM's slide was put in the hands of Robert Stempel, who succeeded Smith as GM's chief executive. A few months later, observers reported a noticeable shift in emphasis from financial to customer priorities.

### Catalysts or Wimps: Human Resource Leadership

The structural literature on leadership amounts to no more than a tiny trickle, but there is a torrent of human resource writing on the subject (for example, Argyris, 1962; Bennis and Nanus, 1985; Blanchard and Johnson, 1982; Bradford and Cohen, 1984; Fiedler, 1967; Fiedler and Chemers, 1974; Hollander, 1978; Hersey, 1984; House, 1971; Levinson, 1968; Likert, 1961, 1967; Vroom and Yetton, 1973). The human resource literature typically focuses on the interpersonal relationship between supervisors and their subordinates and argues for such practices as openness, mutuality, listening, coaching, participation, and empowerment. The leader is viewed as a facilitator and catalyst who motivates and empowers subordinates to perform at their best. The leader's power comes not from position or force but from talent, sensitivity, and service. Greenleaf (1973) argues that followers "will freely respond only to individuals who are chosen as leaders because they are proven and trusted as servants" (p. 4). He adds, "The servant-leader makes sure that other people's highest priority needs are being served. The best test [of leadership] is: do those served grow as persons; do they, *while being served,* become healthier, wiser, freer, more autonomous, more likely themselves to become servants?" (p. 7).

Most of us would prefer to follow leaders who are oriented to service and caring. But we might also wonder whether managers who follow such models will be true leaders. Will they be respected leaders who make a difference, or will they be wimps who are carried along on the current of other people's energy? The risk is real, and there are managers who use participation and caring as excuses not to lead. Still, there are many human resource leaders whose skill and artistry produce extraordinary results. They apply leadership principles such as the following:

*Human resource leaders believe in people and communicate that belief.* Human resource leaders are passionate about "productivity through people" (Peters and Waterman, 1982). They demonstrate this faith in their words and actions and often build it into a philosophy or credo that is central to their vision of their organization. William Hewlitt, co-founder of the enormously successful Hewlett-Packard corporation, put it this way:

> The dignity and worth of the individual is a very important part of the HP Way. With this in mind, many years ago we did away with time clocks, and more recently we introduced the flexible work hours program. This is meant to be an expression of trust and confidence in people, as well as providing them with an opportunity to adjust their work schedules to their personal lives. Many new HP people as well as visitors often note and comment to us about another HP way—that is, our informality and our being on a first-name basis. I could cite other examples, but the problem is that none by themselves really catches the essence of what the HP Way is all about. You can't describe it in numbers and statistics. In the last analysis, it is a spirit, a point of view. There is a feeling that everyone is part of a team, and that team is HP. It is an idea that is based on the individual. It exists because people have seen that it works, and they believe that this feeling makes HP what it is [Peters and Waterman, 1982, p. 244].

When Ren McPherson became chief executive of the Dana Corporation (a manufacturer of automobile components), he eliminated reams of policy manuals and substituted a one-page statement of philosophy that stressed the need for more training and more opportunities for employees. McPherson emphasized the importance of people in virtually every speech and conversation

**Exhibit 8. McPherson's Leadership.**

---

**Talk Back to the Boss**

It's one of Dana's principles of productivity. Bosses don't have all the answers. The worker who does the job always knows more about it than his boss. But all that he knows can't be used unless he's free to talk about it. Especially to his boss.

At Dana, bosses listen. It's part of what we call humanistic management, giving people the freedom to work well, to grow and share the rewards.

You can see the results in our productivity. It's more than doubled in the last seven years.

Productivity alone does not produce profits. But we're balancing our output of parts for the vehicular, service, and industrial equipment markets we manufacture for. So, as well as increasing productivity, we've improved our earnings year after year.

And that's not bad for a bunch of people who talk back to their bosses.

---

*Source:* Dana Corporation.

(Peters and Waterman, 1982) and once ran the advertisement reproduced in Exhibit 8 in a number of major U.S. business publications.

*Human resources leaders are visible and accessible.* Peters and Waterman (1982) popularized the notion of "management by wandering around"—the idea that managers need to get out of their offices and interact with workers and customers. One practitioner of this technique is Patricia Carrigan, the first woman ever to be a plant manager at General Motors. Trained as a clinical psychologist, Carrigan worked for many years in public schools before taking a human resource staff job at GM. In the 1970s, GM developed one of the largest and most extensive quality-of-work-life programs in the world, which created opportunities for atypical managers like Carrigan (Lawler, 1986; Kanter, 1983). Her experience as a human resource management consultant convinced her that she wanted to be a plant manager. She got her chance, and she was successful in turning around two different GM plants, each with a long history of union-management conflict (Kouzes and Posner, 1987).

In both plants, one of her first steps was to go out on the plant floor, introduce herself to production workers, and ask how they thought the plant could be improved. One worker commented that before Carrigan came, "I didn't know who the plant manager was. I wouldn't have recognized him if I saw him." When she left her first plant after three years, the local union gave her a plaque. It said, in conclusion, "Therefore be it resolved that Pat M. Carrigan, through the exhibiting of these qualities as a people person, has played a vital role in the creation of a new way of life at the Lakewood plant. Therefore, be it resolved that the members of Local 34 will always warmly remember Pat M. Carrigan as one of us" (Kouzes and Posner, 1987, p. 36). Not many plant managers get that sort of send-off from their blue-collar union.

Although Roger Smith showed little zeal for human resource management, his counterpart at Ford, Donald Petersen, had a very different orientation. Petersen became president of Ford Motor Company in 1980 and played a major role in the corporation's remarkable comeback in the next several years. Petersen had worked at Ford for much of his life but quit the company twice because he found the culture too combative and politicized. Once he became president, he set about to change the culture: "Progress was slow at first, but Petersen eventually got the warring fiefdoms within Ford to cooperate. He met almost endlessly with managers, beginning each meeting with a sermon on teamwork and quality. He also visited factories to hear what workers had to say and to persuade them that Ford would actually adopt good ideas that trickled up from the rank and file" (Dumaine, 1988, p. 22).

*Effective human resource leaders empower: they increase participation, provide support, share information, and move decision making as far down the organization as possible.* Human resource leaders often like to refer to their employees as "partners," "owners," or "associates." They want to make it clear that employees have a stake in the organization's success and a right to be involved in making decisions. Pat Carrigan credits her success to "partnership with people" and to involving them in decisions. Ren McPherson emphasizes the contribution that every individual can make. Human resource leaders are committed to the concept that individuals want to take responsibility and will do so if they are given the authority and the information that they need. Carrigan, like many other resource managers, created self-managing production teams. McPherson required division managers to meet monthly with everyone in their divisions and to discuss corporate results in detail.

Before leaving the human resource model, we should look at one last example: the well-known case of Donald Burr and People Express Airlines. People Express was the fastest-growing, most successful start-up that the airline industry had ever seen, and Burr, the company's chief executive, was fervently committed to human resource management. He created a company that was organized around work groups, in which people took responsibility for whatever needed doing. Pilots worked ticket counters, and vice-presidents sorted baggage. Salaries were low, but People Express offered high levels of responsibility and automony, exciting work, and a share in the success of the company through an employee stock ownership plan. As the company grew and the value of the stock shot upward, many of its employees became very wealthy—on paper.

But then the bubble burst. The airline industry began to consolidate once again, and competition intensified. As People Express got larger, it suffered from increasing structural confusion, and it made some significant strategic errors. The company went from high-flyer to bankruptcy court in a few months. In human resource terms, Burr's leadership was highly successful. No one in the airline industry had a work force that was more loyal, hardworking, flexible, innovative, and productive. But participation is not enough, and the most committed work force in the world will still fail if its organization has the wrong structure and strategy.

## Summary

Though structural leadership has received less attention than it deserves, it can be a very powerful approach. Structural leaders lead through analysis and design rather than charisma and inspiration. Their success depends on developing the right blueprint for the relationship between their organization's structure and strategy, as well as on finding ways to get that blueprint accepted. Successful structural leaders can become great social architects. But if they pay too little attention to other dimensions of organizational life, they are likely to be dismissed as shortsighted tyrants or insensitive bureaucrats.

Human resource leadership has generated an enormous amount of attention. Until very recently, in fact, human resource concepts dominated the literature on managerial leadership. The human resource literature has focused particularly on interpersonal relationships between superiors and subordinates and on the value of openness, sensitivity, and participation. When they are successful, human resource leaders become catalysts and servant-leaders. They help to build organizations whose success derives from highly committed and productive employees. When they are ineffective, they risk being seen as naive or as weaklings and wimps.

# 22

# *Leaders as Advocates and Prophets*

Lee Iacocca had a meteoric career at Ford Motor Company, rising through a series of sales and marketing triumphs to become president of the company. Then, in July 1978, his boss, Henry Ford II, fired him, reportedly with the simple explanation, "Let's just say I don't like you" (O'Toole, 1984, p. 231). Iacocca's period of unemployment was brief. Chrysler Corporation was desperate for new leadership, and it was convinced that Iacocca was exactly the man it needed.

Iacocca had done his homework before accepting the Chrysler presidency, but the problems were still worse than he anticipated. Chrysler was losing money so fast that bankruptcy was almost inevitable. The only way out seemed to be to get the United States government to guarantee massive loans. It was a tough sell—much of Congress, the media, and the American public were against the idea. Iacocca needed to convince all these groups that it was in their interest, as well as Chrysler's, for the government to intervene. He pulled it off with a remarkable combination of personal artistry and adroit political maneuvering. He successfully employed the following set of rules for political leaders:

*Political leaders clarify what they want and what they can get.* Political leaders are realists above all. They never let what they want cloud their judgment about what is possible. Chrysler's problem was survival, and Iacocca translated that into the realistic goal of getting some breathing room: Chrysler needed help to make it through a couple of difficult years without going under. Chrysler, moreover, did not ask the government for money but for loan guarantees. Iacocca always insisted that the guarantees would cost the taxpayers nothing because Chrysler was going to pay the money back.

*Political leaders assess the distribution of power and interests.* The political leader needs to think carefully about the players, their interests, and their power; in other words, he or she must map the political terrain. Political leaders ask questions such as whose support do I need? How do I go about getting it? Who are my opponents? How much power do they have? What can I do to reduce or overcome their opposition? Is this battle winnable? Iacocca recognized that he needed the support of Chrysler's employees and unions but he also knew that they had few other options. The key players were Congress and the public. He needed Congress to vote the guarantees, and Congress would only do that it if it perceived that Iacocca's proposal had sufficient public support.

*Political leaders build linkages to other stakeholders.* Political leaders focus much of their attention on building relationships and networks. They recognize the value of personal contact and face-to-face conversations. Iacocca knew that he needed linkages with Congress, the media, and the American public, and he set about to build them. He spent hours meeting with members of Congress and testifying before congressional committees. One example was a meeting with thirty-one Italian-American members of Congress. All but one eventually voted for the loan guarantees. According to Iacocca, "Some were Republicans, some were Democrats, but in this case they voted the straight Italian ticket. We were desperate, and we had to play every angle. It was democracy in action" (Iacocca and Novak, 1984, p. 221).

Iacocca gave interviews to anyone in the media who would listen to him. He personally signed Chrysler's advertisements in newspapers and magazines and went on television to make Chrysler's case. Over time, he became America's best-known and most respected chief executive.

*Political leaders persuade first, negotiate second, and use coercion only if necessary.* Wise political leaders recognize that power is essential to their effectiveness, and they know that it needs to be used judiciously. William P. Kelly, director of the U.S. Job Corps in the late 1960s, put it this way: "Power is like the old Esso ad—a tiger in your tank. But you can't let the tiger out, you just let people hear him roar. You use power terribly sparingly because it has a short half-life. You let people know you have it and hope that you don't have to use it" (Ridout and Fenn, 1974, p. 10).

The sophisticated political leader also knows that influence needs to begin with an understanding of others' concerns and interests. What is important to them? How can I help them solve their problems?

Iacocca also recognized that he had to address the widespread belief that Chrysler was a basket case and that federal guarantees would simply throw millions of taxpayers' dollars down a rat hole. Iacocca therefore used advertisements to raise the issue himself and to respond directly to the public's concerns. Does Chrysler have a future? Yes, he said, we've been here fifty-four years, and we'll be here another fifty-four years. Would the loan guarantees be a dangerous precedent? No, he said, the government already had $400 billion in other loan guarantees on the books, and in any event, Chrysler was going to pay its loans back. "You can count on it!" he said over and over. Iacocca also spoke directly to congressional concerns. Chrysler prepared computer printouts showing how many jobs would be lost in every congressional district if Chrysler were to go under. Those arguments were coupled with Iacocca's unique blend of passion and confidence. He never said "we think" or "we might." It was always "we can" and "we will" (O'Toole, 1984, p. 240).

Iacocca got his loan guarantees. Eight years later, in 1987, Chrysler reported earnings of more than $1 billion, ranking it eleventh among all U.S. corporations. The company not only survived, it paid back the loans early.

### Prophets or Zealots? Symbolic Leadership

The symbolic frame provides still a fourth turn of the kaleidoscope of leadership. In this frame, the organization is seen as a stage, a theater in which every actor plays certain roles and attempts to communicate the right impressions to the right audiences. The main premise of this frame is that whenever reason and analysis fail to contain the dark forces of ambiguity, human beings erect symbols—myths, rituals, and ceremonies—to bring order, meaning, and predictability out of chaos and confusion.

Symbolically, the task of leaders is to *interpret experience*. What are the real lessons of history? What is really happening in the world? What will the future bring? What mission is worthy of our loyalty and investment? Data and analysis will never provide completely adequate answers to those questions. Leaders develop interpretations of experience that give meaning and purpose and phrase those interpretations with beauty and passion. Franklin D. Roosevelt reassured a nation in the midst of its deepest economic depression that "the only thing we have to fear is fear itself." At almost the same historical moment, Adolph Hitler assured Germans that their severe economic and social problems were simply the result of betrayal by Jews and communists, and that Germans were a superior people who could still fulfill their nation's destiny of world mastery. Though many Germans saw the destructive paranoia in Hitler's message, millions of their countrymen were swept away by his vision of German conquest.

Burns (1978) was mindful of leaders such as Roosevelt, Gandhi, and Martin Luther King when he coined the distinction between "transforming" and "transactional" leadership. According to Burns, transactional leaders "approach their followers with an eye to trading one thing for another: jobs for votes, or subsidies for campaign contributions" (p. 4). Much rarer, according to Burns, are transforming leaders, who bring out the best in their followers and move them to pursue higher and more universal needs and purposes. Burns's distinction has become so popular that it appears in virtually all the recent writing on leadership and has given rise to a new fad. Whereas ten years ago managers were scrambling to learn how to be participative, now they are told that they must be transformational. Burns's distinction is a profound and useful one, but it is in danger of being transformed into another Hula-Hoop.

Transforming leaders, as Burns describes them, are visionary leaders, and visionary leadership is invariably symbolic. Examination of symbolic leaders reveals that they follow a consistent set of practices and rules.

*Transforming leaders use symbols to capture attention.* When Diana Lam became principal of the Mackey Middle School in Boston in 1985, she knew that she faced a substantial challenge. Mackey had all the usual problems of urban public schools: decaying physical plant, lack of student discipline, racial tension, troubles with the teaching staff, low morale, and limited resources. The only good news was that the situation was so bad that almost any change would be an improvement (Kaufer and Leader, 1987a). In such a situation, symbolic leaders will try to do something visible, even dramatic, to let people know that changes are on the way. During the summer before she assumed her duties, Lam wrote a letter to every teacher to set up an individual meeting. She traveled to meet teachers wherever they wanted, driving two hours in one case. She asked teachers how they felt about the school and what changes they wanted.

She also felt that something needed to be done about the school building because "nobody likes to work in a dumpy place." She decided that the front door and some of the worst classrooms had to be painted. She had few illusions about getting the bureaucracy of the Boston public school to provide painters (though she did get someone to provide paint), so she persuaded some of her family members to help her do the painting. "When school opened, students and staff members immediately saw that things were going to be different, if only symbolically. Perhaps even more important, staff members received a subtle challenge to make a contribution themselves" (Kaufer and Leader, 1987b, p. 3).

When Robert L. Hess became president of Brooklyn College in 1979, he faced a similar situation. The campus had once resembled an Ivy League oasis in the middle of Brooklyn, but years of deferred maintenance had given it a look of decay and decline. One of Hess's first priorities was to clean up the campus and repair the buildings. His reasoning was simple: "I saw as a priority the necessity of rebuilding the image of the school. It was even more important, initially, than recruiting students. The image had to precede the other efforts. The change in the image would have multiplier effects. It would make the rest easy—recruitment, building an alumni network, development. This was an action most in keeping with the myth of the place" (McDade and Gamson, 1987, p. 6).

When Lee Iacocca first became president of Chrysler, one of his first steps was to announce that he was reducing his salary from $360,000 to $1 a year. "I did it for good, cold pragmatic reasons. I wanted our employees and our suppliers to be thinking: 'I can follow a guy who sets that kind of example,'" Iacocca explained in his autobiography (Iacocca and Novak, 1984, pp. 229–230).

*Symbolic leaders frame experience.* In a world of uncertainty and ambiguity, part of the function of symbolic leadership is to provide plausible interpretations of experience. When Martin Luther King spoke at the March on Washington in 1963 and gave his extraordinary "I Have a Dream" speech, his opening line was, "I am happy to join with you today in what will go down in history as the greatest demonstration for freedom in the history of our nation."

How did he know that this was the *greatest* demonstration for freedom? There were many other ways he might have interpreted the meaning of that particular day: "We are here because progress has been slow, but we are not ready to quit yet." "We are here because nothing else has worked." "We are here because it's summer and it's a good day to be outside." Each of those interpretations is about as accurate as the next, but accuracy is not the real issue. King's assertion was bold and inspiring; it told members of the audience that they were making history by their presence at a momentous event.

There is a scene in the film *Gandhi* that shows Gandhi lying in bed, very weak after a long fast that he undertook as a symbolic gesture to oppose a major outbreak of violence between Hindus and Muslims. A Hindu man rushes into the room, obviously distraught, and tells Gandhi, "I am going to hell." Gandhi asks him why. The man replies that Muslims killed his sons, and he went out and killed a small Muslim boy in retaliation. Gandhi winces at the image of adults murdering children, but replies, "I know a way out of hell." He tells the man to find and adopt a small boy who is the size of his dead son. "Only make sure that the boy is Muslim, and that you raise him as one." To assert, "I know a way out of hell," is an extraordinary way to reframe a distraught man's sense of hopelessness and damnation. It illustrates the conviction and courage that often underpin symbolic leadership.

When Charley Gibbons became principal of the Quincy School in Boston in 1982, he introduced himself in his first meeting with the faculty by saying, "The Quincy is a special place at a special time—an enchanted cottage" (Stahl and Johnson, n.d., p. 1). Until Gibbons gave his address, the staff had tended to see the school as more rudderless than enchanted—more an urban warehouse than a cottage. Symbolic leaders recognize that every set of circumstances is open to multiple interpretations. Gibbons, like King and Gandhi, chose an interpretation that provided a constructive and hopeful way to understand what was happening at Quincy, as well as what could happen in the future.

*Symbolic leaders discover and communicate a vision.* One of the most powerful ways in which leaders can interpret experience is by discovering and communicating a vision. A vision is essentially a persuasive and hopeful image of the future that speaks both to the crises of the present and to the hopes and values of followers. Such visions are particularly important in times of crisis and uncertainty. When people are in pain, when they are confused and uncertain, or when they feel despair and hopelessness, they desperately seek meaning and hope.

Where do such visions come from? One view is that leaders must first create a vision and then persuade others to follow it (Bass, 1985; Bennis and Nanus, 1985). An alternative view is that leaders discover a vision that is already present, even if in an inchoate and unexpressed form, among their constituents (Cleveland, 1985). Kouzes and Posner (1987) put it well: "Corporate leaders know very well that what seeds the vision are those imperfectly formed images in the marketing department about what the customers really wanted and those inarticulate mumblings from the manufacturing folks about the poor product quality, not crystal ball gazing in upper levels of the corporate stratosphere. The best leaders are the best followers. They pay attention to those weak signals and quickly respond to changes in the corporate course" (p. 114).

Leadership is two-way street. No amount of charisma or rhetorical skill will enable a leader to sell a vision that reflects only the leader's values and needs. Effective symbolic leadership is possible only for leaders who understand the deepest values and most pressing concerns of their constituents. But leaders still play a critical role. They can bring a unique, personal blend of poetry, passion, conviction, and courage to the articulation of a vision. They can play a key role in distilling and shaping the vision to be pursued. Most importantly, they can choose which stories to tell as a means of communicating the vision.

*Symbolic leaders tell stories.* Often, symbolic leaders embody their vision in a story—a story about *us* and about our past, our present, and our future. "Us" could be a family, the Quincy School, the Sorbonne, the Chrysler Corporation, the people of Thailand, or whatever other audience a leader hopes to reach. The past is usually a golden one, a time of noble purposes, great deeds, heroes and heroines. The present is a time of trouble, challenge, or crisis: a critical moment when we have to make fateful choices. The future is the dream: a vision of hope and greatness, often linked directly to greatness in the past.

This is the sort of story that Mikhail Gorbachev told the Soviet people. In Gorbachev's story, the golden past was the great socialist revolution led by Lenin and the Communist party. The present is a time of crisis because that great legacy has been distorted by Stalinist and bureaucratic conservatism. The Soviet Union is in trouble, Gorbachev said, because it had forgotten its revolutionary heritage. "We need to remove the rust of bureaucratism from the values and ideals of socialism" (Taubman, 1988, p. 1), Gorbachev told Communist party leaders in early 1988. His vision was a restoration of old values through new means—*perestroika* and *glasnost.*

Just as Gorbachev offered a story about the Soviet Union, Ronald Reagan offered Americans a story about America. His golden past was the past of the frontier, of rugged, sturdy, and self-reliant men and women who built a great nation and who took care of themselves and their neighbors without the intervention of a monstrous national government. It was an America of small towns and volunteer fire departments. But America had come to a time of great crisis because "the liberals" had created a monster, a federal government that was levying oppressive taxes and eroding freedom through government regulation and bureaucracy. Reagan offered a vision: a return to American greatness by getting "government off the backs of the American people" and restoring the traditional American values of freedom and self-reliance.

The success of such stories is only partly related to their historical validity or empirical support. The central question is whether they are credible and persuasive to their audiences. A story, even a flawed story, will work if it speaks persuasively to the experience, values, and aspirations of the listeners. This is both the power and the danger of symbolic leadership. In the hands of a Gandhi or a Martin Luther King, the constructive power of stories is immense. Told by a Hitler, their destructive power is almost incalculable. In the wake of the First World War and the Great Depression, Germany in the 1930s was hungry for hope. A number of other stories might have caught the imagination of the German people, but Hitler's passion and single-mindedness brought his story to center stage and carried Europe to the catastrophe of war and holocaust.

## Summary: Integrated Leadership

Each of the frames captures significant possibilities for leadership, but each is incomplete. In the early part of the century, leadership as a concept was rarely applied to management, and the implicit models of leadership were narrowly rational. In the 1960s and 1970s, human resource leadership became fashionable. The literature on organizational leadership stressed openness, sensitivity, and participation. In recent years, symbolic leadership has moved to center stage, and the literature now offers advice on how to become a visionary leader with the power to transform organizational cultures. Organizations do need vision, but it is not their only need and not always their most important one.

In this chapter and the one before it, we have shown that each of the frames provides a powerful set of guidelines to enhance leadership effectiveness. Structural leaders can become great social architects who build an analysis of an organization's environment and its capacities into a powerful structure and strategy. Human resource leaders can become catalysts who lead through caring, support, accessibility, and empowerment. Effective political leaders are advocates who are clear about their agenda and sensitive to political reality and who build the alliances that they need to move their organization forward. Symbolic leaders are artists, poets, or prophets who use symbols and stories to communicate a vision that builds faith and loyalty among an organization's employees and other stakeholders.

Leaders need to understand their own frame and its limits. Ideally, they will also learn to combine multiple frames into a more comprehensive and powerful style. Lee Iacocca's success at Chrysler was built on an extraordinary intuitive understanding of both politics and symbols. Diana Lam brought new vitality to the Mackey School through her understanding of people, power, and symbols.

At the same time, it is unrealistic to expect every manager to be a leader for all times and seasons. Roger Smith, who was a structural leader pure and simple, often displayed a rationalist's inability to understand symbols. He was not impressed when Lee Iacocca cut his own salary to $1 a year. After all, reasoned Smith, Iacocca had stock options that eventually came to be worth millions (Lee, 1988). The fact that Smith was not gifted as a human resource or a symbolic leader was not fatal by itself. What *can* be fatal for leaders is the inability to acknowledge their own limits and to include in their organization people who possess complementary strengths. Wise leaders understand their own strengths, work to expand them, and build teams that together can provide leadership in all four modes—structural, political, human resource, and symbolic.

# 23

# Epilogue: Artistry, Choice, and Leadership

We hope that our book will inspire both inventive management and wise leadership. Managerial leaders will require high levels of personal artistry to respond to challenge, ambiguity, and paradox. They will need a sense of choice and personal freedom that lets them find new patterns and possibilities in everyday thoughts and deeds. They will need the kind of versatility in thinking that fosters flexibility in action. They will need the capacity to act inconsistently when consistency fails, diplomatically when emotions are raw, nonrationally when reason makes no sense, politically when confronted by parochial self-interests, and playfully when pursuing goals and purposes seems counterproductive.

They will face a leadership paradox: how to maintain integrity and mission without making their organizations rigid and intractable. Leading means walking the tightrope between rigidity and spinelessness. Rigidity saps energy, stifles initiative, misdirects resources, and leads ultimately to catastrophes such as the massacre in Tiananmen Square or the revolution in Romania. But, in a world of "permanent white water" (Vaill, 1989), where nothing is solid and everything is changing, it is tempting to follow familiar paths and to use the same old solutions, regardless of how much the problems have changed. Doing what we have always done is comforting. It lets us feel that our world is orderly and that we are in control. But when the old ways fail, as they eventually must, managers often make the mistake of flipping to the opposite extreme: they begin to agree to anything and everything and try to appease everyone. The result is aimlessness, anarchy, and systems so disorganized that concerted, purposeful action becomes impossible.

The best managers and leaders create and sustain a tension-filled balance between two extremes. They combine core values with elastic strategies. They get things done without being done in. They know what they stand for and what they want, and they communicate their vision with clarity and power. But they also know that they must understand and respond to the complex array of forces that push and pull organizations in so many different directions. They see the need to think creatively about how to make things happen. They develop strategies with enough elasticity to respond to the twists, turns, and potholes that they are sure to encounter on the way to the future. Elastic strategies permit and encourage learning. They may be shaped by organizational dynamics, but even as they bend, they create a tension in the direction of the pull. To give a negative example, the lack of elasticity in Roger Smith's strategy was a significant cause of GM's declining fortunes during the 1980s. GM's market share dropped every year, but Smith continued to insist that his strategy was the correct one and that success was right around the next corner.

In the late 1980s, Mikhail Gorbachev personified both sides of the dilemma. He faced enormous economic and political problems, with conservatives assailing him from the right and liberals from the left. He had to respond to threats of secession at home and the collapse of Communist regimes throughout Eastern Europe. *Time* named him Man of the Decade at the same time that critics at home and abroad were attacking him for presiding "over the collapse of the Communist bloc, the sinking of the Soviet economy, and the trashing of socialism" (Barnes, 1990, p. 43).

There was truth to both views; Gorbachev was both underrated and overrated. There is a common but misguided notion that a leader who takes risks and moves into uncharted terrain can somehow see all, know all, and control everything. Keller (1990b) comes closer to the reality: "The greatest leaders are often, in reality, skillful followers. They do not control the flow of history, but by having the good sense not to stand in its way, they seem to. So it is with Mikhail S. Gorbachev, who time and again dazzles the West by accepting reality. These days find Mr. Gorbachev busily acquiescing in the surrender of his party's monopoly, the liquidation of his armies in Eastern Europe, the reunification of Germany, and the defection of an entire republic. Mr. Gorbachev's achievement was having the vision to see the inevitable, and adopting it as his program rather than applying the repressive apparatus at his command to suppress it" (p. 1).

Leadership is always an interactive process between leaders and led. Like all great leaders, Gorbachev was *both* cause and effect of the changes in Russia and Eastern Europe. He could not have done what he did without the support and urging of a substantial "cheering section" (Fenn, 1989) that wanted what he wanted. That cheering section included many intellectuals, managers, dissident members of the Communist party, and common citizens. All believed that the old ways had failed and that new directions were essential. Gorbachev's allies were strongly opposed by other groups—including powerful party officials, old Bolsheviks, and Russian nationalists—that were passionately committed to preserving tradition and continuity. Gorbachev's task was particularly challenging because the balance of power between the liberal and conservative groups was extremely delicate and problematic.

Despite continuing predictions of his impending demise, Gorbachev showed a remarkable capacity to respond flexibly to internal and external pressures, to learn from mistakes, and to change course when necessary. As we wrote this epilogue, Gorbachev was putting increasing pressure on Lithuania to retract its claim of independence. He was walking a tightrope between authoritarian repression on the one hand and the risk of national chaos on the other. A slip from the tightrope was very possible. Even if it occurred, however, Gorbachev would still be numbered among that very small group of leaders who have had a revolutionary impact on our times. He also personifies the complexities that face leaders in the late twentieth century. These leaders need the confidence to confront tangled problems and deep divisions. They must anticipate that they will be buffeted by conflict and that they may unleash forces that they cannot fully control. They need the courage to follow uncharted paths, knowing that they will often be taken by surprise, that events will sometimes outrun them, and that the ultimate destination is only dimly foreseeable.

## Commitment to Core Beliefs

Poetry and philosophy are rarely included in managerial training, and few business schools have asked themselves whether spiritual development is central to their task. It is no wonder that managers are often viewed as chameleons who can adapt to any setting or as dispassionate maneuverers who are guided only by expediency. Analysis and agility are necessary, but they are not enough. Organizations need leaders who can provide a persuasive and durable sense of purpose and direction, rooted deeply in human values and the human spirit. Gorbachev changed courses repeatedly but continually returned to the twin values of *perestroika* and *glasnost,* the symbolic cornerstones of his vision for a more efficient, open, and democratic society.

Leaders need to be deeply reflective, actively thoughtful, and dramatically explicit about their core values and beliefs. Many of America's legendary corporate heroes—Thomas Watson, Walt Disney, Adolphus Busch, David Packard—articulated their philosophies and values in such a striking way that they still live on in the behavior and operations of their respective companies. Whether one agrees with Ronald Reagan or with Franklin Delano Roosevelt, each espoused a stable and cohesive set of values and beliefs. These in turn served as a means of formulating their visions for the direction that America should take.

## Multiframe Thinking

Commitment to both core values and elastic strategies involves a paradox. Franklin Roosevelt's image as lion and fox and Mao's reputation as tiger and monkey were not so much contradictions as signs that they could embrace paradox. They intuitively recognized the multiple dimensions of social organization and moved flexibly to implement their visions. The use of multiple frames permits leaders to see and understand more—*if* they are able to employ the different logics that accompany different frames.

Leaders fail when they take too narrow a view of the context in which they are working. Unless they can think flexibly about organizations and see them from multiple angles, they will be unable to deal with the full range of issues that they will inevitably encounter. Dwight Eisenhower's predisposition to structure and rational discourse blinded him to significant political and symbolic issues in his presidential administration. Jimmy Carter's preoccupation with details and rationality made it hard for him to marshall support for his programs or to capture the hearts of most Americans. Even FDR's multifaceted approach to the presidency—he was a superb observer of human needs, a charming persuader, a solid administrator, a political manipulator, and a master of ritual and ceremony—miscarried when he underestimated the public reaction to his plan to enlarge the Supreme Court.

Multiframe thinking is challenging and, at times, counterintuitive. To see the same organization *simultaneously* as machine, family, jungle, and theater requires the capacity to think in different ways at the same time about the same thing. Like surfers, leaders must always ride the waves of change. If they get too far ahead, they will be crushed. If they fall behind, they will become irrelevant. Success requires artistry, skill, and the ability to see organizations as organic forms in which needs, roles, power, and symbols must be combined to provide direction and shape behavior. The power to reframe will be vital to the leader of the future. The ability to see new possibilities and to create new opportunities will enable leaders to discover choice even when their options seem severely constrained and to find hope even amid fear and despair. Choice is at the heart of freedom, and freedom is essential to achieving the twin goals of commitment and flexibility.

Organizations everywhere are slowly waking to the implications of a shrinking planet and a global economy. The accelerating pace of change continues to produce grave political, economic, and social discontinuities. A world ever more dependent on its organizations now finds that their form and function are evolving too slowly to meet pressing social demands. Without wise leaders and artistic managers to help close the gap, we will continue to see misdirected resources, massive ineffectiveness, and unnecessary human pain and suffering. All these afflictions are already with us, and there is no guarantee that they will not get worse.

We see prodigious challenges for organizations of the future and for those who will guide them, yet we are still optimistic. We hope that this volume will help lay the groundwork for a new generation of managers and leaders who recognize the importance of poetry and philosophy, as well as analysis and technique, and who embrace the fundamental values of human life and the human spirit. Such leaders and managers will be playful theorists who can see organizations through a complex prism. They will be negotiators able to design elastic strategies that simultaneously shape events and adapt to changing circumstances. They will understand the importance of knowing and caring for themselves and those with whom they work. They will, in short, be architects, catalysts, advocates, and prophets and poets.

# References

Abramowitz, S., Tenenbaum, E., Deal, T. E., and Stackhouse, E. A. *High School, 1977*. Washington, D.C.: National Institute of Education, 1978.

Alderfer, C. P. *Existence, Relatedness, and Growth*. New York: Free Press, 1972.

Alderfer, C. P. "A Critique of Salancik and Pfeffer's Examination of Need-Satisfaction Theories." *Administrative Science Quarterly*, 1977a, *22*, 658–669.

Alderfer, C. P. "Organization Development." *Annual Review of Psychology*, 1977b, *28*, 197–223.

Alderfer, C. P. "Consulting to Underbounded Systems." In C. P. Alderfer and C. Cooper, *Advances in Experiential Social Processes*. Vol. 2. New York: Wiley, 1979.

Alderfer, C. P., and Smith, K. K. "Studying Intergroup Relations Embedded in Organizations." Unpublished manuscript, School of Organization and Management, Yale University, 1980.

Aldrich, H., and Pfeffer, J. "Environments of Organizations." In A. Inkeles (ed.), *Annual Review of Sociology, 1976*. Palo Alto, Calif.: Annual Reviews, Inc., 1976.

Alinsky, S. *Rules for Radicals*. New York: Vintage Books, 1971.

Allison, G. *Essence of Decision: Explaining the Cuban Missile Crisis*. Boston: Little, Brown, 1971.

Alterman, E. "Wrong on the Wall, and Most Else." *New York Times,* Nov. 12, 1989, p. E-23.

Argyris, C. *Personality and Organization.* New York: Harper & Row, 1957.

Argyris, C. *Interpersonal Competence and Organizational Effectiveness.* Homewood, Ill.: Irwin, 1962.

Argyris, C. *Integrating the Individual and the Organization.* New York: Wiley, 1964.

Argyris, C. *Intervention Theory and Method.* Reading, Mass.: Addison-Wesley, 1970.

Argyris, C. *The Applicability of Organizational Sociology.* Cambridge, England: Cambridge University Press, 1972.

Argyris, C., and Schön, D. A. *Theory in Practice: Increasing Professional Effectiveness.* San Francisco: Jossey-Bass, 1974.

Argyris, C., and Schön, D. A. *Organizational Learning: A Theory of Action Perspective.* Reading, Mass.: Addison-Wesley, 1978.

Arnold, T. W. *The Folklore of Capitalism.* New Haven, Conn.: Yale University Press, 1938.

Axelrod, R. "More Effective Choice in the Prisoner's Dilemma." *Journal of Conflict Resolution,* 1980, *24,* 379–403.

Baldridge, J. V. *Power and Conflict in the University.* New York: Wiley, 1971.

Baldridge, J. V. "Organizational Change: Institutional Sagas, External Challenges, and Internal Politics." In J. V. Baldridge and T. E. Deal (eds.), *Managing Change in Educational Organizations.* Berkeley, Calif.: McCutchan, 1975.

Baldridge, J. V., and Deal, T. E. *Managing Change in Educational Organizations.* Berkeley, Calif.: McCutchan, 1975.

Bales, F. *Personality and Interpersonal Behavior.* New York: Holt, Rinehart & Winston, 1970.

Bardach, E. *The Implementation Game: What Happens After a Bill Becomes Law.* Cambridge, Mass.: MIT Press, 1977.

Barley, S. R. "The Alignment of Technology and Structure Through Roles and Networks." *Administrative Science Quarterly,* 1990, *35,* 61–103.

Barnard, C. *Functions of the Executive.* Cambridge, Mass.: Harvard University Press, 1938.

Barnes, F. "Gorby's Demons." *New Republic,* Feb. 12, 1990, p. 43.

Barnes, L. B., and Krieger, M. P. "The Hidden Side of Organizational Leadership." *Sloan Management Review*, Fall 1986, pp. 15-25.

Barth, R. "Principals, Teachers, and School Leadership." *Phi Delta Kappan*, 1988, *69* (9), 639-642.

Bass, B. M. *Stogdill's Handbook of Leadership: A Survey of Theory and Research*. New York: Free Press, 1981.

Bass, B. M. *Leadership and Performance Beyond Expectations*. New York: Free Press, 1985.

Bateson, G. *Steps to an Ecology of Mind*. New York: Ballantine Books, 1972.

Bavelas, A., and Barrett, D. "An Experimental Approach to Organizational Communication." *Personnel*, Mar. 1951, pp. 370-371.

Beam, A. "Michael Porter vs. McGraw-Hill." *Boston Globe*, Sept. 20, 1989, p. 40.

Beckhard, R. *Organizational Development*. Reading, Mass.: Addison-Wesley, 1969.

Beer, S. "Death Is Equifinal: Eighth Annual Ludwig Von Bertalanffy Memorial Lecture." *Behavioral Science*, 1981, *26*, 185-196.

Bell, D. *The Cultural Contradictions of Capitalism*. New York: Basic Books, 1976.

Bell, T. E., and Esch, K. "The Fatal Flaw in Flight 51-L." *IEEE Spectrum*, Feb. 1987, pp. 36-51.

Bellow, G., and Moulton, B. *The Lawyering Process: Cases and Materials*. Mineola, N.Y.: Foundation Press, 1978.

Bennis, W. G. *Changing Organizations*. New York: McGraw-Hill, 1966.

Bennis, W. G. *The Leaning Ivory Tower*. San Francisco: Jossey-Bass, 1973.

Bennis, W. G., and Nanus, B. *Leaders: Strategies for Taking Charge*. New York: Harper & Row, 1985.

Bensimon, E. M. "Viewing the Presidency: Perceptual Congruence Between Presidents and Leaders on Their Campuses." Paper presented at meeting of American Educational Research Association, New Orleans, 1988.

Bensimon, E. M. "The Meaning of 'Good Presidential Leadership': A Frame Analysis." *Review of Higher Education*, 1989, *12*, 107-123.

Benson, J. K. "Organizations: A Dialectical View." *Administrative Science Quarterly,* 1977, *22,* 1-21.

Bettelheim, B. *The Uses of Enchantment.* New York: Vintage Books, 1977.

Beyer, J. M., and Trice, H. M. "A Re-Examination of the Relations Between Size and Various Components of Organizational Complexity." *Administrative Science Quarterly,* 1979, *24,* 48-64.

Bion, W. R. *Experiences in Groups.* London: Tavistock, 1961.

Birnbaum, R. *How Colleges Work: The Cybernetics of Academic Organization and Leadership.* San Francisco: Jossey-Bass, 1988.

Blake, R., and Mouton, J. S. *Building a Dynamic Corporation Through Grid Organizational Development.* Reading, Mass.: Addison-Wesley, 1969.

Blake, R., and Mouton, J. S. "A Comparative Analysis of Situationalism and 9,9 Management by Principle." *Organizational Dynamics,* Spring 1982, pp. 20-42.

Blake, R., and Mouton, J. S. *Managerial Grid III.* Houston, Tex.: Gulf, 1985.

Blanchard, K., and Johnson, S. *The One-Minute Manager.* New York: Morrow, 1982.

Blankenship, V., and Miles, R. E. "Organizational Structure and Managerial Decision Behavior." *Administrative Science Quarterly,* 1968, *13,* 106-120.

Blau, P. M., and Schoenherr, R. A. *The Structure of Organizations.* New York: Basic Books, 1971.

Blau, P. M., and Scott, W. R. *Formal Organizations: A Comparative Approach.* San Francisco: Chandler, 1962.

Block, P. *The Empowered Manager: Positive Political Skills at Work.* San Francisco: Jossey-Bass, 1987.

Blum, A. "Collective Bargaining: Ritual or Reality." *Harvard Business Review,* Nov.-Dec. 1961, *39,* 63-69.

Blumberg, P. *Industrial Democracy: The Sociology of Participation.* New York: Schocken, 1968.

Blumer, H. *Symbolic Interaction: Perspective and Method.* Englewood Cliffs, N.J.: Prentice-Hall, 1969.

Bok, S. *Lying: Moral Choice in Public and Private Life.* New York: Vintage Books, 1978.

Bolman, L. "The Client as Theorist." In J. Adams (ed.), *New Tech-*

*nologies in Organization Development.* La Jolla, Calif.: University Associates, 1975.

Bolman, L. "Leader Effectiveness in Group Dynamics Education." In C. L. Cooper (ed.), *Developing Social Skills in Managers.* London: Macmillan, 1977.

Bolman, L. "Leadership Orientations." Unpublished paper, Harvard University, 1989.

Bolman, L. G., and Deal, T. E. *Modern Approaches to Understanding and Managing Organizations.* San Francisco: Jossey-Bass, 1984.

Boulding, K. *Conflict and Defense: A General Theory.* New York: Harper & Row, 1962.

Boulding, K. E. "The Universe as a General System." *Behavioral Science,* 1977, *22,* 299–306.

Bower, J. *Managing the Response Allocation Process.* Boston: Division of Research, Harvard Business School, 1970.

Bower, J. L. "Planning Within the Firm." *The American Economic Review,* 1970, 186–194.

Bower, M. *The Will to Manage: Corporate Success Through Programmed Management.* New York: McGraw-Hill, 1966.

Bowles, S., and Gintis, H. *Schooling in Capitalist America.* London: Routledge, 1976.

Bradford, D. L., and Cohen, A. R. *Managing for Excellence.* New York: Wiley, 1984.

Bradford, L. P., Gibb, J. R., and Benne, K. D. *T-Group Theory and Laboratory Method.* New York: Wiley, 1964.

Bransford, J., Franks, J. J., Vye, N. A., and Sherwood, R. D. "New Approaches to Instruction: Because Wisdom Can't Be Told." In S. Vosniadov (ed.), *Similarity and Analogical Reasoning.* New York: Cambridge University Press, 1989.

Broudy, H. *Truth and Credibility: The Citizen's Dilemma.* New York: Longman, 1981.

Brown, J. L., and Schneck, R. "A Structural Comparison Between Canadian and American Industrial Organizations." *Administrative Science Quarterly,* 1979, *24,* 24–47.

Brown, L. D. *Managing Conflict at Organizational Interfaces.* Reading, Mass.: Addison-Wesley, 1983.

Brown, L. D. "Power Outside Organizational Paradigms: Lessons from Community Partnerships." In S. Srivastva and Associates, *Executive Power: How Executives Influence People and Organizations*. San Francisco: Jossey-Bass, 1986.

Brown, R. "Social Theory as Metaphor: On the Logic of Discovery for the Sciences of Conduct." *Theory and Society*, 1976, *3*, 169–197.

Brown, R. H. "Bureaucracy as Praxis: Toward a Political Phenomenology of Formal Organizations." *Administrative Science Quarterly*, 1978, *23*, 365–382.

Burlingame, M. "Coordination, Control, and Facilitation of Instruction Within Schools." Unpublished paper presented at School Organization and Effects Conference, San Diego, Calif., Jan. 27–29, 1978.

Burns, J. M. *Leadership*. New York: Harper & Row, 1978.

Burns, T., and Stalker, G. M. *The Management of Innovation*. London: Tavistock, 1961.

Burrell, G., and Hearn, J. "The Sexuality of Organization." In J. Hearn, D. L. Sheppard, P. Tancred-Sheriff, and G. Burrell (eds.), *The Sexuality of Organization*. London: Sage, 1989.

Campbell, J. *The Power of Myth*. New York: Doubleday, 1988.

Campbell, J. P., and Dunnette, M. D. "Effectiveness of T-Group Experiences in Managerial Training and Development." *Psychological Bulletin*, 1968, *70*, 73–104.

Caplow, T. *How to Run Any Organization*. New York: Holt, Rinehart & Winston, 1976.

Carlzon, J. *Moments of Truth*. Cambridge, Mass.: Ballinger, 1987.

Chandler, A. D., Jr. *Strategy and Market Structure*. Cambridge, Mass.: MIT Press, 1962.

Chandler, A. D., Jr. *The Visible Hand: The Managerial Revolution in American Business*. Cambridge, Mass.: Harvard University Press, 1977.

Child, J. "Organization Structure and Strategies of Control: A Replication of the Aston Study." *Administrative Science Quarterly*, 1972, *17*, 163–177.

Chin, T. "Whistle-Blower." *Life*, Mar. 1988, pp. 20–22.

Christensen, C. R., and others. *Business Policy: Text and Cases*. (6th ed.) Homewood, Ill.: Irwin, 1987.

Clark, B. R. "The Organizational Saga in Higher Education." In

J. V. Baldridge and T. E. Deal (eds.), *Managing Change in Educational Organizations.* Berkeley: McCutchan, 1975.

Clark, T. D., and Schrode, W. A. "Public-Sector Decision Structures: An Empirically-Based Description." *Public Administration Review,* 1979, *39,* 343–354.

Cleveland, H. *The Knowledge Executive: Leadership in an Information Society.* New York: Dutton, 1985.

Clifford, D. K., and Cavanagh, R. E. *The Winning Performance.* New York: Bantam Books, 1985.

Coch, L., and French, J.R.P. "Overcoming Resistance to Change." *Human Relations,* 1948, *1,* 512–533.

Cohen, E. G., Deal, T. E., Meyer, J. W., and Scott, W. R. "Technology and Teaming in the Elementary School." *Sociology of Education,* Jan. 1979, *52,* 20–33.

Cohen, M., and March, J. G. *Leadership and Ambiguity.* New York: McGraw-Hill, 1974.

Cohen, P. S. "Theories of Myth." *Man,* 1969, *4,* 337–353.

Collins, B. E., and Guetzkow, H. *A Social Psychology of Group Processes for Decision Making.* New York: Wiley, 1964.

Collinson, D. L., and Collinson, M. "Sexuality in the Workplace: The Domination of Men's Sexuality." In J. Hearn, D. L. Sheppard, P. Tancred-Sheriff, and G. Burrell (eds.), *The Sexuality of Organization.* London: Sage, 1989.

Conger, J. A. *The Charismatic Leader: Behind the Mystique of Exceptional Leadership.* San Francisco: Jossey-Bass, 1989.

Corwin, R. "Organizations as Loosely Coupled Systems: Evolution of a Perspective." Unpublished paper, Conference on Schools as Loosely Coupled Organizations, Stanford University, Nov. 1976.

Coser, L. *The Functions of Social Conflict.* New York: Free Press, 1956.

Cox, H. *The Feast of Fools.* Cambridge, Mass.: Harvard University Press, 1969.

Cyert, R. M., and March, J. G. *A Behavioral Theory of the Firm.* Englewood Cliffs, N.J.: Prentice-Hall, 1963.

Dachler, H. P., and Wilpert, B. "Conceptual Dimensions and Boundaries of Participation in Organizations: A Critical Evaluation." *Administrative Science Quarterly,* 1978, *23,* 1–19.

Dalton, M. *Men Who Manage.* New York: Wiley, 1959.

Davis, J. E. "What It's Like to Work for Frank Lorenzo." *Business Week*, May 18, 1987, pp. 76–78.

Davis, M., and others. "The Structure of Educational Systems." Unpublished paper, Conference on Schools as Loosely Coupled Organizations, Stanford University, Nov. 1976.

Deal, T. E., and Celotti, L. D. "How Much Influence Do (and Can) Educational Administrators Have on Classrooms?" *Phi Delta Kappan*, 1980, *61* (7), 471–473.

Deal, T. E., and Kennedy, A. *Corporate Cultures*. Reading, Mass.: Addison-Wesley, 1982.

Deal, T. E., and Nolan R. *Alternative Schools*. Chicago: Nelson-Hall, 1978.

Deal, T. E., and Nutt, S. C. *Promoting, Guiding, and Surviving Change in School Districts*. Cambridge, Mass.: Abt Associates, 1980.

Deal, T. E., and Peterson, K. *The Principal's Role in Shaping School Culture*. Washington, D.C.: General Printing Office, 1990.

Deal, T. E., and Ross, F. "The Effects of an Externally Directed Organizational Change Intervention on the Structure of a Small Elementary School District." Paper presented at annual meeting of the American Educational Research Association, New York, 1977.

Deutsch, M. *The Resolution of Conflict*. New Haven, Conn.: Yale University Press, 1973.

Dittmer, L. "Political Culture and Political Symbolism: Toward a Theoretical Synthesis." *World Politics*, 1977, *29* (4), 552–583.

Doody, A. F., and Bingaman, R. *Reinventing the Wheels: Ford's Spectacular Comeback*. Cambridge, Mass.: Ballinger, 1988.

Dornbusch, S., and Scott, W. R. *Evaluation and the Exercise of Authority*. San Francisco: Jossey-Bass, 1975.

Drucker, P. "Peter Drucker's 1990s: The Futures That Have Already Happened." *The Economist*, Oct. 21–27, 1989, pp. 19–20, 24.

Dumaine, B. "A Humble Hero Drives Ford to the Top." *Fortune*, Jan. 4, 1988, p. 22.

Dunlop, J. T. *Industrial Relations Systems*. Carbondale: Southern Illinois University Press, 1958.

Edelfson, C., Johnson, R., and Stromquist, N. *Participatory Plan-*

*ning in a School District.* Washington, D.C.: National Institute of Education, 1977.

Edelman, M. J. *Politics as Symbolic Interaction: Mass Arousal and Quiescence.* Orlando, Fla.: Academic Press, 1971.

Edelman, M. J. *The Symbolic Uses of Politics.* Madison: University of Wisconsin Press, 1977.

Elden, M. "Client as Consultant: Work Reform Through Participative Research." *National Productivity Review,* Spring 1983, 136–147.

Elden, M. "Sociotechnical Systems Ideas as Public Policy in Norway: Empowering Participation Through Worker-Managed Change." *Journal of Applied Behavioral Science,* 1986, *22,* 239–255.

Ellul, J. *Propaganda.* New York: Basic Books, 1965.

Elmore, R. F. "Organizational Models of Social Program Implementation." *Public Policy,* 1978, *26,* 185–228.

Enderud, H. G. "The Perception of Power." In J. G. March and J. Olsen (eds.), *Ambiguity and Choice in Organizations.* Bergen, Norway: Universitetsforlaget, 1976.

Engel, G. V. "Professional Autonomy and Bureaucratic Organization." *Administrative Science Quarterly,* 1970, *15,* 12–21.

Etzioni, A. *A Comparative Analysis of Complex Organizations.* New York: Free Press, 1961.

Farnham, A. "Migratory Habits of the 500." *Fortune,* Apr. 24, 1989, p. 400.

Fayol, H. *General and Industrial Management.* (C. Stours, trans.) London: Pitman, 1949. (Originally published 1919.)

Fenn, D. H. "How Government Works: Inside the Black Box." Lecture, Institute for Educational Management, Cambridge, Mass., July 1989.

Fernandez, J. W. *Persuasion and Performances: The Play of Tropes in Culture.* Bloomington: Indiana University Press, 1986.

Fiedler, F. E. *A Theory of Leadership Effectiveness.* New York: McGraw-Hill, 1967.

Fiedler, F. E., and Chemers, M. *Leadership and Effective Management.* Glenview, Ill.: Scott, Foresman, 1974.

Firestone, W. A. "Butte-Angels Camp: Conflict and Transformation." In R. Herriot and N. Gross (eds.), *The Dynamics of*

*Planned Educational Change.* Berkeley, Calif.: McCutchan, 1977.

Fisher, R., and Ury, W. *Getting to Yes.* Boston: Houghton Mifflin, 1981.

Fleishman, E. A., and Harris, E. F. "Patterns of Leadership Behavior Related to Employee Grievances and Turnover." *Personnel Psychology,* 1962, *15,* 43–56.

Floden, R. E., and Weiner, S. S. "Rationality to Ritual." *Policy Sciences,* 1978, *9,* 9–18.

French, J.R.P., and Raven, B. H. "The Bases of Social Power." In D. Cartwright (ed.), *Studies in Social Power.* Ann Arbor, Mich.: Institute for Social Research, 1959.

French, W., and Bell, C. *Organization Development.* Englewood Cliffs, N.J.: Prentice-Hall, 1973.

French, W., and Bell, C. *Organization Development.* (2nd ed.) Englewood Cliffs, N.J.: Prentice-Hall, 1978.

Freud, S. *On Dreams.* New York: Norton, 1952.

Friedlander, F., and Brown, L. D. "Organization Development." *Annual Review of Psychology,* 1974, *25,* 313–341.

Frost, P. J. *Organizational Culture.* Beverly Hills, Calif.: Sage, 1985.

Frost, P. J. "Power, Politics, and Influence." In L. W. Porter and others (eds.), *The Handbook of Organizational Communication.* Beverly Hills, Calif.: Sage, 1986.

Frost, P. J., Mitchell, V. F., and Nord, W. R. *Organizational Reality: Reports from the Firing Line.* Glenview, Ill.: Scott, Foresman, 1986.

Fullan, M., Miles, M., and Taylor, G. *Organization Development in Schools: The State of the Art.* Washington, D.C.: National Institute of Education, 1981.

Galbraith, J. *Designing Complex Organizations.* Reading, Mass.: Addison-Wesley, 1973.

Galbraith, J. *Organization Design.* Reading, Mass.: Addison-Wesley, 1977.

Gamson, W. A. "A Theory of Coalition Formation." *American Sociological Review,* 1961, *26,* 373–382.

Gamson, W. A. *Power and Discontent.* Homewood, Ill.: Dorsey Press, 1968.

Gardner, J. W. *Handbook of Strategic Planning.* New York: Wiley, 1986.

Gardner, J. W. *The Moral Aspects of Leadership.* Washington, D.C.: Independent Sector, 1987.

Gardner, J. W. *On Leadership.* New York: Free Press, 1989.

Gaventa, J. *Power and Powerlessness: Quiescence and Rebellion in an Appalachian Valley.* Urbana: University of Illinois Press, 1980.

Gephart, R. P. "Status Degradation and Organizational Succession: An Ethnomethodological Approach." *Administrative Science Quarterly,* 1978, *23,* 553–581.

Gibb, J. R. "A Research Perspective on the Laboratory Method." In K. D. Benne, L. P. Bradford, J. R. Gibb, and R. O. Lippitt (eds.), *The Laboratory Method of Changing and Learning.* Palo Alto, Calif.: Science and Behavior Books, 1975.

Glanzer, M., and Glaser, R. "Techniques for the Study of Group Structure and Behavior: Empirical Studies of the Effects of Structure in Small Groups." *Psychological Bulletin,* 1961, *58* (1), 1–27.

Goffman, E. *The Presentation of Self in Everyday Life.* New York: Doubleday, 1959.

Goffman, E. *Frame Analysis.* Cambridge, Mass.: Harvard University Press, 1974.

Goodman, D. "Doctor Fights Order to Quit Maine Island." *Boston Globe,* Oct. 15, 1983, pp. 1, 8.

Gouldner, A. "Metaphysical Pathos and the Theory of Bureaucracy." *American Political Science Review,* 1955, *49,* 496–507.

Gouldner, A. W. "Organizational Analysis." In R. K. Merton, L. Broom, and L. S. Cottrell, Jr. (eds.), *Sociology Today.* New York: Basic Books, 1959.

Graeff, C. L. "The Situational Leadership Theory: A Critical View." *Academy of Management Review,* Apr. 1983, pp. 321–338.

Greenleaf, R. K. "The Servant as Leader." Newton Center, Mass.: Robert K. Greenleaf Center, 1973.

Gulick, L., and Urwick, L. (eds.). *Papers on the Science of Administration.* New York: Institute of Public Administration, Columbia University, 1937.

Hackman, J. R., and Morris, C. "Group Tasks, Group Interaction

Process, and Group Performance Effectiveness: A Review and Proposed Integration." Technical Report no. 7. New Haven, Conn.: School of Organization and Management, Yale University, 1974.

Hackman, J. R., and Oldham, G. R. *Work Redesign*. Reading, Mass.: Addison-Wesley, 1980.

Hackman, J. R., Oldham, G. R., Janson, R., and Purdy, K. "A New Strategy for Job Enrichment." In L. E. Boone and D. D. Bowen (eds.), *The Great Writings in Management and Organizational Behavior*. New York: Random House, 1987.

Hall, D. T. *Careers in Organizations*. Pacific Palisades, Calif.: Goodyear, 1976.

Hall, R. H. "The Concept of Bureaucracy: An Empirical Assessment." *American Journal of Sociology*, 1963, *49*, 32–40.

Hall, R. H. *Organizations: Structures, Processes, and Outcomes*. (4th ed.) Englewood Cliffs, N.J.: Prentice-Hall, 1987.

Hall, R. H., Haas, J. E., and Johnson, N. J. "An Examination of the Blau-Scott and Etzioni Typologies." *Administrative Science Quarterly*, 1967, *12*, 118–139.

Hambleton, R. K., and Gumpert, R. "The Validity of Hersey and Blanchard's Theory of Leader Effectiveness." *Group and Organization Studies*, June 1982, pp. 225–242.

Hamburger, H. *Games as Models of Social Phenomena*. New York: W. H. Freeman, 1979.

Hampton, W. J., and Norman, J. R. "General Motors: What Went Wrong. Eight Years and Billions of Dollars Haven't Made Its Strategy Succeed." *Business Week*, Mar. 16, 1987, p. 102.

Hannan, M. T., and Freeman, J. "The Population Ecology of Organizations." *American Journal of Sociology*, 1977, *82*, 929–966.

Hannan, M. T., and Freeman, J. *Organizational Ecology*. Cambridge, Mass.: Harvard University Press, 1989.

Hansot, E. "Some Functions of Humor in Organizations." Unpublished paper, Kenyon College, 1979.

Harragan, B. L. *Games Mother Never Taught You: Corporate Gamesmanship for Women*. New York: Rawson, Wade, 1977.

Hedberg, B.L.T., Nystrom, P. C., and Starbuck, W. H. "Camping on Seesaws: Prescriptions for a Self-Designing Organization." *Administrative Science Quarterly*, 1976, 41–65.

Heffron, F. *Organization Theory and Public Organizations: The Political Connection.* Englewood Cliffs, N.J.: Prentice-Hall, 1989.

Henderson, R. M., and Clark, K. B. "Architectural Innovation: The Reconfiguration of Existing Product Technologies and the Failure of Established Firms." *Administrative Science Quarterly,* 1990, *35,* 9–30.

Hersch, S. M. *The Target Is Destroyed: What Really Happened to Flight 007 and What America Knew About It.* New York: Random House, 1986.

Hersey, P. *The Situational Leader.* New York: Warner Books, 1984.

Hersey, P., and Blanchard, K. H. *The Management of Organizational Behavior.* (3rd. ed.) Englewood Cliffs, N.J.: Prentice-Hall, 1977.

Herzberg, F. *Work and the Nature of Man.* Cleveland, Ohio: World, 1966.

Hirschman, A. O. *Exit, Voice, and Loyalty.* Cambridge, Mass.: Harvard University Press, 1970.

Hoffman, M. S. *The World Almanac and Book of Facts.* New York: Pharos, 1988.

Hollander, E. P. *Leadership Dynamics.* New York: Free Press, 1978.

Holusha, J. "No Utopia, but to Workers, It's a Job." *New York Times,* Jan. 29, 1989, sec. 3, p. 1.

Honsot, E. "Some Functions of Humor in Organizations." Unpublished paper, Kenyon College, 1979.

Hoskins, G. *The Awakening of the Soviet Union.* Cambridge, Mass.: Harvard University Press, 1990.

House, R. J. "The Path-Goal Theory of Effectiveness." *Administrative Science Quarterly,* 1971, *16,* 321–338.

Iacocca, L., and Novak, W. *Iacocca.* New York: Bantam Books, 1984.

Jackall, R. *Moral Mazes: The World of Corporate Managers.* New York: Oxford University Press, 1988.

Jacobson, L., and Rosenthal, R. *Pygmalion in the Classroom: Teacher Expectation and Pupils' Intellectual Development.* New York: Holt, Rinehart & Winston, 1968.

Jenkins, D. *Job Power: Blue and White Collar Democracy.* New York: Doubleday, 1973.

Johnson, S. M. "Merit Pay for Teachers: A Poor Prescription for Reform." *Harvard Educational Review*, 1984, *54*, 175–185.

Jung, C., and others. *Man and His Symbols*. New York: Doubleday, 1964.

Kahn, R. L., and others. *Organizational Stress*. New York: Wiley, 1964.

Kamens, D. H. "Legitimating Myths and Education Organizations—Relationship Between Organizational Ideology and Formal Structure." *American Sociological Review*, 1977, *42*, 208–219.

Kanter, J. *Management-Oriented Management Information Systems*. Englewood Cliffs, N.J.: Prentice-Hall, 1977.

Kanter, R. *Men and Women of the Corporation*. New York: Basic Books, 1977.

Kanter, R. *The Change Masters: Innovations for Productivity in the American Corporation*. New York: Simon & Schuster, 1983.

Katz, D., and Kahn, R. L. *The Social Psychology of Organizations*. New York: Wiley, 1966.

Katz, D., and Kahn, R. L. *The Social Psychology of Organizations*. (2nd ed.) New York: Wiley, 1978.

Katzell, R. A., and Yankelovich, D. *Work, Productivity, and Job Satisfaction*. New York: Psychological Corporation, 1975.

Kaufer, N., and Leader, G. C. "Diana Lam (A)." Boston University, 1987a.

Kaufer, N., and Leader, G. C. "Diana Lam (B)." Boston University, 1987b.

Keeley, M. "Organizational Analogy: A Comparison of Organismic and Social Contract Models." *Administrative Science Quarterly*, 1980, *25*, 337–362.

Keidel, R. W. "Baseball, Football, and Basketball: Models for Business." *Organizational Dynamics*, Winter 1984, pp. 5–18.

Keidel, R. W. *Game Plans, Sports Strategies for Business*. New York: Berkley Book, 1987.

Keidel, R. W. *Corporate Players: Designs for Working and Winning Together*. New York: Wiley, 1988.

Keller, B. "Of Famous Arches, Beeg Meks, and Rubles." *New York Times*, Jan. 28, 1990a, pp. 1, 12.

Keller, B. "While Gorbachev Gives In, the World Marvels at His Power." *New York Times,* Feb. 11, 1990b, p. 4-1.

Kidder, T. *The Soul of a New Machine.* Boston: Little, Brown, 1981.

Kohlberg, L. "The Claim to Moral Adequacy of a Highest Stage of Moral Judgment." *Journal of Philosophy,* 1973, *70,* 630-646.

Kopelman, R. E. "Job Redesign and Productivity: A Review of the Evidence." *National Productivity Review,* 1985, *4* (3), 237-255.

Kotter, J. P. *The General Managers.* New York: Free Press, 1982.

Kotter, J. P. *Power and Influence: Beyond Formal Authority.* New York: Free Press, 1985.

Kotter, J. P. *The Leadership Factor.* New York: Free Press, 1988.

Kouzes, J. M., and Posner, B. Z. *The Leadership Challenge: How to Get Extraordinary Things Done in Organizations.* San Francisco: Jossey-Bass, 1987.

Kristoff, N. "China Update: How the Hardliners Won." *New York Times Magazine,* Nov. 12, 1989, pp. 38-71.

Landau, M., and Stout, R., Jr. "To Manage Is Not to Control: Of the Folly of Type II Errors." *Public Administration Review,* 1979, *39,* 148-156.

Lawler, E. E., III. *High-Involvement Management: Participative Strategies for Improving Organizational Performance.* San Francisco: Jossey-Bass, 1986.

Lawrence, A. T., and Weckler, D. A. "Can NUMMI's Team Concept Work for You? Part I: A Bicultural Experiment." *Northern California Executive Review,* Spring 1990, pp. 12-17.

Lawrence, P., and Lorsch, J. *Organization and Environment.* Boston: Division of Research, Harvard Business School, 1967.

Lax, D. A., and Sebenius, J. K. *The Manager as Negotiator.* New York: Free Press, 1986.

Leavitt, H. J. "Some Effects of Certain Communication Patterns on Group Performance." *Journal of Abnormal and Social Psychology,* 1951, *46,* 38-50.

Leavitt, H. J. *Managerial Psychology.* (4th ed.) Chicago: University of Chicago Press, 1978.

Lee, A. *Call Me Roger.* Chicago: Contemporary Books, 1988.

Leifer, R., and Huber, G. P. "Relations Among Perceived Environmental Uncertainty, Organization Structure, and Boundary-

Spanning Behavior." *Administrative Science Quarterly*, 1977, *22*, 235–247.

Leitch, J. *Man-to-Man: The Story of Industrial Democracy*. New York: Forbes, 1919.

Lepawsky, A. *Administration: The Art and Science of Organization and Management*. New York: Knopf, 1955.

Levinson, H. *The Exceptional Executive*. Cambridge Mass.: Harvard University Press, 1968.

Levinson, H., and Rosenthal, S. *CEO: Corporate Leadership in Action*. New York: Basic Books, 1984.

Lewin, K., Lippitt, R., and White, R. "Patterns of Aggressive Behavior in Experimentally Created Social Climates." *Journal of Social Psychology*, 1939, *10*, 271–299.

Lichtman, C. M., and Hunt, R. G. "Personality and Organization Theory: A Review of Some Conceptual Literature." *Psychological Bulletin*, 1971, *76*, 271–294.

Lieberman, M. A., Yalom, I. D., and Miles, M. B. *Encounter Groups: First Facts*. New York: Basic Books, 1973.

Lifson, T., and Takagi, H. *Mitsubishi Corporation: Organizational Overview*. Boston: HBS Case Services, 1981.

Likert, R. *New Patterns of Management*. New York: McGraw-Hill, 1961.

Likert, R. *The Human Organization*. New York: McGraw-Hill, 1967.

Lipsky, M. *Street-Level Bureaucracy*. New York: Russell Sage Foundation, 1980.

Lohr, S. "Mix of Vodka and Gorbachev Revives Old Soviet Industry." *New York Times*, July 23, 1989, p. 1.

Love, J. F. *McDonald's: Behind the Arches*. New York: Bantam Books, 1986.

Lukes, S. *Power: A Radical View*. New York: Macmillan, 1974.

Lynn, L. E., Jr. *Managing Public Policy*. Boston: Little, Brown, 1987.

McCaskey, M. B. *The Executive Challenge: Managing Change and Ambiguity*. Marshfield, Mass.: Pitman, 1982.

McClelland, D. C. *Power: The Inner Experience*. New York: Irvington, 1975.

Maccoby, E. E., and Jacklin, C. N. *The Psychology of Sex Differences*. Stanford, Calif.: Stanford University Press, 1974.

Maccoby, M. *The Leader*. New York: Ballantine Books, 1981.

McConnell, M. *Challenger: A Major Malfunction*. New York: Doubleday, 1987.

McDade, S., and Gamson, Z. "Brooklyn College (A)." Cambridge, Mass.: Institute for Educational Management, 1987.

McGregor, D. *The Human Side of Enterprise*. New York: McGraw-Hill, 1960.

Machan, D. "DEC's Democracy." *Forbes*, Mar. 23, 1987, pp. 154, 156.

Machiavelli, N. *The Prince*. New York: Penguin, 1961. (Originally published 1514.)

McKelvey, W., and Aldrich, H. "Populations, Natural Selection, and Applied Organizational Science." *Administrative Science Quarterly*, 1983, *28*, 115.

McLennan, R. *Managing Organizational Change*. Englewood Cliffs, N.J.: Prentice-Hall, 1989.

McManus, M. L. "Two Worlds of Organization Development: Contrasting East-West Organizational Intervention." Paper presented at First International Conference on International Organization Development, Toronto, 1978.

McNeil, K. "Understanding Organizational Power: Building on the Weberian Legacy." *Administrative Science Quarterly*, 1978, *23*, 65-90.

Maier, N. "Assets and Liabilities in Group Problem Solving." *Psychological Review*, 1967, *74*, 239-249.

Mangham, I. L. *Interactions and Interventions in Organizations*. New York: Wiley, 1978.

Mangham, I. L., and Overington, M. A. *Organizations as Theatre: A Social Psychology of Dramatic Appearances*. New York: Wiley, 1987.

Manning, P. *Police Work: The Social Organization of Policing*. Cambridge, Mass: MIT Press, 1979.

March, J. G. "The Technology of Foolishness." In J. G. March and J. Olsen (eds.), *Ambiguity and Choice in Organizations*. Bergen, Norway: Universitetsforlaget, 1976.

March, J. G., and Olsen, J. *Ambiguity and Choice in Organizations*. Bergen, Norway: Universitetsforlaget, 1976.

March, J. G., and Simon, H. *Organizations*. New York: Wiley, 1958.

Marrow, A. J., Bowers, D. G., and Seashore, S. E. *Management by Participation*. New York: Harper & Row, 1967.

Marshall, M. V. "An Introduction to the Marketing Concept of Managing an Institution's Future." Cambridge, Mass.: Institute for Educational Management, 1984.

Martinez, L. P. "Principal as Artist: A Model for Transforming a School Community." Unpublished dissertation, December 1989.

Marx, R., Stubbart, C., Traub, V., and Cavanaugh, M. "The NASA Space Shuttle Disaster: A Case Study." *Journal of Management Case Studies*, 1987, *3*, 300–318.

Maslow, A. H. *Motivation and Personality*. New York: Harper & Row, 1954.

Mason, R., and Mitroff, I. *Challenging Strategic Planning Assumptions*. New York: Wiley, 1981.

Medvedev, Z. A. *Gorbachev*. New York: Norton, 1986.

Mercer, J. L., and Koester, E. H. *Public Management Systems*. New York: AMACOM, 1978.

Meyer, J., and Rowan, B. "Institutionalized Organizations: Formal Structure as Myth and Ceremony." *American Journal of Sociology*, 1977, *30*, 431–450.

Meyer, J., and Rowan, B. "The Structure of Educational Organizations." In M. W. Meyer and Associates, *Environments and Organizations: Theoretical and Empirical Perspectives*. San Francisco: Jossey-Bass, 1978.

Meyer, J., Scott, W. R., and Deal, T. E. "Institutional and Technical Sources of Organizational Structure: Explaining the Structure of Educational Organizations." In H. Steen (ed.), *Organization and Human Services: Cross-Disciplinary Perspectives*. Philadelphia: Temple University Press, 1981.

Meyer, M. "Two Authority Structures of Bureaucratic Organization." *Administrative Science Quarterly*, 1968, *13*, 211–228.

Miller, D., and Friesen, P. H. *Organizations: A Quantum View*. Englewood Cliffs, N.J.: Prentice-Hall, 1984.

Miller, J. G. *Living Systems*. New York: McGraw-Hill, 1978.

Mintzberg, H. *The Nature of Managerial Work.* New York: Harper & Row, 1973.

Mintzberg, H. *The Structuring of Organizations.* Englewood Cliffs, N.J.: Prentice-Hall, 1979.

Mintzberg, H. *Power in and Around Organizations.* Englewood Cliffs, N.J.: Prentice-Hall, 1983.

Mirvis, P. H. "Organization Development: Part I—An Evolutionary Perspective." *Research in Organizational Change and Development,* 1988, *2,* 1–57.

Mitroff, I. I. *Stakeholders of the Organizational Mind: Toward a New View of Organizational Policy Making.* San Francisco: Jossey-Bass, 1983.

Mitroff, I. I., and Kilmann, R. H. "Stories Managers Tell: A New Tool for Organizational Problem Solving." *Management Review,* 1975, *64* (7), 18–28.

Moeller, J. "Bureaucracy and Teachers, Sense of Power." In N. R. Bell and H. R. Stub (eds.), *Sociology of Education.* Homewood, Ill.: Dorsey Press, 1968.

Money, J., and Ehrhardt, A. A. *Man and Woman, Boy and Girl.* Baltimore, Md.: Johns Hopkins University Press, 1972.

Moore, S. F., and Meyerhoff, B. G. *Secular Ritual.* Assen, The Netherlands: Van Goerum, 1977.

Morgan, G. "Paradigms, Metaphors, and Puzzle Solving in Organization Theory." *Administrative Science Quarterly,* 1980, *25,* 605–622.

Morgan, G. *Images of Organization.* Beverly Hills, Calif.: Sage, 1986.

Morgan, G. *Riding the Waves of Change: Developing Managerial Competencies for a Turbulent World.* San Francisco: Jossey-Bass, 1988.

Morganthau, T. "Saying 'No' to New Coke." *Newsweek,* 1985, *105* (25), 32–33.

Morrow, A. A., and Thayer, F. C. "Collaborative Work Settings: New Titles, Old Contradictions." *Journal of Applied Behavioral Science,* 1977, *13,* 448–457.

"The Multinational, Eastern Style." *The Economist,* June 24, 1989, pp. 63–64.

Murphy, J. T. *Managing Matters: Reflections from Practice.* Monograph. Cambridge, Mass.: Graduate School of Education, Harvard University, 1985.

Murphy, J. T. "The Unheroic Side of Leadership: Notes from the Swamp." *Phi Delta Kappan*, 1988, *69* (9), 654-659.

Myers, I. *Introduction to Type*. Palo Alto, Calif.: Consulting Psychologists Press, 1980.

Nord, W. R. "The Failure of Current Applied Behavioral Science—A Marxian Perspective." *Journal of Applied Behavioral Science*, 1974, *10*, 557-569.

Nussbaum, B., and Dobrzynski, J. H. "The Battle for Corporate Control." *Business Week*, May 18, 1987, pp. 102-109.

O'Connell, S. "Sayings of Chairman Ken." Unpublished paper submitted to Symbolism in Organizations Course, Graduate School of Education, Harvard University, 1983.

Oliver, T. *The Real Coke, the Real Story*. New York: Random House, 1986.

Olsen, J. "The Process of Interpreting Organizational History." In J. G. March and J. Olsen (eds.), *Ambiguity and Choice in Organizations*. Bergen, Norway: Universitetsforlaget, 1976a.

Olsen, J. "Reorganization as a Garbage Can." In J. G. March and J. Olsen (eds.), *Ambiguity and Choice in Organizations*. Bergen, Norway: Universitetsforlaget, 1976b.

"On a Clear Day You Can Still See General Motors." *The Economist*, Dec. 2, 1989, pp. 77-78, 80.

Ong, W. "'Latin Language Study as a Rennaissance Puberty Rite." In G. Spindler (ed.), *Education and Culture*. New York: Holt, Rinehart & Winston, 1963.

Ortner, S. "On Key Symbols." *American Anthropologist*, 1973, *75*, 1338-1346.

Ortony, A. *Metaphor and Thought*. Cambridge, Mass.: Cambridge University Press, 1979.

O'Toole, P. *Corporate Messiah: The Hiring and Firing of Million-Dollar Managers*. New York: Morrow, 1984.

Ouchi, W. G. *Theory Z*. Reading, Mass.: Addison-Wesley, 1981.

Owen, H. *Spirit: Transformation and Development in Organizations*. Maryland: Abbott, 1987.

Parenti, M. *Democracy for the Few*. New York: St. Martin's Press, 1977.

Parsons, T. *Structure and Process in Modern Societies.* New York: Free Press, 1960.

Pascale, R., and Athos, A. *The Art of Japanese Management.* New York: Simon & Schuster, 1981.

Paterson, T. T. *Management Theory.* New York: Business Publications, 1969.

Perrow, C. *Organizational Analysis: A Structural View.* Pacific Grove, Calif.: Brooks/Cole, 1970.

Perrow, C. *Complex Organizations: A Critical Essay.* Glenview, Ill.: Scott, Foresman, 1972.

Perrow, C. *Complex Organizations: A Critical Essay.* (2nd ed.) Glenview, Ill.: Scott, Foresman, 1979.

Perrow, C. *Complex Organizations: A Critical Essay.* (3rd ed.) New York: Random House, 1986.

Peters, T. J., and Austin, N. *A Passion for Excellence.* New York: Random House, 1985.

Peters, T. J., and Waterman, R. H. *In Search of Excellence.* New York: Harper & Row, 1982.

Pettigrew, A. M. *The Politics of Organizational Decision Making.* London: Tavistock, 1973.

Pfeffer, J. *Organizational Design.* Arlington Heights, Ill.: AHM, 1978.

Pfeffer, J., and Salancik, G. *The External Control of Organizations: A Resource Dependence Perspective.* New York: Harper & Row, 1978.

Pinder, C. C., and Moore, L. F. "The Resurrection of Taxonomy to Aid the Development of Middle-Range Theories of Organizational Behavior." *Administrative Science Quarterly,* 1979, *24*, 99–118.

Pondy, L. R., and Mitroff, I. "Beyond Open Systems Models of Organization." In B. M. Staw (ed.), *Research in Organizational Behavior.* Greenwich, Conn.: JAI Press, 1979.

Porter, E. "Notes for Looking for Leadership Conference." Paper presented at Looking for Leadership Conference, Graduate School of Education, Harvard University, Dec. 1989.

Porter, L. W., and Lawler, E. E. *Managerial Attitudes and Performance.* Homewood, Ill.: Irwin, 1968.

Pressman, J. L., and Wildavsky, A. B. *Implementation.* Berkeley: University of California Press, 1973.

Pugh, D. S., Hickson, D. J., and Hinings, C. R. "An Empirical Taxonomy of the Structure of Work Organizations." *Administrative Science Quarterly,* 1969, *14,* 115–125.

Pugh, D. S., Hickson, D. J., Hinings, C. R., and Turner, C. "Dimensions of Organizational Structure." *Administrative Science Quarterly,* 1968, *13,* 65–105.

Pümpin, C. B. *The Essence of Corporate Strategy.* Brookfield, Vt.: Gower, 1987.

Radin, C. A. "New Haven Blues: Yale President's Colors Not True to Tradition." *Boston Globe,* Apr. 23, 1989.

Rallis, S. "Different Views of Knowledge Use by Practitioners." Unpublished qualifying paper, Graduate School of Education, Harvard University, 1980.

Ranson, S., Hinings, B., and Greenwood, R. "The Structuring of Organizational Structures." *Administrative Science Quarterly,* 1980, *25,* 1–17.

Reddin, W. J. *Managerial Effectiveness.* New York: McGraw-Hill, 1970.

Rice, A. K. *Productivity and Social Organization: The Ahmedabad Experiment.* London: Tavistock, 1958.

Rice, A. K. *The Enterprise and Its Environment.* London: Tavistock, 1963.

Ridout, C. F., and Fenn, D. H. "Job Corps." Boston: HBS Case Services, 1974.

Ritti, R. R., and Funkhouser, G. R. *The Ropes to Skip and the Ropes to Know.* Columbus, Ohio: Grid, 1979.

Ritti, R. R., and Funkhouser, G. R. *The Ropes to Skip and the Ropes to Know.* (2nd. ed.) Columbus, Ohio: Grid, 1982.

Rosenthal, R., and Jacobson, L. *Pygmalion in the Classroom: Teacher Expectations and Pupils' Intellectual Development.* New York: Holt, Rinehart & Winston, 1968.

Ross, F., and Deal, T. E. "The Effects of an Externally Directed Change Intervention on the Structure of a Small Elementary School District." Unpublished paper, American Educational Research Association, Apr. 1977.

Rossiter, C. *1787: The Grand Convention*. New York: New American Library, 1966.

Rubin, J. Z., and Brown, B. R. *The Social Psychology of Bargaining and Negotiation*. San Diego, Calif.: Academic Press, 1975.

Salancik, G. R., and Pfeffer, J. "An Examination of Need-Satisfaction Models of Job Attitudes." *Administrative Science Quarterly*, 1977, *22*, 427–456.

Salancik, G. R., and Pfeffer, J. "A Social Information Processing Approach to Job Attitudes and Task Design." *Administrative Science Quarterly*, 1978, *23*, 224–253.

Sapolsky, H. *The Polaris System Development*. Cambridge, Mass.: Harvard University Press, 1972.

Sayles, L. R. "Matrix Organizations: The Structure with a Future." *Organizational Dynamics*, Autumn 1976, pp. 2–17.

Schein, E. H. *Process Consultation*. Reading, Mass.: Addison-Wesley, 1969.

Schein, E. H. *Career Dynamics: Matching Individual and Organizational Needs*. Reading, Mass.: Addison-Wesley, 1978.

Schein, E. H. *Organizational Culture and Leadership: A Dynamic View*. San Francisco: Jossey-Bass, 1985.

Schelling, T. *The Strategy of Conflict*. Cambridge, Mass.: Harvard University Press, 1960.

Schlesinger, J. M. "NUMMI Keeps Promise of No Layoffs by Setting Nonproduction Workdays." *Wall Street Journal*, Oct. 29, 1987, p. 30.

Schneider, B., and Alderfer, C. "Three Studies of Measures of Need Satisfaction in Organizations." *Administrative Science Quarterly*, 1973, *18*, 498–505.

Schwartz, H. S. "The Clockwork or the Snakepit: An Essay on the Meaning of Teaching Organizational Behavior." *Organizational Behavior Teaching Review*, 1986, *11*, 19–26.

Scott, W. G., and Mitchell, T. R. *Organization Theory: A Structural and Behavioral Analysis*. Homewood, Ill.: Irwin, 1972.

Scott, W. R. *Organizations: Rational, Natural, and Open Systems*. Englewood Cliffs, N.J.: Prentice-Hall, 1981.

Seeger, J. A., Lorsch, J. W., and Gibson, C. F. "First National City Bank Operating Group (A) and (B)." Boston: HBS Case Services, 1975.

Selznick, P. *TVA and the Grass Roots.* Berkeley: University of California Press, 1949.

Selznick, P. *Leadership and Administration.* New York: Harper & Row, 1957.

Selznick, P. *Law, Society, and Industrial Justice.* New York: Russell Sage Foundation, 1969.

Sennett, R. *Authority.* New York: Knopf, 1980.

Silverman, D. *The Theory of Organizations.* New York: Basic Books, 1971.

Simon, H. A. *Administrative Behavior.* New York: Macmillan, 1947.

Simon, H. A. *Administrative Behavior.* (2nd ed.) New York: Free Press, 1957.

Simon, H. A. *The New Science of Management Decisions.* New York: Harper & Row, 1960.

Simon, H. A. *The Sciences of the Artificial.* Cambridge, Mass.: MIT Press, 1969.

Simon, R. "The Fabric of Our Lives." *The Family Therapy Networker,* July-Aug. 1989, pp. 30-33.

Sloan, A. P., Jr. *My Years with General Motors.* New York: Macfadden, 1965.

Smale, A. "Yugoslavia's Chaotic Finances." *Boston Globe,* Oct. 18, 1987, p. 103.

Smith, H. *The Power Game.* New York: Random House, 1988.

Smith, R. "It's No Fun Running No. 1 When You're Taking the Heat." *Fortune,* Aug. 3, 1987, pp. 26-27.

Soderlind, R. "Polish Leader Calls for Unity." *Boston Globe,* Sept. 10, 1980, p. 1.

Spady, W. "The Authority System of the School and Student Unrest." In G. W. Gordon (ed.), *Uses of the Sociology of Education.* Chicago: National Society for the Study of Education, 1974.

Stahl, E., and Johnson, S. M. "The Josiah Quincy School." Graduate School of Education, Harvard University, n.d.

Stogdill, R. *Handbook of Leadership.* New York: Free Press, 1974.

Tannenbaum, R., and Schmidt, H. W. "How to Choose a Leadership Pattern." *Harvard Business Review,* 1958, *36* (2), 95-101.

Taylor, F. W. *The Principles of Scientific Management.* New York: Harper & Row, 1911.

Terry, R. *Leadership: A Preview of a Seventh View.* Humphrey Institute of Public Affairs, University of Minnesota, 1986.

Thompson, J. D. *Organizations in Action.* New York: McGraw-Hill, 1967.

Thorsrud, E. "Democracy at Work: Norwegian Experiences with Nonbureaucratic Forms of Organization." *Journal of Applied Behavioral Science,* 1977, *13,* 410–421.

Thorsrud, E. "The Scandinavian Model: Strategies of Organizational Democratization in Norway." In B. Wilpert and A. Sorge (eds.), *International Perspectives on Organizational Democracy.* New York: Wiley, 1984.

Tomkins, S. S. *Affect, Imagery, Consciousness.* New York: Springer, 1962.

Topoff, H. R. "The Social Behavior of Army Ants." *Scientific American,* Nov. 1972, pp. 71–79.

Tregoe, B. B., and Zimmerman, J. W. *Top Management Strategy.* New York: Simon & Schuster, 1980.

Trice, H. M., Belasco, J., and Alutto, J. A. "The Role of Ceremonials in Organizational Behavior." *Industrial and Labor Relations Review,* 1969, *23,* 40–51.

Trist, E. L., and Bamforth, K. L. "Some Social and Psychological Consequences of the Long-Wall Method of Coal-Getting." *Human Relations,* 1951, *4,* 3–38.

Trost, Admiral A. H. "Leadership Is Flesh and Blood." In L. Atwater and R. Penn, *Military Leadership: Traditions and Future Trends.* Annapolis, Md.: Action Printing and Graphics, 1989.

Tushman, M. L. "Special Boundary Roles in the Innovation Process." *Administrative Science Quarterly,* 1977, *22,* 587–605.

Udy, S. H. "Administrative Rationality, Social Setting, and Organizational Development." *American Journal of Sociology,* 1962, *68,* 299–308.

Umanzio, P. "The Demise of the Joint Labor-Management Council." Unpublished analytic paper, Graduate School of Education, Harvard University, 1980.

Urwick, L. "Organization as a Technical Problem." In L. H. Gulick (ed.), *Papers on the Science of Administration.* New York: Columbia University Press, 1937.

Vaill, P. B. "The Purposing of High-Performance Systems." *Organizational Dynamics*, Autumn 1982, pp. 23–39.

Vaill, P. B. *Managing as a Performing Art: New Ideas for a World of Chaotic Change.* San Francisco: Jossey-Bass, 1989.

Van Maanen, J. *Organizational Careers: Some New Perspectives.* New York: Wiley, 1977.

Van Maanen, J. "The Fact of Fiction in Organization Ethnography." *Administrative Science Quarterly*, 1979, *24*, 539–550.

Vaughn, D. "Autonomy, Interdependence, and Social Control: NASA and the Space Shuttle Challenger." *Administrative Science Quarterly*, 1990, *35*, 225–257.

Vogt, E. Z., and Abel, S. "On Political Rituals in Contemporary Mexico." In S. F. Moore and B. G. Meyerhoff (eds.), *Secular Rituals.* Assen, The Netherlands: Van Goreum, 1977.

Von Bertalanffy, L. *General System Theory.* New York: Braziller, 1949.

Vroom, V. H. *Work and Motivation.* New York: Wiley, 1964.

Vroom, V. H., and Yetton, P. W. *Leadership and Decision Making.* Pittsburgh: University of Pittsburgh Press, 1973.

Walton, R. E., and McKersie, R. B. *A Behavioral Theory of Labor Negotiations.* New York: McGraw-Hill, 1965.

Wambaugh, J. *The Blue Knight.* Boston: Little, Brown, 1972.

Warwick, D. P. *A Theory of Public Bureaucracy: Politics, Personality, and Organization in the State Department.* Cambridge, Mass.: Harvard University Press, 1975.

Weatherford, J. M. *Tribes on the Hill: The United States Congress—Rituals and Realities.* Granby, Mass.: Bergin and Garvey, 1985.

Weber, M. *The Theory of Social and Economic Organization.* (T. Parsons, trans.) New York: Free Press, 1947.

Weick, K. E. *The Social Psychology of Organizing.* Reading, Mass.: Addison-Wesley, 1969.

Weick, K. E. "Educational Organizations as Loosely Coupled Systems." *Administrative Science Quarterly*, 1976a, *21*, 1–19.

Weick, K. E. "On Repunctuating the Problem of Organizational Effectiveness." Unpublished paper, Cornell University, 1976b.

Weick, K. E. "Cognitive Processes in Organizations." In B. E. Staw (ed.), *Research in Organizational Behavior*. Greenwich, Conn.: JAI Press, 1981.

Weinberg, M. W. "Continental Airlines, (A)." Boston: HBS Case Services, 1984.

Weiner, E. "Lorenzo to Leave Airline Industry in Deal Selling Continental Stock." *New York Times,* Aug. 10, 1990, pp. A-1, D-8.

Weiner, S. "Participation, Deadlines, and Choice." In J. G. March and J. Olsen (eds.), *Ambiguity and Choice in Organizations.* Bergen, Norway: Universitetsforlaget, 1976.

Weiss, C. H. *Social Science Research and Decision Making.* New York: Columbia University Press, 1980.

Westerlund, G., and Sjostrand, S. *Organizational Myths.* New York: Harper & Row, 1979.

"Why Image Counts: A Tale of Two Industries." *Business Week,* June 8, 1987, pp. 138-139.

Whyte, W. F. *Money and Motivation.* New York: Harper & Row, 1955.

Whyte, W. F. *Organizational Behavior.* Homewood, Ill.: Irwin, 1969.

Wiener, N. *The Human Use of Human Beings: Cybernetics and Society.* New York: Avon Books, 1967.

Wilkins, A. "Organizational Stories as an Expression of Management Philosophy." Unpublished thesis, Business School, Stanford University, 1976.

Wilson, W. "The Study of Administration." *Political Science Quarterly,* June 1987, pp. 209-210.

Wimpelberg, R. K. "Managerial Images and School Effectiveness." *Administrators' Notebook,* 1987, *32,* 1-4.

Woodward, J. *Industrial Organization: Theory and Practice.* New York: Oxford University Press, 1965.

Woodward, J. (ed.). *Industrial Organizations: Behavior and Control.* Oxford, England: Oxford University Press, 1970.

"World Airways, Inc., DC8-8-63F, N80ZWA, King Cove, Alaska, 1974." National Transportation and Safety Board Accident Report. Washington, D.C.: NTSB, n.d.

Wrigley, L. *Diversification and Divisional Autonomy.* D.B.A. thesis, Business School, Harvard University, 1970.

Yeltsin, B. N. "School Reform: Ways to Accelerate It." *Uchitelskaia gazeta,* Sept. 25, 1986, pp. 1–2.

Zaslavskaya, T. *The Second Socialist Revolution.* Bloomington: Indiana University Press, 1990.

# Name Index

Abel, S., 264
Abramowitz, S., 276
Agnew, S., 217–218
Alderfer, C., 125
Alderfer, C. P., 125, 188, 311, 313
Aldrich, H., 234
Alinsky, S., 229–230, 237
Allen, G., 108
Alsing, C., 292, 293, 294, 296, 298, 300, 301, 302
Alterman, E., 188
Argyris, C., 53, 127–130, 131, 135, 136, 138, 140, 142, 151, 152, 153, 154, 157, 158, 159, 178, 239–240, 311, 312, 313, 430
Arnold, T. W., 267, 284
Austin, N., 83, 251, 269, 411, 412
Axelrod, R., 219

Baldridge, J. V., 195, 196, 255, 273
Bales, F., 143
Barley, S. R., 68
Barnard, C., 267
Barnes, F., 447
Barnes, L. B., 410
Barreta, A., 132–133, 134, 135, 136–139
Barrett, D., 104

Barth, R., 410
Barth, S., 324
Bass, B. M., 141, 412, 442
Bateson, G., 267
Bavelas, A., 104
Beam, A., 79, 80
Beer, S., 310, 312–313
Bell, D., 230
Bell, T. E., 183, 184, 185, 210
Bellow, G., 208, 217
Bennis, W., 178, 192, 311, 406, 407, 411, 412, 430, 442
Bennis, W. G., 368–370, 375
Bensimon, E. M., 340–341, 410
Bettelheim, B., 256
Bieber, O., 176
Bion, W. R., 143
Birnbaum, R., 311, 318
Blake, R., 142, 413–416, 419
Blanchard, K., 430
Blanchard, K. H., 412, 417–420
Blau, P. M., 48
Block, P., 178, 192, 219–221
Bluestone, I., 164
Blum, A., 285, 286
Blumberg, P., 155
Blumer, H., 253
Boisjoly, R., 210

# Subject Index